LAW AND SCIENCE

CURRENT LEGAL ISSUES 1998

Volume 1

LAW AND SCIENCE

CURRENT LEGAL ISSUES 1998
Volume 1

Edited by

HELEN REECE
Lecturer in Laws,
University College London

OXFORD UNIVERSITY PRESS
1998

Oxford University Press, Great Clarendon Street, Oxford OX2 6DP
www.oup.co.uk

Oxford New York

Athens Auckland Bangkok Bogota Bombay Buenos Aires
Calcutta Cape Town Dar es Salaam Delhi Florence Hong Kong Istanbul
Karachi Kuala Lumpur Madras Madrid Melbourne Mexico City
Nairobi Paris Singapore Taipei Tokyo Toronto Warsaw
and associated companies in
Berlin Ibadan

Oxford is a registered trade mark of Oxford University Press

Published in the United States
by Oxford University Press Inc., New York

British Library Cataloguing in Publication Data
Data available

Library of Congress Cataloguing in Publication Data
Data available

ISBN 0–19–826794–0

1 3 5 7 9 10 8 6 4 2

Typeset by Cambrian Typesetters, Frimley, Surrey
Printed in Great Britain
on acid-free paper by
Biddles Ltd., Guildford and King's Lynn

CONTENTS

GENERAL EDITOR'S PREFACE

1997 is the fiftieth year of the series of lectures at University College London given and published under the title *Current Legal Problems*. In recent years the annual volume of lectures had been joined by a second devoted to consideration of contemporary developments in the law. When the Editors of *Current Legal Problems* were considering ways of marking the jubilee they came up with the notion of replacing this second volume with one which was more generally thematic but which, like *CLP*, would publish proceedings first given 'live' at University College London. The idea of a series of international and inter-disciplinary colloquia on Current Legal Issues was born and the first in a series, entitled 'Law and Science', took place on 30 June and 1 July 1997. As ever, the Editors are grateful for the support and encouragement of our publishers.

Responsibility for the organization of the programme for this first colloquium was placed in the hands of Helen Reece, with the assistance of the Editors, and she has also been responsible for editing this first volume of published *Current Legal Issues*. The very considerable response which the call for papers elicited and the high quality of papers given at the colloquium prompted the Editors to arrange for the publication of a second, companion, volume of proceedings which Dartmouth is publishing as *Science In Court*. Preparations are presently in hand for the second Current Legal Issues colloquium on 'Law and Literature' to take place at University College London on 29–30 June 1998. Plans are proceeding for colloquia on 'Law and Medicine' in 1999 and on 'Law and Religion' to coincide with the millennium.

The Editors would welcome expressions of interest in these colloquia and offers of participation.

Andrew D. E. Lewis

EDITOR'S INTRODUCTION

This volume addresses the intersection between law and science, two monolithic institutions which generally compete for, but sometimes coincide in presenting, an authoritative analysis of the world. The contributors to this volume take different views as to who is the victor in this contest. According to Lewis Wolpert, it is indisputable that science is the best way of understanding the world. He argues that science, unlike art and by analogy law, is progressive in that it increasingly approximates to an understanding of the nature of the world. In contrast, Tony Ward uses an analysis of three case studies, namely insanity, nervous shock, and radiation, to conclude that legal truth is different from scientific truth but that, as far as the legal arena is concerned, they both give way to what he describes as lay truth, while Michael King and Felicity Kaganas are less optimistic about the possibility of any discipline gaining an understanding of reality. Lewis Wolpert makes a robust attack on this relativism in the form which it takes in the scientific sphere, namely what he describes as the Strong Programme in the Sociology of Science. This is a fairly easy target. As Wolpert points out, the applications of science to technologies such as electronics or jet aircraft should give us all some confidence that reality is involved. Yet, although Wolpert limits his defence of objectivity to the scientific sphere, a broader defence is needed. The fallacy of the relativist outlook is easiest to expose in the scientific arena, but the fact that it has managed to make so much headway even in such hostile territory is testament to how firmly it has established itself elsewhere. Defence of objectivity in science must be merely a prelude to a full frontal attack on relativism in other areas including the law. It is more difficult to hold on to a materialist analysis in the social sciences but it is just as necessary. James Penner, in his paper on cognitive science, makes an interesting contribution by examining evidence from linguistic theory which he argues could suggest a universal moral framework. While perhaps we are unlikely to find that even a linguistic core cuts across all cultures, it is refreshing to read a contribution which focuses on human commonality rather than difference.

While Wolpert is on solid ground in his attack on sociology of science, his ground is perhaps more shaky when he turns to philosophy of science. He asserts that philosophers of science have made no contribution to an understanding of science this century. If he is right about this then he must include his own contribution within this assessment, because his paper in this volume and much of his other writing is work within the discipline of philosophy of science. The claims that he makes, to take a couple of examples, that science is the best way to understand the world or that science is different from technology, are not scientific claims but rather claims about the nature of science. What Wolpert must therefore be arguing for is for different and better philosophers and philosophy of science. The philosophy of any discipline is in effect an understanding of that discipline at a more abstract level; to stand back from the coal-face can never be a pointless enterprise, although it may be often, or even always, an unsuccessful one.

This is to put the worst-case scenario, for it may be the case that philosophy of science can provide solutions to legal problems, if not to scientific ones. In my own contribution and in Richard Goldberg's, philosophy of probability is plundered to shed light on complex questions of causation with, I would suggest, some success. In any case, even if philosophy of science cannot provide answers to legal questions, it is incontrovertible that law has to provide answers to questions posed by philosophy of science. To take one example, several of these papers grapple with the question of when expert evidence should be admissible, and all of the authors agree that at the very least the evidence should not be admitted unless it is 'good science'. But what is good science? Tony Ward tells us that the law has made a distinction between the potentially flawed authority of individual scientists and the invincible authority of the institution of science. Such a distinction is as inevitable as it is necessary, but it means that it cannot be assumed that anything which any scientist does is automatically good science. Criteria must be found, and this is a question for the philosophers. If Wolpert is right that falsification is a flawed yardstick then this is an issue of crucial importance to the law, because, as James Richardson and Gerald Ginsburg explain, falsification has been endorsed in America as part of the test for the admissibility of expert evidence in the recent case of *Daubert v. Merrell Dow Pharmaceuticals Inc.*[1]

Expert testimony is one of the most prominent areas in which science and law collide. Several of the papers pull apart the implications of expert evidence. Richardson and Ginsburg in their paper on brainwashing evidence draw a sharp distinction between popular support for a scientific view, often influenced by media coverage, and objectivity. It is refreshing to see an approach which is prepared to accept the social and behavioural sciences as being as scientific as the natural sciences but which correspondingly demands the same rigorously scientific standards of them. From this starting-point, Richardson and Ginsburg are highly critical of evidence of such syndromes as 'destructive cultism' which do not meet scientific standards, since to the extent that they are testable they are falsified and to any greater extent than this they are untestable because theories about these syndromes make contradictory predictions about the behaviour which, it is argued, provides evidence of the syndrome. This was taken to an extreme in a case which they cite, that of the son of one of the leading proponents of 'destructive cultism' who joined a cult, leading his father to argue that he was suffering from mental illness and furthermore that the mind-control techniques were so powerful that they could disguise mental illness, so that it did not show up on diagnostic tests.

Fiona Raitt's paper is in marked contrast in its approach to syndrome evidence. Raitt takes the view that there is no reason to assume that the legal system in the form of judge and jury is competent to assess human behaviour unaided by scientific testimony, since the views of human behaviour may be based on prejudice. She suggests that syndrome evidence can be very useful in dispelling popular myths, regarding evidence of battered women's syndrome and sexual abuse syndrome in this positive light. She argues that the criterion should be not whether the evidence is helpful but simply whether the evidence is reliable, since if it is reliable it cannot be other than helpful. But what if the expert evidence is itself based on prejudice and myth, as Richardson and Ginsburg convincingly argue in relation to 'destructive cultism'

[1] 113 S. Ct. 2786 (1993); 125 L. Ed. (2d) 469 (1993).

and sexual abuse accommodation syndrome, and as Paul Roberts does in relation to battered women's syndrome? Roberts tends to side with Richardson and Ginsburg with his argument that expert evidence on behavioural and social matters may as often reinforce as challenge common prejudices. Even where the evidence itself is well-informed, he suggests that it may have the potential for mischief in that it may put into the jurors' minds illegitimate lines of thought. His approach differs from Raitt's; she generally favours a liberal approach to admitting expert evidence on the basis that at the very least it will do no harm, while he argues that there needs to be a more secure foundation than simply a feeling that jurors have common prejudices about human behaviour. He reminds us that political correctness cannot substitute for scientific rigour and suggests that as jurors become more enlightened there will be less need for expert evidence. King and Kaganas take this argument in a different but related direction with their suggestion that it may be the law itself which creates the prejudice and therefore the need for experts, specifically through drawing a distinction between dangers, which cannot be avoided, and risks, for which the law seeks responsibility. But when we turn to Jane Holder and Sue Elworthy's contribution we find that this distinction between risks and dangers has become outmoded: with the development of the precautionary principle, highlighted in Holder and Elworthy's discussion of the BSE débâcle, the law seems to be seeking responsibility for dangers as much as risks, for the precautionary principle demands that if there is a danger then aversive action should be taken. Indeed the argument can be taken further: Holder and Elworthy convincingly argue that the law is dealing not with risk but with 'virtual risk', which, it could be argued, leads to the undermining of scientific knowledge. In a complementary historical chapter, John McEldowney argues that we have much to learn from the nineteenth-century approach to the connection between science, particularly in the form of statistics, and environmental law.

Roberts' contribution raises important questions about expert evidence. The argument is often made that expert evidence is dangerous because experts' views may be given too much weight because of their status. But Roberts emphasizes in his paper that this is not the only reason that expert evidence may exert too much influence. He demonstrates the ways in which testimony is allowed to circumvent fundamental legal principles, such as the rule against admitting evidence of bad character or the hearsay rule, simply because it is introduced by an expert. Expert evidence may be dangerous as much because of what the expert is allowed to say as it is because of who is saying it. Roberts ends his paper by examining the implications which this discussion has for the broader issue of who decides questions of procedure, given that they can be fundamental constitutional questions. This contribution reminds us of a crucial distinction between law and science, that law is intimately connected with morality. Heidi Feldman provides an interesting discussion of the light which science can shed on ethical questions, specifically the identity and character of the reasonable person, but ultimately Lewis Wolpert is right to defend scientists against charges of social irresponsibility. Science deals in objective reality; therefore it is for scientists to reveal as much as they can about reality, and for the law to determine what should be made of the discoveries. Perhaps this division of labour is too simplistic, but if it is taken as a model, it is apparent that law and science are bound together and that mutual understanding is essential. If this volume contributes to that understanding then it will have performed an invaluable service.

Helen Reece

TABLE OF CASES

TABLE OF STATUTES

NOTES ON CONTRIBUTORS

James Penner is a Lecturer in Law at the London School of Economics. He was awarded a D.Phil. from Oxford University in 1992 for his dissertation on the philosophical foundations of property law. He was a visiting scholar in the Department of Philosophy and Centre for Cognitive Science at Rutgers University in 1996, and has been awarded a Nuffield Foundation Social Science Research Fellowship to write a book on cognitive science, philosophy of mind, ethics, and law.

Heidi Li Feldman is Visiting Associate Professor of Law at Georgetown University Law Center. She received her JD from the University of Michigan in 1990 and her Ph.D. in Philosophy, also from the University of Michigan, in 1993. Heidi Feldman is currently working on a book that will pursue a naturalistic, ethico-psychological analysis of central concepts in American tort law.

Richard Goldberg is a Lecturer in Law at the University of Birmingham and he has also taught in the University of London at King's College, the London School of Economics, and Queen Mary and Westfield College. He was awarded a Ph.D. from King's College London in 1997, on causation, risk and scientific evidence in medicinal-product liability. His special interests are in the areas of medicinal-product liability and intellectual property, particularly in respect of pharmaceuticals.

Helen Reece is a Lecturer in Laws at University College London. Her current research interests include philosophy of science, particularly questions of causation and probability. This interest stems from the Masters which she took in Logic and Scientific Method in the Department of Philosophy at the London School of Economics, for which she was awarded Distinction in 1994. The article in this volume is a development of an article which was published in the Modern Law Review in 1996 and which was awarded the Wedderburn Prize.

John McEldowney is Reader in Law at the University of Warwick. He is the co-author of *Environment and the Law* (Essex, 1996) and has written extensively on privatization and regulation issues.

Jane Holder and Sue Elworthy are respectively Lecturer in Laws and Co-Director of the Centre for the Law of the European Union, Faculty of Laws, University College London and Research Associate in the School of Public Administration and Law at The Robert Gordon University, Aberdeen. They are the co-authors of *Environmental Protection: Law in Context* (London, 1997) and co-editors of *Perspectives on the Environment* (Aldershot, 1995). Jane Holder is also the editor of *The Impact of EC Environmental Law in the United Kingdom* (Chichester, 1997).

Fiona Raitt is a solicitor and Senior Lecturer in the Department of Law at the University of Dundee and also Director of Studies of the Diploma in Legal Practice in that Department, where she teaches Evidence. Recent publications include articles on law and psychology, battered women's syndrome, and rape trauma syndrome. She is the co-author of the second edition of *Evidence* and is currently co-writing a theoretical text entitled *Psychology and Law: the Implicit Relation*, due to be published in 1999.

Paul Roberts is a Lecturer in Law at the University of Nottingham, where he teaches Criminal Justice, Criminology, Criminal Law, and the Law of Evidence. His recent publications include articles on character evidence, the burden of proof, and the admissibility of expert evidence, and he is co-author of *The Role of Forensic Science Evidence in Criminal Proceedings* (RCCJ Research Study No. 11, 1993).

Michael King and Felicity Kaganas are respectively Professor and Lecturer at the Centre for the Study of Law, the Child and the Family, Department of Law, Brunel University. Michael King has written extensively on interdisciplinary issues involving law and behavioural sciences, including a book entitled *Psychology in and out of Court* (Oxford, 1986). His most recent book, *A Better World for Children?* (New York, 1997) applies autopoietic theory to issues of children's welfare. Felicity Kaganas has published on legal and policy issues concerning children's welfare both in the United Kingdom and South Africa.

Tony Ward is a Senior Lecturer at De Montfort University, Leicester. His Ph.D. thesis, completed last year, deals with the relationship between psychiatry and criminal law in the nineteenth and early twentieth centuries. He previously worked for the organization INQUEST, which provides advice and campaigns for reform in relation to coroners' courts and deaths in custody.

Gerald Ginsburg is Chair of the Interdisciplinary Ph.D. Program in Social Psychology, Professor of Psychology and member of the Advisory Board of the Center for Justice Studies at the University of Nevada, Reno. His two primary areas of research are the study of scientific evidence in trial courts, and the social and psycho-physiological study of emotion. He is the co-author (with James Richardson, Shirley Dobbin and Sophia Gatowski) of a 1995 article in *Judicature* on the impact of the *Daubert* decision on social and behavioural science evidence. JAMES RICHARDSON, JD, Ph.D., is Director of the Master of Judicial Studies Program for trial judges, offered by the University of Nevada, Reno, in conjunction with The National Judicial College and the National Council of Juvenile and Family Court Judges. He teaches Social Science Evidence in that program. He is also Professor of Sociology and Judicial Studies, working with the Sociology undergraduate program and the Social Psychology doctoral level program at the University. He specializes in Sociology of Religion and Sociology of Law, as well as in the area of social movements. His research interests include the use of evidence in the courts.

Lewis Wolpert is Professor of Biology as Applied to Medicine in the Department of Anatomy and Developmental Biology of University College London. His research interests are in the mechanisms involved in the development of the embryo. He was originally trained as a civil engineer in South Africa. He is currently Chairman of the Committee for the Public Understanding of Science. His most recent book is *The Unnatural Nature of Science* (London, 1992) and he writes a column in *The Independent on Sunday*.

COGNITIVE SCIENCE, LEGAL THEORY, AND THE POSSIBILITY OF AN OBSERVATION/THEORY DISTINCTION IN MORALITY AND LAW

*J. E. Penner**

For people committed to control and manipulation, it is quite useful to believe that human beings have no intrinsic moral and intellectual nature, that they are simply objects to be shaped by state and private managers and ideologues—who, of course, perceive what is good and right. Concern for intrinsic human nature poses one of the barriers in the way of manipulation and control . . . human rights are rooted in human nature.

Noam Chomsky[1]

Introduction

An observation/theory distinction is a distinction between beliefs which we are able justifiably to form on the basis of observations, that is, true perceptions of the world more or less uncoloured by our desires, beliefs, theories, ideologies, cultures, etc., and beliefs which we form on the basis of attempts to explain or understand

* I gratefully acknowledge the support of the Economic and Social Research Council, grant no. R000221765, in carrying out the research upon which this paper is based. I also thank Richard Barton, Alison Diduck, Michael King, Brian Langille, Elizabeth Penner, Jonathan Sutton, Ernest Weinrib, and participants at a seminar at Sussex University, at the UCL Law and Science Seminar, and at the Toronto Legal Theory Workshop, for their comments on and criticisms of earlier versions of this paper.

[1] N. Chomsky, *Language and the Problems of Knowledge* (Cambridge, Mass., 1988), 165–6.

our observations, that is, our various theories, ideologies, or cultural world views. In the case of morality, the existence of observational beliefs would depend upon our minds being set up to 'perceive' or 'grasp' certain moral concepts or propositions without being taught a particular theory of morality,[2] or without being indoctrinated into a particular ideological or cultural perspective. Now observations depend on the universal perceptual and cognitive apparatus that humans share. By contrast, our theories, ideologies, and cultural perspectives vary like mad. Thus an observation/theory distinction provides one indicator (perhaps the only sensible indicator) of a distinction between a moral human nature and cultural moral variation. Whether we have a moral human nature is, to say the least, an important question, and I take it for granted here that if we have a moral human nature then that obviously concerns the law, since the law is generally regarded as institutionalizing certain norms because of their moral character.

Here I will consider first whether the metaphoric theory of concepts that George Lakoff develops from the results of cognitive science, and which Steven Winter adopts in his work on legal theory, can deliver a workable observation/theory distinction of this kind. I conclude that it cannot. I then tentatively propose that the results of cognitive science do provide reason for believing that one can draw an observation/theory distinction in morality. The first thing I will do, however, is briefly and roughly describe what cognitive science is.

Cognitive Science, Briefly

For a decent history of cognitive science, I recommend Howard Gardner's *The Mind's New Science*,[3] but here is a very brief and partial caricature. Before the 1950s psychology was dominated by behaviourists, whose goal was to explain human behaviour without recourse to the mental, that is, without recourse to the idea that the mind, through various faculties, performed various operations which were causally relevant in the determination of human

---

2 Gilbert Harman thinks not, though I will not specifically address his work here. See Harman, 'Ethics and Observation' in G. Sayre-McCord (ed.), *Essays on Moral Realism* (Ithaca & London, 1988), 119.

3 H. Gardner, *The Mind's New Science* (New York, 1985).

behaviour. Very roughly, if one can explain behaviour as (publicly observable) responses to (publicly observable) stimuli, like screaming 'ouch' and withdrawing one's hand from a hot plate, then one can forgo all this mystical 'in the head' stuff. While this might appear today as a somewhat odd constraint for psychologists to impose upon themselves (what other branch of science would so manifestly deny their own object of study, for heaven's sake?) there were a few related reasons for it, which looked good at the time. First, the predecessor form of psychology, which did take the mental seriously, was even worse: introspectionist psychology. Its methodology was to train researchers to observe their own mentation, and describe it scientifically. The difficulty of finding a grounding for any kind of scientific rigour in this approach would appear insurmountable, and on that score behaviourist psychology was clearly superior. Philosophy assisted. For quite a while there was a popular view amongst philosophers, a view probably best exemplified by Ryle's *The Concept of Mind*,[4] which was that the conventional understanding of the mind as 'something in the head' that was causally determinative of behaviour, was a mistake. Speaking about 'minds' was, roughly, the use of a *façon de parler* which really referred to the observable experience of human behaviour. Finally, no one had any kind of decent description of what thinking consisted of or how it might work.

So what happened? First of all, the deep-seated problems of behaviourism became just too obvious to ignore. Gardner regards an address by Karl Lashley on 'Cerebral Mechanisms in Behaviour', given to a conference held at the California Institute of Technology in 1948, as one of the most significant turning points; Lashley argued that behavioural explanations based on simple associative chains of stimulus and response would never account for certain complex human capabilities, such as the ability to speak a language.[5] Noam Chomsky's review of B. F. Skinner's *Verbal Behaviour* was also profoundly significant.[6] With respect to almost every aspect of Skinner's theory, Chomsky pointed out how thoroughly Skinner's behaviourist explanation helped itself to characterizations of stimulus and response to which it was simply

---

[4] G. Ryle, *The Concept of Mind* (London, 1949).

[5] See Gardner, *New Science*, n. 3 above, 11–14.

[6] N. Chomsky, 'A Review of B. F. Skinner's Verbal Behaviour' (1959) 35 *Language* 26.

not entitled on any unambiguous (i.e. rigorous) definition of its own terms. It was nothing if not thorough. As Fodor put it, 'no term was left unstoned'.[7] Secondly, Alan Turing's invention of a computing machine provided a theoretically respectable model of cognition, that is of *cognition as computation*, which idea remains *the* foundation of 'classical' cognitive science to this day: on the 'classical' view,[8] cognitive science is the empirical study of the human mind on the view that the mind's cognitive processes are computational.[9]

Computation is the manipulation of symbols by reference to their syntactic structure, as opposed to their semantics, or meaning. Here is a computational operation:

> If A then B;
> A
> Therefore B.

A and B are symbols which are manipulated by the operation of a rule of inference, 'if then'. For the manipulation to work, it does not matter what the semantics of A and B are, i.e. what they stand for or refer to. They simply have to be identifiable symbols. A and B might stand for 'smoke' and 'fire', or 'lawyers' and 'exorbitant billing', or any other pair. The computational operation runs on the symbols, not on what they are symbols for. That the mind might be a computer, that is, a rule-governed symbol manipulator, seems plausible in view of Chomsky's work in linguistics, which

---

[7] J. A. Fodor, *A Theory of Content and Other Essays* (Cambridge, Mass., 1990), 54.

[8] More recently, an alternative computer-based model of cognition has been loudly proclaimed, the 'connectionist' or 'neural network' model of cognition, although whether it is any good is controversial: see J. Fodor and Z. Pylyshyn, 'Connectionism and Cognitive Architecture: A Critical Analysis' (1988) 28 *Cognition* 3; P. Smolensky, 'The Constituent Structure of Connectionist Mental States: A Reply to Fodor and Pylyshyn' (1987) 26 *Southern J of Philosophy* (Suppl.) 137.

[9] What has happened in philosophy remains something of an open question, since while whatever logical positivist and verificationist precepts lay behind Ryle's views are now disfavoured, following on from some interpretations of the later Wittgenstein there are some who espouse a kind of logical or conceptual behaviourism, under which the ontological status of things like minds still turns, pretty much, on our behaviour, though now all the proof of this pudding is to be found in the eating of our *linguistic* behaviour. For a critical view of 'logical behaviourism', see J. A. Fodor and C. Chihara, 'Operationalism and Ordinary Language' in J. A. Fodor, *Representations: Philosophical Essays on the Foundations of Cognitive Science* (Brighton, 1981), 35.

reveals that human linguistic ability involves a strong syntax/ semantics distinction. His famous nonsense sentence, 'Colourless green ideas sleep furiously', illustrates how grammatical well-formedness, that is, syntactical correctness, is independent of semantic meaningfulness. While the sentence is literally meaningless, it is well-formed.[10]

'Cognitive science' describes a sort of research programme more than a discipline in itself, drawing upon work in philosophy, psychology, artificial intelligence, linguistics, anthropology, and neuroscience. What binds cognitive scientists together is, to quote Gardner, first 'the belief that, in talking about human cognitive activities, it is necessary to first speak about mental representations and to posit a level of analysis wholly separate from the biological or neurological, on the one hand, and the sociological or cultural, on the other', and secondly, the belief that the '[electronic] computer . . . serves as the most viable model of how the human mind functions'.[11]

Concepts as Mental Representations

The way in which I will set about hunting down an observation/theory distinction in morality is to explore what cognitive science tells us about concepts. As I have mentioned, Winter and Lakoff propose a metaphoric theory of concepts, and the question I ask is whether that delivers a sound observation/theory distinction. First, however, I should say a little about what concepts are, and what cognitive science has to say about them.

Concepts are mental objects, the objects of thought, that represent to our mind anything which we can think about, like aeroplanes. ('Represent' does not mean present a little image, as if our minds were movie screens; 'represent' is neutral as to the mode of presentation.) *Words*, in contrast, are linguistic symbols that express concepts. The concept AEROPLANE represents, more or less accurately, the *property* of being an aeroplane (which all aeroplanes share; by virtue of instantiating such property aeroplanes

---

[10] See e.g. N. Chomsky, *Syntactic Structures* (The Hague, 1957); N. Chomsky, *Aspects of the Theory of Syntax* (Cambridge, Mass., 1965).
[11] Gardner, *New Science*, n. 3 above, 6.

are aeroplanes). According to the computational model, concepts are syntactic objects (that is symbols) that represent properties; thus they make properties (that is, properties in the real world) available to the mind, and thus to the mind's computational processes, by representing them. The nature of this conceptual or representational apparatus or faculty, and the way in which mental processes operate at this representational level—that is, how people think with these symbols—draw inferences according to rules which operate on these symbols, structure their knowledge or beliefs framed in terms of these symbols, store and later retrieve symbolic representations—that is, have memories, and so on—are therefore one of the main objects of study for cognitive scientists, in particular cognitive psychologists. In short, the nature of concepts is a big deal.

To take just one example where the study of concepts by cognitive scientists has produced interesting results, we can consider the way in which concepts are *categories*. By representing properties, concepts naturally categorize things according to those properties. That is, if something has the property X, then it falls within a set of things with that property: thus applying the concept of X to something that has the property X categorizes that thing as an X, or as having X-hood. Thus concepts are abstract in the sense that they apply to all the particulars which instantiate those properties, and thus our concepts categorize the world into various kinds. Eleanor Rosch and her associates found that humans do not appear to apply concepts/categories on the basis of necessary and sufficient conditions for category membership.[12] Rather, we appear to apply our concepts on the basis of prototypes or stereotypes—a robin is a 'better' bird, and more easily characterized as such, than is a penguin, even though we know that robins and penguins are both birds. This 'prototype' effect in the way we categorize concepts seems completely general, even 'promiscuous'. That is, even for concepts which can be explicitly defined in terms of necessary and sufficient conditions for category membership, and which we might very well have learnt by being taught these necessary and sufficient conditions, concepts like 'odd number', experimental subjects will find some category members as better exemplars of the category than

---

[12] For a review see *ibid.*, 340–8.

others: apparently, three is a much better example of an odd number than is twenty-three.[13]

The relevance of this for the law should be fairly apparent, for much of the day-to-day work of the law consists of determining the correct categorization of a legal dispute or problem—for example, 'Is this a tort problem or a property problem?', 'Is this a "sale" for the purposes of the Sale of Goods Act?', etc. It may suggest, for example, that the way in which students are introduced first to 'paradigm' cases and then to more peripheral 'extensions' of doctrine in the case-based method of teaching appropriately mirrors the way in which individuals apply concepts in other domains. It is worth pointing out that the prototype theory is a theory of concept *application*. It is quite neutral on the question whether the concepts *qua* categories which we have exhibit a prototype structure themselves.[14] That is, our categories may well be perfectly sharp sets, with precise criteria as to category membership, although our acquisition and application of those categories might depend upon the use of prototypes. So, for example, it seems clear that while a robin is a better bird in the sense that we can identify a robin as a bird more quickly than we can identify a penguin as one, it remains the case that both robins and penguins are birds, one as much as the other.

Steven Winter, George Lakoff, and the Metaphoric Theory of Concepts

It is now time to consider the views of Steven Winter, perhaps the strongest proponent of the view that cognitive science has important implications for legal theory. Winter draws almost exclusively on George Lakoff for his information on cognitive science, and Lakoff takes a particular line on the way in which the mind represents the world for the purposes of cognitive operations. Lakoff believes that most of our concepts are structured metaphors, metaphors which reflect our experience as beings who exist in particular kinds of bodies. Winter has written quite extensively,

---

[13] S. L. Armstrong, L. R. Gleitman, and H. Gleitman, 'What Some Concepts Might Not Be' (1983) 13 *Cognition* 263–308.
[14] See G. Rey, 'Concepts and Stereotypes' (1983) 15 *Cognition* 237; E. Margolis, 'A Reassessment of the Shift from the Classical Theory of Concepts to Prototype Theory' (1994) 51 *Cognition* 73.

but the most thorough statement of his views on this subject is to be found in his 1989 paper, 'Transcendental Nonsense, Metaphoric Reasoning, and the Cognitive Stakes for Law'.[15] Here Winter applies Lakoff's theory of conceptual representation, based on metaphor, to various issues in legal theory.

OBJECTIVISM AND SUBJECTIVISM

In order to understand how Lakoff's and Winter's views might implicate an observation/theory distinction, it is necessary first to explore how they situate their work in the debate between 'objectivism' and 'subjectivism'. Winter puts it this way:

The traditional view of law is largely dependent upon objectivist assumptions about reasoning and categorization. . . . I use the term 'objectivist' to capture a general position that has three familiar sub-parts. First, it treats the world as filled with determinate, mind-independent objects with inherent characteristics unrelated to human interactions. Second, it understands categorization either as about natural sets of objects in the world or, when it recognizes categorization as humanly constructed, as about objects with ascertainable properties or criteria that establish their commonality. Finally, it treats reasoning as about propositions and principles that are capable of 'mirroring' those objects and accurately describing their properties and relations. . . . The objectivist position is seen in contradistinction to either that of the subjectivist or that of the radical relativist. By 'subjectivist' I refer to an approach that treats doctrines, rules, and categories as mere expressions of an actor's purposes, desires, or beliefs, and thus as virtually infinitely manipulable. In general, the positions I refer to as ' relativist' assert that reasoning and categorization are not natural or given, but rather are relative to particular languages, cultures, histories, or conceptual schemes.[16]

And Lakoff (with Johnson) says this:

What the myths of objectivism and subjectivism both miss is the way in which we understand the world through our interactions with it. What objectivism misses is the fact that understanding, and therefore truth, is necessarily relative to our cultural conceptual systems and that it cannot be framed in any absolute or neutral conceptual system. Objectivism also misses the fact that human conceptual systems are metaphorical in nature

---

[15] S. L. Winter, 'Transcendental Nonsense, Metaphoric Reasoning, and the Cognitive Stakes for Law' (1989) 137 Univ. Penn. LRev. 1105.

[16] Winter, 'Transcendental Nonsense', n. 15 above, 1107–8.

and involve an imaginative understanding of one kind of thing in terms of another. What subjectivism specifically misses is that our understanding, even our most imaginative understanding, is grounded in our successful functioning in our physical and cultural environments.[17]

The way forward is a *via media* called *experientialism*:

[E]mpirical work . . . provides evidence for experientialism—an approach to human understanding that is simultaneously relativist and realist. The central insight of this approach is that human knowledge is grounded in our direct physical and social experience with the world, but is elaborated *indirectly*, largely by means of metaphor and the extension of idealised cognitive models.[18]

'Experientialism' expresses the fact that our representations of the world reflect our experience as embodied, physical creatures:

The claim is that reason, language, and knowledge can be understood only in terms of the cognitive process. That process is *embodied*; it arises directly from physical experience. The process is not 'objective' in the sense of transcendental truth, but rather is dependent on the kind of bodies that we have and the ways in which those bodies interact with our environment. It is grounded in a reality that to a very large degree is shared by all human beings. This claim is, therefore, relativist *and* realist—relativist *but not* nihilist. The experientialist view is relativist in that it does not depend upon, and in fact rejects, an objectivist, correspondence view of meaning and reality. . . . But this does not mean that there is no reality or that 'anything goes'. Rather, it means that there is no *objective* description of reality separate from our conceptual schemes. . . . Experientialism posits that we form that basic conceptual structure by means of our physical interactions with our environment.[19]

At first glance, this looks like a promising approach to the recognition of a sound observation/theory distinction. Experientialism appears to offer a distinction between beliefs which humans are able to justifiably form on the basis of observational interactions with the world as embodied creatures, and what humans believe because through thought and imagination (framed in terms of metaphors) they have developed various theories, or explanations, or cultural perspectives which thoroughly shape human activity,

---

[17] G. Lakoff and M. Johnson, *Metaphors We Live By* (Chicago & London, 1980), 186.
[18] Winter 'Transcendental Nonsense', n. 15 above, 1115, emphasis in original.
[19] *Ibid.*, 1130–2, emphasis in original.

like scientific or legal practice. The problem, however, is that the metaphoric conceptual apparatus they posit doesn't work.

THE METAPHORIC THEORY OF CONCEPTS

The metaphoric theory of concepts or mental representations is as follows: our representational or conceptual system has two kinds of concepts, which are related in such a way as to produce an hierarchical conceptual system:

(1) *experiential concepts*: these are more or less direct representations of our bodily experiences, and thus are largely determined by the physical structure of our bodies, in particular our sensory apparatus; and

(2) *metaphoric concepts*: these are more abstract concepts, like LOVE, or ARGUMENT, which are represented as *metaphoric mappings* from the first kind of concepts.

Winter explains how the two sorts of concepts provide an hierarchical representational apparatus:

Because the human mind understands new input in terms of and by comparison to existing knowledge, the cognitive process begins with unmediated, directly encountered experience. Meaning is elaborated by imaginative extension of this experience to understand and conceptualize other, more abstract domains. . . . [This process] yields a sense of knowledge and meaning as neither arbitrary nor determinate, but rather as systematic and imaginative. . . . The particular metaphoric elaborations of these basic experiences to structure and talk about both purposive activities and life are not inescapable, required, or determinate aspects of human logic. Rather, we start out with a stock of relatively stable and well-defined experiences that are shared by all human beings, given the general structure and functioning of the human organism in its environment. These basic experiences serve as the preconceptual material of imagination and rationality. Most of the complex concepts that concern us, however, are understood *indirectly* by means of our more directly experienced realities. Thus abstract purposes are understood in terms of movement along a path toward a goal, and the finitude of life is conceptualized as a journey to a final end. Embodied experiences may be elaborated to construct meaning in many different fashions; different cultures or sub-cultures may use the raw materials of experience to conceptualize their world in different ways. More abstract concepts are likely to show the greatest cultural variation because they are indirect, imaginative extensions of the physical and social experiences that ground them. Thus, experientialism recognizes no 'privileged understanding of rationality' in the sense that one way of thinking and talking better represents the world around us.[20]

Unfortunately, things are not so simple. The picture is complicated by a particular sort of conceptual structure called an 'Idealized Cognitive Model', or ICM:

An ICM is a 'folk' theory or cultural model that we create and use to organize our knowledge. It relates many concepts that are inferentially connected by means of a single conceptual structure that is experientially meaningful as a whole. For example, our understanding of the words 'buy', 'sell', 'cost', 'goods', 'advertise', 'credit', and the like, are made meaningful by an ICM of a *commercial transaction* that relates them together as a structured activity.[21]

One of the questions that we must ask, therefore, in trying to understand the Lakoff/Winter model of conceptual representation is: how do ICMs differ from the conceptual complexes which are just metaphoric mappings, i.e. to what extent are the 'inferential connections' themselves metaphoric? Secondly, how does one decide which is which? On what evidence is COMMERCIAL TRANS-ACTION an experiential concept, a metaphoric concept, or an ICM? At one point, in discussing the Hart/Fuller 'No vehicles in the park' debate, Winter purports to solve the problem by referring to the 'ICM of *vehicle*',[22] so it seems that words which we normally regard as expressing concepts, here 'vehicle', may instead express ICMs, in which case it may be better to treat ICMs as a third kind of concept, one structured in a different way from metaphoric mapping. (It should be pointed out that Winter's characterization of vehicle is not consistent. Two pages later he says vehicle is a 'simple' term, whatever that means.)[23]

In order to get to grips with all of this, it is worthwhile taking an example of a metaphorical mapping. Take a look at the Appendix to this essay, in which Lakoff shows how a particular concept, LUST, is to be understood as a metaphoric concept.[24]

Here Lakoff presents his linguistic evidence for a conceptual

---

20 *Ibid.*, 1133–4, emphasis in original.
21 *Ibid.*, 1152, emphasis in original.
22 *Ibid.*, 1178, emphasis in original.
23 *Ibid.*, 1180; see also *ibid.*, 1194 where he speaks of the 'ICM of property'.
24 G. Lakoff, *Women, Fire, and Dangerous Things* (Chicago, 1987), 409–11.

representation of LUST which is structured in terms of metaphoric mappings from different source concepts; i.e. the concept we have of LUST *is* nothing more than a congeries of metaphoric mappings. Thus our concept of LUST is composed of metaphoric mappings from FOOD, ANIMAL, HEAT, INSANITY, FUNCTIONING MACHINE, GAME, WAR, and PHYSICAL FORCE.

METAPHORIC CONCEPTS IN THE LAW

Now I want to convince you that this is simply hopeless as explanation of a concept like LUST, and that the metaphoric theory's failure here can be generalized to any other example, because it is flawed in principle. First, however, I want briefly to explore how Winter uses this idea of metaphoric representation to attack some issues in legal theory, so that we have an idea of the significance for law of accepting this view of our complex concepts.

In 'Transcendental Nonsense', Winter claims that:

1. Legal discourse is shot through with just the kind of conventional phrases which Lakoff identifies as metaphoric mappings and which we recognize in the case of LUST.[25] According to Winter, on the basis of this evidence we should conclude that our understanding of law is neither objectivist nor subjectivist but experiential, and that many of our legal concepts are metaphoric.
2. In the light of this, we should alter our understanding of what law is, and this will have obvious consequences for legal theory. Roughly, we are to understand that the law is a creation of human cognition, in which the experience of our lived lives is transformed through the metaphoric nature of our reasoning to produce various ICMs which guide our thought and behaviour. Thus our law is in a sense objective, since these ICMs are created on the back of our actual, historical, shared, and embodied, human experience, but also contingent, because our metaphorical mappings may change as our experiences or cultural circumstances do.

One of Winter's examples of a metaphor change which alters the ICM by which legal doctrine is understood is the case of the

---

[25] Winter, 'Transcendental Nonsense', n. 15 above, 1162–71.

American First Amendment which protects free speech.[26] Before the turn of the century, speech was understood to be like the flow of a river, and the constitutional protection of speech therefore amounted to a prohibition on dams: it was conceived of in terms of a prohibition on restraint prior to publication. If, however, the speech was 'bad' in some way, for example, seditious, there was no unconstitutionality in punishing it once it was published. Following Holmes' dissent in *Abrams* v. *United States*,[27] however, the prevalent metaphor for speech became the market-place, as in 'the market-place of ideas'. Speech was to be conceived of as wares offered for sale, and good products, or true speech, would capture the market in an atmosphere of unfettered competition. On this view, even post-publication restraints on speech are regarded as constitutionally suspect, since such restraints interfere in the workings of the market-place.

Thus metaphor provides us with an understanding of the transformative potential of law. Winter tells us how our communal and committed lived experiences provide the source for metaphorical transformative potential, so that the violent apparatus of the legal state is never immune from real progress in creating a more tolerant and free society.[28]

Four Arguments against Metaphoric Representation

Assuming we now have some idea of what Winter is up to, I would like to turn to the work of Lakoff, on whom he depends. The reason for going to the source directly is not just Winter's dependence on Lakoff, but primarily that Lakoff provides more explicit examples of metaphoric mappings along with the evidence which accounts for them. In criticizing the metaphoric model of concepts I will draw heavily first on a paper by Gregory L. Murphy, 'On Metaphoric Representation',[29] and secondly upon Jerry Fodor's work on the nature of concepts. The main thrust of

---

[26] *Ibid.*, 1188–90.   [27] 250 US 616 (1919), cited in *ibid.*, 1188.

[28] See in particular Winter, 'Transcendental Nonsense', 1228–33.

[29] G. L. Murphy, 'On Metaphoric Representation' (1996) 60 *Cognition* 173–204. See also the response: R. W. Gibbs, 'Why Many Concepts are Metaphorical' (1996) 61 *Cognition* 309–19. Murphy replied: G. L. Murphy, 'Reasons to Doubt the Presence of Evidence for Metaphoric Representation' (1997) 62 *Cognition* 99–108.

these criticisms is that on any plausibly rigorous formulation, the idea that many of our concepts are these complex metaphoric mappings is simply untenable.

First, to clear away some possible misinterpretations: no one in their right mind would deny that humans use metaphors extensively, nor that we often do so in reasoning or thinking about things. Nor would anyone deny that much of our thinking is a matter of making sense of our experience. So in criticizing the Lakoff model of concepts I am making no claims about either the nature of metaphor, which is in itself a very difficult subject, or the role of metaphors in thinking generally. What we are concerned with here is the idea that our mental representations, that is, our concepts, *are* complexes of metaphorical mappings. It is a different, and empirical, question whether our concepts may be shaped over time by the metaphorical way in which they are used.

The two views we are counterposing, then, are these: first, the Lakoffian model, in which the concept RIGHTS is a reasonably stable structural composite, the components of which are metaphors; these metaphors are grounded in basic bodily experiences. The directness of this mapping occurs, presumably, because we understand basic bodily experiences better than abstract things like rights; secondly, the opposing, conventional model of concepts, in which concepts are representations which have an identity that is independent of the metaphors we can use to think about, express, or describe the properties they represent. Thus there is a content, a semantics, for the concept RIGHTS which is independent of whatever metaphors concerning rights we may use; on this view, if it were not for its independent semantic identity, there would be no way in which we would understand what a 'rights' metaphor was about, much less discern whether it was an apt metaphor.

Argument 1

Consider Lakoff's examination of the concept of LUST in the Appendix. The evidence Lakoff presents for metaphoric concepts is, to say the least, shaky. There are two aspects to this: first, it is not clear that the examples which Lakoff cites as metaphors are metaphors; secondly, the evidence is circular.

As to the first point, consider the particular lust-mapping phrases which I have underlined. It is not at all obvious to me that these even are metaphors. The point is not simply that etymologically speaking, some of these are dead metaphors—'Don't be cold to me' for 'Don't be emotionally unresponsive to me'—and are now conventionally literal. The point is that some of these are straightforwardly literal. Lakoff seems to have decided that any use outside the most typical context for the use of a word is metaphoric. But although, as I mentioned earlier, stereotype or prototype effects are abundant in the human *application* of categories, these effects are not to be taken as implicating the *identity* of those objects to which the category properly applies; atypical members of a conceptual category are still full and proper members of the category. So it may well be that, according to the way we generally think, ostriches and penguins are lousy examples of birds; they are, nevertheless, both still birds as much as any other birds are.

In a similar way, although I suppose humans pounce less than tigers do, a human may still pounce. And notice this so-called metaphor about pouncing; the literal reading is that the person in question looks like he's 'ready to pounce', not that he's actually pouncing.

The same I think goes for the expressions 'sex-starved', 'sexual appetite', 'drooling', 'luscious', 'hunger', 'pawing', 'nuzzling', 'preys', 'loser', 'fled', 'fend off', and 'surrendered'. In the phrases Lakoff cites these words may not be used in the contexts we would employ in teaching children, just as we would probably not show a child a picture of a penguin first to teach it the meaning of the word 'bird'. Nevertheless, just as we would want the child to be able to use 'bird' in respect of penguins at the end of the day (and this is exactly what happens), we want children to use words like 'nuzzle' or 'surrender' or 'flee' or 'luscious' in all those circumstances in which they properly apply, even if those circumstances are atypical.

A somewhat different difficulty arises with Lakoff's characterization of the phrases under the rubric 'LUST IS INSANITY'. It seems plausible to me from my experience of lust or infatuation that a state of mental disorientation or obsession is experienced which, in stronger form of course, is supposed to characterize craziness or insanity. In other words, these may be straightforward examples of hyperbole, not metaphor, in the same way that describing a tall person as a 'giant' is an example of hyperbole, not metaphor.

These criticisms, which directly challenge Lakoff's characterization of his data, can be supplemented. Another way of disputing the metaphoric description of these phrases is to rely upon the idea of polysemy, that is, that words have a number of related meanings: for example, the word 'rise' is understood to have related but distinct meanings in the sentences 'The bird rose into the air' and 'Inflation is rising'. The first concerns physical rising, the second concerns a more abstract mathematical notion of increase. What relates the two conceptual contents or word-meanings is their structural similarity; neither is a metaphor for the other. The other view, upon which my remarks on the metaphoric treatment of 'pounce', 'luscious', 'fled' and so on, tacitly relied, may be called monosemy. This is the view that these words apply to the phenomena in question because they instantiate the very same property.[30] The point is, as Murphy points out,[31] that Lakoff never explores other possible characterizations of the expressions upon which he relies which would suggest that they are simply not metaphors at all.

The second problem with the evidence is that it is circular. Murphy describes Lakoff's *modus operandi*:

[A] cultural metaphor is identified on the basis of various idioms and collocations, such as *I destroyed her argument; he lambasted me in class; she undermined my position.* Then a metaphoric representation is proposed on the basis of these data, such as ARGUMENT IS WAR. What predictions or consequences are derived from this metaphoric representation? ... [I]t is further idioms and collocations: *He can't defend against that argument*, etc. There is an absence of other psychological data given in support of this view. Lakoff identifies five types of evidence for the metaphoric representation view. ... Notably, none of them provides a nonlinguistic measure of conceptual structure. Standard theories of concepts have had implications for findings in induction, problem-solving, object recognition, conceptual development, and memory, among other areas. It would be useful to see evidence for metaphorical concepts from these domains, in order to escape the linguistic circularity.[32]

Argument 2

The basic-abstract relation which is supposed to ground the direction of the mapping is implausible given the evidence. A metaphor

---

[30] For a strong defence of the view that concepts are generally monosemic, see C. Ruhl, *On Monosemy: A Study in Linguistic Concepts* (Albany, NY, 1989).

[31] Murphy, 'On Metaphonic Representation', n. 29 above, 189.

[32] *Ibid.*, 183–4.

is directional: there is one thing being talked about, called either the topic or the target, and some metaphorical material which is applied to it, called either the vehicle or the source. Thus in 'She's quite a dish', 'she' is the topic or target and 'is a dish' is the source or vehicle. The relation which is supposed to connect the two, say that this woman is 'appetizing', somewhat like a plate of food is, is sometimes called the ground. The problem is that on Lakoff's theory of metaphoric mapping, the topics and vehicles are often the wrong way round given his experientialist commitments. The vehicle is often more complex, disembodied, or abstract than the topic which, according to Lakoff and Winter, we must necessarily understand metaphorically because it is so complex, disembodied, or abstract.

Take again the case of LUST. It just seems implausible that the vehicle FUNCTIONING MACHINE (ESPECIALLY A CAR) is somehow more embodied and experiential than is LUST. The same can be said of insanity. I have experienced lust, but not, so far, actual insanity, and I think this state of affairs is true of most people. How then could the latter be more familiar experientially than the former? Much the same could be said about LUST IS A GAME, since games are artificial practices that really are composed of abstract rules.

Common examples of Lakoff's metaphorical representations are emotion concepts, like anger or love. But it has been pointed out that emotions are generally

experienced by children much earlier and much more extensively than the domains that are said to structure them. Since the experiential basis of thought is a tenet of the metaphorical representation view, it is extremely puzzling why it is that emotions are not directly represented via our experiences of them, and instead are represented in terms of warfare, journeys, insanity, sickness, animal behaviour, pressure in closed containers, and so on.[33]

Argument 3

The metaphoric theory of concepts creates a serious false/contradictory information problem. It simply does not make sense to hold that some concepts consist of metaphoric mappings because

---

[33] *Ibid.*, 191, citing A. Ortony, 'Are Emotion Metaphors Conceptual or Lexical?' (1988) 2 *Cognition and Emotion* 95.

the possession of such concepts would entail the possession of multiple false and contradictory beliefs.

Consider the metaphoric mapping LUST IS HUNGER; THE OBJECT OF LUST IS FOOD. Now the idea is that I understand LUST in terms of what I understand about hunger and food. The question is, what aspects of hunger or food are properly mapped or transferred to inform me about the nature of LUST? If there is no independent identity for LUST, no constraints which the concept of LUST *itself* imposes, then everything I know about food must (should? may?) be treated as true also of lust. So, for example, I know that food is nutritious. So, therefore, I should believe that having sex is nutritious. I know that most people eat several times during the day, and so I should also believe that people satisfy their lusts several times during the day. If you don't eat a fair helping of food and often, you will die, and thus if you don't have a fair helping of sex and often, you will die. And so on. There is no way of determining that any of these mappings is incorrect if nothing about the concept of LUST itself makes them so. Note that there is no way out of this problem by positing that the mappings themselves are somehow metaphoric, such that the mapping only transfers some aspects of FOOD to LUST, for that only leads to an infinite regress: what determines which elements of LUST are properly part of the FOOD/LUST metaphor which is applied directly to lust? There must be some stable concept of the LUST/FOOD mapping, and we begin all over again.

One might, however, remind oneself that Lakoff typically provides multiple metaphors, as we have with LUST, and so argue that *the intersection of many metaphors* fixes the content of the concept, by triangulation, metaphorically speaking. So in the same way that we might say that the complex concept 'red wine' is the intersection of red things and wines, LUST is the intersection of things which are food, things which are games, things which are functioning machines, and so on. Lakoff and Winter make no such claim, and it is probably wisest not to do so, for it does not look promising.[34] For this to work, the intersection itself cannot

---

[34] The rules by which complex concepts may be created from simple ones comprise more than the rule of intersection, of course, and these combinatorial rules are complicated; e.g., many examples of adjectival modification of noun which seem superficially to follow the same rule as does 'red wine' cannot simply be treated as intersection. Consider 'big ant' and 'fake Rembrandts': the set of big

be a *metaphoric* intersection: the intersection must be of a particular property or set of properties which actually 'triangulates'. But, of course, the intersection of the concepts HUNGER, HEAT, INSANITY, WAR, a GAME, and so on, does not reveal any plausible complex concept, for there is no such thing which is literally hungry, hot, insane, war, a game, and so on.

Indeed, rather than affording any kind of solution to the indeterminacy problem, the multiplicity of metaphoric mappings only makes things worse. With no independent identity for LUST which constrains what we are to believe about LUST based on what we believe about FOOD, we not only have a representational structure for the concept which leads us to have many false beliefs, we have one which leads us to have many false *and contradictory* beliefs.

LUST, so we are told, is HUNGER, HEAT, INSANITY, WAR, a GAME, and so on. In wars or games, we expect people to act rationally to secure their self-interest; on the other hand, insane people are typically regarded as acting irrationally in ways that rarely serve their self-interest. The metaphors, therefore, are in direct conflict. It is simply impossible to have a stable concept structured in this way, that is, a stable concept about which we must believe P and not P simultaneously in order to possess it. Unless a concept has an independent representation which may manifest various aspects which are relevantly similar to the metaphoric vehicles in the mappings, the metaphoric mapping simply has no focus, and therefore cannot give the concept any stable, determinate, and coherent identity.[35]

Argument 4

There is, finally, a more technical problem concerning the individuation of concepts. The metaphoric model of concepts delivers concepts which are far too 'fine-grained'.

An excessive fine-grainedness of concepts is a problem which

---

ants is not the intersection of the sets 'big things' and 'ants', for ants are not big, they are small: the set of fake Rembrandts is not the intersection of the sets 'fake things' and 'Rembrandts', for fake Rembrandts are not Rembrandts. The point in the text may be developed thus: the most obvious combinatorial rule does not work, and it is incumbent upon Lakoff and Winter, if they want to go down this route, to provide one that does. No particular rule appears to suggest itself, and they have the burden of argument.

[35] See Murphy, 'On Metaphonic Representation', n. 29 above, 180–2, 184–8.

can arise in any semantic theory, that is, a theory which purports to explain what words or sentences mean. If, for example, I explain that the content of the concept FOOD that you have is *constituted* by all your beliefs about food, then that theory of concepts is too fine-grained. It slices concepts too thinly because it individuates concepts in such a way that we have many more distinguishable, separate concepts than we want. Why? Well, if your concept FOOD is constituted by all the beliefs you have about food, it is most unlikely that your concept FOOD will be the same as my concept FOOD, since you and I will surely have some different beliefs about food. I may believe, for example, because once upon a time I knew things like this, that the energy we get from food is ultimately made available for cellular processes in the form of adenosine triphosphate, and you may not. If our concept of FOOD were to depend upon, in the sense of being at least in part constitutively composed of, such beliefs, then you and I would have different concepts of FOOD: as regards our FOOD-thoughts, and our use of the word 'food', we would be operating under different conceptual schemes. Thus when we talked using the word 'food', we would be talking at cross-purposes. There is, on this score, a similar difficulty with one's own concepts; each time you learned a new fact about FOOD, your concept of food would change. Thus your memories about FOOD 'in the past' would no longer be available to you as memories about FOOD now, and your current FOOD beliefs could never actually be in conflict with your old FOOD beliefs. Indeed, it doesn't really make sense to say that you could learn a new fact about FOOD, for such learning would alter what you were learning about.

There are currently, I think, roughly three ways of dealing with the problem of excessive fineness of grain vis-à-vis the belief-constitutive semantics sketched above. The first is to deny that one must necessarily have any particular beliefs to possess the concept. This is the position of Jerry Fodor, a conceptual 'atomist'.[36] While Fodor does not deny that *de facto* one may have to possess some beliefs or other concepts in order to possess any particular concept X, he does deny that any particular beliefs or other concepts are necessary constitutive elements

---

[36] See Fodor, *Representations*, n. 9 above, ch. 10; J. A. Fodor, *Concepts: Where Cognitive Science Went Wrong* (Oxford, forthcoming).

of the concept itself. So he distinguishes possession conditions from semantic content. So, on Fodor's view, your having different beliefs from mine about food is not a problem, since the content of the concept is not dependent on the particular beliefs you may have about the property it represents. A second approach is to deny that any belief whatsoever about food, like the belief that one's Aunt Ethel eats it, is constitutive of the concept FOOD. On this view, only a certain few beliefs which it is plausible that all concept-possessors have are constitutive. The problem with this approach will be recognized by anyone familiar with Quine's criticism of the analytic-synthetic distinction. If one wishes to hold that only some particular beliefs about a concept are conceptually necessary aspects of its representational content, while the rest are not, one seems to be arguing that some beliefs are true in virtue of meaning alone, for example, that bachelors are unmarried men. To distinguish these beliefs from all the other contingent beliefs about the property which the concept represents, one requires a principled way of telling them apart, that is, a workable analytic/synthetic distinction, and there does not appear to be one on the horizon. The third option is to say that we do not need to rely upon concept *identity* at all, that is, the idea that you and I share the same concept or that you and you as you were ten minutes ago do. All we need is the notion of concept *similarity*. Thus your concept FOOD and mine are close enough for jazz, that is, sufficiently similar to describe our food behaviour so that we understand that it is food we both seek after a hard day of delivering academic papers, or to say that I get my point across when I say, 'Let's have a pint first, and then we'll get some food'. This may seem a promising way out, but unfortunately no one has the first shred of an idea how to make the notion of conceptual similarity work without tacitly trading on the implicit existence of concept *identities*.[37] That is, the only notion of similarity we have outside of degree concepts like HOT or TALL (and FOOD is not such a concept) is 'identical in some respects': that is, X is similar to Y in that X shares some of the features of Y. Unfortunately, if X 'shares some of the features' of Y, that means that X and Y have

---

[37] See in particular J. A. Fodor and E. Lepore, *Holism: A Shopper's Guide* (Oxford, 1992), 17–22, 189–202.

those features identically. So we're stuck with conceptual identity, it seems, whether we like it or not.[38]

The point of raising all of this is that if there is a problem of
excessive fine-grainedness of concepts when we regard *beliefs* as
constitutive of concepts, then the Lakoff/Winter metaphorical
representation view has this problem as well, though the problem
is framed in terms of the constitutive metaphors which together
compose the concept. Although Winter and Lakoff talk about
conventional metaphors, given their belief that what makes a
metaphor salient is the way in which the experiential vehicle
makes sense of the topic which is abstract or difficult to understand, what makes a metaphoric mapping appropriate seems to be
nothing more than the fact that the metaphor works, that there is
some similarity between the topic and the vehicle which we find
somewhat enlightening. And this does not appear to be any more
restrictive a constraint than is imposed by individuating concepts
according to any or all of the beliefs that one holds. After all, I
should assume that there will be just as many metaphors I am
willing to accept, some lousy, some quite informative, *as*
metaphors, that is, as expressing some aspect of the topic via its
similarity to the vehicle, as there will be statements about the topic
I am willing to believe are true; indeed, it is possible that the scope
of difference between individual concept-possessors is multiplied
extensively if any metaphor one is willing to accept is constitutive,
for after all, as is often said, everything is like everything else in
some way. As a result, it is highly unlikely that differently situated
metaphoric concept-possessors would ever share the same
concept. The metaphors we understand, and thus are willing to
accept, are, as Lakoff and Winter point out, likely to be local and
culturally specific. Thus, despite what seems plausible and even
obvious, for example that both the !Kung tribesman and I can
both realize that Fred over there is behaving in a lustful fashion to

---

[38] By the same token, reference to Wittgenstein's idea of family resemblance
does not get us anywhere here, for the notion of family resemblance explicitly
depends upon the identity of different identifiable features and relationships. As
Wittgenstein puts it, '[a]nd we can extend our concept of number as in spinning a
thread we twist fibre on fibre. And the strength of the thread does not reside in the
fact that some one fibre runs through its whole length, but in the overlapping of
many fibres': L. Wittgenstein, *Philosophical Investigations* (G. E. M. Anscombe
(trans.), Oxford, 1958). In order to make the thread, we require the individual
fibres.

Beatrice, on Lakoff's and Winter's view we could not understand each other's concept of lust, since it seems most unlikely he will understand that a lustful person is a functioning motor car. For the same reason we must hold that my great-grandfather's concept of lust changed when he learned of the invention of the motor car.

For all of these reasons, it seems that the metaphoric theory of conceptual representation is fatally flawed. The problem does not lie primarily in Lakoff's and Winter's paying special attention to our 'experiential understanding'. It lies in their positing a realm of 'concepts' which are fairly obviously the results of different evanescent episodes of creative thinking. In his reply to Murphy's criticism of metaphoric representation, Gibbs pretty much gives the game away. He says:

> The so-called problem of multiple metaphors can be easily handled if we view concepts not as fixed, static structures but as temporary representations that are dynamic and context-dependent. Under this view, concepts are temporary, independent constructions in working memory created on the spot from generic and episodic information in long-term memory. Because temporary conceptualizations are doing the traditional work of concepts in controlling categorization behavior, it is important in this view to refer to these as *concepts*, and to use knowledge for referring to the body of information in long-term memory from which concepts are constructed.[39]

This just cannot be right. Treating temporary constructions in working memory as *concepts* would virtually guarantee that the fineness-of-grain problem could never be adequately solved, for these temporary constructions would categorize objects on a different basis each time the concept was applied. Concepts are not merely one-off categorization devices, but simply must be implicated in the way in which we have beliefs, desires, and expectations, store things in memory, and reason. If humans are to be even minimally rational, our concepts must be relatively stable symbolic representations which enter into all of the processes of categorization, belief, desire, memory, and so on.[40]

---

[39] Gibbs, 'Metaphorical Concepts', n. 29 above, 313 (emphasis in the original).

[40] Another way of putting this, suggested to me by Jonathan Sutton, is that concepts must be stably *bivalent*: they must either apply or not apply, over indefinite periods of time and in different circumstances. Otherwise they do not serve to represent properties.

As far as I know, Lakoff and Winter do not adopt these views of Gibbs, but their reliance upon metaphorical representations may ineluctably lead them to the same position. If, as seems true, and as Gibbs seems to endorse, metaphoric representation is a more or less temporary act of expression, rather than the manifestation of stable conceptual content, then their hope of framing conceptual schemes as systems of metaphoric representations is bound to fail.

An Observation/Theory Distinction in Law and Morality and the Innateness of Moral and Legal Concepts

Does cognitive science, then, provide any reason for believing that there may be an observation/theory distinction in the domain of morality and law? That is, is there reason for believing that there is some sort of principled distinction between moral knowledge which is secured because of our status as embodied creatures situated in a world with which we naturally interact in a limited number of ways, and knowledge that we have because of the power of our minds to reason, think, speculate, theorize, draw analogies, and so on? In this final part, I want to say a few very speculative things about how cognitive science may indeed suggest the existence of such a distinction.

In the first place, what we must do is take the non-theoretical concept base seriously, but not confuse it with an experientialist base—Lakoff and Winter are not the only ones to have made this mistake. Reading 'sensory concept' for 'experiential concept' was also a mistake of reductionist empiricists who believed that all human beliefs and concepts could ultimately be reduced to various associations of primitive, experiential concepts, like 'red' for instance. This project failed, utterly, and the failure is regarded by most philosophers as principled: that is, not only is it the case that it did not work, the fact of the matter is that it cannot work because it is misconceived. The facts of the matter appear to be that human minds are set up to appreciate and represent reality in terms of a vast array of primitive concepts that our experience triggers or 'releases', concepts which we are already programmed to acquire. In this sense, the concepts which we get are ones we already have simply by virtue of being the kinds of creature we are. In other words, many of our concepts are *innate*.

The central issue concerning the innateness of concepts can be framed in terms of a dispute between empiricists and rationalists over the extent and nature of the primitive conceptual base. According to the former, all primitive concepts are triggered by sensory experience, and all other concepts are complex constructions built by the mental combinatorial apparatus with constituents from this primitive base. While rationalists also recognize a primitive conceptual base, it is much larger than that of the empiricist sensory base, not being limited to sensory concepts. The essence of this dispute turns on whether the empiricist claim that the non-sensory concepts that humans acquire are learnt (that is, generated by the standard inductive process of hypothesis formation and confirmation from experience) is more or less plausible than the rationalist claim that a great many non-sensory concepts are triggered by various environmental factors. The evidence seems to support the rationalist claim:[41] first, there is the well-recognized problem of the poverty of the stimulus; the rate at which children acquire lexical concepts, that is, those concepts which are not obviously structured complexes of other constituent concepts (like 'brown cow')—in other words, the rate at which children acquire really *new* words—makes it highly unlikely they could do so as a process of hypothesis formation and confirmation. 'Pre-literate children, who are limited to ambient speech, must be lexical vacuum cleaners, inhaling a new word every two waking hours, day in day out.'[42] Secondly, given the variety of actual human experience, the empiricist story makes it remarkable that the conceptual repertoire of humans is so largely invariant. That is, besides the *rate* at which children learn the language of their parents, they all learn (roughly) the *same* language, despite the fact that the paucity of linguistic data with which children are presented would empirically support the acquisition of a literally infinite number of languages and conceptual vocabularies. The upshot, as Fodor puts it, is that 'the concept isn't coming from the environment, it's coming from the organism. All the environment does is provide the triggers that release the information'.[43]

---

[41] See Fodor, *Representations*, n. 9 above, ch. 10.
[42] S. Pinker, *The Language Instinct* (London, 1994), 151.
[43] Fodor, *Representations*, n. 9 above, 280.

Now the question is: is there any reason to believe that our *moral* conceptual repertoire is somehow different from the rest of our conceptual repertoire that, though it appears to be the case that our grasp of the world in various domains, from the characterization of artefacts, to natural kinds, to physical concepts like causation, motion, rigidity, to colour perception, to number and geometrical concepts, and so on, depends upon innate principles, should the possibility of innateness not be extended to the domain of morality?

In order to test this possibility, we must understand what we ought to be looking for. No one doubts that many of our concepts (think of a concept like PROTON) are dependent upon our having already acquired more basic concepts. So we are looking for the possibility that there are innate moral concepts which a child can grasp on the basis of merely observing its (social) environment, or at least on the basis of getting no better explicit instruction from its elders than it gets in its own language. Thus, one wants to be able to discern a basic level of moral concepts, the acquisition of which can lay the foundations for the acquisition of less easily 'observable' concepts, or indeed of what we might call 'theoretical' concepts which are not observable at all, but which necessarily relate to more basic concepts. Having acquired the basic concepts, the right mental and social environment is provided for the acquisition of more 'theoretical' moral concepts. Thus the idea would be that a child might pick up a list of specific dos and don'ts, e.g. don't hit others or take their things from them, before it learns the concept RIGHTS, if indeed it ever does.[44]

One bit of evidence one might look for is the existence of a basic conceptual level. I have discussed the nature of basic level concepts and the existence of basic level legal/moral concepts elsewhere;[45] roughly the idea is this: our concepts exist in hierarchies. For example, we have natural kind hierarchies like poodle, dog, animal, living thing, which run from the more specific to the more abstract. There is no logical or philosophical reason why any particular level of a hierarchy should be particularly important.

---

[44] Remember, *no one* had the concept of 'rights' which we do until, apparently, the late 16th or early 17th century. See J. Finnis, *Natural Law and Natural Rights* (Oxford, 1980), 206–10.

[45] J. E. Penner, 'Basic Obligations' in P. B. H. Birks (ed.), *The Classification of Obligations* (Oxford, 1997), 91.

But in human cognition a certain level is, which is called the 'basic' level. Concepts at this level are learnt first, reflect 'gestalt' observational properties (that is, they are grasped as wholes, for instance on the basis of general shape), provide the most ready access to stored knowledge, and so on. Interestingly, the basic level is not the most specific level, nor the most abstract: we enter into the hierarchy in the middle, which happens to be a particularly salient level. Thus children learn DOG before POODLE or ANIMAL, and basic concepts like DOG appear to be more productive 'entry points' into our knowledge than are concepts higher up or lower down in the hierarchy. The evidence from all kinds of domains seems to suggest that there is a basic level of concepts, which reflects *both* the sensory properties of the world *and* our human interests.[46]

As for the existence of basic moral or legal concepts, the evidence is slim, but positive.[47] In the two empirical investigations carried out there appears to be fair evidence for a basic level for moral/legal categories, just as for all the others. It seems pretty clear that CRIME is a super-ordinate concept, that is, one higher up the hierarchy than the basic level. With respect to a basic legal or moral concept like LARCENY, the idea, roughly, is that humans understand a concept of LARCENY (though not the particular label 'larceny' of course) on the basis of exposure to the phenomenon of larceny in various ways. And larceny is not a merely perceptual property. As we all know, it takes more to identify a case of larceny than merely to look at an event such as someone's taking some object from the possession of someone else. As a basic-level concept, it is not acquired through having mastered a 'theory' or 'conceptual' scheme which explains what a CRIME is and how LARCENY is a species of CRIME. At the very least then, the empirical work that has been done does not suggest that moral or legal categories are somehow special in not exhibiting a basic conceptual level.

---

[46] For a review, see G. Murphy and L. E. Lassaline, 'Hierarchical Structure in Concepts and the Basic Level of Categorization' in K. Lambert and D. Shanks (eds.), *Knowledge, Concepts, and Categories* (London, forthcoming).

[47] See A. Rifkin, 'Evidence for a Basic Level in Event Taxonomies' (1985) 13 *Memory & Cognition* 538; M. W. Morris and G. L. Murphy, 'Converging Operations on a Basic Level in Event Taxonomies' (1990) 18 *Memory & Cognition* 407.

A second place where one might look for evidence of the possibility of innate moral concepts is in psychological data in related
areas. Here I want briefly to mention some work on the theory of
mind. The 'theory of mind' refers to the capacity of individuals to
recognize the existence of other minds that have their own individual beliefs, their own independent psychological reality, as it were.
Simon Baron-Cohen has convincingly argued that there is a
'mental module' which governs the acquisition of a theory of
mind, that is, an independent mental faculty which can be specifically absent in certain individuals due to brain trauma or pathology.[48] The most striking case is that of autistic persons. People
with autism fail to acquire a theory of mind, that is, an understanding of the independent reality of other minds, not only at the
normal developmental age of three or four, but usually well into
their teens; many never manage it. The point about raising the
theory of mind module here is to dispel the notion that somehow
social faculties, and the concepts that arise from our having them,
are *a priori* immune from consideration as innate faculties because
they are necessarily the result of explicit socialization. One cannot
socialize an autistic person into getting a theory of mind, and
although intelligent autistic persons develop a myriad of strategies
in dealing with others, by their own account their experience of
those dealings is akin to dealing with another species in terms of
all sorts of basic social interactions.[49] While the defects of autism
are not to be translated directly as equivalent to the failings of a
'moral' mental module, autism does make children quite oblivious
to their often startling violations of appropriate social behaviour.
It is therefore not crazy to suggest that similar observational and
conceptual faculties might underpin the acquisition of concepts
which could more obviously be regarded as 'moral'.

If it is true that there are innate moral concepts, and furthermore that there may be a discernible distinction to be drawn
between basic moral concepts and more 'theoretical' ones, then I
want further to suggest that we can picture the work of moral
philosophy as 'moral science', and that furthermore this science
may be very well served by the methodology of common-law
decision-making.

---

[48] S. Baron-Cohen, *Mindblindness: An Essay on Autism and the Theory of Mind* (Cambridge, Mass., 1995).   [49] *Ibid.*, 139–43.

By common-law decision-making, I wish to refer to a process of moral enquiry which may be characterized by certain features of the way in which the law is developed in common law legal systems (though, of course, not only there). First, the subject-matter of common-law decisions are real-life events of social conflict, that is, conflicts over the correct or just norms to be applied. Secondly, these events are framed in terms of narratives, by which I mean nothing more than that the events are understood to take place in the world in which common-sense causation operates. Common-sense causation comprises both the causation of the natural world, whereby we understand that flying cricket balls can crack skulls, and common-sense or 'folk' psychological explanation, by which we explain A's behaviour when he socks B in the jaw by A's belief that socking B in the jaw will hurt B and by A's desire to achieve that result. Thirdly, the decisions of common-law judges are justified on the basis of 'local', not theoretical, reasons. That is, my reading of most of the cases at common law is that judges, faced with litigants who expect reasons to be persuasive to them regardless of whatever allegiances they may have to overarching moral theories like utilitarianism, tend by and large to produce reasons which take as their explicit or implicit starting-points fairly specific injunctions which concern the particular area or category of law which they perceive to bear on the instant problem. So, for example, if a plaintiff claims that he should be compensated because, before the formation of an actual contract with the defendant, he performed services towards the contract of which the defendant was aware, and because the defendant allowed him to carry on even after the defendant was well aware that he was no longer going to enter into the contract, I do not imagine the judge would begin his opinion with a disquisition on autonomy. I expect that his relevant starting-point would be the laws of contract, restitution, and estoppel, and indeed, rather specific areas or rules of those laws which might govern the 'narrative' of pre-contractual relations between commercial actors. Framing the decision in broad and abstract terms of the 'Who is my neighbour?' variety occurs infrequently, and if the subsequent career of Lord Atkin's judgment in *Donoghue* v. *Stevenson*[50] is anything to go by, that infrequency

---

[50] [1932] AC 562.

should be welcomed. The typical judicial opinion does not look very much like theory construction, which is why, perhaps, the injunctions of people like Hohfeld to judges and lawyers to adopt a more rigorous and abstract use of terms like 'rights' have not been notably successful.[51]

What I am suggesting is that, by and large, in general, *roughly*, the history of the development of the mass of common law doctrine has occurred employing concepts which are at, or close to, the basic level. That is, the common law operates to develop the law not as a theoretical exercise, but at a more common-sense or 'observational' level, simply because, as a function of its institutional nature, judges are faced with real situations, real 'narratives' that is, rather than philosophical hypotheticals (truth *is* stranger than fiction), and they are required to give reasons which, despite the legal jargon (which is not that impenetrable after all, once the terms of art are mastered), are supposed to, and usually do, explain the basis of the decision to the litigants, who are regular folks, not philosophers.

Perhaps a comparison will be illustrative. Common-law moral decision-making can be compared to modern empirical linguistics. After Chomsky, linguistics operates essentially on the basis of one 'theoretical' postulate (which might, of course, turn out to be wrong, though don't hold your breath): the human language faculty is a *specific* biological property of human beings, more precisely, of the human mind/brain, and is therefore amenable to empirical investigation to see how it works. By specific biological property, I mean that the language faculty is, in the standard terminology, *modular*: it is a particular organ of the mind/brain, in the same way that the liver is a particular organ. It can be usefully studied (really, *only* usefully studied) if recognized to be a distinct functional mechanism which, while interacting with other organs of the mind/brain, has its own particular features and functional characteristics. The idea that the ability to acquire and use language is simply a matter of general intelligence, whether framed in terms of an association device, or an hypothesis forming

---

[51] W. N. Hohfeld, *Fundamental Legal Conceptions as Applied in Legal Reasoning and Other Essays* (New Haven, 1923). Hohfeld might, of course, have simply got rights wrong (a view I favour). See J. E. Penner, 'The "Bundle of Rights" Picture of Property' (1996) 43 UCLA LRev. 711 for a consideration of the effect of the 'bundle of rights' thesis on the theoretical appreciation of property.

and confirming device, or something else again, which individuals *just apply* to the problem of verbal communication, seems hopeless in light of the facts. And in order to understand this faculty, the day-to-day work of linguistics involves studying the actual speech that humans produce in their different languages (almost all linguists examine comparable instances in different languages) to try to work out the innate rules which govern speech production and interpretation. In order to do so, linguists rely heavily on what speakers of particular languages regard as 'well-formed' grammatically. Thus particular rules of the universal grammar, which can and do display different parametric values in different human languages, are discovered through the systematic observation of grammatical speech production. If we have a moral faculty which allows us to acquire certain moral concepts or principles, which may, like the rules of universal grammar, have different parametric values which can be set in different cultures, the development of the common law is akin to a process of moral narrative investigation in which the moral sense of 'well-formedness' according to the parametric values set in a particular society are realized and explained in the light of new situations of moral conflict which present a kind of data for examination. Very rarely, I suggest, do individuals have truly opposing moral intuitions about a particular case or narrative that appears. The disputes are in a sense about explanation. How do we achieve the 'well-formed' result given the other 'commitments' our particular moral grammar has made, that is, given the other parameters on moral judgement we have, as a culture, already set? It may be that in some cases we decide that the parameters remove the injustice from the sway of the common law entirely. For example, given other legal-moral commitments, a society may no longer legitimately hold that a coercive, institutionalized response is morally appropriate for bad behaviour in marriages which leads to a breakdown; instead a regime of no-fault divorce is the only appropriate one. In other cultures different parametric settings may demand that divorces should only be granted upon the finding that one party is an utter rogue. To take another possible example, it may be the case that the growth of insurance for accidents *does* alter what our legitimate moral commitments might be vis-à-vis compensation for personal injury through the institution of negligence law. The suggestion is that the most salient *moral* reasons for the law to switch to no-fault divorce or abolish the action for personal injury in negligence law (perhaps legally requiring individuals to take out first-party insurance)[52] are appreciable via local considerations which reflect the current 'well-formedness' of quite specific moral principles.

This may appear to suggest that abstract, philosophical enquiry into the nature of morality and what morality really requires of us is of little use. I should say quite the opposite. While there may well be a salient distinction between observation (what I have suggested might be akin to the linguistic sense of well-formedness) and theory in morality, that does not impugn the value of theory, or what might be called more abstract and speculative explanation. For it is on the back of this that it would appear that we achieve much moral progress. For example, the notion of rights is a very abstract one, just like the notion of a proton is, but it might well be the case that the notion of rights reflects moral reality as much as we currently believe the notion of protons is indispensable to understanding the physical world. And the notion of rights, I would argue, has had a profoundly beneficial influence in forcing a more rigorous, and therefore just, characterization of our moral principles and concepts at the basic level. In this sense, moral theory, or abstract moral explanation, is indispensable to moral progress, and should never be discounted. But we should be wary of the hegemony of theory at the same time. The 'observational' basis[53] of morality is not something that can be overthrown, lest we lose all connection to the only way we can morally experience or grasp the world. To give just one illustration, about which I have written quite closely elsewhere,[54] the distinction between different things that we allow to be treated as property, and our actions (or services to others) which normally we do not, may be basic. Thus a resistance to treating chattels and human actions as just examples or species of a genus 'value' may not simply be a resistance to imbibing a theory which would have them so, say a theory which treats the satisfaction of preferences (of whatever kind) as a foundational building block. Thus our resistance to treating rape as just a kind of theft may not simply be

---

52 See P. S. Atiyah, *The Damages Lottery* (Oxford, 1997).
53 Which might be the best way of understanding the notion of moral intuition.   54 See Penner, 'Basic Obligations', n. 45 above.

a theoretical resistance, but innate, because based on our basic conceptual apparatus. If what I have said above is right, it may be very important to take this kind of resistance seriously.

It might be appropriate to conclude by pointing out that 'theory' might have different forms, some good, some not so good. It does sound like a throw-back to the nineteenth century, but perhaps it is time to revive the term 'legal scientist', and its cognate 'moral scientist': for these terms suggest that the purpose of legal and moral theorizing is to investigate and explain something that exists independently of what we might wish or what is in our control. Anyway, depending upon your various intellectual commitments, you may find all of this either tantalizing or outrageous. It is, however, worth exploring, and that is what I am currently up to.

Appendix

LUST IS HUNGER: THE OBJECT OF LUST IS FOOD

He is <u>sex-starved</u>.
You have a remarkable <u>sexual appetite</u>.
She's quite a *dish*.
Hey, *honey*, let's see some *cheesecake*.
Look at those *buns*!
What a piece of *meat*!
She had him <u>*drooling*</u>.
You look <u>*luscious*</u>.
Hi, *sugar*!
I *hunger* for your touch.

A LUSTFUL PERSON IS AN ANIMAL

Don't touch me you *animal*!
Get away from me, you <u>*brute*</u>!
He's a *wolf*.
He looks like he's ready to <u>*pounce*</u>.
Stop <u>*pawing*</u> me.
Wanna <u>*nuzzle*</u> up close?
He <u>*preys*</u> upon unsuspecting women.
He's a real *stud*—the Italian *Stallion*!
Hello, my little *chickadee*.
She's a *tigress* in bed.
She looks like a *bitch on heat*.
You bring out the *beast* in me.

LUST IS HEAT

I've got the *hots* for her.
She's an old *flame*.
Hey, baby, *light my fire*.
She's *frigid*.
Don't be *cold* to me.
She's *hot stuff*.
He's still carrying a *torch* for her.
She's a *red hot mama*.
I'm *warm* for your form.
She's got *hot pants* for you.
I'm *burning* with desire.
She's *on heat*.
He was *consumed* by desire.

LUST IS INSANITY

I'm *crazy* about her.
I'm *madly* in love with him.
I'm *wild* over her.
You're driving me *insane*.
She's <u>*sex-crazed*</u>.
He's a real *sex-maniac*.
She's got me *delirious*.
I'm a <u>*sex addict*</u>.

A LUSTFUL PERSON IS A FUNCTIONING MACHINE (ESPECIALLY A CAR)

You *turn me on*.
I got my *motor runnin'*, baby.
Don't leave me *idling*.
I think I'm *running out of gas*.
Turn my crank, baby.

LUST IS A GAME

I think I'm going to *score* tonight.
You won't be able to *get to first base* with her.
He's a <u>*loser*</u>.
I *struck out* last night.
She wouldn't *play ball*.
Touchdown!

LUST IS WAR

He's known for his *conquests*.
That's quite a *weapon* you've got there.
Better put on my *war paint*.
He <u>*fled from her advances*</u>.
He has to <u>*fend off*</u> all the women who want him.
She <u>*surrendered*</u> to him.

SEXUALITY IS A PHYSICAL FORCE; LUST IS A REACTION TO THAT

She's *devastating*.
When she grows up, she'll be a *knockout*.
I was *knocked off my feet*.
She *bowled me over*.
What a *bombshell*!
She's *dressed to kill*.
I could feel the *electricity* between us.
She *sparked* my interest.
He has a lot of *animal magnetism*.
We are *drawn* to each other.
The *attraction* was very strong.

SCIENCE, REASON, AND TORT LAW

Looking for the Reasonable Person

Heidi Li Feldman

Introduction

Remember the reasonable person of ordinary prudence who acts with due regard for the safety of others ('the reasonable person')? Appellate opinions constantly invoke this creature, sometimes explicitly developing his character and personality traits, sometimes providing information about him by deciding how he would behave in particular circumstances. Yet very few scholars have investigated the identity of 'the reasonable person', the agent who animates tort law. While academics have explored the conditions for reasonable risk-taking,[1] they have not taken the judicial cue to do so by investigating the personality of the reasonable person of ordinary prudence who acts with due regard for the safety of others. The doctrinal sketch provides a rudimentary ethico-psychological profile, but hardly more than that. I contend that we can arrive at a much richer understanding of the moral and epistemic outlook of 'the reasonable person' as it appears in tort doctrine. With such an understanding, we would better appreciate

---

[1] See e.g. R. A. Epstein, 'A Theory of Strict Liability' (1973) 2 J Legal Studies 151 (arguing that exposing others to risk is never reasonable in the sense of being an excuse to avoid liability to one injured directly by one's actions); G. P. Fletcher, 'Fairness and Utility in Tort Theory' (1972) 85 Harvard LR 537 (arguing that risk-taking is unreasonable when it is non-reciprocal); E. J. Weinrib, 'Toward A Moral Theory of Negligence Law' (1983) 2 Law and Philosophy 37 (arguing that risk-taking that violates Kantian principles is unreasonable); R. Posner, 'A Theory of Negligence' (1972) 1 J Legal Studies 29 (arguing that risky activity is unreasonable when it is economically inefficient); J. Coleman, *Risks and Wrongs* (Cambridge, 1992), 303–86 (arguing that unreasonableness in risk-taking has both moral and economic dimensions).

how modern negligence law conceives of and evaluates individual decisions about activities that risk injury to others. It would then be easier to decide a panoply of issues prominent in scholarship and policy debates today: whether we should retain, reform, or reject the modern legal approach to negligent behaviour.

The current paper takes a tiny step toward a more ambitious project: a naturalistic, ethico-psychological analysis of the reasonable person of ordinary prudence who acts with due regard for the safety of others. Ultimately, I aim for an analysis that places our understanding of this concept, including its social function and uses, within a broader empirical understanding of the natural world. I do not seek a simplistic reduction of 'the reasonable person' to a scientific formula. Rather, I aim to integrate our understanding of this doctrinal concept with relevant research from science, especially the social sciences, and from philosophy, especially ethics and the philosophy of mind. Yet my project remains broadly naturalistic in that it attempts to understand the doctrinal conception of 'the reasonable person' by using empirical information about people and drawing upon philosophical theories themselves concerned to accommodate such information. I hope to arrive at an analysis of the doctrine that comports with and may contribute to current work in anthropology, psychology, cognitive science, evolutionary biology, and philosophy of mind, political philosophy, and ethics. In each of these fields, researchers investigate issues directly relevant to tort law's 'reasonable person'.

Anthropologists investigate cultural entities such as 'the reasonable person'. Psychologists, cognitive scientists, and evolutionary biologists study human cognition and reason, how these capacities develop in individual persons and humans as a species, and the conditions that foster good cognition and reasoning. Philosophers of mind develop normative standards for cognition and reason and explore the relationship between empirical information about these capacities and proposed norms to govern them. Political philosophers and ethicists examine the relationship between epistemic rationality (rationality in belief formation) and practical rationality (rationality in action), and the interplay of the descriptive and the normative in the concepts, principles, and norms that govern both individual and social practices. Despite its somewhat overwhelming scope, this array of scholarship promises to bear on the best understanding of tort's concept of the reasonable person. Let me briefly highlight the potential relationship between 'the reasonable person' and each of the fields mentioned above. I mention some possible connections, attempting to be illustrative rather than exhaustive.

In *Explaining Culture*, the prominent anthropologist Dan Sperber proposes a research programme for explaining cultural representations. Sperber's research programme is both nuanced and ambitious, and I will not do it justice here. But I hope to say enough about the Sperberian programme to demonstrate its relationship to my large-scale project. Sperber suggests that anthropologists should develop an epidemiology of cultural representations, that is, an account of culture that explains why certain representations endure over time and across people—sometimes even throughout different cultures—while others do not.[2] Representations include all sorts of ideas, concepts, notions, stories, rituals, and so forth.[3] Embedded in common law tort doctrine, 'the reasonable person of ordinary prudence who acts with due regard for the safety of others' is one such cultural representation.

Researchers working within a Sperberian programme would trace the pathways running from and to individual mental representations and shared public representations. This would necessitate research into what goes on in the minds of individuals as they interact with their environment, which, in turn, would require research into the environment they inhabit. So, a cultural-epidemiological study of 'the reasonable person' would examine both the psychological and ecological conditions that explain this representation's endurance in the common law. A naturalized analysis of the representation could contribute to the cultural-epidemiologist's investigation into the conditions for its maintenance and

---

[2] According to D. Sperber (*Explaining Culture: A Naturalistic Approach* (Oxford, 1996), 61):

An epidemiology of representations would establish a relationship of mutual relevance between the cognitive and the social sciences, similar to that between pathology and epidemiology. This relationship would in no way be one of reduction of the social to the psychological. Social-cultural phenomena are, on this approach, ecological patterns of psychological phenomena. Sociological facts are defined in terms of psychological facts, but do not reduce to them.

[3] Sperber himself defines 'representation' very generally. He writes: 'an object is a representation *of* something, *for* some information processing device' (*ibid.*).

transmission. In turn, cultural-epidemiological information about 'the reasonable person' could increase our grasp of how laypeople and jurists conceive of this legal representation.

Consider now the fields devoted, in whole or part, to the study of the human mind and its capacities: psychology, cognitive science, philosophy of mind, and evolutionary biology. Note that 'the reasonable person' portrays a specific individual—fictitious, certainly, but a specific individual none the less. The representation itself reminds us that this individual possesses a particular psychological outlook and the capacity to cognize and reason. Cast in this light, those fields that investigate human psychology, cognition, and reasoning—either at the level of the individual or the species— offer resources for analysing the nature of the person portrayed. As with the Sperberian research programme within anthropology, certain research programmes within each of these fields appear especially helpful in the quest for a naturalized analysis of 'the reasonable person'. In a subsequent segment of this paper, I will examine in some detail one such research programme within psychology, developed by Daniel Kahneman, Amos Tversky, Richard Thaler, and Jack L. Knetsch among others.

The common law invokes 'reasonable person' as a normative standard, to be applied by laypeople to resolve particular disputes over accidental injury. Yet the tort representation couches the standard of care in descriptive terms, depicting a fictitious person and inviting the jury to compare an actual litigant's conduct to how this person would have acted in the litigant's circumstances at the time of the accident. Many moral philosophers have relied on the strategy of idealizing a person who then serves as a normative standard for actual actors.[4] Additionally, some ethicists have studied the relationship between the descriptive and the evaluative.[5] Others have focused specifically on the moral dimensions of reasonableness.[6] Each of these philosophical inquiries has the potential to illuminate 'the reasonable person' and the negligence standard they set.

[4] See e.g. J. Rawls, *A Theory of Justice* (Oxford, 1973), 17–21, 136–49; P. Railton, 'Moral Realism' (1986) 95 *Philosophical Review* 163–207.
[5] See e.g. 'Goodness and Choice' in P. Foot, *Virtues and Vices* (Berkeley, 1978), 132–47; B. Williams, *Ethics and the Limits of Philosophy* (Cambridge, 1985), 129–55.
[6] See e.g. J. Rawls, *Political Liberalism* (New York, 1993), 48–53.

While a full-strength ethico-psychological analysis of 'the reasonable person' requires comprehensive interdisciplinary treatment, the confines of the current paper permit only narrower study. First, I survey an alternative treatment of 'the reasonable person', the law and economics analysis. This analysis serves as both foil and model for the approach I propose. Secondly, I turn to social psychology for a preliminary assessment of the identity of the reasonable person of ordinary prudence who acts with due regard for the safety of others. In this section, I also use social psychological results to examine the place of the Learned Hand test in the thinking of 'the reasonable person'. Thirdly, I discuss one way the ethico-psychological analysis might account for the normative aspect of 'the reasonable person'. Finally, I conclude with an early estimation of the merits of the ethico-psychological project.

Lessons from Law and Economics

To date, the social science most widely brought to bear on tort law has been economics. This fact by itself would make it worthwhile to examine the analysis of negligence and reasonable risk-taking through law and economics before undertaking another analysis involving the social sciences. But the approach of law and economics to tort law deserves a careful look for another reason. For many scholars, this school of thinking about tort law presents a paradox. The perspective of law and economics on torts simultaneously attracts and repels. Scholars apparently uncomfortable with it nevertheless end up capitulating to it, in whole or part.[7] I find this ambivalence instructive. If we could isolate the attractive features of the approach to negligence through law and economics

---

[7] This stance toward law and economics is apparent in many of Jon Hanson's collaborations. Hanson and his co-authors often adopt the law and economics framework and then, while working within it, argue against the conclusions reached by stalwart devotees. See S. P. Croley and J. D. Hanson, 'The Nonpecuniary Costs of Accidents: Pain-and-Suffering Damages in Tort Law' (1995) 108 Harvard LR 1785; S. P. Croley and J. D. Hanson, 'Rescuing the Revolution: The Revived Case for Enterprise Liability' (1993) 91 Michigan LR 683; J. D. Hanson and K. D. Logue, 'The First-Party Insurance Externality: An Economic Justification for Enterprise Liability' (1990) 76 Cornell LR 129. See also G. Calabresi, *The Costs of Accidents* (London, 1970), 18–20, 24–6; Coleman, *Risks and Wrongs*, n. 1 above, ix–xi.

from the repellant ones, an ethico-psychological analysis might profit by incorporating the former and avoiding the latter.

The law and economics movement borrows primarily from one current in contemporary economics—mainstream neo-classical micro-economics.[8] While economists working in this tradition might well criticize some of the ways scholars of law and economics have applied its tenets, it remains the case that law and economics together have adopted the distinctive commitments of neo-classical economics. These include methodological individualism; rational choice theory; and an ambition to provide predictive explanations for actual individual behaviour. Somewhat perversely, these commitments endow the analysis of negligence by law and economics with both its most appealing features and its major drawbacks.

According to law and economics, negligence consists of risk-taking that fails to maximize overall social welfare, usually understood as utility[9] and occasionally as wealth.[10] Individuals seek to maximize their own welfare. In the absence of market failure, produced by problems such as transaction costs and imperfect information, private parties concerned only with maximizing their own welfare could, simply through bargaining with one another, realize maximal social welfare: a state in which no one could be better off without somebody else becoming worse off. Legal measures to prevent negligence become necessary only when individual welfare-maximizing behaviour fails to maximize social welfare. Hence, the function of tort law is to align incentives for maximization of individual welfare with the goal of maximization of social welfare. A properly functioning tort law corrects for market failure by forcing risk-takers to internalize negative externalities which their activities impose on others.

The foregoing account displays the distinctive commitments of neo-classical economics. The account explains a social institution—tort law—always with reference to the behaviour of individ-

---

[8] See e.g. S. Shavell, *Economic Analysis of Accident Law* (Cambridge, 1987). A highly respected legal economist, Shavell commits to both the substantive and methodological principles of neo-classical micro-economics. See *ibid.*, vii, 1–3.

[9] *Ibid.*, 2.

[10] See R. A. Posner, 'Utilitarianism, Economics, and Legal Theory' (1979) 8 J Legal Studies 103; *idem*, 'The Ethical and Political Basis of the Efficiency Norm in Common Law Adjudication' (1980) 8 Hofstra LR 487.

ual persons. Tort law's negligence standard responds to a co-ordination problem among individuals, each pursuing their own interests. Law and economics contends that, over time, courts have developed a standard for negligence meant to solve this problem. Scholars within law and economics may disagree over how conscious that development has been or how well the current standard succeeds, but they agree on the form of an economic interpretation of tort law: personal welfare-maximization drives individual behaviour; aware of this at some level, appellate judges fashion legal standards to align individual incentives with maximization of social welfare. The interpretation holds tight to methodological individualism: it explains both extra-legal behaviour and the emergence of legal standards in terms of the attitudes and actions of individual persons. Methodological individualist analyses need not deny the plausible claim that social institutions and practices shape individual attitudes and behaviour. Methodological individualism insists only that an analysis clearly delineate the relationship between the existence of a social entity and the attitudes and behaviour of individual human beings; in sum, that social entities are fundamentally the creatures of individual agents and not the other way around, notwithstanding the complex causal interconnections between individuals' beliefs, attitudes, and actions and social institutions and practices. This insistence is quite attractive. Any methodological individualist account avoids the need to postulate cultural entities entirely detached from the human agents who inhabit that culture. This is an advantage, because it is hard to see how such wholly detached entities could come into being or systematically interact with members of a culture.

Neo-classical economic analysis presupposes a particular conception of individual rationality. According to neo-classical principles, rational actors seek to maximize their own welfare in accordance with the axioms of rational choice. The axioms of rational choice can be variously presented. The basics: rational actors prefer outcomes with higher payoffs to ones with lower payoffs. These preferences are consistent across choice situations. They are also transitive, so that if A is preferred to B, and B is preferred to C, then A is preferred to C. Rational actors will select dominant outcomes and strategies. Thus, a rational actor selects a prospect, if there is one, that is better than another in one situation, and at least as good as that alternative in all others. The presupposition that actual people do and should conform to these axioms propels neo-classical economic analysis, including the law and economics interpretation of negligence law. Negligence law responds to conditions that prevent actual people from bargaining with one another so as to maximize their respective individual welfare. Because it corrects this problem, a properly functioning tort standard facilitates rational action and is thereby justified as well as explained.

In contrast to our scrutiny of methodological individualism in the context of law and economics, the neo-classical conception of rationality becomes problematic when we examine it embedded in an account of negligence law. As an account of rationality, the neo-classical economic conception is itself controversial, vulnerable to charges of descriptive inaccuracy and normative ugliness. Both scholars and laypeople question the validity of this understanding of human rationality. Since the economic conception of rationality powers the account of negligence law by law and economics, that account inherits its troubles.

Regardless of the particular strengths or weaknesses of the economic conception, however, superimposing *any* specialized conception of rationality on to an account of negligence law raises potential problems. Negligence law seems to have its own outlook on rationality. The 'reasonable person' predates interdisciplinary examination, and reference to reason and rationality lies at the heart of this doctrinal representation. This creates a presumption in favour of an analysis that starts from the internal perspective of tort law, seeing whether the common law of negligence has generated a coherent, distinctive, plausible conception of rationality. It might turn out that a conception of rationality indigenous to tort law duplicates the economic conception. This would bolster the adequacy of the law and economics approach to negligence. But by presupposing an identity between tort law's conception of rationality and the economic one, law and economics begs a controversial and significant question. Even if we cannot cultivate an indigenous conception of rationality from the common law of negligence, we need not incorporate the economic one, unless we determine both that tort requires a conception of rationality and that the economic one is the best available. At best, then, the superimposition of the economic conception of rationality is premature.

Despite the drawbacks of too readily importing the economic conception of rationality into an analysis of negligence law, we can appreciate the appeal of doing so if we turn our attention to the value that informs this conception of rationality: welfare-maximization. This value seems compelling, at both the individual and the social levels: whatever welfare consists in, being best off seems best. It seems attractive therefore to interpret negligence law as a device for making everybody as best off as possible. Furthermore, if we maintain welfare-maximization as the exclusive value for individual behaviour and for the tort system, it appears that we can give a unified, elegant explanation of individual action and a unified, elegant criterion for deciding upon the nature of negligence. To cap it all, we get a neat match between individual motivation for action and normative justification for the negligence standard. One can appreciate the impact of an analysis that reduces to an apparently singular value that both motivates and justifies. Ultimately this stark reductionism may fail to do justice to the range of values implicit in tort doctrine, yet the virtue of elegance should not be forgotten in developing an alternative to the analysis of negligence by law and economics.

From the foregoing dissection, we can extract some of the most and least attractive features of law and economics as an approach to understanding the law of negligence. Law and economics teaches the appeal of methodological individualism, the significance of human welfare, and the import of elegance and unity in a theoretical account of negligence. It also illustrates the dangers of too hastily importing specialized, non-legal conceptions of rationality into our understanding of tort law and the drawbacks of reductionism as an analytical strategy. With these lessons in mind, I begin the ethico-psychological analysis.

The Psychology of the Reasonable Person of Ordinary Prudence Who Acts with Due Regard for the Safety of Others

Psychology concerns itself with, among other things, the intentional states and intentional acts of human beings. A mental state or a physical behaviour is intentional when it has content or meaning, when it is about something. Quintessential intentional states include beliefs and desires. A belief is a state of mind about how the world is; a desire is about how one would like things to be. Purposeful, deliberate acts typically express intentionality. When, for example, one drinks a glass of water to quench one's thirst, one's act differs from an automatic reflex, such as breathing in one's sleep, or, to put the contrast more starkly, from the physical movements of a plant swaying in the wind.

'The reasonable person' depicts an intentional actor. Such a person believes and desires and, at least sometimes, acts with purpose. This means that psychological investigation into intentional states and actions can illuminate the identity of tort's reasonable person. Of course, the reasonable person is a very unusual individual—idealized and incomplete. To decide which psychological research promises insight into the reasonable person, we need a preliminary sense of who the reasonable person is.

Starting from the doctrinal representation itself, we know that this individual is reasonable, prudent (but not especially so), aware of others, and concerned with their safety. Furthermore, these are his only traits. When a jury compares a defendant's conduct to his, they define the reasonable person's situation according to the defendant's circumstances at the time of the incident. But these additional features are contingent. Unlike those specified in the doctrinal representation they are not inherent characteristics of the reasonable person. To understand the identity of 'the reasonable person' across individual cases—an identity whose constancy courts stress[11]—we should concentrate on the reasonable person's enduring attributes, looking to psychological research relevant to these. Reason and prudence are, in part, cognitive capacities, enabling certain types of judgement and evaluation. (Just by this phrasing, it should be clear that I intend no sharp distinction between cognition and evaluation, a dichotomy sometimes drawn.) Reason makes us more than passive vessels of our beliefs: we can reflect upon our beliefs, modify them in the light of evidence, draw inferences based upon them, and so forth. Prudence makes us appreciate that the world presents hazards and obstacles as well as opportunities. Reason and prudence—among other capacities—permit us to navigate the world sensibly and thereby further our ends.

---

[11] The seminal case stressing the unity and constancy of the 'reasonable person's' identity is *Vaughan* v. *Menlove*, 132 Eng. Rep. 490 (C.P. 1837), in which the court rejects a characterization that would shift according to the attributes of particular defendants.

For over twenty years, psychologist Daniel Kahneman and his collaborators—most notably, Amos Tversky, Richard Thaler, and Jack L. Knetsch—have investigated the beliefs, desires, and decisions of ordinary people making decisions about loss and gain under conditions of uncertainty—ordinary people called upon to exercise reason and prudence. The aim of the authors has been to see whether people's actual decision principles obey the axioms of rational choice theory—the formal underpinning of neo-classical micro-economics. Their work has demonstrated that people's actual behaviour consistently diverges from these axioms, in systematic ways. My own interest in this empirical social psychological research does not lie directly in its implications for rational choice theory. Kahneman and his co-authors' results bear on the identity of the reasonable person of ordinary prudence who acts with due regard for the safety of others. By definition, this person exercises reason and prudence in deciding what risks to take. Although an idealization, tort law's 'reasonable person' is still an abstracted version of an ordinary person. Good information about actual people offers insight into the capacities, beliefs, and judgements of tort's central figure.

After performing a range of experiments designed to reveal how people make decisions under circumstances of uncertainty, Daniel Kahneman and Amos Tversky concluded that people divide the process of such decision-making into two stages.[12] In the editing phase, decision-makers rely on framing to code the stakes of choice. They perceive outcomes as positive or negative in relationship to a neutral reference outcome or state.[13] Whether or not a decision-maker regards a given outcome as a loss or a gain depends upon the reference point, which the frame generates. In any given choice situation, the neutral reference tends to be dictated either by a description given to the decision-maker or by the conditions to which he has become adapted.[14] Social norms and individual expectations and aspirations can also play a role in setting reference points.[15] In any event, if the frame shifts, so can

[12] D. Kahneman and A. Tversky, 'Prospect Theory: an Analysis of Decision Under Risk' in P. K. Moser (ed.), *Rationality in Action,* Contemporary Approaches (Cambridge, 1990), 140, 151; A. Tversky and D. Kahneman, 'Rational Choice and the Framing of Decisions' (1986) 59 *J of Business* S257.

[13] A. Tversky and D. Kahneman, 'The Framing of Decisions and the Psychology of Choice' (1981) 211 *Science* 456. [14] *Ibid.*

[15] *Ibid.*

the reference point, and the same final outcome may be re-coded as either a loss or gain compared to the new reference point.

People do not translate across different frames of the same facts. Nor do they operate with any canonical representation of a decision, which they then might use as a basis for translation.[16] Furthermore, Kahneman and Tversky discovered that framing effects persist even after people become aware of them—more like visual illusions than computational error.[17]

The Kahneman–Tversky experiments also revealed systematic patterns in how people evaluate outcomes of choice. People perceive and care about outcomes *qua* losses and gains, rather than simply as final states of wealth or welfare.[18] Moreover, people dislike loss more than they like gain. Kahneman, Tversky, and their co-authors call this tendency 'loss aversion'.[19] Note that it differs from risk aversion. A person who is averse to loss may choose relatively risky options in order to avoid outcomes perceived as loss. In fact, people are generally risk-seeking in order to avoid losses; they are only systematically risk-averse to achieve or retain gains.[20]

Loss aversion regularly produces other systematic consequences, including endowment effects, status quo biases, and higher toleration for opportunity costs than concrete losses.[21] Explaining these in turn: experimental tests show that once someone regards an item as part of his endowment, this in itself increases its value to him. Due to endowment effects, holders of goods value them more highly than buyers do. People will not pay as much for something they do not have as they will demand for the same item if they already possess it. Indeed, people generally prefer the status quo to any change at all, whether a gain or loss— the status quo bias. Finally, people would rather maintain the

[16] Tversky and Kahneman, 'Rational Choice', n. 12 above, S256.

[17] *Ibid.*, S260.

[18] Kahneman and Tversky, 'Prospect Theory', n. 12 above, 151.

[19] R. H. Thaler, A. Tversky, D. Kahneman, and A. Schwartz, 'The Effect of Myopia and Loss Aversion on Risk Taking: An Experimental Test' (1997) *Q J Econs* 648.

[20] Kahneman and Tversky, 'Prospect Theory', n. 12 above 162–4.

[21] D. Kahneman, J. L. Knetsch, and R. H. Thaler, 'Experimental Tests of the Endowment Effect and the Coase Theorem' (1990) *J Political Economy* 1325–46; D. Kahneman, J. L. Knetsch, and R. H. Thaler, 'The Endowment Effect, Loss Aversion, and Status Quo Bias' (1991) *J Econ. Perspectives* 193–206.

contents of their current endowment and give up even a fairly large opportunity to increase their endowment if the opportunity poses even relatively slight risk of loss.

Both framing and loss aversion pertain to the psychology of 'the reasonable person'. To the extent that this person perceives situations as presenting choices under conditions of uncertainty—and this appears to be his perspective on the world—Kahneman and Tversky's research suggests that he decides what to do in the light of a reference point, from which he assesses possible losses and gains. Furthermore, 'the reasonable person' cares about losses and gains instead of states of the world understood in isolation from previous states of the world. He evaluates comparatively. 'The reasonable person' cares more about losses than gains, to the point that he strongly dislikes any prospect of losing what he already has even for the sake of attempting great gain, but if threatened with loss, he will take great risk to avoid it. 'The reasonable person' will also be subject to endowment effects and status quo bias. He will therefore be reluctant to risk people's current level of well being, even if doing so stands some chance of improving their well being. Likewise, he will even forego opportunity to increase others' overall safety-level rather than expose them to risk of injury beyond current reference levels.

Until the reasonable person is situated, we do not know much about the reference point compared to which the reasonable person assesses losses and gains. Once a court appeals to 'the reasonable person', however, it has fuller information: the defendant's circumstances at the time of the incident play a large part in setting the frame. Since people tend to adopt frames rather passively, nothing indicates that the reasonable person would be more highly reflective about framing effects in the moment than would any other person, including the defendant. Yet even though we cannot know specifically the frames that set the reasonable person's reference point in each situation he faces, we do know one crucial element in all of his decision frames. The reasonable person's frame always includes a measured but serious concern for the safety of others. Combined with loss aversion this means 'the reasonable person' will be especially sensitive to imposing losses upon others and not particularly concerned with actually affording them gain.

Tversky and Kahneman also researched how people appraise probabilities, discovering that people tend to rely on certain heuristics rather than basic principles of statistics. The heuristics reduce the complexity of assessing outcomes, although they can lead to systematic errors in calculating probabilities. I want to examine this research for its consequences for the Learned Hand test.[22] This is one of the subsidiary doctrines American courts use to understand the behaviour of the reasonable person of ordinary prudence who acts with due regard for the safety of others. As is well known, the Hand test asks whether the burden of precaution was more or less than the probability of loss posed by a tort defendant's conduct. While scholars of law and economics have treated the Hand test as a proto-typical cost-benefit analysis, judges have understood it somewhat differently. Learned Hand himself resisted too quantitative an understanding of the approach:

It is indeed possible to state an equation for negligence in the form, $C = P \times D$ [in] which C is the care required to avoid risk, D, the possible injuries, and P, the probability that the injuries will occur, if the requisite care is not taken. But of these factors care is the only one ever susceptible of quantitative estimate, and often that is not. The injuries are always a variable within limits, which do not admit of even approximate ascertainment and, although probability might theoretically be estimated, if any statistics were available, they never are and, besides, probability varies with the severity of the injuries. It follows that all such attempts are illusory, and, if serviceable at all, are so only to centre attention upon which one of the factors may be determinative in any given situation.[23]

While Hand may not have anticipated developments in the techniques of cost-benefit analysis, his observations about shortages of relevant information remain accurate. Furthermore, ordinary people do not employ sophisticated—or basic—statistical methods when assessing probability.

Tversky and Kahneman found that people use three main heuristics, highlighted as follows. Relying on *representativeness*, people evaluate the probability of a result according to its similarity to the process or class from which it originates. People also depend upon *availability*, assessing probability according to how readily they can recall instances of the possible outcome. Finally, people evaluate probability by *adjusting from an initial anchor*, so

22 *United States* v. *Carroll Towing*, 159 F.2d 169 (2d. Cir. 1947).
23 *Mosian* v. *Loftus*, 178 F.2d 148, 149 (2d Cir. 1949).

their final determinations remain relatively close to that starting-point. Tversky and Kahneman observed these heuristics among experienced social scientists as well as laypeople. Such data supports Tversky and Kahneman's conclusion that principles of statistics such as sampling and regression toward the mean are not intuitive, nor do people tend to induce them from life experience.

The persistence of these heuristics suggests that tort law's reasonable person would resort to them when considering probability of losses potentially caused by their activities. Courts paint the Learned Hand test as a way of identifying how the reasonable person behaves; they do not attribute this way of thinking to the reasonable person directly. Yet presumably the value of the test as an indicator of how the reasonable person would behave depends in part on an assumption that the reasonable person's conduct conforms to the principles of choice implicit in the test. When 'the reasonable person' assesses the likelihood of loss, he uses the heuristics of representativeness, availability, and adjustments to anchors. This comports with Learned Hand's observations in *Mosian*, quoted above. The algebraic Hand test does highlight features likely to be noticed and considered by 'the reasonable person' when they pursue a risky activity; but it is psychologically implausible to assume that the reasonable person engages in sophisticated cost-benefit analysis, or even uses basic statistical methods, to assess probable outcomes depending upon precautions taken.

The Psychological, the Descriptive, and the Normative

We can investigate reasonableness from two directions, one descriptive and the other normative. We need not rest content with an account of reasonableness derived exclusively from empirical investigation. We can also ask whether a descriptive account based on actual behaviour captures the normative force of reasonableness. Likewise, we know the negligence standard based on 'the reasonable person' is meant to govern our actions, not just depict our actual behaviour. Having relied on empirical social science to develop a preliminary psychological profile of 'the reasonable person', it is incumbent upon me to defend a profile so rooted in the descriptive, and to explain how it can preserve the normative role played by 'the reasonable person' in the law of negligence.

Any analysis of the standard set by 'the reasonable person' must allow for its dual aspect—part descriptive, part normative. On the one hand, an analysis that ties 'the reasonable person' too tightly to the intentional states and actions of real people empties the standard of negligence of normative force, making it superfluous. On the other, an analysis that detaches 'the reasonable person' too completely from real people's intentional states and actions undermines the prospect of anybody actually measuring up to it, threatening to collapse an alleged fault standard into something extremely close to strict liability.

Law and economics pursues the happy middle ground by incorporating into 'the reasonable person' principles of rational choice, which do and should guide their decisions about risky activity. The problem with this strategy is that empirical testing indicates that these principles do not guide people's choices about risk and loss under conditions of uncertainty. Moreover, people appear to be consistently and systematically incapable of reasoning according to the axioms of rational-choice theory or assessing probability with the accuracy required by the theory. Even in market environments, people do not readily learn to reason according to rational choice theory.[24] In short, law and economics proposes an analysis of 'the reasonable person' that makes meeting the negligence standard virtually impossible for most people most of the time.

The ethico-psychological analysis does not suffer from this problem. This analysis imputes to 'the reasonable person' actual decision-makers' attitudes towards and evaluations of risk, loss, and probability. The ethico-psychological analysis maintains the normativity of the standard of 'the reasonable person', however. Recall the full representation: the reasonable person of ordinary prudence who acts with due regard for the safety of others. Reasonableness and ordinary prudence are not the only components of this person's psyche. Equally integral is his due regard for the safety of others. Nothing in Kahneman and Tversky's or Kahneman, Knetsch, and Thaler's results suggests that actual people cannot or regularly do not act with such regard. At the same time, nothing in this social psychological literature suggests that actual people always do exercise due regard for the safety of

[24] Kahneman and Tversky, 'Rational Choice', n. 12 above, S274–5.

others. Thus, his due regard for others has the potential to endow a standard based on 'the reasonable person' with authentic normativity, asking of people something they can achieve, although they often do not—the exercise of due regard for the safety of others.

We must now entertain the question of what constitutes due regard for others from the perspective of the reasonable person of ordinary prudence. Reasonableness has an ethical overtone as well as an epistemic one. Ultimately, philosophical study of reasonableness as an ethical quality must be introduced into a full ethico-psychological analysis of the reasonable person of ordinary prudence who acts with due regard for the safety of others. For now, however, I continue my exploration of social psychology in an effort to better understand how 'the reasonable person' understands due regard for the safety of others.

Another portion of Daniel Kahneman's research, conducted primarily with Jack L. Knetsch and Richard Thaler, investigates people's perceptions of fairness in market transactions. This work bears a more attenuated relationship to the psychology of 'the reasonable person' than Tversky and Kahneman's earlier studies, because negligence regulates the law of behaviour not generally construed as market activity.[25] Nonetheless, judgements of fairness in market transactions may provide a baseline for judgements of fairness in other contexts, particularly in those involving treatment of people outside one's circle of intimates. Torts generally involve strangers in this sense, and so do market transactions, which usually occur outside the familial or social setting.

Kahneman, Knetsch, and Thaler surveyed people's opinions about a variety of market transactions, ranging from the consumer setting, to landlord–tenant interactions, to labour relations. They discovered that people applied two basic 'rules of fairness' regardless of general milieu or the size and nature of the firm (that is, a large department store and a small hardware store, or a mass producer and an individual craftsman).[26] Both rules invoke the

---

[25] Some scholars of law and economics interpret all behaviour as market activity, but I take it that this distinguishes their view from the ordinary understanding of the domain of the market. If the law-and-economics interpretation is correct, then the Kahneman–Knetsch–Thaler results do bear directly on the outlook of the 'reasonable person'.

[26] D. Kahneman, J. L. Knetsch, and R. Thaler, 'Fairness as a Constraint on Profit Seeking: Entitlements in the Market' (1986) 76 *Amer. Econ. Rev.* 728.

idea of a reference point. According to one, it is unfair for a firm to exploit increases in market power to alter terms of a reference transaction at the direct expense of a customer, tenant, or employee.[27] According to the other, it is fair for a firm to maintain its profit at the reference level by raising prices or rents or reducing wages.[28] Kahneman, Knetsch, and Thaler claim some evidence that people, including those who operate firms, act on these judgements.

Generalizing from the market setting—but cautiously–these rules suggest that people judge it unfair for one party to exploit its power to inflict direct losses on others; but they judge it permissible for a party to maintain its wealth even if this is at a cost to others. If this is correct, and people abide by these rules somewhat regularly, we can add to our profile of 'the reasonable person'. If the reasonable person occupies a powerful position vis-à-vis others, he will not take this as licence to expose them to risk. At the same time, neither will the reasonable person actively promote others' safety at his own expense, at least not if this would require a sacrifice of his reference level of wealth.

The results of the Kahneman–Knetsch–Thaler research suggest that 'the reasonable person' combines self-interest in its most traditional aspect with consideration for others. To assess the plausibility of this general combination, my larger project will examine whether it is plausible to conclude that the capacity for such a psychological combination has evolved in humans. I will also refine my discussion of the many ways in which self-interest and consideration for others might possibly mingle, and the ways in which they ought to mingle, at least according to the law of tort.

A Tentative Appraisal of the Ethico-Psychological Project

While it would be quite premature to comprehensively assess the strengths and weaknesses of the ethico-psychological analysis of 'the reasonable person', or even to attempt a complete comparison to the law-and-economics alternative, a preliminary accounting is in order. As developed so far, the ethico-psychological approach

---

[27] Kahneman, Knetsch, and Thaler, 'Fairness as a Constraint', 729–30.
[28] *Ibid.*, 730, 732.

fares rather well when measured against the law-and-economics analysis. More generally, this dip into the ethico-psychological approach suggests fruitful lines of extension and admittedly also a few potential problems.

Introducing social psychological research into our understanding of 'the reasonable person' respects the requirements of methodological individualism. Kahneman and his collaborators examine the behaviour and thinking of individuals to generate their descriptive theory of decision-making under uncertainty and their descriptive theory of fairness. In neither case do they rely on epistemic or ethical norms that exist wholly independent of the thoughts and actions of individual agents. While Kahneman, Tversky, Thaler, and Knetsch acknowledge the interplay between individual psychology and the social environment, they do not detach the social from the individual and assign the social intentional status of its own.

Because it works from a descriptive theory of human rationality rather than a normative one, the ethico-psychological analysis avoids the pitfall of superimposing a technical and perhaps controversial conception of rationality on 'the reasonable person'. This could create the countervailing problem, discussed in the previous section, of depriving the ethico-psychological account of the resources to explain the normativity of tort law's representation of 'the reasonable person'. As I argued, however, turning to the representation of 'due regard for the safety of others' opens the possibility of examining the normativity of the larger representation from another angle. While I barely began such an examination in the present paper, further review of psychological and philosophical research into empathy, altruism, and judgements of fairness promises at least the potential of an analysis that does justice to the normative dimension of 'the reasonable person'.

This paper does not address the question whether welfare is the most important or even the only value realized in the law of tort. I assume the significance of welfare to the law of tort. The ethico-psychological analysis does, however, shed important light on what welfare means to 'the reasonable person'. Contrary to assumptions of law and economics, for 'the reasonable person' the carriers of value are losses and gains relative to a reference point, rather than states of affairs characterized independently of context. Shifting to this understanding of welfare increases the complexity of the analysis, because we have to investigate framing thoroughly, both in general and in specific cases, to understand the relationship between risk-taking and welfare for 'the reasonable person'. We relinquish some elegance and unity once we complicate the meaning or measurement of welfare. But this sacrifice may be worth it. Surely it is actual welfare—not a tidy idea of welfare—that figures significantly in the law of tort, and actual welfare appears to be a complex phenomenon.

So far, the ethico-psychological analysis compares nicely to the law-and-economics alternative. It retains some of the most compelling commitments of law and economics, such as methodological individualism. It gives up an extremely parsimonious understanding of welfare, which involves some loss of elegance of unity, but does so in favour of an understanding arguably more relevant to the law of tort. It avoids some of the most contentious aspects of law and economics by replacing the neo-classical conception of rationality with a descriptive account based on empirical social science.

Plenty of work remains, however, before we can rest assured that the ethico-psychological analysis will prove preferable to the law and economics analysis of 'the reasonable person', let alone fully satisfactory in its own right. Aside from introducing learning from additional disciplines, further information from psychology must be considered. Equally pressing are methodological issues. For example, I plan to consider the reliability of *any* ethico-psychological profile of a fictitious character—particularly one drawn rather sketchily in law, rather than fully fleshed out in literature. Given the vagaries in understanding the psyches of actual individuals, we might wonder about the validity of the effort to understand the psyche of a fictional person. Also on the methodological front, I will inspect the relationship between an ethico-psychological analysis of 'the reasonable person' and the larger corpus of tort case law. At the minimum, a satisfactory analysis should illuminate the law of negligence, providing good grounds for retaining or modifying all or some of it.

The current paper merely begins the move toward a fully-fledged ethico-psychological analysis. I have shown how to conduct the project, begun a substantive profile of 'the reasonable person', and demonstrated its appeal and potential fruitfulness. Still searching for 'the reasonable person'—but a few steps closer.

THE ROLE OF SCIENTIFIC EVIDENCE IN THE ASSESSMENT OF CAUSATION IN MEDICINAL PRODUCT LIABILITY LITIGATION

A Probabilistic and Economic Analysis

Richard Goldberg

Introduction

The role of scientific evidence in proving causation is becoming increasingly significant in tort litigation. This role is particularly relevant when assessing causality in cases involving liability for medicinal products. The present paper discusses the importance of the use of probabilistic evidence in such cases and suggests that statistical devices, such as Bayes' Theorem, could be useful in medicinal product liability litigation for solving causation problems which are recalcitrant to non-numerical solutions.

In view of the economic importance of the pharmaceutical industry, and the increasing occurrence of medicinal product liability litigation, the paper ends with a theoretical analysis, addressing the hypothesis of whether the use of probabilistic approaches to causation and medicinal products promotes economic efficiency.

The Importance of Causation in Medicinal Product
Liability Litigation

GENERAL

As we approach the end of the twentieth century, liability for medicinal products constitutes a major source of health-care litigation in most countries, particularly in the United States and to a lesser extent in the United Kingdom. The attribution of cause is a central issue in litigation concerning liability for medicinal products. The importance of establishing causation in such cases is considerable. Causation, if proved, will probably lead to settlement or victory.[1]

THE ROLE OF CAUSATION IN NEGLIGENCE

However, the traditional position in negligence in relation to causation means that the causation hurdle will be virtually impossible to overcome in the majority of cases concerning medicinal products.[2] This is partly because the difficulties in proving causation are magnified where medicinal products are involved. As Teff and Munro have observed,

Drugs are always potentially dangerous due to their toxicity. They are often taken by people who are already ill and who may be unusually susceptible to further ailments. Unlike many other products, they may cause injury in unpredictable ways, depending on the individual user's constitution. They may not be taken according to the instructions. The

---

[1] M. Mildred, 'Representing the Plaintiff' in G. Howells (ed.), *Product Liability, Insurance and the Pharmaceutical Industry: An Anglo-American Comparison* (Manchester, 1991), 27. However, this will not necessarily be so. For example, in the HIV–Haemophilia litigation, although the causal agent of the infection was clear, i.e. HIV-infected blood fractions, the question still remained as to whether the provision of the product or its prescription by a doctor was negligent *'at the time the infection was caused'*: *id.*, 'Class Actions' in C. J. Miller (ed.), *Product Liability and Safety Encyclopaedia* (London, 1997), Div. IIIA, para. 147.

[2] See *Wilsher* v. *Essex Area Health Authority* [1988] 1 All ER 871 at 881–2 (the burden of proof remains on the plaintiff to prove the causal link between the defendant's negligence and his injury). *Wilsher* was a case involving possible competing causes. For an overview of the representative case law in this area see R. Goldberg, 'Causation and Medicinal Products—A Legal and Probability Analysis' (1996) Consumer LJ 57 at 57–61.

user may be allergic to a particular drug. Alternatively, what appears to be an allergy may in fact be a toxic reaction.[3]

The difficulties of proving causation were recently noted by the Court of Appeal in an appeal by the plaintiffs from the judgment of Ian Kennedy J, who had struck out the plaintiffs' actions against prescribers of Benzodiazepines, on the basis that the actions were vexatious and an abuse of the process of the court.[4] Stuart-Smith LJ observed that there were 'very considerable problems on causation'.[5] Such problems involved

distinguishing between the effects of the drug and the underlying condition for which it was prescribed, the problems caused by previous addiction to Benzodiazepine drugs other than those prescribed by the defendants, and distinguishing between symptoms due to the drugs, or in some cases, other drugs or excess alcohol, and the fact that many plaintiffs may suffer at least some withdrawal symptoms in any event.[6]

STRICT LIABILITY AND CAUSATION

Causation has remained a problem, even in the light of strict liability for defective products. The EC Product Liability Directive,[7] and the UK Consumer Protection Act 1987 Part 1, which gives effect to it, adopt a strict liability scheme for defective products: the claimant in a medicinal product liability case will have to prove, for products supplied from 1 March 1988,[8] that (a) the product was defective, (b) the plaintiff's injury was caused by the defective product,[9] and (c) the defendant either produced the product or was a party with the same liability as the actual producer.[10] Moreover, the person injured by a defective medicinal

---

[3] H. Teff and C. R. Munro, *Thalidomide: The Legal Aftermath* (Hants, 1976), 135–6.

[4] *AB and others v. John Wyeth & Brother Ltd and others (No 2)* [1994] 5 Med. LR 149 and LEXIS 13 Dec. 1996.   [5] *Ibid.*, at 153.

[6] *Ibid.* See also the similar observations of Stuart-Smith LJ in respect of the difficulties in proving causation in *AB and others v. John Wyeth & Brother Ltd*, n. 4 above; *AB and others v. Roche Products Ltd* (LEXIS 13 Dec. 1996).

[7] 85/374/EEC on the approximation of the laws, regulations and administrative provisions of the Member States concerning liability for defective products [1985] OJ L210/29.

[8] When the Consumer Protection Act 1987 ('CPA') came into effect. S. 50(7) CPA states that no person is to be liable for a defective product supplied by its producer before the coming into force of Pt 1, i.e. 1 Mar. 1988.

[9] *Ibid.* s. 2(1).   [10] *Ibid.* s. 1(2); s. 2(2); s. 2(3).

product must prove the damage, the defect and the causal relationship between them.[11] The damage must have been caused
'wholly or partly by a defect' in the medicinal product.[12]

Thus the difference from negligence is that under a negligence
action breach of duty must cause the harm, whereas under the
Consumer Protection Act 1987 the *defect* must cause the
damage.[13] It seems that each Member State will rely on its own
theory of causation as established in its civil liability system,
though it has been noted that some kind of semi-autonomous
European understanding of causation could be established from
common elements of the Member States' legal systems.[14]

It seems that the area of strict liability and causation is affected
by the same sort of complexity as existed prior to the Consumer
Protection Act 1987, in the context of negligence. Indeed, it has
been argued that the lack of clarity concerning the operation of
causation under the Consumer Protection Act might result in a
greater obstacle to the securing of compensation than even the
inclusion of the Act's development risk defence.[15] With the difficulties of causation in both negligence and strict liability in mind,
we now turn to alternative approaches to the causation problem
looked at from the perspective of probability.

Proportional Liability

THE ROLE OF PROPORTIONAL LIABILITY IN THE CONTEXT OF CAUSATION AND MEDICINAL PRODUCTS

The problematic nature of drug-induced causation has posed the
question as to whether the traditional standard of proof on a

[11] Consumer Protection Act 1987, s. 2(1), implementing Art. 4 of the
Directive.   [12] *Ibid.* s. 2(1).

[13] It is therefore incorrect to state, as has one author, that under the CPA, 'a
plaintiff is still required to establish a causal link between the *defendant's act or
omission* and the former's loss' (emphasis added): P. Ferguson, *Drug Injuries and
the Pursuit of Compensation* (London, 1996), 125.

[14] S. Whittaker, 'The EEC Directive on Product Liability' (1985) 5 Yearbook
Europ. Law 233 at 247.

[15] B. S. Markesinis and S. Deakin, *Tort Law* (3rd edn, Oxford, 1994), 553.
For discussion of the development risk defence, see R. Goldberg, 'The
Development Risk Defence and Medicinal Products' (1991) 36 J Law Soc. Scotland
376.

balance of probabilities is really an appropriate or indeed accurate way of assessing drug causality. Professor David Kaye has examined the usefulness of the standard of both the balance of probabilities and that of proportional liability using the concept of what he describes as an expected loss function. He considers that the preponderance of evidence standard minimizes expected losses and error in both single defendant cases and those involving multiple defendants. In relation to the latter cases, he suggests that this is subject to important exceptions, in particular in the Diethylstilboestrol ('DES') cases, where the 'preponderance of evidence standard' produces 'biased results'. In such cases, Professor Kaye submits that proportional liability is the only approach that does not compensate undeserving victims and awards an accurate sum to each victim in question.[16]

In the cases involving alleged adverse drug reactions associated with the oestrogenic hormone DES, there were many potential defendants and the type of harm became increasingly difficult to attach to the drug, due to the considerable number of its manufacturers.[17] The proportional liability approach to establishing causal link has been considered as a solution to this difficult conundrum. Rosenberg moots proportional liability as a replacement for the traditional requirement as to the preponderance of the evidence in tort:

Under such a standard, courts would impose liability and distribute compensation in proportion to the probability of causation assigned to the excess disease risk in the exposed population, regardless of whether that probability fell above or below the 50 per cent threshold and despite the absence of individualised proof of the causal connection.[18]

The probability of causation would be derived from dividing excess risk[19] by the total risk, that is, by the sum of excess and

[16] See D. Kaye, 'The Limits of the Preponderance of the Evidence Standard: Justifiably Naked Statistical Evidence and Multiple Causation' (1982) 2 Amer. Bar Foundation Research J. 487 at 498–502, 504, 507–9, 514.

[17] There were 200 to 300 manufacturers of DES because neither DES nor its production method were subject to the protection of intellectual property rights and the basic materials were freely available: See N. Sheiner, 'DES and a Proposed Theory of Enterprise Liability' (1978) 46 Fordham LR 963 at 976.

[18] D. Rosenberg, 'The Causal Connection in Mass Exposure Cases: A "Public Law" Vision of the Tort System' (1984) 97 Harvard LR 851 at 856.

[19] Also known as 'attributable risk', calculated by subtracting the level of risk of the unexposed population (background risk) from the level of risk of the exposed population (total risk): see J. Sanders, 'From Science to Evidence: The

background risk.[20] Variations of this approach have been tried yet subsequently rejected in the courts.[21] One of the main objections to proportional liability has been the requirement of identification of risks that might be difficult to quantify.[22]

LIABILITY FOR THE TORTIOUS CREATION OF RISK

It is thus clear that there remains considerable difficulty surrounding the use of traditional causation solutions to resolve such complex issues, though proportional liability has been increasingly proposed as an appropriate response in many medicinal product liability cases.[23] Indeed, the most radical version of probability mooted is that of liability for the tortious creation of risk, which eliminates the actual harm requirement of tort law by assessing liability according to the degree of risk imposed on the plaintiff as opposed to the amount of harm suffered by the plaintiff.[24]

In the United Kingdom, there is no liability in tort or delict for increasing risks. Indeed, the courts have established that causal connection with the defendant's wrongful conduct is an essential requisite of liability, additional to the foreseeability of the type of harm.[25] It would seem that UK courts would be resistant to using

Testimony on Causation in the Bendectin Cases' (1993) 46 Stanford LR 1 at 23; T. Brennan, 'Causal Chains and Statistical Links: The Role of Scientific Uncertainty in Hazardous Substance Litigation' (1988) 73 Cornell LR 469 at 508.

[20] The proportionality rule thus comes as close as possible to preserving the value of individual entitlements to personal security and autonomy: Rosenberg, 'Causal Connection', n. 18 above, 860–2.

[21] See *Hotson* v. *Fitzgerald* [1985] 3 All ER 167; *Hotson* v. *East Berkshire Area Health Authority* [1987] 1 All ER 210 (CA), reversed by *Hotson* v. *East Berkshire Area Health Authority* [1987] 2 All ER 909 (HL).

[22] C. Newdick, 'Strict Liability for Defective Drugs in the Pharmaceutical Industry' (1985) 101 Law QR 405 at 424.

[23] See e.g. in respect of Bendectin, L. Lasagna and S. R. Shulman, 'Bendectin and the Language of Causation' in K. R. Foster, D. E. Bernstein and P. W. Huber (eds.), *Phantom Risk: Scientific Inference and the Law* (Cambridge, Mass., 1993), 116. This seems, however, to conflict with the book's conclusion that traditional standards of proof should be maintained: *ibid.*, 434–5.

[24] See K. Abraham, 'What is a Tort Claim? An Interpretation of Contemporary Tort Reform' (1992) 51 Maryland LR 172, 181. Advocates of a philosophical approach to probability have argued that risk does not generally constitute harm in itself: S. R. Perry, 'Risk, Harm and Responsibility' in D. G. Owen (ed.), *Philosophical Foundations of Tort Law* (Oxford, 1995), 321 at 336–8.

[25] H. L. A. Hart and T. Honoré, *Causation in the Law* (Oxford, 1985), lxvii, 282–3; *McKew* v. *Holland and Hannen & Cubitts (Scotland) Ltd* [1969] 3 All ER 1621 at 1623 (per Lord Reid).

probabilistic apportionment of risk without additional corroborative evidence indicating that the general statistics fairly represented the individual case in issue.[26] Such an argument points to a dichotomy between statistical chance and personal chance, the answer to which is to refine the probabilities in respect of a class of persons or in respect of individual members of that class.[27] Robinson has considered it unnecessary to establish absolute magnitudes of risk and regards rough estimates of relative magnitudes as being sufficient, since the task is to assess causal responsibilities to provide a more equitable and efficient method of apportioning losses in multiple causation cases.[28] Nevertheless, in the absence of accurate prior probabilities it would seem that there remain the problems of overcompensation and over-deterrence or under-compensation and under-deterrence.

Bayes' Theorem and Medicinal Products

The late Sir Richard Eggleston examined the importance of Bayes' Theorem in questions involving probability.[29] The Theorem allows us to determine how our evaluation of probability based on initial assumptions can be modified in the light of more data. It is submitted that this methodology can be used in the context of medicinal products and causation,[30] in order to refine general statistical evidence into that peculiar to the particular individual in the case in issue.[31] Such general scientific evidence is obtained from doctors and pharmacists who are obliged to record such information and communicate it to the Committee on Safety of Medicines and other drug-data collecting services.[32]

---

[26] See G. Robinson, 'Multiple Causation in Tort Law: Reflections on the DES Cases' (1982) 68 Virginia LR 713 at 765 for such resistance in the American courts.   [27] See p. 61–7.

[28] Robinson, 'Multiple Causation', 767.

[29] R. Eggleston, *Evidence, Proof and Probability* (2nd edn, London, 1983), 22–4.

[30] For a clear discussion of the use of this theorem in this context see D. Lane *et al.*, 'The Causality Assessment of Adverse Drug Reactions Using a Bayesian Approach' (1987) 2 *Pharmaceutical Medicine* 265 at 265–83.

[31] For the distinction between statistical chances and personal chances, see T. Hill, 'A Lost Chance for Compensation in the Tort of Negligence by the House of Lords' (1991) 54 Mod. LR 511 at 511–12, 514–16. See further H. Reece, 'Losses of Chances in the Law' (1996) 59 Mod. LR 188, and p. 88.

[32] Such other drug-data collecting services include the General Practice Research Database and also the Boston Collaborative Drug Surveillance Programme: H. Jick, *A Major Resource for Drug Safety Studies* (Carshalton, Surrey, 1995).

Bayes' Theorem is an important branch of applied statistics which can be developed out of conditional probability. Bayes' Theorem expresses the relationship between the probability of a proposition (A) evaluated *before* the utilization of new data (B) (prior probability) and the probability of the same proposition evaluated *after* the utilization of the new data (posterior probability). Thus:

$$\text{Posterior Probability of A given B} = \frac{\text{Prior Probability of A}}{1} \times \frac{\text{Probability of B given A}}{\text{Unconditional Probability of B}}$$

$$\text{i.e. } P(A/B) = P(A) \times \frac{P(B/A)}{P(B)}$$

The main possible use of Bayes' Theorem in the context of causation and medicinal products is in refining statistics regarding evidence of general causal links between a drug and an injury into statistics establishing a specific causal link between the drug and the adverse drug reaction in the case in question.[33] However, it would seem that the biggest criticism of Bayes' theorem is the difficulty of arriving at a sufficiently accurate evaluation of a pre-existing probability to which experimental data can be applied.[34]

Perhaps the most interesting potential use of Bayes' Theorem is refining what may be termed statistical chances into 'personal chances' which are peculiar to a particular individual.[35] For example, if a defendant had not negligently given an overdose of anaesthetic to a child suffering from cancer resulting in that child's death there might have been a 40 per cent statistical chance of recovery from the cancer if the anaesthetic had been correctly given.[36] Arguably, Bayes' Theorem could be applied to the 40 per cent statistical chance to obtain an accurate assessment of the personal chance in that case.

[33] See the application by the author of Bayes' Theorem in the context of medicinal products: Goldberg, 'Causation and Medicinal Products', n. 2 above 69–70.

[34] Eggleston, *Evidence*, n. 29 above, 171.

[35] I. Kennedy and A. Grubb, *Medical Law: Text with Materials* (2nd edn, London, Dublin, Edinburgh, 1994), 488; Hill, 'A Lost Chance', n. 31 above at 512.

[36] See J. King, 'Causation, Valuation and Chance in Personal Injury Torts Involving Pre-existing Conditions and Future Consequences' (1981) 90 Yale LJ 1353 at 1370 (concerning a plaintiff claiming that, by virtue of the intervention of the defendant's tortious conduct, the plaintiff lost the chance to recover from the pre-existing condition or to avoid an untoward consequence of it).

In the context of medicinal products and causation, it is possible to obtain a measure of probability through the application of Bayes' Theorem. Such a statistical chance could be refined and personalized into a 'personal chance' unique to an individual, using specific factors embodied in the likelihood ratio.

The likelihood ratio of a test can be defined as:

$$\frac{\text{The true positive incidence of the test}}{\text{The false positive incidence of the test}}$$

The probabilities in the likelihood ratio (LR) can be decomposed into factors in the light of specific case information in respect of patient history LR(Hi), timing LR(Ti), characteristics of the adverse event LR(Ch), the response to dechallenge (that is, discontinuing the drug) LR(De), and the response to rechallenge (that is, restarting the drug) LR(Re). The likelihood ratio is calculated by obtaining the product of all the individual likelihood ratio factors.

Diagrammatically this can be expressed by:

$$LR = LR(Hi) \times LR(Ti) \times LR(Ch) \times LR(De) \times LR(Re)$$

(Caveat: components, i.e. Hi etc., must be statistically independent).

The use of all these factors is dependent on the specific case information which is available. If all specific case information in respect of the factors is available, the posterior odds[37] may be calculated as follows:

$$\text{Posterior Odds} = \text{Prior Odds} \times LR(Hi) \times LR(Ti) \times LR(Ch) \times LR(De) \times LR(Re).$$

Thus the posterior odds can be further refined by combining the prior odds, based on background information, and the likelihood ratios, based on case-specific information, to produce as accurate a posterior probability as possible.[38] It would seem that

---

[37] The relationship between odds and probability is:

$$\text{Odds} = \frac{\text{Probability}}{1 - \text{Probability}}$$

Thus the probability of 0.9 = odds of 9:1.

[38] B. Donatini, I. Le Blaye and P. Krupp, 'Causality Assessment of Spontaneous Reporting: Correlation Between Bayesian and Other Approaches' (1993) 7 *Pharmaceutical Medicine*, 255, 256.

particularly important known risk factors could be introduced into the calculation[39] such as kidney and liver function, age, gender, genetic aberration, or nutritional deficiency.[40] The list of factors indicating a proximate causal relationship[41] will assist in the personalizing of the data.

Finkelstein and Fairley, two of the early protagonists of Bayes' Theorem, proposed its use in trials 'in order to translate the data into a form congenial to scrutiny by jurors'.[42] This was heavily criticized in a powerful rejoinder by Tribe, in which, although he considered that the costs of trying to integrate mathematics into the fact-finding process of legal trials outweighed its benefits, he refrained from ruling out the 'carefully limited use of probabilistic proof in special circumstances'.[43] In recent years, support for the use of the Theorem in the resolution of legal problems has increased.[44] Indeed, it has been argued that Bayes' Theorem 'offers an instrument for picking the thought process apart',[45] providing a convincing rejoinder to the criticism that a probability approach to dealing with legal issues cannot interpret evidence. It is able to provide a 'normative approach' to legal decision-making,[46] though implementation of it in legal practice is difficult. As one of the major protagonists of Bayes' Theorem has argued, the results of the Bayesian model are not inconsistent with those that result when a court or jury evaluates the weight of conflicting evidence

[39] See M. N. G. Dukes and B. Swartz, *Responsibility for Drug-Induced Injury* (Amsterdam, New York, Oxford, 1989), 19.

[40] See Goldberg, 'Causation and Medicinal Products', n. 2 above, 68.

[41] Dukes and Swartz, *Responsibility*, n. 39 above, 41–5.

[42] M. Finkelstein and W. Fairley, 'A Bayesian Approach to Identification Evidence' (1970) 83 Harvard LR 489 at 517.

[43] L. Tribe, 'Trial by Mathematics: Precision and Ritual in the Legal Process' (1971) 84 Harvard LR 1329 at 1377. However, such circumstances would have to be extraordinary. Tribe objected to the use of Bayes' Theorem at trial because its methods generated an 'intrinsic bias' within the trial process. However, he conceded that the Bayesian approach might not display an intrinsic bias *outside* the trial process in circumstances where its use could be subjected to continuing scrutiny over time: 1356–7.

[44] For a comprehensive examination of the merits and demerits of using Bayes' Theorem when dealing with the uncertainty of fact finding, see P. Tillers and E. D. Green (eds.), *Probability and Inference in the Law of Evidence* (Dordrecht, 1988).

[45] B. Robertson and T. Vignaux, 'Probability—The Logic of the Law' (1993) 13 OJLS 457 at 471.

[46] S. Fienberg and M. Schervish, 'The Relevance of Bayesian Inference for the Presentation of Statistical Evidence and for Legal Decision Making' (1986) 66 Boston Univ. LR 771 at 794.

in accordance with legal norms.[47] Although hardly a convincingly positive reason for using Bayes' Theorem, it would seem to be one which would support its use in certain circumstances. It is arguable, however, that the standard of proof in England of the balance of probabilities is 'even more susceptible to a probabilistic interpretation' than its American counterpart, the preponderance of the evidence standard,[48] and that the English courts should consider carefully the use of Bayes' Theorem as a working tool in fact-finding.[49] An attempt to correlate existing causality assessment methods and Bayes' Theorem approach to drug causality suggests that a non-numerical approach is sufficiently accurate for a causality assessment based on spontaneous reports. Donatini *et al.* also suggest that Bayes' Theorem should be used if there is doubt regarding causality using non-numerical approaches.[50] So it would seem that Bayes' Theorem, in the specific context of problems concerning causation and medicinal products, may assist where a non-numerical approach has failed.

Depending on the availability of data from a test or sample, Bayes' Theorem can thus help to establish more personalized chances.[51] However, a further consideration is the question of a

---

[47] R. Lempert, 'The New Evidence Scholarship: Analyzing the Process of Proof' in Tillers and Green, *Probability*, n. 44 above, 76. Lempert observes that the arguments of those who reject the use of the Bayesian model in trials suggest that statistical evidence has no place at all in trials (*ibid.* at 63). His following reply indicates an awareness of the day-to-day practical importance of probabilistic evidence in trials: '[t]hose who criticise Bayesian models of the legal process and the suggested application of the Bayesian approaches at trial must confront the reality that statistical evidence is offered in trials every day' (*ibid.*).

[48] Fienberg and Schervish, 'Bayesian Inference', n. 46 above at 780.

[49] See for support for the use of Bayes' Theorem in courts requiring an accurate assessment of a drug's causal role in particular cases: Lane *et al.*, 'The Causality Assessment', n. 30 above at 265, 282.

[50] Donatini *et al.*, 'Spontaneous Reporting', n. 38 above at 255–6, 262–4. The interdisciplinary Vaccine Safety Committee of the Institute of Medicine adopted an 'informal Bayesian approach' to assessing case reports in its review of the scientific and medical literature on specific risks to children associated with vaccines: K. R. Stratton, C. J. Howe and R. B. Johnston (eds.), *Institute of Medicine, Adverse Events Associated with Childhood Vaccines: Evidence Bearing on Causality* (Washington, DC, 1994), 3, 25.

[51] Allen has stressed the importance in civil trials of permitting the parties to determine how far they wish the particularity of the relevant facts to be pushed, but that it is the parties, and not the State, who must decide the extent to which they wish to explore the particularities of the case: R. J. Allen, 'A Reconceptualization of Civil Trials' in Tillers and Green, *Probability*, n. 44 above, 45–6. However, it is arguable that the State does have an interest in the particularity of evidence, since

possible synergistic relationship between the combined background risk and the defendant's fault, which is a distinct problem
in respect of causation and medicinal products.[52] Despite such
difficulties, there would thus seem to be potential in the use of
such a statistical analysis in the attempt to improve probabilistic
assessments of causal link, particularly in drug-induced injury
cases.

Nevertheless, the focus from the position of legal scholarship
has mainly been on the use of logic, probability, and inference to
resolve issues of forensic science, in the criminal law but not the
civil law context.[53] It would seem that Bayes' Theorem could be of
the greatest potential use in medicinal product liability cases
involving causation, since the epidemiological evidence associated
with adverse reactions naturally lends itself towards being used as
part of a statistical refinement process. Moreover, the fact that
proof in a civil court must be established on a balance of probabilities would suggest that the Bayesian approach to legal decision-
making might be more appropriate in a civil arena than a criminal
one, where the concept of certainty assumes much greater importance.[54] Bayes' Theorem recognizes that absolute certainty cannot

this will affect the quality of decision by the fact-finder. This would be of particular importance in the area of drug-product liability and causation.

[52] Synergism's challenge to legal concepts is, however, constrained by the difficulties in identifying such interactions: J. Stapleton, *Disease and the Compensation
Debate* (Oxford, 1986), 58–9.

[53] See the masterly monograph of Robertson and Vignaux, advocating the use
of Bayes' Theorem in assessing scientific evidence principally in a criminal context:
B. Robertson and G. A. Vignaux, *Interpreting Evidence: Evaluating Forensic
Science in the Courtroom* (Chichester, 1995), 22, 29, 219–220. It is Robertson and
Vignaux's thesis that expert evidence must be correctly interpreted by a court and
that the best way of achieving this is to utilize the LR to describe the strength of
the evidence. They also advocate that scientific evidence concerning an issue
'should be combined with other evidence relating to the same issue' and that the
most effective way of doing so is to express the evidence in LR form. In addition,
Robertson and Vignaux have observed that the importance of the LR is that it
determines relevance and probative value, the key determinants of admissibility of
expert evidence. Robertson and Vignaux have also argued that it is not essential to
have precise numbers for each of the probabilities to assess the LR. This would
seem, however, arguable in complex cases involving the establishment of causation
in relation to medicinal products. Indeed the need for statistics with a strong
evidential foundation for the calculation of the LR has recently been expressed: see
K. Grevling, Book Review, 'Robertson and Vignaux, *Interpreting Scientific
Evidence: Evaluating Forensic Science in the Courtroom*' (1996) 112 Law QR 509
at 510.

[54] Allen, 'Reconceptualization', n. 51 above at 51.

be provided for by science. But there is, however, a need for greater accuracy in decision-making by the courts, and Bayes' Theorem may at least help to achieve that.[55]

In the light of the economic importance of the pharmaceutical industry and the increasing occurrence of medicinal product liability litigation, this paper attempts to address the hypothesis that a probabilistic approach to causation in relation to medicinal products promotes economic efficiency. This hypothesis will be matched against other economic theories to determine which of those are consistent with its approach. The hypothesis will then be considered as a solution to the practical problems of inefficiency in pharmaceutical product liability litigation stemming from the uncertainties of determining injury causation.

Economic Analysis

THE IMPORTANCE OF EFFICIENCY

It is this writer's submission that the use of statistical methods of establishing causal link in cases involving alleged adverse effects of medicinal products would promote economic efficiency. An attempt will be made to show that this approach is consistent with an economic analysis of causation.

It seems clear, from an early stage in the development of law and economics, that causation was inherently linked to efficiency through the internalization of costs. Calabresi wrote, in one of the seminal articles on law and economics, that 'tort costs should be borne by the activity which causes them'.[56] This proposition remains entirely correct today when looked at in the context of

---

[55] For further reading, see M. Redmayne, Review Article, 'Science, Evidence and Logic' (1996) 59 Mod. LR 747. Redmayne recommends a cautious recognition of Bayes' Theorem but regards it as problematic since it assumes that the fact-finder will have 'unlimited cognitive capabilities'. However, he considers that it is a useful 'analytical tool' in providing insights into the fact-finding process. The fact that Bayes' Theorem discloses the complexity of situations with which it 'copes poorly' is ironically a positive value of it (756, 759). Cf. my view that Bayes' Theorem is most useful in dealing with *complex* situations involving causation and drugs that are recalcitrant to non-numerical solutions: Goldberg, 'Causation and Medicinal Products' n. 7 above at 69.

[56] G. Calabresi, 'Some Thoughts on Risk Distribution and the Law of Torts' (1961) 70 Yale LJ 499 at 533.

the pharmaceutical industry. However, it is also arguable that the efficiency theory can be criticized on the ground that it champions wealth maximization over other goals, including compensation and the protection of the poor.[57]

Landes and Posner's economic analysis of causation in tort law stresses the importance of economic efficiency in determining the cause of an injury. They state:

If the basic purpose of tort law is to promote economic efficiency, a defendant's conduct will be deemed the cause of an injury, when making him liable for the consequences of the injury would promote an efficient allocation of resources to safety and care; and when it would not promote efficiency for the defendant to behave differently, then the cause of the accident will be ascribed to an 'act of God' or some other force on which liability cannot rest. In this view, the injurer 'causes' the injury when he is the cheaper cost avoider; not otherwise.[58]

Wright has argued that the efficiency theory is inconsistent with the requirement of causation and that any attempt to reconcile the two is both 'unscientific and unrealistic'.[59] The basis of this criticism is that the use of 'probabilistic cause'[60] is regarded as flawed since it is not proof that it was the cause of the actual result in question. It is merely 'proof that it increased the risk or probability of the result's occurring'. Legal economists are thus criticized for 'assum[ing] a functional relationship, but . . . never fill[ing] it out with a mathematical description of any *specific* causal generalization'. Wright continues: '[I]dentification of *actual* instances of causation . . . is missing from the efficiency theory.'[61] However, an important observation left unnoticed by Wright is the fact that probabilistic methods of causation can refine statistics into those specific to a particular situation, using Bayes' Theorem. Bayes' Theorem is one approach which can 'mathematically manipulat[e] . . . causal generalizations'[62] by the refinement of statistics to

57 J. Stapleton, *Product Liability* (London, 1994), 159–60.

58 W. M. Landes and R. A. Posner, 'Causation in Tort Law: An Economic Approach' (1983) 12 J Legal Studies 109 at 110; *id.*, 'Causation' in W. M. Landes and R. A. Posner, *The Economic Structure of Tort Law* (Cambridge, Mass., London, 1987), 229.

59 R. Wright, 'The Efficiency Theory of Causation and Responsibility: Unscientific Formalism and False Semantics' (1987) 63 Chicago-Kentucky LR 553.

60 i.e. causation inferred by statistical probability.

61 See n. 59 above at 555, 560–2 (emphasis added).

62 *Ibid.* at 561.

produce specific causal generalizations. Bayes' Theorem also appears to be a response to Wright's criticism that legal economists are unable to reconcile the *ex post* focus of causation with the *ex ante* focus of efficiency theory, since Bayes' Theorem can operate using statistics *ex ante*, on a futuristic basis, or *ex post*, after the principal data has been obtained.

THE CHEAPEST COST AVOIDER AND ITS RELATION TO CAUSATION

Economic theory necessitates that any market deterrence approach to liability places injury costs on the party who is best able to assess whether avoidance of risks is cheaper than bearing costs. That party is termed the ' "cheapest cost avoider" of an accident who would be held responsible for the accident costs under the market deterrence standard'.[63] It is apparent that causal link is generally required to establish the cheapest cost avoider since, '[t]o put it another way, how can a person be the cheapest cost avoider of an injury if his actions do not increase [or decrease] the chances that the injury will occur?'[64] It is submitted that the reconciliation of the requirements of the efficiency theory with the traditional requirements of causation can only transpire when probabilistic causation and statistics are used to show that on a balance of probabilities a *particular* product (say a medicinal product) caused the *particular* loss complained of by the plaintiff.[65] The present writer supports the view of Calabresi that 'causal linkage', that is, 'a prediction of future risk', is required to ascertain the identity of the cheapest cost avoider.[66] Stapleton attacks Calabresi's attempt to render the traditional causation requirement an 'acceptable vehicle for achieving efficiency' for being an approach predicated upon a 'centrally flawed' reliance on probabilistic linkage. Stapleton states that such an approach is wrong since it requires the identification of those 'but for' factors which 'increase the probability of the event occurring' and that because all such factors are necessary for an outcome, 'relative to what can one factor be said to have increased the chance of harm once it has

---

[63] G. Calabresi, 'Concerning Cause and the Law of Torts: An Essay for Harry Kalven, Jr' (1975) 48 Univ. Chicago LR 69, 84.   [64] *Ibid.* at 84.

[65] Cf. Stapleton, *Product Liability*, n. 57 above, 120.

[66] Calabresi, 'Concerning Cause', n. 63 above at 85.

occurred?'[67] It is arguable, however, that Stapleton gives an unduly harsh interpretation of Calabresi's theory in this context. It is true that Calabresi states that market deterrence[68] relies heavily on 'causal linkage' to identify the cheapest cost avoider. This element is crucial, according to Calabresi, but this is not the case in respect of the 'but for' relationship. 'But for' cause is relied on by market deterrence as a way of determining on an ad hoc basis the burden to be placed on the cheapest cost avoider. It has a 'limited significance'. The 'but for' test is not to be regarded 'as an absolute requirement in case by case determinations'. *A fortiori*, Calabresi continues,

[W]here it is difficult to prove a *but-for* relationship or where either of two independent defendants was a sufficient cause of the harm and hence neither was a necessary (*but-for*) cause, it is, at the very least, doubtful whether blind adherence to the requirement that the victim prove a *but-for* relationship serves the purposes of market deterrence.[69]

It is submitted that Calabresi correctly states that causal linkage is relevant to selecting the cheapest cost avoider since causal linkage represents the 'predictability as to how much the recurrence of one activity, relative to others, increased the risk of injury'.[70] Stapleton's criticism, mentioned earlier, is that because all factors are necessary for an outcome, 'relative to what can one factor be said to have increased the chance of harm once it has occurred?' The weakness in this argument is that Stapleton is referring to 'but for' factors, while Calabresi is in fact referring to *probabilistic* measures of incidence. Stapleton's criticism can only be addressed by *probabilistic* approaches which embrace statistical significance.

Stapleton considers that it is generally the manufacturer rather than the victim who is the cheapest cost avoider and that therefore internalization of costs to the cheapest cost avoider is appropriate. This would appear to be appropriate in pharmaceutical product liability cases since it will indeed most often be the manufacturer who is deemed the cheapest cost avoider. However, the greatest challenge to the cheapest cost avoider concept is the extent to which traditional causal theory approximates to the cheapest cost

---

[67] Stapleton, *Product Liability*, n. 57 above, 120–1.
[68] i.e. deterring economically inefficient conduct through the market.
[69] Calabresi, 'Concerning Cause', n. 63 above at 86–7.
[70] *Ibid.* at 89.

avoider. Stapleton regards the cheapest cost avoider as an *ex ante* concept since it is the cheapest cost avoider whose behaviour *in future* 'most cheaply makes a difference to the incidence of the relevant losses'.[71] By contrast, cause explains the occurrence of loss in the past. Stapleton provides an example to demonstrate that the concept of cause does not always identify the cheapest cost avoider in the context of medicinal products. A drug is found to cause adverse drug reactions in some of those who are administered it which are unforeseeable before their first manifestation. However, further investigation reveals that such adverse drug reactions are suffered by a precisely identifiable group of users, for example, red-haired males. Stapleton argues that although the past victims of such reactions will never be regarded as their cause we may regard red-haired males as the cheapest cost avoiders in the future. It is submitted, however, that this is incorrect since the cheapest cost avoider remains the manufacturer, and is not red-haired males in the future, *until* the manufacturer puts a warning on a product. This action is the cheapest way to avoid cost and therefore the cheapest cost avoider is still the manufacturer and the manufacturer remains the cause of the adverse reactions. Then and only then, if a red-haired male takes the product in spite of the warning, is he the cheapest cost avoider. Moreover, the red-haired male would probably also be the cause under the traditional causation test since his act of taking the drug is now a voluntary one and one that would break the chain of causation.[72] Cause still seems to approximate to the cheapest cost avoider in the context of medicinal products, suggesting that there is consistency between the efficiency theory and traditional causal rules in the context of drugs. Stapleton believes that cases in which the future cheapest cost avoider is not reconciled with the traditional causation requirement will be rare and that the traditional causal requirement is an 'acceptable vehicle' to ascertain the cheapest cost avoider.[73] Stapleton appears correct in noting that the Product Liability Directive[74] is difficult to justify in efficiency

[71] Stapleton, *Product Liability*, n. 57 above, 125–6.

[72] Alternatively, it may be a doctor who becomes the cheapest cost avoider at the same time as being a learned intermediary in the context of certain medicinal products, his act amounting to a break in the chain of liability and thus of causation.

[73] Stapleton, *Product Liability*, n. 57 above, 125–6.

[74] See n. 7 above.

terms since 'liability is not even directed to the party causally responsible for the condition of the product which injured the victim'. In the Product Liability Directive, there is merely a sub-set of potentially relevant causes, namely, the manufacturer of the product, the component manufacturer, the importer, and the own-brand supplier, the latter two having little causal relevance and being unlikely to be the cheapest cost avoider.[75] Nevertheless, in most cases involving pharmaceuticals under the Directive, the cheapest cost avoider and the cause of the condition of a defective product will be the manufacturer; hence, the Directive will not result in a dilution of economic incentives, as it may for other products.

The identity of the cheapest cost avoider cannot be readily discovered in latent damage cases, including medicinal products involving multiple possible causes, in which epidemiological data produces less than even odds, rendering proof of causation, on the balance of probabilities under the traditional test, impossible. Moreover, imposing liability twenty years after supply may not have any deterrent effect since the product may no longer be marketed.[76] It is submitted that the cheapest cost avoider could only be identified in such cases where the epidemiological data is statistically refined by probabilistic methods, such as Bayes' Theorem, to identify the *probability* that a product caused an adverse event. The solution would then be considered in terms of *probabilities* of cause and not in terms of traditional causation. It would also mean that the manufacturer could be proportionately liable as a cheapest cost avoider for a loss, reducing the possibility of over deterrence in such cases.

LANDES AND POSNER'S ECONOMIC MODEL OF CAUSATION

(i) The Basis of the Economic Model—the Learned Hand Formula

Economic theorists like Posner say that their approach to tort problems is compatible with the law of negligence, at least with respect to the Learned Hand formula of Judge Learned Hand in *United States* v. *Carroll Towing Co.*[77] In that case, Judge Learned

---

[75] Stapleton, *Product Liability*, n. 57 above, 126.
[76] *Ibid.*, 149.
[77] 159 F.2d 169 (2d Cir. 1947).

Hand laid down that 'if the probability of harm be called P; the injury L and the burden [of adequate precautions] B; liability depends upon whether B is less than L multiplied by P: i.e., whether $B < PL$'.[78] The Learned Hand formula could be relevant to the problems of escalating costs of drug innovation in the pharmaceutical industry. The experience over the past thirty years of clinical injury caused directly by the introduction of new drugs, for example, thalidomide, Practolol, Opren, and other non-steroidal anti-inflammatory drugs, has necessitated increasingly complicated and costly safety requirements from the drug regulatory authorities. These have involved more pre-clinical and clinical trials before new drugs have been able to obtain product licences, thus extending the pre-marketing phase by years and increasing costs by millions of pounds. It could be argued that this is inherent in the development of more powerful drugs, with greater potential for therapeutic benefit but, on the other side of the coin, more liable to cause potentially graver injury (increasing L), more frequently (increasing P). Thus B (the burden of adequate precautions) must inevitably rise. This consideration has led to understandable pressure from the drug industry to extend the effective patent life of new drugs as compensation in order to prevent the inhibition of new drug development.[79]

However, expected accident costs must be compared at the margin by measuring the costs and benefits of small increments in safety and ceasing investing in more safety where another £1 spent would yield a £1 or less in extra safety. Negligence-based liability encourages a marginal approach since it is difficult in practice to get information on more than small changes in the manufacturer's safety precautions.[80]

(ii) *Landes and Posner's Economic Model Analysed—its Reconciliation with a Probabilistic Approach to Causation*

Landes and Posner attempt to produce a refinement of the Learned Hand formula ($B < PL$) to take account of factors which

---

[78] *Ibid.* at 173.

[79] See the resulting Council Regulation which came into force on 2 Jan. 1993 in the UK and all other Member States except Greece, Portugal, and Spain, introducing a supplementary protection certificate ('SPC') for medicinal products: Regulation 1768/92 [1992] OJ L182/1.

[80] R. A. Posner, *Economic Analysis of Law* (4th edn, Boston, Toronto, London, 1992), 148–9, 164.

affect the probability of an accident. They express the Hand formula in marginal terms as:

$$- \emptyset_z \, (p/v - p/nv) \, D = B_z$$

where $\emptyset$ = probability of violating the standard of care
$- \emptyset_z$ = marginal reduction in the probability of violating the
applicable standard of care
z = additional inputs of care to reduce $\emptyset$

p/v = probability of an accident in the event an injurer violates the standard of care
p/nv = probability of an accident if an injurer does not violate the standard of care
D = victim's damages if accident occurs
B_z = marginal cost of additional inputs of care

They conclude that an efficient level of care depends on the difference between p/v and p/nv. If p/v − p/nv is 0, the optimal level of care (z*) is 0, and the defendant's failure to take care should not be deemed actionable negligence or the *cause* of the accident. However, if p/v − p/nv is positive, z* is also positive, provided the cost of the first unit of z is less than the expected reduction in damages resulting from the first unit. An injurer is deemed to be negligent or to have caused the injury if the optimal level of care is such that the benefits from the additional efforts to comply with the standard of care (left hand side of the equation) are greater than (>) B_z, the marginal costs of efforts, i.e. benefits > costs.[81]

Although Landes and Posner are correct in saying that the refinement of the Learned Hand Formula allows us to analyse cases without invoking causal concepts,[82] it replaces the idea of causal concepts with the need to utilize *probabilistic* concepts, since the probability that the defendant's failure to take care has caused the accident is determined by the difference between p/v and p/nv. It would now appear to be necessary, in complex cases, to invoke statistical constructs such as Bayes' Theorem to ascertain the probability that an accident will occur if care is not taken (p/v) and the probability it will occur even if care is taken (p/nv).

---

[81] Landes and Posner, 'Economic Approach', n. 58 above at 111–14.
[82] *Ibid.*

(iii) Landes and Posner's Economic Model Applied to Cases Involving Causation and Medicinal Products

(a) Bendectin

In the overwhelming majority of cases no statistically significant association has been shown between the administration of Bendectin and childhood defects. Indeed, the difficulty of proving causation is compounded by the fact that congenital abnormalities manifest themselves in 1 to 7 per cent of newborn children, even in the absence of exposure to known teratogens.[83] On Landes and Posner's economic model, p/v – p/nv (i.e. the probability that a child would suffer congenital abnormalities as a result of, say, failure to warn of an adverse effect of Bendectin administered, minus the probability of a possible adverse effect given the proper warning and non-administration of Bendectin to pregnant women) is near 0. In such cases, the cost of legal proceedings, the deterrence of socially valuable conduct in administering the drug, and the requirement on the potential injurer to use excessive care are the factors suggesting that liability is unwarranted.[84]

(b) Thalidomide

On the Landes and Posner economic model, it is more probable than not that phocomelia in the children of pregnant women administered thalidomide would not have occurred if before clinical testing the manufacturer had subjected the drug to teratogenicity tests, and then had warned pregnant women in the light of such tests against using the drug (i.e. p/v – p/nv is substantial).[85] However, this

---

[83] L. Lasagna, 'The Chilling Effect of Product Liability on New Drug Development' in P. W. Huber and R. E. Litan (eds.), *The Liability Maze: The Impact of Liability Law on Safety and Innovation* (Washington, DC, 1991), 339.

[84] Landes and Posner, 'Economic Approach', n. 58 above at 122. Landes and Posner illustrate the comparable situation, where it was unclear whether an accident would have occurred if the defendant had not been negligent, with the case of *New York Cent. R. Co. v. Grimstad* 264 F. 334 (2d Cir. 1920). In that case, the Circuit Court of Appeals, Second Circuit, held that the death of a captain of a barge was not due to the failure to equip the barge with life preservers or buoys, in the absence of evidence to show that the presence of such appliances would have saved the deceased (*ibid.* at 335).

[85] See Landes and Posner's reference to the traumatic cancer case of *McGrath v. Irving* 265 N.Y.S. 2d 376 (1965) at 377–8. In that case, the plaintiff received an injury to her throat as a result of hitting the side of the car in which she was a passenger, and swallowed glass which the court held on a preponderance of evidence had caused an epidermoid carcinoma of the larynx.

presupposes that such pre-clinical teratogenicity tests were routine procedures at that time for drugs used in pregnancy. Sadly, although thalidomide was recommended for use in pregnancy, such teratogenicity tests were not then routine requirements.[86]

(c) Pertussis Vaccine

The administration of pertussis vaccine has occasionally been associated with the problem of encephalopathy. In *Bonthrone* v. *Millan*, Lord Jauncey emphasized unknown causes to eliminate a possible causal link between pertussis vaccine and brain damage.[87] On the Landes and Posner economic model, it was impossible to ascertain whether p/v – p/nv was positive or zero.[88]

(d) Diethylstilboestrol (DES)

In the DES cases, the identity of the injurer was unclear, since there were numerous manufacturers of the drug. In such circumstances, a strict application of the Landes and Posner economic model is not feasible. There was the added complication that although a subsequent direct link was shown between DES and vaginal cancer in the daughters of the women who were administered the drug, this effect manifested itself many years after initial exposure. However, market-share liability should theoretically be consistent with the economics of Landes and Posner's modification of the Learned Hand formula in that it creates incentives for companies to take care and to show that their act did not cause the plaintiff's injury.[89] If this can be shown, the defendant can escape liability for its market share of the product, thus creating incentives for care.[90]

---

[86] W. Sneader, *Drug Discovery: The Evaluation of Modern Medicines* (Chichester, New York, 1985), 32. Teratogenicity tests did not form part of a standard screening procedure in 1958: Teff and Munro, *Thalidomide*, n. 3 above, 32.

[87] (1985) 2 *The Lancet* ii 1137 at 1138.

[88] See Landes and Posner's reference to the parallel decision of *Doumitt* v. *Diemer* 23 P.2d 918, 920 (1933) (where it was considered impossible to tell whether a scar was caused by tuberculosis or by use of X-rays) (Landes and Posner, 'Economic Approach', n. 58 above at 123).

[89] *Ibid.* at 124–5. Here, Landes and Posner address the problem of 'cases where the identity of the injurer is unclear'.

[90] See *Sindell* v. *Abbott Laboratories* 607 P.2d 924, 930 (1980); cf. Schwartz, who states that *Sindell* has turned out to be not economically feasible in that eventual awards are not sufficiently large to justify the delays, uncertainties, and costs in the legal process: G. Schwartz, 'The Beginning and the Possible End of the Rise of Modern American Tort Law' (1992) 26 Georgia LR 601 at 688.

However, the DES decision of *Hymowitz* v. *Eli Lilly* seems economically incorrect since it imposes liability on a manufacturer despite his showing that his product had not caused the plaintiff's injury, since it had not been used.[91]

SHAVELL, THE EFFICIENCY THEORY AND CAUSATION

The idea that manufacturers should be liable only for the accidents that they cause is supported by Shavell, on the basis that restricting the scope of liability on causation grounds prevents discouragement from engaging in a socially worthwhile activity.[92] This is of particular importance in the area of causation and medicinal products, since in the absence of an effective ability to establish no liability on causation grounds, many pharmaceutical companies will be discouraged from engaging in the production of innovative treatments, particularly in respect of high-risk patient groups. Nevertheless, despite the causation requirement, it seems apparent that the difficulty in establishing causation accurately has resulted in uncertainties in product liability litigation and withdrawal of treatment in the areas of pregnancy drugs, vaccines, orphan drugs, contraceptives, and medical devices.[93] Restricting liability on the grounds of causation is of increasing relevance where there is a greater probability that an accident involving an alleged injurer was not caused by that injurer, for example, cancer in the context of multifactorial causes including a defective medicinal product and a patient susceptible to cancer.[94]

The Solution in Practice—Reform of how Science is Used in Court to Determine Injury Causation

It has been argued by the RAND Corporation in their report *Product Liability and the Economics of Pharmaceuticals and Medical Devices* that the current liability system promotes inefficient incentives through their distortion by factors such as the difficulty of proving injury causation.[95]

---

[91] 541 N.Y.S.2d 941, 950 (Ct. App. 1989).
[92] S. Shavell, *Economic Analysis of Accident Law* (Cambridge, Mass., London, 1987), 108.   [93] Lasagna, 'Chilling Effect', n. 83 above at 334–5.
[94] Shavell, *Economic Analysis*, n. 92 above, 109.
[95] S. Garber, *Product Liability and the Economics of Pharmaceuticals and Medical Devices* (Santa Monica, 1993), 180–1.

In respect of high-risk products, such as contraceptives, vaccines, and products for pregnancy-related illnesses, misperceptions of liability are generated by 'decisions reflecting controversial science', which establish liability in the absence of concrete epidemiological evidence. As a result, liability in respect of some products is overestimated and, in relation to others, underestimated. The unpredictability of the eventual liability costs of such products results in the deterrence of companies from producing socially valuable medicinal products. The RAND report argues that improving the quality of scientific evidence to determine injury causation is the key to reform in this area. The report recognizes the need to 'promote economic efficiency' by a new approach. Such reforms would need to 'strengthen the beliefs of company decision-makers that injuries caused by their products will be recognised as such [whilst allaying] concerns that companies will be held liable for injuries not caused by their products'. The report concludes: 'improving the scientific basis for legal determination of liability is a policy initiative that could strengthen efficient deterrence while attenuating inefficient deterrence'.[96]

It is submitted that the use of probabilistic statistical methods, such as Bayes' Theorem, may improve the scientific basis for the determination of injury causation, together with the use of court-appointed experts to interpret such evidence for the assistance of the courts.[97] This has already been recognized by Lasagna, who notes the need for either assistance with the evaluation of epidemiological evidence through court experts or the adoption of 'a more discrete evidentiary standard that would reflect more accurately the realities of causation'.[98]

The courts have shown a tendency to be uncomfortable with probabilistic assessments and multiple causation.[99] In a recent

---

[96] Garber, *Product Liability*, pp. xxiv, 184–5, 194.

[97] See R. Goldberg, 'Scientific Evidence, Causation and the Law—Lessons of Bendectin (Debendox) Litigation' (1996) 4 Med. LR 32, 57–9.

[98] Lasagna, 'Chilling Effect', n. 83 above, 356. Cf. support for traditional causation, except 'in unusual circumstances', but such circumstances would not include those in which identification of the defendant is possible: J. Henderson and A. Twerski, 'A Proposed Revision of Section 402A of the Restatement (Second) of Torts' (1992) 77 Cornell LR 1512 at 1518, 1535.

[99] H. Grabowski, 'Product Liability in Pharmaceuticals: Comments on Chapters Eight and Nine' in Huber and Litan (eds.), *The Liability Maze*, n. 83 above, 363.

criminal case, *Regina* v. *Adams*,[100] Rose LJ expressed the view, in a reserved judgment, that use of Bayes' Theorem was inadmissible in a criminal case since 'it trespassed on an area peculiarly and exclusively within the jury's province, namely the way in which they evaluated the relationship between one piece of evidence and another'. He observed that Bayes' Theorem might be an appropriate and useful tool for statisticians, but that it was not appropriate for use in jury trials or as a means to assist the jury. In the first place, the Theorem's methodology required that items of evidence be assessed separately according to their bearing on the guilt of the accused before being combined in the overall formula. Secondly, and more fundamentally, the attempt to determine guilt or innocence on the basis of a mathematical formula applied to each separate piece of evidence was an inappropriate approach for the jury's task.

Two points should be noted. Firstly, Bayes' Theorem is not evaluating the guilt or innocence of the accused in such a case. It is merely a method of evaluating evidence that can be used by judge and jury in making the ultimate decision on the guilt or innocence of the accused. Secondly, despite the criticisms of Rose LJ, it is submitted that it would be a useful tool to assist the judge in his deliberations on whether a drug caused damage in a civil case, where the standard of proof is the balance of probabilities. The judge could use the Theorem and court experts or panels to aid him in his deliberations. Such experts would include those with statistical experience in the area at issue. In this way, economic efficiency would be promoted in practice. A corresponding reduction in Legal Aid resources at present wasted on frivolous litigation could also transpire so that such resources could be redirected to more deserving cases. The Legal Aid Fund would be alerted to the use of such evidence and would be able to make its own decisions on the basis of it.

Conclusion

This paper has attempted to address the importance of the role of scientific evidence in proving causation in medicinal product liability litigation. It has examined the importance of the use of probabilistic evidence in such litigation. Three propositions have emerged from this study. First, the established legal approaches to

---

[100] *The Times*, 9 May 1996.

causation are inadequate when complex issues of drug causality fail to respond to non-numerical solutions. Secondly, a probabilistic approach to discovering the cause of adverse reactions to medicinal products is the most effective since it is a quantitative approach and one which should promote more certainty in judicial decision-making. Thirdly, the need to refine probabilistic statistics based on epidemiological studies to reflect the personal circumstances of a particular patient given a particular drug is best served by Bayes' Theorem. Although not embraced by the criminal courts, the theorem is potentially useful as a tool to refine statistics in order to establish the most accurate probability of a specific causal link between a drug and an injury in civil litigation, where proof of causation operates on a lesser standard than criminal law, that is, that of the balance of probabilities.

A theoretical analysis has attempted to show that the use of statistical approaches to the ascertainment of causal link in cases involving medicinal products promotes the efficiency theory of law and economics. The analysis appears to show that, in the majority of cases, cause seems to approximate to the Calabresian concept of the cheapest cost avoider in the context of causation and medicinal products. The Landes and Posner economic model of causation, devised as a refinement of the Learned Hand formula, has been found to be consistent with a probabilistic approach to causality, and illustrations of the model's application to cases involving causation and medicinal products have been given. The idea that manufacturers of medicinal products should be liable only for the accidents that they cause in *probabilistic* terms is consistent with Shavell's interpretation of the efficiency theory and causation.

It has also been demonstrated that there is considerable support for efficient decision-making and resolution of causal problems in practice. Such an approach is necessary to counter the problem of inefficient product liability, resulting from both inappropriate and ill-conceived incentives by companies, creating inconsistent and incongruous judicial decisions.

Incentives to introduce developed medicinal products or to invest in clinical trials have been shown to be sensitive to unusual product liability risks. In the light of such problems, theories of economic efficiency have been presented as consistent with probabilistic methods of ascertaining cause in cases involving scientific evidence, causation and medicinal products.

PEDRO JUAN CUBILLO V. COMMONWEALTH OF AUSTRALIA: RIGHT RESULT, WRONG METHOD

Helen Reece

Introduction

From 1957 to 1958, Pedro Juan Cubillo was a private in the Australian army, engaged in constructing and dismantling atomic explosion test sites and equipment. In 1982, he was diagnosed as having renal-cell carcinoma. About ten years later, he brought proceedings against the Commonwealth of Australia, claiming that his cancer had been caused by ionizing radiation, to which he had been exposed as a result of his employer's negligence.[1] The Commonwealth of Australia denied both that there had been any breach of duty and that any such breach of duty had caused Cubillo's cancer. Cubillo failed to satisfy Foster J either of breach or of causation. The issue which dominated the case, however, was that of causation, proof of which was bound to be an uphill struggle, especially given that Cubillo had been smoking more than twenty cigarettes a day for over thirty-five years before his cancer was diagnosed. On an application of the ordinary rules of proof, Cubillo could never have won: he was clearly unable to show that but for the exposure to radiation, it was more likely than not that he would not have developed cancer of the kidney.[2] The interesting question, however, is whether this would have been a suitable case to relax causation requirements, allowing the

---

[1] *Pedro Juan Cubillo v. Commonwealth of Australia*, NSW District Registry, General Division, 14 Dec. 1995.

[2] *Barnett v. Chelsea and Kensington Hospital Management Committee* [1969] 1 QB 428. But see *March v. E & M H Stramare Party Ltd and Another* (1991) 171 Commonwealth Law Reps. 506 for the opinion that the 'but for' test is not the exclusive test in negligence.

plaintiff to recover if he could show that his employers had materially contributed to (the chance of) his developing cancer. Foster J considered the precedents for this, principally *McGhee* v. *National Coal Board*[3] and *Birkholz* v. *R J Gilbertson Pty Limited*,[4] but distinguished them. A re-examination of the precedents will show that, although Foster J was right to distinguish the precedents, he did so on the wrong grounds: the crucial distinction is whether we are dealing with a deterministic or an indeterministic scenario.[5]

Cubillo on Ordinary Rules of Proof

Cubillo's case was that he had been exposed to alpha rays, and more specifically to one particular alpha ray, plutonium 239. It was not in dispute that alpha rays had been produced by the tests, nor was it in dispute that although alpha rays have little penetrative capacity, external exposure being therefore of little significance, if they enter the human body then they do have carcinogenic potential. It was therefore Cubillo's contention that inhalation or ingestion of plutonium 239 had caused his cancer.

The first link in the chain for Foster J was to determine whether Cubillo had worked in areas in which plutonium 239 was present. On this point he found for Cubillo. However this finding led to the question of the amount of plutonium 239 in the area. Here Foster J was satisfied that the contamination was not significant. Plutonium 239 has a long half-life in excess of 24,000 years. Therefore the amount of plutonium 239 detected currently gave a good indication of the amount present at the relevant time. Substances are radioactive because they emit radioactive ions into the atmosphere as they decay; the measure of radiation, therefore, is the rate of decay, measured in disintegrations per second; the original unit for measuring radioactivity was the curie, based on the rate of decay of one gram of radium. An aerial survey conducted in 1990 gave an upper bound of 1.6 micro curies of plutonium 239 per square metre at a distance of one kilometre from the explosion. The nearest distance at which Cubillo could have been exposed to plutonium 239 was 2.7 kilometres, at which

---

[3] [1972] 3 All ER 1008.
[4] (1985) 38 South Aust. State Reporter 121.
[5] H. Reece, 'Losses of Chances in the Law' (1996) 59 Mod LR 188.

distance the level of radiation would have been less. This had to be reduced by a factor of 10 to take into account research relating to plutonium 239 used in particular types of weapons. Taking into account all of these factors, the maximum amount of plutonium 239 present in the area in which Cubillo worked was 0.2 micro curies per square metre.

To give a meaningful indication of the harmfulness of this amount, it needs to be converted into a 'dose level'. This is carried out in two stages; first, the amount of energy deposited when radiation passes through tissue, known as the absorbed dose, is measured in 'rads', one rad being 0.01 joules of energy per kilogram; second, this measurement is refined by taking into account how damaging the particular type of radiation is biologically: rather than measuring dose, the 'rem', or 'rad equivalent man', and the sievert, which is equivalent to 100 rems, measure 'dose equivalent'. The dose received by Cubillo was estimated as at a maximum of 0.2 millisieverts, calculated in the absence of a respirator: this compared with the anticipated annual dose that an individual receives from natural background radiation of 0.23 rem.

The next question was whether plutonium 239 could have entered Cubillo's body. Here, Foster J was satisfied in Cubillo's favour that there might have been occasions on which, because of heat and discomfort, respirators were removed, and that on one or more of such occasions, Cubillo could have wiped his face with a dusty glove, thus transferring dust to his lips, and then licked his lips. Therefore it was possible that Cubillo had inhaled or ingested plutonium 239. Again, the issue became the amount of plutonium 239 that Cubillo could have taken into his body. Foster J found that this would have been very small, for two main reasons. First, the evidence showed that plutonium 239 was always dispersed along with fission products, of which plutonium 239 itself would make up a small proportion. Four of the personnel involved in similar operations to Cubillo, if not more hazardous ones, had been tested for the presence of iodine 131 in their thyroids, iodine 131 being a fission product which rapidly finds its way to the thyroid. No iodine 131 was detected, from which finding it could be inferred that these men, and therefore Cubillo, had not ingested or inhaled plutonium 239. Secondly, Foster J returned to his finding that Cubillo could have ingested plutonium 239 by licking his lips. He found that in this scenario, the amount of dust which would have led Cubillo to lick his lips would have been insignificant, and of this amount only 0.001 per cent of a plutonium compound would have been transferred across the gut wall, with the rest being harmlessly excreted. Thus Foster J concluded that Cubillo could not have ingested or inhaled a large amount of plutonium 239.

Foster J then considered the amount of plutonium 239 which would have entered his kidney as a proportion of the amount which entered his body. Undisputed material from the International Commission on Radiological Protection showed that the kidney was not a potential target organ for plutonium 239, a potential target organ being the organ which a radionuclide seeks out and which therefore receives the highest dose. Thus, of the 0.001 per cent of the ingested or inhaled plutonium 239 which would have passed through the gut wall into the blood stream, only one per cent would end up in the kidney. As well as supporting the hypothesis that the dose to the kidney itself had been small, the fact that the potential target organ for plutonium 239 was bone rather than the kidney, coupled with the absence of bone cancer among the servicemen working alongside Cubillo, provided additional support for the finding that only a small amount of plutonium 239 had been inhaled or ingested during the tests. Foster J concluded that the dose to the kidney itself would have been between 12 rem, which was less than the amount of radiation emitted by brick walls in an ordinary house every second, and 0.002 rem, which was about 3 per cent of the dose which the kidney would receive in a year from natural background radiation.[6] Therefore the dose to the kidney itself was very small.

The remaining question was whether the entry into Cubillo's kidney of a small amount of plutonium 239 could have caused cancer in his kidney. This question had to be addressed against a background of possible causes, of which three others were considered: Cubillo's smoking, his drinking and that the cancer was idiopathic, that is, had no particular cause. The theory put forward on behalf of Cubillo was that the ingestion of a small particle of

---

[6] Diagnostic X-rays expose tissue to a trauma of between 0.03 and 2.5 rem depending on procedure: J. DiStefano, 'Dangerous Doses?' (1987) 16 The Brief 27 at 30.

plutonium 239 on one occasion would have been sufficient to cause carcinogenic changes to Cubillo's kidney if he had a particular genetic predisposition to radiation-induced cancer of the kidney, there being no simple relationship between radiation dose and carcinogenesis. Foster J found that there was almost unanimous agreement that risk was proportional to dose,[7] such agreement being supported by the evidence from experiments on animals, in which attempts to induce renal tumours by exposure to ionizing radiation had shown that the animals' physiological systems failed completely before tumours developed in their kidneys, from which it could be inferred that the kidney is not a radio-sensitive organ. This inference suggested that if Cubillo had received a dosage of radiation sufficient to cause renal-cell carcinoma, he would have suffered other reactions including radiation burns, possible hair loss and loss of immune function. The experiments on animals were backed up by an epidemiological study which had followed up 15,000 people who had been given X-rays exposing them to a very high level of radiation, an average of 600 rads, directed to the same side of their spine as their kidneys, so that their kidneys were amongst the organs which received the highest dose of radiation. Thirty-five of them developed kidney cancer. The conclusion was that there was a 10 per cent increase in the relative risk of developing cancer of the kidney for each 100 rads of radiation. This conclusion was compatible with other studies, such as one from Germany, in which the results from patients

---

[7] See D. Farber, 'Toxic Causation' (1987) 71 Minnesota LR 1219 at 1243 and Note, 'Tort Actions for Cancer: Deterrence, Compensation, and Environmental Carcinogenesis' (1981) 90 Yale LJ 840 at 850 for support for the view that the risk of disease is normally related to the amount of exposure. See DiStefano, 'Dangerous Doses?', n. 6 above at 30 for the comment that dose is the crucial element in proving causation and at 31 for the view that the majority of scientific opinion is that low-level doses of radiation present minimal risk. But see Note, 'Tort Actions', above at 850 for the view that there is no safe level of exposure to carcinogens. See H. Latin, 'The "Significance" of Toxic Health Risks: An Essay on Legal Decisionmaking Under Uncertainty' (1982) 10 Ecology Law Q 339 at 369 for the view that no valid theory of extrapolation from high doses to low doses has achieved reasonable scientific consensus. See E. Schwartzbauer and S. Shindell, 'Cancer and the Adjudicative Process: The Interface of Environmental Protection and Toxic Tort Law' (1988) 14 Amer. J Law and Medicine 1 for the argument that linear extrapolation from high dose to low dose is illogical, so that a low dose may be completely harmless. See K. R. Foster and P. W. Huber, *Judging Science: Scientific Knowledge and the Federal Courts* (Massachusetts, 1997), 57, for the suggestion that at low levels, ionizing radiation can be beneficial for human health.

treated by the injection of radium into their bloodstream also indicated that kidney cancer resulted only from a very high dose.

But what of the argument that Cubillo could have had a kidney which was particularly sensitive to radiation? Foster J found that there was no evidence of the existence of individuals particularly prone to developing cancer of the kidney from exposure to a small amount of radiation, nor was it possible, because people with this genetic make-up would have died long ago as a result of exposure to background radiation. Moreover, the evidence from experiments on animals showed that the level of radiation required to produce kidney tumours was associated with prior sclerosis or scarring of the kidney: since an examination of Cubillo's kidney disclosed no such damage, this suggested that Cubillo's cancer had not been caused by radiation. There was also no indication of any special feature in Cubillo's case which distinguished him from the 60,000 new cases of cancer in Australia each year, so that his cancer could be regarded as idiopathic, especially bearing in mind his age, which in 1982 would have given him a 1 in 20 chance of developing cancer. The factor which did set him apart from the general population was his heavy smoking, which doubled the risk.

But Cubillo argued that his smoking strengthened his case, because it could well have assisted radiation to cause his cancer, through synergism, a process by which two carcinogens present together have an effect which is greater than simply their sum, because they can accelerate the effect of each other. However Foster J rejected the synergism theory on the basis that the effect of each factor in the presence of the other could only be assessed by examining its effect in the absence of the other, so the radiation first must have had a carcinogenic effect on its own before it could act synergistically. Foster J assessed the increase in the risk of cancer of the kidney as a result of a dose of radiation of the relevant magnitude as between 0.002 and 0.000006. The most that synergism could mean, therefore, was that it increased Cubillo's risk of developing cancer of the kidney, given his age and his smoking history, by two-thousandths.

This evidence was sufficient for Foster J to feel satisfied that Cubillo's cancer had not been caused by exposure to plutonium 239. However, in support of his conclusion, he considered the evidence from five epidemiological studies, all of which compared individuals who had been exposed to radiation with both the general population and a control group. A UK study of 21,358 participants in UK nuclear-weapons tests found an increase in the incidence of and mortality from leukaemia only. An Australian study of 2,440 participants in the UK tests found that the only increase was in relation to skin cancer. A second Australian survey of the death certificates of 1,560 participants found that the only increase in mortalities from cancer was in relation to lung cancer, but that there was also an excess of mortalities in relation to other smoking related diseases. A New Zealand study of 528 participants found that there was a higher incidence of, and mortality from, all types of cancers including kidney cancer, but the number was not regarded as statistically significant. Moreover, the largest study, of 121,000 survivors from Hiroshima and Nagasaki, found no statistically significant increase in cancer of the kidney following exposure to ionizing radiation.

Foster J concluded that Cubillo's cancer was either idiopathic or caused by his heavy smoking:

I am satisfied, on the whole of the evidence, that Cubillo's renal cell carcinoma was not caused by exposure to ionising radiation at Maralinga acting either directly or synergistically.

Should the Rules of Causation Have Been Relaxed?

Cubillo could not show that his cancer was caused by his exposure to radiation. But an alternative submission advanced on his behalf was that where his employers had breached their legal duty to protect Cubillo from the risk of injury from radiation and where this breach of duty resulted in a substantial increase in the risk of cancer, in the absence of evidence as to the exact cause of the cancer, a substantial increase in risk was a sufficient basis for the inference that his employers' breach of duty had materially contributed to the cancer. Although it was not strictly necessary for Foster J to deal with this submission, having found that there was no breach of duty, he did so in order to reinforce his finding on causation.

The precedents which Cubillo relied upon for this submission, and which Foster J attempted to distinguish, were *Birkholz* v.

R J Gilbertson Pty Limited,[8] *McGhee* v. *National Coal Board*,[9] *Bonnington Castings* v. *Wardlaw*,[10] *Western Australia* v. *Watson*[11] and *Bennett* v. *Minister of Community Welfare*.[12] The latter two of these cases will not be discussed further because they lent no support to Cubillo's submission: *Western Australia* v. *Watson* was a case in which the trial judge had found at first instance that the plaintiff's asbestosis had been caused by his employer's breach of duty, and this finding was not challenged on appeal; *Bennett* v. *Minister of Community Welfare* concerned successive independent causation, and whether the second causal event was a *novus actus interveniens*.

Foster J attempted to distinguish the precedents in two ways. First, he asserted that *Bonnington Castings Ltd* v. *Wardlaw*, *McGhee* v. *National Coal Board* and *Western Australia* v. *Watson* all 'concerned causation of a disease by cumulative causes'. The implication, consistent with his earlier conclusion that Cubillo's cancer was not a product of synergy between smoking and radiation exposure,[13] was that Cubillo's case concerned causation of a disease by one of a number of discrete causes.

In *McGhee* the plaintiff, who had worked for many years as a labourer in the defendants' brickworks, was found to be suffering from dermatitis. In the House of Lords there was no dispute that the dermatitis was attributable to the dust from the works nor that the defendants were in breach of duty in failing to provide showers. The position was that if the defendants had provided showers then the plaintiff would still have been exposed to dust at work (the 'innocent' dust) but would not have retained the dust on his skin on his way home each day (the 'guilty' dust). The defendants argued that the plaintiff could not show that the 'innocent' dust would not have been enough to cause the dermatitis. The House of Lords held that the plaintiff did not need to prove that it was more likely than not that the absence of showers had caused the disease; it was enough for him to show that the defendants' breach of duty had materially contributed to the (risk of) dermatitis.

In distinguishing *McGhee* on the basis that it was a case of

---

[8] See n. 4 above.   [9] See n. 3 above.
[10] [1956] AC 613.   [11] [1990] Western Australian Reps. 248.
[12] (1992) 176 Commonwealth Law Reps. 408.   [13] See n. 10 above.

cumulative causation, Foster J adopted the orthodox explanation of *McGhee*. This was the reason that the House of Lords gave in *Wilsher* v. *Essex Area Health Authority*[14] for their decision that *McGhee* was inapplicable to the facts of *Wilsher*. Foster J quoted from Lord Bridge's speech, with which the other Lords agreed, in support of his interpretation:

> *McGhee* v. *National Coal Board* laid down no new principle of law whatever. . . . . Adopting a robust and pragmatic approach to the undisputed primary facts of the case, the majority concluded that it was a legitimate inference of fact that the defenders' negligence had materially contributed to the pursuer's injury. The decision, in my opinion, is of no greater significance than that and to attempt to extract from it some esoteric principle which in some way modifies, as a matter of law, the nature of the burden of proof of causation which a plaintiff or pursuer must discharge once he has established a relevant breach of duty is a fruitless one.[15]

This was also the way in which one of the judges in *Birkholz*, Matheson J, distinguished *Birkholz* from *McGhee*:

> McGhee's case was concerned with cumulative causes, not alternative causes. As I understand the evidence, the appellant here contracted brucellosis as a result of an infection incurred on one occasion, and not as a result of an accumulation of organisms over a period of time.[16]

The reason that this is the orthodox explanation is that it is the easy way out. It is an uncontentious legal principle that negligence which makes a material contribution to the damage founds liability:

---

[14] [1988] 1 All ER 871.

[15] *Ibid.* at 881–2. The explanation given by Foster J of the decision in *McGhee*, that it was a case of cumulative causes, is equivalent to the explanation provided by the House of Lords in *Wilsher*, that *McGhee* was a case where the negligence had made a material contribution to damage, because if causes are cumulative then they all contributed to the effect, whereas if they are discrete then each one only increases the risk of the effect, since one of them caused the effect alone.

[16] N. 4 above at 142–3. Other commentators who rely on this explanation are: J. Fleming, *Law of Torts* (8th edn, Sydney, 1992), 199; J. Holder, 'The Sellafield Litigation and Questions of Causation in Environmental Law' (1994) Current Legal Problems 287 at 302; M. Jones, *Textbook on Torts* (5th edn, London, 1996), 181; R. Wright, 'Causation in Tort Law' (1985) 73 Calif. LR 1735 at 1814; M. Brazier (ed.), *Clerk and Lindsell on Torts* (17th edn, London, 1995), 43 and 447; H. Hart and T. Honoré, *Causation in the Law* (2nd edn, Oxford, 1985), 410; P. Balen, 'Causation Problems' (1994) 138 Solicitors' Journal 742 at 743.

N = defendant was negligent
C = another cause
L = plaintiff suffered a loss
R = plaintiff recovers

$$[(N \wedge C) \leftrightarrow L] \rightarrow R.$$

The principle is merely a restatement of the proposition that legal causes have to be necessary not sufficient causes:

$$[(N \wedge C) \leftrightarrow L] \rightarrow (\sim N \rightarrow \sim L) \rightarrow R.[17]$$

Foster J was right to regard *Bonnington Castings* v. *Wardlaw* as an example of this principle; indeed, the principle was enshrined in *Bonnington Castings*. In that case the plaintiff contracted pneumoconiosis by inhaling particles of silica present in the air as a result of the steel castings which his employers produced. When he sued his employers, the House of Lords found that they were to blame only for the dust from the swing grinders and not for the dust from the pneumatic hammers. The House of Lords held that a material contribution by the dust from the swing grinders was sufficient to establish liability and was prepared to infer, rightly or wrongly, that the pneumoconiosis was caused by an accumulation of dust:[18]

The medical evidence was that pneumoconiosis is caused by a gradual accumulation in the lungs of minute particles of silica inhaled over a period of years. That means, I think, that the disease is caused by the whole of the noxious material inhaled and, if that material comes from two sources, it cannot be wholly attributed to material from one source or the other. . . . In my opinion, it is proved not only that the swing grinders may well have contributed but that they did in fact contribute a quota of silica dust which was not negligible to the pursuer's lungs and therefore did help to produce the disease.[19]

---

[17] See A. Grubb, 'Causation and Medical Negligence' (1988) Cambridge LJ 350 at 351.

[18] A. Palmer, 'Causation in the High Court' (1993) 1 Torts LJ 9 at 22; E. Adeney, 'The Challenge of Medical Uncertainty: Factual Causation in Anglo-Australian Toxic Tort Litigation' (1993) 19 Monash Univ. LR 23 at 37; A. Phillips, 'Further Reflections on Medical Causation' (1988) 1 SLT 325 at 325.

[19] N. 10 above at 621 and 623 per Lord Reid. *Bonnington Castings* was followed in *Nicholson* v. *Atlas Steel Co. Ltd* [1957] 1 All ER 776 on very similar facts and in *Power* v. *Snowy Mountains Hydro Electric Authority* [1957] State Reps. (NSW) 9. But see Jones, *Torts*, n. 16 above, 178 and 182, Adeney, 'Challenge of Uncertainty', n. 18 above at 34 and Holder, 'Sellafield', n. 16 above at 299–300 for the view that *Bonnington Castings* represents a departure from the 'but for' test.

Therefore if *McGhee* can be interpreted as a case where it was proved that the 'guilty' dust and the 'innocent' dust acted in concert to cause the dermatitis, then *McGhee* becomes an unexceptionable negligence case[20] and readily distinguishable from Cubillo's case. The problem is that in *McGhee* there was absolutely no basis for making,[21] and not a single one of the Lords was prepared to make, the inference that the 'guilty' dust had made a material contribution to the dermatitis. This was most clearly acknowledged by Lord Reid:

In the present case the evidence does not shew—perhaps no one knows—just how dermatitis of this type begins. It suggests to me that there are two possible ways. It may be that an accumulation of minor abrasions of the horny layer of skin is a necessary precondition for the onset of the disease. Or it may be that the disease starts at one particular abrasion and then spreads, so that multiplication of abrasions merely increases the number of places where the disease can start and in that way increases the risk of its occurrence. I am inclined to think that the evidence points to the former view. But in a field were [*sic*] so little appears to be known with certainty *I could not say that that is proved.*[22]

The case was made to look like an orthodox material contribution case by several different techniques. The judges redefined the terms:[23]

The effect of such abrasion of the skin is cumulative in the sense that the longer a subject is exposed to injury *the greater the chance* of his developing dermatitis.[24]

. . .

In my view, a failure to take steps which would bring about a material reduction of the risk involves, in this type of case, a substantial contribution to the injury.[25]

---

[20] See G. Robertson, 'Overcoming the Causation Hurdle in Informed Consent Cases: The Principle in *McGhee* v. *National Coal Board*' (1984) 22 Univ. of Western Ontario LR 75 at 87.

[21] Palmer, 'Causation', n. 18 above at 21.

[22] N. 3 above at 1010 (emphasis added).

[23] See Robertson, '*McGhee*', n. 2 above at 87 for recognition of this. See Wright, 'Causation in Tort Law', n. 16 above at 1814 for an example of such redefinition.

[24] N. 3 above at 1010, per Lord Reid (emphasis added). Adeney, 'Challenge of Uncertainty', n. 18 above at 33 falls into this trap. See Palmer, 'Causation', n. 18 above at 22. [25] N. 3 above at 1014, per Lord Simon.

They also indulged in self-contradictory statements:

[T]here could be little doubt that the ... dermatitis resulted from a combination, or accumulation, of two causes. ... The appellant's expert was unable to attribute the injury to the second of these causes for he could not say that if the appellant had been able to wash off the dust by showers he would not have contracted the disease.[26]

Or they just avoided the issue:

In the circumstances of the present case it seems to me unrealistic and contrary to ordinary common sense to hold that the negligence which materially increased the risk of injury did not materially contribute to causing the injury. ... In the circumstances of the present case, the possibility of a distinction existing between (a) having materially increased the risk of contracting the disease and (b) having materially contributed to causing the disease ... is ... far too unreal to be recognised by the common law.[27]

Lord Salmon went further with this self-deception, equating liability for materially increasing the risk with the uncontroversial proposition that the negligence does not have to be a sufficient cause:

[W]hen it is proved, on a balance of probabilities, that an employer has been negligent and that his negligence has materially increased the risk of his employee contracting an industrial disease, then he is liable ... notwithstanding that the employer is not responsible for other factors which have materially contributed to the disease.[28]

In reality, as was acknowledged by Lord Reid, *McGhee* is a case of material increase in risk[29] not material contribution to damage and so cannot be distinguished from *Cubillo* on that basis:

The evidence is to the effect that the fact that the man had to cycle home caked with grime and sweat added *materially to the risk* that this disease

---

[26] N. 3 above at 1012. This statement is equivalent to the following contradiction: $[(N \wedge C) \leftrightarrow L] \wedge \sim[(\sim N \wedge C) \rightarrow \sim L]$.

[27] *Ibid.* at 1017 and 1018, per Lord Salmon.

[28] *Ibid.* at 1018.

[29] See E. Handsley, 'Market Share Liability and the Nature of Causation in Tort' (1993) 1 (1) Torts LJ 24 at 41, W. Wilson, 'A Note on Causation' (1976) SLT 193 at 193, J. Logie, 'Proof of Causation in Medical Negligence Cases' (1988) 1 SLT 25 at 27, Phillips, 'Reflections', n. 18 above at 326 and C. Pugh and M. Day, *Toxic Torts* (London, 1992), 36 for recognition of this.

might develop. . . . Nor can I accept the distinction . . . between materially increasing the risk that the disease will occur and making a material
contribution to its occurrence.[30]

This is ultimately the basis on which Lord Wilberforce decided
the case,[31] admitting that making the inference that the negligence
had materially contributed to the disease was 'something of a
fiction'.[32] This has been recognized by the courts in other cases.
Lord Mackay in *Hotson* v. *East Berkshire Area Health Authority*
acknowledged that *McGhee* had been dealt with by sleight of
hand.[33] The Court of Appeal faced up to this in *Wilsher*, as a
result of which they applied *McGhee* rather than attempting to
distinguish it:

I think it essential to note that, in that case, the original exposure to brick
dust and the failure to provide adequate washing facilities were treated as
separate causes.[34]

Secondly, Foster J argued that all of the precedents were

cases in which the plaintiff's disease or condition could only have been
caused by one agent, namely contact with infected cattle, brick dust, silica
dust and asbestos dust respectively. It was established in each case that
the plaintiff had come into contact with these dangerous agents in the
course of his employment.[35]

---

[30] N. 3 above at 1011 (emphasis added). See M. Parascandola, *The
'Indeterminate Plaintiff': Statistical Evidence and Causal Inference in Medicine and
the Law* (unpub. Phd thesis, Cambridge Univ., 1996), 163 and Phillips,
'Reflections', n. 18 above at 326 for recognition that this distinction was rejected
in McGhee.

[31] N. 3 above at 1012. This is recognized by Adeney, 'Challenge of
Uncertainty', n. 18 above at 33.

[32] N. 3 above at 1013. This has also been recognized by B. Markesinis and S.
Deakin, *Tort Law* (3rd edn, Oxford, 1994), 261, Holder, 'Sellafield', n. 16 above
at 300, H. Luntz, A. Hambly and R. Hayes, *Torts: Cases and Commentary* (2nd
edn, Sydney, 1985), 562 and Jones, *Torts*, n. 16 above at 178.

[33] [1987] 2 All ER 909 at 916.

[34] [1986] 3 All ER 801 at 832 per Glidewell LJ. See M. Stauch, 'Causation,
Risk, and Loss of Chance in Medical Negligence' (1997) 17 OJLS 205 at 215 for
the view that *Wilsher* is indistinguishable from *McGhee*. See Palmer, 'Causation',
n. 18 above at 22 for the view that *McGhee* was 'unconvincingly reinterpreted' by
the House of Lords in *Wilsher* as a case of cumulative causation. See Handsley,
'Market Share Liability', n. 29 above at 41 for the view that *Wilsher* represented a
narrower reinterpretation of *McGhee*. See Pugh and Day, *Toxic Torts*, n. 29
above, 37 for the view that *Wilsher* approved *McGhee* but in a rather restricted
way. [35] N. 3 above.

In contrast, Cubillo's was not 'a case in which the cause of the disease could be attributed to only one agent, namely, exposure to radiation.'[36]

In *Birkholz*,[37] the plaintiff contracted brucellosis after having worked in the defendants' abattoirs for two or three years. At first instance, Mohr J found that the plaintiff had become infected through his employment, but dismissed the plaintiff's claim on the basis that there was no reasonably practicable method by which his employers could have obviated the risk. On appeal by the plaintiff, the Full Supreme Court held that in order to succeed, the plaintiff had to show only that his employers could have alleviated the risk, not that they could have removed it. The evidence was that the disease could be transmitted from infected cattle to humans in a number of different ways, such as contact between human skin, particularly if it is broken, and the tissue or blood of an infected cattle; as a result of drinking milk from an infected animal; through inhaling an aerosol of infected tissue; or through an infected animal sneezing on the human. Mohr J had felt unable to determine how the plaintiff had been infected, but the Full Supreme Court felt able to find that it was more probable than not both that the appellant contracted the disease by touching the blood and tissue of the animals, and that if gloves had been provided alongside proper information about the risk of infection the plaintiff would not have been infected. This finding made it unnecessary for the Full Supreme Court to discuss *McGhee*; however, all three of the Lords gave an indication of how they would have decided the case had they been unable to determine the method of infection, two indicating that they would have applied *McGhee* and found for the plaintiff and Matheson J indicating that he would have distinguished *McGhee*.

None of the Lords attached any relevance to the fact that the disease had been caused by one agent. As was seen above,[38] Matheson J distinguished *McGhee* on the basis that *Birkholz* concerned discrete causes. King CJ argued that *McGhee* was

---

[36] See also Brazier, *Clerk and Lindsell*, n. 16 above, 44. Similarly, Jones, *Torts*, n. 16 above, 182, argues that the number of risk factors or the specificity of the risk is important and Adeney, 'Challenge of Uncertainty', n. 18 above at 49, 50 and 52 argues that the decision in *McGhee* is only applicable when there is only one substance which could have caused the injury.

[37] N. 4 above.   [38] See n. 16.

applicable on what can most charitably be described as a legal realist basis:

Has the failure to take those precautions been shown to have caused or materially contributed to the contracting of the disease by the appellant? It might be argued as a matter of strict logic, that the fact that given precautions would substantially diminish the risk, does not prove that failure to take those precautions materially contributed to the appellant's infection unless it can be established how that infection occurred. But the law's view of causation is less concerned with logical and philosophical considerations than with the need to produce a just result to the parties involved.[39]

. . .

However precisely the disease was contracted, the substantial increase in the risk of his contracting it resulting from the respondent's failure to discharge its legal obligations, should be regarded in a realistic, practical and legal sense, if not in a strictly logical sense, as materially contributing to the contracting of the disease.[40]

Moreover, in neither *Bonnington* nor *McGhee* itself did the judiciary rely on the explanation that there was only one agent.

However, the reasons which the judges in a case give for their decision do not determine the *ratio decidendi*. Moreover, if it is true that in *Birkholz*, *Bonnington* and *McGhee*, there was only one agent then it was not crucial in any of these cases for the courts to point out this unifying factor. In particular, in *Birkholz*, two out of the three judges were concerned to apply rather than to distinguish *McGhee* and so can hardly be castigated for not making explicit all of the common features. It could be argued that Foster J was simply drawing out a unifying factor which had been left implicit and which had not arisen before. In this context, it is perhaps more telling that when the House of Lords wanted to distinguish *McGhee* in *Wilsher*, in which they could very easily have relied on there being more than one agent, they did not put great emphasis on this. In *Wilsher* the plaintiff, a premature baby who was kept alive by being given extra oxygen, almost completely lost his sight as a result of developing retrolental fibroplasia ('RLF'). He claimed that this condition had been caused by an excess of oxygen tension in his bloodstream. The House of Lords accepted both that excess oxygen could cause RLF and that in this case the defendants had administered excess oxygen. However it was also accepted that RLF could occur in premature babies without any administration of oxygen since it was linked with several other conditions, namely apnoea, hypercarbia, intra ventricular haemorrhage and patent ductus arteriosus, all of which the plaintiff had suffered from. The House of Lords, overturning the Court of Appeal's decision that *Wilsher* was indistinguishable from *McGhee*, held that the plaintiff had failed to show that the excess oxygen had caused or materially contributed to the onset of RLF: all the plaintiff could show was that it was one of a number of possible causes. As seen above, the method which they unanimously used to distinguish *McGhee* was Foster J's first distinguishing feature, that the causes were cumulative in *McGhee* and discrete in *Wilsher*. However, they did quote and approve, although without commenting on, Sir Nicolas Browne-Wilkinson VC's dissenting speech from the Court of Appeal, in which he distinguishes *McGhee* from *Wilsher* on the basis of the number of agents:

To apply the principle in *McGhee* v. *National Coal Board* [1972] 3 All ER 1008, [1973] 1 WLR 1 to the present case would constitute an extension of that principle. In *McGhee* there was no doubt that the pursuer's dermatitis was physically caused by brick dust. . . . There was only one possible agent which could have caused the dermatitis, viz brick dust, and there was no doubt that the dermatitis from which he suffered was caused by that brick dust. In the present case the question is different. There are a number of different agents which could have caused the RLF. Excess oxygen was one of them. The defendants failed to take reasonable precautions to prevent one of the possible causative agents (e.g. excess oxygen) from causing RLF. But no one can tell in this case whether excess oxygen did or did not cause or contribute to the RLF suffered by the plaintiff. The plaintiff's RLF may have been caused by some completely different agent or agents, e.g. hypercarbia, intra ventricular haemorrhage, apnoea or patent ductus arteriosus. In addition to oxygen, each of those conditions has been implicated as a possible cause of RLF. . . . The position, to my mind, is wholly different from that in *McGhee*, where there was only one candidate (brick dust) which could have caused the dermatitis . . .[41]

---

[41] N. 34 above at 882. Stauch, 'Causation, Risk', n. 34 above at 215 interprets this to mean that the greater the number of candidate conditions and the more limited the defendant's control over those conditions, the less willing the courts will be to impose liability. However, given that the defendants in *McGhee* were not to blame for the dust at work it seems illogical to take into account any control which they had over it. M. McInnes, 'Case Comment: *Wilshir* [sic] v. *Essex Area*

There is therefore some limited authority for this point of distinction. More importantly, even if there were not, a legal distinction is not wrong for being novel. The problem for Foster J's point of distinction really comes when we ask how we decide what an agent is. 'Agent' is defined by the Shorter Oxford Dictionary as 'the material cause or instrument'. Even leaving aside the formal definition, it is difficult to see how the concept of agency can be given a meaning which is independent of the concept of causation.[42] Once we have recognized that agency is synonymous with causation, Foster J's distinction boils down to the statement that in *Cubillo* there was more than one cause while in the precedents there was only one cause.[43] Once the distinction has been reformulated in this way, it is obviously faulty because it depends on how the causes are categorized. All of the precedents can be described as cases with more than one cause: *McGhee* can be classed as a case with two possible causes, the dust at work and the dust on the way home; indeed this is how the House of Lords did characterize it:

[T]here could be little doubt that the appellant's dermatitis resulted from a combination, or accumulation, of two causes; exposure to dust while working in hot conditions in the kiln and the subsequent omission to wash thoroughly before leaving the place of work.[44]

Birkholz can be classed as a case with four possible causes, contact between human skin and infected tissue or blood, drinking milk from infected cattle, inhaling an aerosol of infected tissue and

Health Authority: Wiping Away *McGhee*'s Benevolent Smile' (1989) 47 The Advocate 759 at 762 interprets *Wilsher* as limiting *McGhee* to the situations where there is one risk and *Wilsher* as applying where there is more than one risk; Phillips, 'Reflections', n. 18 above at 326 argues that *Wilsher* is different because it involved 1 negligent risk factor out of 5, rather than 1 out of 2 and that even after *Wilsher* it is sufficient to show a material increase in risk so long as there are not too many risk factors.

[42] See D. Davidson, 'Agency' in R. Binkley, R. Bronaugh and A. Marras (eds.), *Agent, Action and Reason* (1971), esp. 15–16 for support for this view.

[43] See e.g. Rogers, *Winfield and Jolowicz on Tort* (14th edn, London, 1994), 151; Wilkinson, '*Reay and Hope* v. *British Nuclear Fuels plc*' (1994) Water Law 22; Boon, 'Causation and the Increase of Risk' (1988) 51 Mod. LR 508 at 513; B. Coote, 'Chance and the Burden of Proof in Contract and Tort' (1988) 62 Australian LJ 761 at 765; Holder, 'Sellafield', n. 16 above at 302; M. Khan, 'What's To Become of Medical Negligence in England?' [1995] 3 Malayan LJ lix at lxii; Phillips, 'Reflections', n. 17 above at 326.

[44] N. 3 above at 1012, per Lord Wilberforce.

through an infected animal sneezing on the human, and *Bonnington* can be classed as a case with two possible causes, the dust from the swing grinders and the dust from the pneumatic hammers, as indeed it was categorized:

> I cannot agree that the question is: which was the most probable source of the respondent's disease, the dust from the pneumatic hammers or the dust from the swing grinders? It appears to me that the source of his disease was the dust from both sources.[45]

> . . .

> [T]he silica dust discharged from the swing grinders contributed to the harmful condition of the atmosphere . . . and was therefore a contributory cause of the disease.[46]

In contrast, *Cubillo* can be classed as a case with only one possible cause, the pre-cancerous cell changes to Cubillo's kidney.

It is ironic that Foster J's second distinction, that there is only one agent, turns out to contradict his first distinction that the causes were cumulative: for there to be cumulative causes presupposes that there is more than one cause. Distinguishing different agents is a precondition to the argument that the agents acted together.[47] This highlights the problem with the first distinction: we could only argue that there were two agents and therefore that the causes were cumulative if in *McGhee* the dust at work was distinguishable from the dust on the way home by way of its *effect* on the plaintiff. And the corollary of this is that we can sensibly talk of one agent when it is impossible to distinguish among the particles of dust in relation to their effect on the plaintiff. So, by way of illustration, if we discovered that particles of dust came in two different shades of grey but that the colour made no difference to their effect then I think that we would say that there was only one agent of the disease, the dust of whatever colour. But in contrast, if we found that there were two different types of dust, one of which caused dermatitis if an individual was exposed for however short a period and the other of which caused dermatitis

---

[45] N. 10 above at 621, per Lord Reid.

[46] *Ibid.* at 623, per Lord Tucker.

[47] Fleming, *Law of Torts*, n. 16 above, 199 and Adeney, 'Challenge of Uncertainty', n. 18 above at 49 argue in contrast that in *McGhee* it could be inferred that the causes operated cumulatively because they were of the same kind, i.e. dust.

only if the exposure was over a sustained period, I think we could distinguish two agents of dermatitis, even if the two types of dust were apparently identical.

Foster J falls into the common trap set by the orthodoxy with his first distinction, but his instincts are good. He believes that there is one agent in *McGhee* because he regards the dust as indistinguishable in its effect on the plaintiff, regardless of its source.

The Distinction is Determinism

I have argued elsewhere that the courts allow recovery for loss of a chance if and only if they are confronted with an indeterministic scenario.[48] More precisely, judges allow recovery in all situations where they have a degree of belief of at least 0.5 in the proposition that but for the defendant's negligence the plaintiff would not have suffered his loss. However, in indeterministic situations, judges allow recovery even if they have a degree of belief of less than 0.5 in the above proposition, but only if they have a degree of belief of at least 0.5 in the proposition that the defendant's negligence significantly increased the objective probability, that is, probability as a property of the external world and independent of human knowledge or belief, that the plaintiff would suffer the loss. How do we decide whether an event is indeterministic? We cannot know for certain, but an event which could not have been predicted at any point in the past, cannot be predicted in the present even given unlimited time, resources, and evidence, and which we cannot imagine how we would predict in the future even given the success of present research programmes, is indeterministic for all human purposes, or quasi-indeterministic.[49] On close inspection, it emerges that this theory also explains the distinction between *Cubillo* and the precedents and particularly the decision in *McGhee*.

McGhee was a quasi-indeterministic scenario. At the heart of the House of Lords' decision in *McGhee* was the realization that it was impossible to determine which particles of dust had caused the dermatitis:

---

[48] Reece, 'Chances', n. 5 above. [49] *Ibid.* at 193–4.

[L]ittle is known as to the exact causes of dermatitis. The experts could say that it tends to be caused by a breakdown of the layer of heavy skin covering the nerve ends provoked by friction caused by dust, but had to admit that they knew little of the quantity of dust or the time of exposure necessary to cause a critical change.[50]

. . .

It is, in the present state of medical knowledge, impossible to say that if the appellant had taken a shower he would certainly not have got the disease, and it is equally impossible to say that another man, in exactly the same case as the appellant, would on the contrary certainly have got it. . . . *This is a case in which the actual chain of events in the man's body leading up to the injury is not clearly known.*[51]

There was also some recognition of this in Lord Bridge's interpretation of *McGhee* in *Wilsher*:

The precise mechanism of causation of the disease however, was not known and the furthest the doctors . . . were able to go was to say that the provision of showers would have materially reduced the risk of dermatitis. They were unable to say that it would probably have prevented the disease.[52]

There was a similar recognition in Bollen J's interpretation of *McGhee* in *Birkholz*:

'Where knowledge of the material facts is incomplete, it is legitimate to take a broad practical view and proof of a material increase of the risk of injury will suffice for proof of material contribution to the injury suffered.' . . . I think that this is a correct statement of the effect of *McGhee* v. *National Coal Board*.[53]

If *McGhee* is a quasi-indeterministic case, it is certainly one in which the judges had a degree of belief of at least 0.5 in the proposition that the negligence had increased the quasi-objective

---

[50] N. 3 above at 1012, per Lord Wilberforce.

[51] *Ibid.* at 1015 and 1016, per Lord Kilbrandon (emphasis added).

[52] N. 14 above at 878.

[53] N. 11 above at 146 (references omitted). See Robertson, '*McGhee*', n. 20 above at 85 for the argument that the basis for the decision was that the limitations of medical knowledge rendered it impossible to overcome the evidential difficulty. See also Brazier, *Clerk and Lindsell*, n. 16 above, 44 & 45; G. Fridman, *Torts* (London, 1990), 332 & 333 for the argument that the basis for the decision in *McGhee* was that the evidence of causation was absent and the mechanism by which the disease had been caused was unclear. See *Jaszkowski* v. *Goldsworthy Mining Ltd* [1992] 8 State Reps. (WA) 1, in which Healy J distinguished *Wilsher* from the instant case on the basis that in that case there was an absence of direct evidence.

probability. Lord Kilbrandon in particular regarded this increase in probability as *known*.[54]

In *Birkholz*, two of the judges regarded the case as analogous to *McGhee*. One of them, Bollen J, recognized that in order to make the analogy it was of utmost importance that it was impossible to show how the plaintiff had contracted brucellosis:

Is he then to be denied a remedy because he could not prove the precise cause of his illness? I say 'could not prove' deliberately. For I think that the appellant did all he could to put the fullest information about the cause of his illness before the learned trial Judge. All evidence must be judged by the capacity of a party to produce information. I have studied the evidence. I do not see that the appellant could have produced more information. I speak in the qualitative sense. No doubt he could have multiplied the experts whom he called. But that would not (on the present assumption) have identified the precise cause of his illness.[55]

. . .

[A]ssuming that a plaintiff has done all he can to provide full information to the Court, I think that the basing of the legal concept of causation on practical considerations is consistent with justice.[56]

It is, however, *McGhee* that is the paradigm of a case in which a loss of a chance approach is appropriate. As Lord Kilbrandon recognized, no differences had been identified between those who did and those who did not develop dermatitis when exposed to the same amount of dust for the same period.[57] The causal process by which particles of a substance lead to a disease in a random sample of the people exposed to the substance is unlikely to be humanly determinable, making *McGhee* at least quasi-indeterministic, and may well be a genuinely indeterministic process, similar to the decay of a uranium atom.[58]

Additional support for this interpretation of *McGhee* is contained in Lord Salmon's speech, whose discussion of the probabilities involved in *McGhee* sounds far more like estimations of objective risk than expressions of degrees of belief:

Suppose . . . it could be proved that men . . . would be exposed to a 52 per cent risk of contracting dermatitis even when proper washing facilities were provided. Suppose it could also be proved that that risk would be

[54] N. 3 above at 1015.   [55] N. 4 above at 145.
[56] *Ibid*. at 146–7.   [57] See n. 51 above.
[58] See Reece, 'Chances', n. 5 above at 195.

increased to, say, 90 per cent when such facilities were not provided. It would follow that if the decision appealed from is right, an employer who negligently failed to provide the proper facilities would escape from any liability to an employee . . . notwithstanding that the employers had increased the risk from 52 per cent to 90 per cent. The negligence would not be a cause of the dermatitis because even with proper washing facilities . . . it would still have been more likely than not that the employee would have contracted the disease. . . . If, however, you substitute 48 per cent for 52 per cent the employer could not escape liability, not even if he had increased the risk to, say, only 60 per cent. Clearly such results would not make sense.[59]

These results would not make sense if they are objective chances. There is little to choose between objective chances of 48 and 52 per cent. It is far more relevant to ask to what extent the action increased the risk. But if the figures were interpreted as degrees of belief then the results would make sense and would have been accepted by the House of Lords. Degrees of belief in a proposition of 90 per cent, 60 per cent and 52 per cent all indicate that, on balance, one believes in the proposition, albeit more or less strongly, while a degree of belief of 48 per cent means that one does not believe the proposition.

We have already noted that Foster J's second point of distinction, while wrong, leads us to the right answer. Having established the true point of distinction, we are now able to pinpoint precisely the insight contained in the incorrect explanations. It is not that *McGhee* is a case where we know that the causes are acting cumulatively but rather that it is a case where we do not know that they are not acting cumulatively.[60] There is a strong connection between this state of belief and indeterminism, because when we are faced with an agent which may be acting either cumulatively or discretely, it is generally very hard to see our way forward to identifying the token cause.

But Parascandola argues that it would be mistaken to regard *McGhee* as favouring a 'chancy approach to causation'[61] because

---

[59] N. 3 above at 1018. See B. Legum, 'Increased Risk of Cancer as an Actionable Injury' (1984) 18 Georgia LR 563 at 569 for a similar approach.

[60] See F. Trindade and P. Cane, *The Law of Torts in Australia* (2nd edn, Melbourne, 1993), 453, for the argument that *McGhee* was reinterpreted in *Wilsher* on the basis that it was *possible* that the dermatitis had been caused by the cumulative effect of the sources of risk.

[61] *Indeterminate Plaintiff*, n. 30 above, 163.

'the reasons given for adopting the risk principle show that it was merely a way of stretching legal rules to aid the plaintiff and not acceptance of a different (non-deterministic) concept of causation.'[62] This misses the point, which is why the judges felt inclined to stretch the legal rules to aid the plaintiff in the case of *McGhee*, and when they feel this in other cases. It has transpired that they feel this urge when the situation is indeed indeterministic. Parascandola himself recognizes that the reason the courts stretched the legal rules was that the evidence was insufficient as a result of medical uncertainty.[63] I have made it clear in my earlier work that the judges have only an intuitive grasp of the distinction with which they themselves are working.[64] This also deals with another criticism which has been made, that my argument overlooks the empirical impossibility of discovering whether the situation is indeterministic:[65] of course the courts may make the wrong decision in individual cases, but it is the distinction between indeterminism and determinism with which they are instinctively grappling.

Is *Cubillo* Deterministic?

The precedents, then, are cases where the rules of causation could be relaxed on the basis that the cases were at least quasi-indeterministic. The question then becomes whether Foster J got it right or wrong in the case of *Cubillo*: can *Cubillo* be regarded as a case where it was determined that the radiation did not cause the kidney cancer?

This can be argued in a number of different ways. It is impossible to suggest that we can discover the cause of individual cancers,[66] but it is possible to argue that given the success of present research programmes, we will be able to do so, that the development of cancer is not a random process. This was the approach taken by Gonthier J in the Supreme Court of Canada in *Lawson* v. *Laferrière*.[67] In this case the defendant doctor negligently failed to inform the plaintiff that she had cancer. The plaintiff, who had died by the time of the decision, had argued that if she had known she had had cancer, she would have had follow-up treatments and

---

[62] *Ibid.*, 164. [63] *Ibid.*
[64] Reece, 'Chances', n. 5 above at 189.
[65] Stauch, 'Causation, Risk', n. 34 above at 222.
[66] DiStefano, 'Dangerous Doses?', n. 6 above at 28 & 31.
[67] (1991) 78 Dominion Law Reps. (4th) 609.

regular check-ups, but she had been unable to prove that she would have recovered under these circumstances. Gonthier J dismissed her case, but he recognized that in order to do so he needed to distinguish it from a random scenario:

Even though our understanding of medical matters is often limited, I am not prepared to conclude that particular medical conditions should be treated for purposes of causation as the equivalent of diffuse elements of pure chance.[68]

Clearly however, Gonthier J is rejecting the loss-of-chance approach for all medical cases rather than in relation to cancer in particular, and it is hard to argue that the development of cancer is more determinable than the development of dermatitis or brucellosis.

Importantly, however, in order to distinguish *Cubillo*, it is not necessary to show that the cause of the cancer was determined but only that it was determined that the cause was not radiation. In contrast to McGhee and Birkholz, although the majority of the evidence was probabilistic in *Cubillo*, there was some case-specific evidence. There was the finding that Cubillo himself would have suffered other reactions to radiation such as radiation burns, possible hair loss, and loss of immune function had the dose been sufficient to cause renal-cell carcinoma. There was also the finding that there would have been visible changes to Cubillo's kidney, namely prior sclerosis and scarring.

The final way in which *Cubillo* can be distinguished is that even if it was not determined that the radiation did not cause his cancer, so that there was an objective chance that this was the cause, the chance did not meet the requisite level of significance. Foster J found that the maximum increase in risk attributable to the radiation was 0.002. This increase in risk is almost a hundred times smaller than the smallest chance which has been judicially protected, which was in *Fisher* v. *Knibbe*, in which compensation was awarded for a chance of 0.15.[69] The question of the size of

---

[68] (1991) 78 Dominion Law Reps. (4th) 609 at 654 and 656. See Reece, 'Chances', n. 5 above at 195.

[69] [1989] 6 Western Weekly Law Reps. (Canada) 130, in which case a solicitor who had been negligent in allowing his client's case to become time-barred was ordered to pay his client 15% of the damages which his client would have been awarded had the case been successful, the 15% representing the chance that his client would have won the case. See Adeney, 'Challenge of Uncertainty', n. 18 above at 32 for discussion of the necessity for the contribution to be material. See

the chance that the radiation caused the cancer is not distinct from the question whether it is determined that the radiation did not cause Cubillo's cancer: in dealing with a risk of such a tiny magnitude, for all human purposes it is determined that the radiation did not cause the cancer.

It seems then that the distinction which I have drawn between deterministic and indeterministic scenarios can explain Foster J's reluctance to apply *McGhee* in *Cubillo*, and that *McGhee* itself lends additional support to my hypothesis. However this hypothesis has attracted some criticism.

Previously, I have argued that the legal system, and particularly the burden and standard of proof, are founded on the assumption of determinism. Therefore when this assumption is not maintainable, the burden and standard of proof have no basis, so when confronted with an indeterministic scenario, it becomes necessary for courts to adjust their world view. However, given that the courts are wedded to deterministic analysis, they naturally make as small an adjustment as is possible, which is to retain causation as a deterministic concept but to alter the phenomenon found to have been caused, so that in an indeterministic case, it is the chance of the event which is found to have been caused.[70]

Parascandola argues that 'underlying these attitudes is an assumption that causation is always deterministic and that laws of nature are never statistical'.[71] He is right that there is a quite explicit assumption that part of the definition of causation is determinism, but there is no corresponding assumption that the laws of nature are never statistical: indeed the fundamental assumption underlying the hypothesis which I have presented is that there are situations in which we can never move beyond probabilities. It is rather the case that *he* makes the assumption that the laws of nature are *always* statistical,[72] as a result of which he sees the equation of causation with determinism as too restrictive of causation.

Parascandola argues that the most serious defect of an approach

M. Mandell and S. Carlin, 'The Value of a Chance: The Evolution and Direction of Chance in Tort Law' (1986) 20 Suffolk Univ. LR 203 at 204 for the argument that all chances should be recognized, including mere possibilities.

[70] Reece, 'Chances', n. 5 above at 204–6.

[71] *Indeterminate Plaintiff*, n. 30 above, Foreword.

[72] M. Parascandola, 'Evidence and Association: Epistemic Confusion in Toxic Tort Law' (1996) 63 *Philosophy of Science* S168 at S174.

which equates causation with determinism is that it cannot make sense of the causal claims of medical science because on this approach, for example, smoking does not cause cancer: 'The result is that one can never rightly claim, even in principle, that anyone developed cancer because of their smoking.'[73] He argues that to make sense of paradigmatic claims of medical science, such as the claim that smoking causes cancer, we need a concept of causation that includes statistical elements.[74]

The first point to make in response is that I am not committed to this being the only, or the best, approach to causation in indeterministic scenarios; I simply pointed out that it is the approach which the courts will tend towards, since it is the smallest concession away from the world view to which they are committed. However, as against this approach to causation Parascandola gives little justification for his argument that it is a defect of the theory that it does not allow the claim that an individual's cancer was caused by an individual's smoking; he simply points out that this is the consequence of this approach; for him, this is unacceptable on the simple basis that he wants to be able to say that John's smoking causes John's cancer; this is the direction in which his intuitions about causation take him. For me, this is no price to pay. It is not that we are limited in our expression of the relation between John's smoking and John's cancer in terms of causation; it is simply that we need to say that John's smoking caused an increase in the risk that John would contract cancer. This seems a far more accurate expression of the relationship; on the present state of medical knowledge it is right that we cannot say that John's smoking caused John's cancer, but only that his smoking increased the risk that he would contract cancer. Parascandola finds this particularly difficult to accept when we are dealing with a small chance that John's smoking did not cause John's cancer. He argues that it is unacceptable that 'the slightest element of chance precludes all causation'.[75] But it seems quite right to me that if there is a random element then we cannot say that A caused B, only that A caused the overwhelming chance of B. All causation is not precluded; we can make use of the concept, but the phenomenon found to have been caused is altered.

---

[73] *Indeterminate Plaintiff*, n. 30 above, 30. See also 136.
[74] Ibid., Foreword.   [75] Ibid., 32.

Given that Parascandola is operating mainly on the level of an intuitive argument, it is a valid response that my intuitions about causation are in completely the opposite direction. For me, the idea that we would try to attribute John's cancer directly to his smoking seems to me quite distasteful and indeed positively macabre. Given the intuitive nature of the discussion so far, it is also no criticism of the courts that their intuition accords with my own.

However Parascandola is not arguing purely on the instinctive level. He suggests that the most serious consequence of my approach for the law is that it does not allow plaintiffs to recover for actually contracting cancer.[76] Clearly it does, as *McGhee* itself demonstrates.

He also argues that these accounts leave no place for a notion of degrees of causal strength, but he goes on almost immediately to give the answer to this problem himself, although he finds it unsatisfying, when he says: 'one might reply that the strength of causes can still be measured by how much they raise the chances of their effects'.[77] This is completely right: a pollutant which causes a 90 per cent chance that an individual will develop cancer is clearly far more causally potent than a pollutant which causes a 0.09 per cent chance.

We certainly need a concept of causation which can cope with statistical associations but it does not follow that the concept of causation itself must be probabilistic.

It seems that the case of *Cubillo* was readily distinguishable from the precedents. Foster J accordingly reached the right result, even if not by quite the right route.

---

[76] Ibid., 137. See also Stauch, 'Causation, Risk', n. 34 above at 222 where he argues that my approach does not explain how the chance lost is to be quantified statistically: generally where this is a difficulty it seems that the courts allow full recovery.

[77] *Indeterminate Plaintiff*, n. 30 above, 32.

THE ENVIRONMENT, SCIENCE, AND LAW

John McEldowney

Introduction

The environment poses diverse problems and challenges requiring a scientific[1] explanation. Science[2] provides many of the assumptions that underlie most environmental laws and is frequently used by policy-makers to justify decision-making. The authority of science is sought to support various claims, counter-claims and assumptions about the environment.

Well-publicized problems such as acid rain, global warming, depletion of the ozone layer, and loss of biodiversity are examples of scientific research explaining the nature and scope of anthropogenic impacts on the environment. Scientific data and analysis provide us with an understanding of the environment. In fact, only rarely do environmental problems not depend on some scientific explanation.

During the eighteenth and nineteenth centuries environmental law grew out of demands of public health and a limited response to problems of pollution. Solutions to environmental problems developed in a piecemeal fashion. In recent times environmental law has continued to evolve in an organic way, responding to new scientific developments and the development of new processes. Scientific knowledge has improved to the point that environmental law has begun to become less reactive and more proactive. In that regard environmental law and regulation is

---

[1] See S. Jasanoff, *Science at the Bar: Law, Science and Technology in America* (Cambridge, Mass., 1995); also T. O'Riordan (ed.), *Environmental Science for Environmental Management* (Essex, 1995); J. A. Hannigan, *Environmental Sociology* (London, 1995); J. F. McEldowney and S. McEldowney, *Environment and the Law* (Essex, 1996).

[2] D. E. Bernstein, 'Junk Science in the United States and the Commonwealth' (1996) 21 Yale J Intern Law 123.

increasingly dependent on scientific understanding and the continual development of new techniques for assessing the quality of the environment.

In this paper it is intended to explore the foundations of the relationship of the environment, science, and law. An historical approach is adopted with a particular focus on the rise of statistical studies which informed the development of the social sciences and provided a bridge between mathematical science and law. Interest in political economy in the seventeenth century gave rise to the development in the eighteenth century of mathematical inquiry applied to social problems. Interest in statistical study formed the focus of the rise of the statistical movement and the creation of a number of statistical societies both nationally and provincially in the middle of the nineteenth century. The statistical societies provided a national and international forum based on an interdisciplinary collaboration of science, mathematical probability, and law. They provided the basic framework for reform, particularly of the laws on public health[3] and pollution. The scientific method of collecting evidence to prove a hypothesis informed the methodology of the Royal Commission and parliamentary inquiry. This was an unparalleled period where law and science provided a forum for common issues to be analysed.

Particular emphasis is given in this paper to the question of how science and law may require differing methodology and levels of proof. Assessing the inter-relationship[4] between law and science requires increasingly specialized knowledge.[5] The intellectual foundations of environmental law rooted in the eighteenth and nineteenth centuries require a fresh appraisal to understand how law and science may best be integrated to meet the challenges of the 1990s.

---

[3] See E. Chadwick, *Report on the Sanitary Condition of the Labouring Population of Great Britain, with an introduction by M. W. Flinn* (Edinburgh, 1965).

[4] *This Common Inheritance, UK Annual Report*, Cm. 1995 no. 2822.

[5] See W. Lepenies, *Between Literature and Science: The Rise of Sociology Ideas in Context* (Cambridge, 1989); Gerd Gigerenzer *et al.*, *The Empire of Change: How Probability Changed Science and Everyday Life, Ideas in Context* (Cambridge, 1989).

Science and Law: the Analytical Method

The common-law tradition was particularly adept in encompassing scientific methodology. Before examining the role of science and concerns about the environment it is useful to locate the discourse of scientific methodology as part of the common law.[6] The development of the common law rested on remedies and generally avoided directly defining rights and wrongs. The judges, responsive to the need to develop legal rules, attempted to interpret the needs and problems of society through flexible solutions applied in individual cases. Much of the development of English law depended on the ability of the law to grant a suitable remedy in an individual case. Whilst remedies may have offered solutions to practical problems often these were constructed in narrowly defined ways and limited by procedure and form. No codified set of statutes or doctrine existed.

The English common law[7] was particularly influenced by the practitioner's concerns. This may explain how its survival and the haphazard nature of its development was achieved. The common law was remarkably anti-theoretical in its approach. Notions of policy, justice, and legal doctrine found in the common law were determined by procedure and form rather than through reasoned or theoretical principles. From an impartial point of view the law had to find an appropriate remedy to solve the case.

Attempts to systemize English law came from two directions. One approach, influenced by Blackstone, attempted to add continental ideas about rights to the reasoning implied in the common law. The other approach, dominated by Bentham, aimed to provide a codification of principles. Whilst different directions may be detected in the approaches there was common ground. The methodology of science and the reasoning of statistical study were influential in the writings of both Blackstone and Bentham. This ensured that scientific methodology was integral to the analytical methodology and legal reasoning employed in the development of the common law.

Blackstone encouraged the idea that English law was 'a science

---

[6] See J. F. McEldowney, *Public Law* (2nd edn., London, 1998), ch. 7; M. Loughlin, *Legality and Locality* (Oxford, 1996).
[7] See S. Amos, *A Systematic View of the Science of Jurisprudence* (London, 1872).

which distinguished the criteria of right and wrong'.[8] His attempts to reconcile the historical development of the common law with a flexible and rule-bound system gave rise to an analytical method. This proved to be very influential, especially when later adopted by Dicey in his analysis of the English Constitution.[9] The essential of Blackstone's legacy found that English law could be formed from a deductive system of reasoning incorporating natural-law principles. This required a mathematical approach to law forming a deductive method of analysis. It favoured the formality of legal rules and the formal reduction of the resolution of any dispute to specific points.

It is not surprising to find that at the end of the eighteenth century, a time when scientific discovery and science attracted the attention of the age, many lawyers had become empiricists. Whether this was coincidence or not is difficult to determine. What was remarkable was that lawyers found that through detailed empirical investigation law was treated as practical and relevant rather than theoretical and abstract.[10] The law on pleading was a clear example of the view that the legal system was a functioning set of rules that provided the tools for the practitioner to fashion remedies for the client. Writers considered 'the science of pleading', rooted in the belief that the precision of rules would give rise to the revelation of truth. The system of writs furthered the idea that correct procedure gave rise to an accurate record and that this laid the foundations of law.[11]

On a broader analysis empirical methodology lay at the root of deciding cases. The development of case law followed from the efforts to systematize. The idea that English law could be found in decided cases rested on the development of a reliable and comprehensive system of law reports. The system of *stare decisis* and the doctrine of precedent rested on judicial reasoning being applied by analogy to cases with similar facts. Technical and formal rules, applied in an analytical and scientific way, rooted the common law to the empiricist tradition and the logic of the judges.

---

[8] W. Blackstone, *Commentaries*, vol. x, 5–6.

[9] See J. F. McEldowney, 'Dicey in Historical Perspective—A Review Essay' in P. McAuslan and J. F. McEldowney (eds.), *Law, Legitimacy and the Constitution* (London, 1985).

[10] Also influential was the writing of Montesquieu (1689–1755): *De l'esprit des lois* (Paris, 1748).

[11] See *Mirehouse* v. *Rennell* (1833) 1 Cl. and F. 527 at 546.

Within this tradition lay considerable self-doubt and disenchantment. The desire for a clearly defined set of rules for judges to apply prompted many English lawyers to examine the value of the civil law as a source of principles and jurisprudence. Generally there was considerable reluctance to reconcile the common law with the civil law system in all its forms.

Bentham's disillusionment with the common law came from his identification of the inadequacy of the procedural rules, the absence of clear principles and the lack of comprehensiveness. His pursuit of the universal codification of English law proved a lifetime work which ultimately ended in frustration. There is evidence to show that in determining the contents of codes and their application Bentham shared the techniques implied in the scientific method as a means to determine concepts and ideas. Lobban explains, 'An Introduction [to the Principles of Morals and legislation] was perceived by Bentham to be a "metaphysical" work, standing in relation to the substantive law as a treatise of pure mathematics stood to natural philosophy.'[12]

Bentham's codification project was ultimately rejected, despite many attempts through numerous Royal Commissions and law reform initiatives. Bentham had sought to devise a science of principles derived from the immutable laws of human nature. In his principles of utility may be found the science of law reform. Diagnosing a wide range of social reforms from prisons to the workhouse, from education to the courts and from the substantive criminal law to a codified constitution, Bentham's ambitious aim was that through codification a legislative solution to the problems of society might be found.

As a result, English law resisted the attempt to provide a single jurisprudence of rights and remedies. The jurisprudence of Blackstone, Bentham, Austin, and Dicey allowed lawyers to conceive law through an analytical jurisprudence rooted in an empirical tradition bearing many characteristics of scientific proof. Strict procedural rules determined the precise point of dispute for deliberation by the court. Judges attempted to discover through deductive reasoning the resolution of the dispute from the material facts presented by the litigants in each case. So much lay outside

---

[12] M. Lobban, *The Common Law and English Jurisprudence 1760–1850* (Oxford, 1991), 155.

the control of any single system of rules. The litigant determined the cases that came to court and the facts each case presented. The judges responded to the challenge in a haphazard way, drawing on a wide range of sources and ideas to find solutions. The jury added to the lack of predictability of outcome. The common law built on the reasoning common to 'ordinary men' and the rules of procedure that guided the discourse set the agenda for judges. The absence of a systemized English law and a coherent theoretical underpinning of the principles of law underlines the importance of the analytical method used in the common law. This brings us to the question of how the foundations of science and economic management played such an important role in shaping the character of environmental law in the mid-nineteenth century.

The Foundations of Science and Economic Management

The publication of the work of William Petty (1623–87) and John Graunt (1620–74) in 1662[13] marked a new approach to the study of society.[14] Their new approach, described as 'the science of political arithmetic', focused on three elements of what soon led to the generation of natural laws that governed the social sciences. Through this means the study of economic, social, and political problems could develop on a par with the study of the physical sciences. The three elements in Petty and Graunt's study comprised the following: first, the collection of statistical data; secondly, the application of statistical or empirical research to a particular problem; and thirdly, the development of natural laws that could predict the outcome of events from known data. As we shall see in more detail below, public health, sanitation, and pollution fell within the social problems that came to be addressed through statistical study.

Petty began his analysis with a study of public finances[15] and, through studies of population and wealth, drew up a comprehensive understanding of the economy.[16] The significance of Petty

---

[13] *Natural and Political Observations on the Bills of Mortality* (London, 1662).

[14] M. J. Cullen, *The Statistical Movement in Early Victorian Britain* (London, 1975), 1–6.

[15] W. Petty, *Treatise of Taxes and Contributions* (London, 1662).

[16] See R. Smith, *The Fontana History of the Human Science* (London, 1997), 308–9.

and Graunt's work should not be considered in isolation from the work of other scholars. French writers, notably Antoine de Montchrestein (1575–1621),[17] attempted to consider the role of the state and the economy as part of a scientific understanding of political and economic questions. It was the interrogation of how economies developed and how society could be measured that initiated studies into techniques for collecting appropriate scientific data. This was related partly to measurement of the economy as a whole[18] and partly to the development, in the eighteenth century, of schemes of insurance. In 1762, the Society for Equitable Assurances for Lives and Survivorships was established in Britain and the development of life-tables to make actuarial calculations began.

Medical inquiries into smallpox,[19] later studies on insanity and into the causes of poverty and destitution were all based on statistical study. Boards of Public Health were formed to fill the gaps left by inadequate Poor Law provision and identified by local statistical surveys. Notably, from 1780 to 1830 several developments formed the foundation of the application of statistical and scientific data to social problems. The national census was instituted in 1800. National criminal statistics for England and Wales began to be published by the Home Office in 1810, followed by Scotland in 1812 and eventually regular returns from 1832. Significantly, official and private statistical surveys co-existed. Parliamentary select committees added to their task the compilation of a statistical basis for parliamentary information. Soon what had been *ad hoc* and the response to individual inquiry became routine.

Government departments responded to the curiosity encouraged by the provision of statistical information. The Board of Trade established a Statistical Department in 1832 covering the development of trade and manufacturers. Other departments of government soon followed with the establishment of statistical divisions: the Colonial Office, the Home Office, the Inspector-General of Imports and Exports. Private organizations also engaged in the

[17] A. de Montchrestein, *Traité de l'economie politique* (Paris, 1615).
[18] W. Playfair, *The Commercial and Political Atlas of 1787* (London, 1787).
[19] W. Black, *Observations Medical and Political on the Smallpox* (London, 1830).

collection of statistical data.[20] Parliament took an important step in the Registration Act 1836, which provided a General Register Office to index, collate, and record the returns on births, deaths, and marriages. Official recognition of statistical information led to debates as to what the data should be used for and how it might be analysed. Military, as well as civilian, use of statistics was apparent as army statistics became regularly collected from 1834.

The Statistical Movement in the Nineteenth Century and the Environment

(A) Environmentalism and Public Health

The revolution that transformed England from an agrarian to an industrial society is well documented.[21] The creation of the Poor Law Commission in the 1830s and 1840s established the remit of government into concerns about the poor and their environment. Urbanization and industrialization were considered an achievement and evidence of British ingenuity and innovation, the success of which depended on the Victorian work ethic. From the perspective of humanitarian concerns, frequently unhealthy and unsafe working practices placed the new industrialism in a bad light. The rise of trade unions highlighted the plight of the poor, the unsatisfactory nature of the employment of children and the unhealthy working conditions of many. The development of new towns and cities placed a strain on existing water and sanitation systems. Poor food hygiene in shops and in the home and poor living conditions contributed to many epidemics such as influenza, diarrhoea, and tuberculosis. This is described as follows:

While the woeful state of the environmental condition of urban Britain must have been pellucidly clear to anyone who had either eyes to observe the squalid living conditions or the filthy urban air or a nose to smell the effluent covering the street of the waste matter dumped immediately

---

[20] The best examples, given by Cullen, *Statistical Movement*, n. 14 above, 23, were the various leading hospitals: Bethlem, Greenwich, St Thomas's, St Bartholomew's and St Luke's.

[21] W. M. Frazer, *A History of English Public Health 1834–1939* (London, 1950); R. A. Lewis, *Edwin Chadwick and the Public Health Movement 1832–1854* (London, 1952); M. W. Flinn, *Public Health Reform in Britain* (London, 1968).

outside houses, it was that most feared disease, cholera, which dramatically and cruelly drew the attention of the public and more importantly, the government to the unsatisfactory state of the external environment and the deleterious effect it could have on human health.[22]

The cholera outbreak in 1831–2 claimed 32,000 lives[23] and marked the beginning of environmental legislation intended to ameliorate the sanitary conditions which were identified in the 1842 Parliamentary Report on the *Sanitary Condition of the Labouring Population of Great Britain*.

The major intellectual influences behind the rise in environmentalism were Bentham and, undoubtedly, Edwin Chadwick, through his concerns about public health. Chadwick's case was weakened by the claims he made from statistical information that often failed to be supported by an analysis of the statistics. Acrimonious disputes arose between Chadwick and members of the Poor Law Commission. These shortcomings did not lessen the appeal of statistical information, particularly to support the lobbying activities of the public health reformers.

Unquestionably, statistical information provided a new confidence for law reformers. Social problems and their amelioration through law reform touched humanitarian concerns about the welfare of ordinary people. It is obvious that the various law reform movements built on the work of the statistical movement, although quite often engaged in independent agendas. Cullen, in his major study of statistical societies, chronicles one of the main challenges that confronted the use of statistical information at this time. A common belief, in fact unsupported by statistical data and later to be rejected by medical knowledge, was that disease could be eliminated through the application of the miasma theory. The miasma theory advanced the view that the removal of all putrefaction decomposition would succeed in the removal of disease. Miasmatics, as they were known, believed that 'the essential prophylactic against cholera was to cleanse the external environment of refuse, excremental and organic matter'.[24] A series of Nuisance Removal Acts and the Public Health Act 1848 were products of the application of the theory. Local authorities were given powers to construct sewers, remove nuisances and to license

---

[22] F. McManus, *Environmental Health Law* (London, 1994), 3.
[23] *Ibid.*, 4.   [24] *Ibid.*, 3.

slaughterhouses and lodgings. A central government department, the General Board of Health, received default powers to regulate and enforce local authority powers and duties. Statistical study was therefore a powerful weapon in the hands of those that chose to apply it. Even when the statistical data appeared to be unsupportive of the views advanced, this did not prevent statistical data from being used.

Equally obvious from a study of the legislation in mid-Victorian Britain is that statistical study was the catalyst for a number of major legislative initiatives. These include the Sewage Utilization Act 1865 and the Sanitary Act 1866 which gave local authorities additional powers to provide and maintain drains and sewers. Special drainage districts were established with regulatory powers for their maintenance. The Public Health Act 1872 provided for the division of the country into sanitary areas with local authority enforcement powers. Consolidation of the law came in the Public Health Act 1875, which provided comprehensive legislation for England and Wales on all aspects of public health.[25]

The law on housing was similarly reformed. Local authorities received powers to demolish unfit housing and erect buildings for the use of working-class tenants.[26] This landmark legislation laid the foundations of public housing in the United Kingdom.

Similarly, on food standards and safety, environmental health considerations became a major focus of the legislation from 1872. The Adulteration of Food and Drugs Act 1872 and the Sale of Food and Drugs Act 1875 set standards for the manufacture, sale, and consumption of food and drink.

A study of the Reports of the Poor Law Commissioners reveals how statistical data was accumulated and used to service different dogmas and platforms of reform. The disparate nature of these studies ranging from local to national surveys reveals how the study of disease and its causes linked the science of medicine with the social science of law reform.

Statistical study was also applied to crime, and the causes of crime. Drawing a link among poverty, crime, and social degradation was not difficult. Cullen has pointed out:

---

[25] In Scotland, see the Public Health (Scotland) Act 1897.
[26] See the Housing of the Working Classes Acts 1885 and 1890. See also the Shafestbury Act 1851 and the Landlord and Tenant Law Amendment Act, Ireland, 1860.

Chadwick expanded upon, but in no way originated, the environmentalist argument that sanitary reform would produce a more stable and thrifty working class. Overcrowding was seen as a 'cause of extreme demoralization and recklessness, and recklessness, again as a cause of disease'. . . . Both moralistic and environmentalist conceptions were inherent in the statement that many new convicts arrived 'in a state of disease from intemperance and bad habits' and were 'improved by the effect of cleanliness, dryness, better ventilation, temperance and simple food'.[27]

(B) The Statistical Movement and the Environment

At the centre of the application of science to the social sciences through the study of statistics lay the term 'moral statistics'. Today this term has fallen into disuse. Commonly used in the nineteenth century, the term applied to education, crime, and religion. The House of Commons became the focal point of the debate and collection of statistics that covered a wide-ranging analysis of the causes of poverty, crime, and unemployment. An important element in the growth in statistical study was the formation of the numerous statistical societies during the nineteenth century. These societies were motivated by the study of social problems and their alleviation. The statistical movement, as it became known, marked a unique period in intellectual activity. The movement was both national and international in its activities. It was also multidisciplinary and complementary to the various popular causes of the time. Intellectuals from differing disciplines combined to study through statistical data common social, economic, and legal problems. In the British Isles the statistical section of the British Association for the Advancement of Science was formed in Cambridge in 1833. This led to the foundation of the London Statistical Society,[28] renamed the Royal Statistical Society in March 1834. The idea was to have provincial societies meeting regularly and comprising scientists, economists, and statisticians. The Manchester Statistical Society first met in September 1833. Five years later the Statistical Society of Ulster was established as part of the Belfast Natural History and

---

[27] Cullen, *Statistical Movement*, n. 14 above, 63.
[28] The Statistical Society of London had set up a census committee which included William Farr and G. R. Porter.

Philosophical Society. The Social Inquiry and Statistical Society of Ireland began life in 1847 as the Dublin Statistical Society.[29] Significantly, the Dublin Statistical Society was modelled on the Statistical Section of the British Association. The Dublin Society[30] had a large number of prominent Irish lawyers among its membership.

The Statistical Societies facilitated lawyers, historians, philosophers, and economists in studying the wide-ranging nature of the major social and economic problems of the nineteenth century.[31] This included the study of political economy and its application to current social problems. The Irish famine was at its height in 1847 and it was a logical step to set up a society devoted to the study of economics in Ireland.[32]

Statistical study was also influential in the development of the law schools and the University teaching of law. 'Historical jurisprudence', a term which is usually associated with Savigny (1779–1861), undoubtedly had a powerful influence on leading lawyers of the period. Dr Clive Dewey explains the importance of the study of historical jurisprudence:

[29] Prof. R. D. C. Black, *History of the Society, The Statistical and Social Inquiry Society of Ireland, Centenary Volume 1847–1947* (Dublin, 1947).

[30] This international dimension of the Dublin Society was reflected in the honorary membership offered to John Stuart Mill and Nassau Senior in 1849.

[31] Cullen, *Statistical Movement*, n. 14 above.

[32] See Black, *Society*, n. 29 above, for an historical explanation of the Society and its importance. The account which follows takes much from the information provided by Prof. Black's study. Also see M. Shannon, *Historical Memoirs* (Dublin, 1970), which provides an important biographical source for the Society's membership. The importance of law reform is discussed in R. D. C. Black, *Economic Thought and the Irish Question 1817–1970* (Cambridge, 1960); J. F. McEldowney, 'William Neilson Hancock 1820–1888' [1985] Irish Jurist 378–402. According to Black, the influential members of the statistical movement in Ireland included the following: Joseph Napier (1804–82), born Belfast 1804, Irish Attorney-General 1852, Vice-Chancellor of Dublin University 1867–82, Lord Chancellor of Ireland 1858–1859 (see A. C. Ewald, *Life of Sir Joseph Napier Ex Lord Chancellor of Ireland* (Dublin, 1892)); Thomas O'Hagan (1812–85), Lord Chancellor of Ireland 1868–1874 (see J. F. McEldowney, 'Lord O'Hagan 1812–1885: A Study of his Life and Period as Lord Chancellor of Ireland 1868–1874' (1979) XIV Irish Jurist (NS) 360; Hugh Law (1818–83), Lord Chancellor of Ireland 1881–83, Prof. of English Law, Queen's College Galway, 1849–58, drafted the Irish Church Act 1869 and Land Act (Ireland) 1870, Solicitor-General 1872–79, Attorney-General, 1880; Revd. Franc Sadlier (1774–1851), BA 1795, Trinity College Provost 1837–1851, Prof. of Mathematics and Greek Trinity College, Dublin, 1805.

But the bias of the law schools—in Oxford, Cambridge, Dublin and London—was towards historical jurisprudence. The great legal discoveries of the time were made on the frontiers of historical research: and the leading law teachers—Maine, Pollock, Vinogradoff, Bryce, Maitland, Hancock and Richey were all historical jurists.[33]

The principal doctrine of the historical school emphasizes the role of the lawyer. Lawyers formulate technical and precise legal principles and provide the expertise in the drafting of laws. The content of the laws that are drafted should reflect the interests of the community as a whole. In this task the lawyer becomes an important law-maker by diagnosing problems and providing solutions. The ability of the lawyer to correctly diagnose social problems is dependent on how the lawyer understands the way in which laws evolve. In this respect the study of custom is regarded as an essential feature of the process of understanding law and social problems. Legislation became the most direct and effective means to assist in the development of society. Hence Maine's famous dictum that 'the movement of the progressive societies has hitherto been a movement from status to contract'[34] in which he highlighted how legislation might shape the form society might take. Consequently responsibilities for the environment and public health might be given a higher priority over the vested interest of property or ownership.

Environmental interests dominated the work of the various statistical societies, notably in the areas of public health, poverty, pollution, and sanitation, as noted above, for example, in the Dublin-based Social Inquiry and Statistical Society, James Haughton's paper in 1863, 'Some Remarks on the Unsatisfactory Tenure of Land by our Farmers at Home and a Few Concluding Observations on the Administration of the Poor Law in England and in Ireland';[35] a year later J. K. Ingram read a paper on the 'Comparison between the English and Irish Poor Law with respect to the Conditions of Relief'.[36]

Statistical study sought to combine the development of the

---

[33] C. Dewey, 'Celtic Agrarian Legislation and the Celtic Revival: Historicist Implications of Gladstone's Irish and Scottish Land Acts 1870–1886' (1974) 64 *Past and Present* 31 at 36.
[34] H. Maine, *The Early History of Institutions* (London, 1875), 355.
[35] (1863) III *J Dublin Statistical Society* 343.
[36] (1864) IV *J Statistical and Social Inquiry Society of Ireland* 43.

industrialized society with the environmental impact of that development. Railways, street lighting, improved sanitation, hospital improvements, education of women, the regulation of Friendly Societies, the care of the mentally handicapped, the production of sugar and beetroot, and the condition of small farmers attracted papers and discussion in the work of the society.

It is undoubtedly the case that the zenith of the statistical societies was in the nineteenth century. Both local and central government found that they depended on the work of the major statistical societies and discovered common cause in finding and proposing reforms beneficial to the general needs of society. An interesting observation is that the statistical societies were in fact private organizations and bridged the gap between the private and public sector. As the century came to an end the legislative achievements of the statistical movement looked impressive. Almost simultaneously with their new-found success the influence and enthusiasm for statistical societies ebbed away.

An unparalleled combination of circumstances had resulted in the joining of law and science in common causes. Undoubtedly the foundations of environmental law had benefited from the use of statistical data to develop major legislation. The question remains as to the legacy that statistical study has left.

Science and Law: Probability and Risk

In the nineteenth century statistical study provided a bridge between law reformer, social scientist, and science. Inter-disciplinary work was desirable as part of the innovative first steps taken in the development of a new discipline and in the adoption of a clear legislative strategy.

In the present century, the world of science appears uncertain when compared to the enthusiasm that accompanied the pioneering search for new data and understanding in the past century. Statistical study grouped around the statistical society fails to attract admirers today to compare to those that championed it in the past. The scepticism of the present day is not shared by everyone. Science retains a certain mysticism and profits from its own believers. It offers many attractive claims. It is easily identifiable with the physical reality of the natural world and is portrayed as truthful when based on positive and verifiable outcomes.

However, there are increasing signs of disillusionment. The reality appears to be that science is quite unable to deliver such high expectations and values of truth and fact. Science may depend as much on subjective assessment as on objective fact. It is as capable of having the facts distorted as any other knowledge-based subject.

SCIENCE AND THE ENVIRONMENT: A DISCOURSE ON RISK

The rise and fall of the statistical movement has not diverted modern advances. Modern developments based on statistical probability include predictive models based on statistical data. At the heart of the relationship between science and law is the question of assessing risk and predicting outcomes from known or ascertainable data. How to assess and interpret scientific evidence is a fundamental inquiry. Courts provide an examination of what has occurred and only rarely evaluate future risks. In contrast environmental law must attempt to predict outcomes and take steps in anticipation of risks. Some current examples serve to reinforce the link between the assessment of science and law. Principles such as 'the polluter pays', techniques such as 'eco-labelling', and the development of environmental impact assessment and integrated pollution control are examples of the distinct contribution environmental law is making to the general development of new concepts in law. Environmental lawyers place reliance on scientific data and methodology in measuring, monitoring, and understanding anthropogenic impacts on the environment. Science is used to help predict outcomes and deal with the impact, often unpredictable, of man's activities on the environment. Scientists increasingly need to understand the impact of legal rules on the environment.[37] The development of suitable legal rules and standards to serve the needs of the scientist presents one of the formidable challenges for the future.

[37] M. Tolba and O. A. El-Kholy, *The World Environment 1972–1992* (London, 1992), 804–5; A. Haagsma, 'The European Community's Environmental Policy: A Case-study in Federalism' (1989) 12 Fordham International LJ 311; R. E. Hester and R. M. Harrison (eds.), *Waste Treatment and Disposal* (London, 1995); R. Kerry Turner, D. Pearce and I. B. Bateman, *Environmental Economics* (London, 1994); A. Kiss and S. Shelton, *Manual of European Environmental Law* (Cambridge, 1993); L. Kramer, *European Environmental Law Casebook* (London, 1993).

At international, European, and national level, environmental policies are being shaped, albeit belatedly, that begin to take account of the challenges to the environment towards the end of the present century and beyond. The UN Earth Summit in 1992 drew attention to the need for international action to tackle global problems such as climate change, biodiversity, and forest loss. This highlights the fact that man's environmental impacts do not recognize national boundaries and that action is required at an international level. The end of this century has seen the realization that environmental protection and conservation rest heavily on the implementation of policies such as clean technology, waste-minimization and sustainable development. In January 1994 the UK Government embarked on a national strategy for sustainable development.[38]

Contemporary examples underline the need to examine the value judgements that underlie various assumptions about science and law. Assessing scientific evidence in order to draw conclusions involves two issues of fundamental importance: first, the concept of the burden and standard of proof and secondly, the recognition that in identifying uncertainty and calculating risk there are implications for law and the science that underpins it.

The standards set by the burden of proof involve lawyers and scientists in a dialogue over methodology and emphasis. In the environmental context Page has drawn an important contrast between two principles. The first concerns what he calls 'limiting false positives' and the second is 'limiting false negatives'. Limiting false positives concerns an hypothesis which appears to be true when it is in fact untrue. Limiting false negatives occurs when there is insufficient evidence for an hypothesis which is in fact proved to be correct.[39]

Most experimental science appears to focus on the limiting of false positives. This goal is shared by those who see the criminal justice system as based on the premise that it is undesirable to convict an innocent person even though this may mean allowing a guilty person to go free. The prosecution must meet a high standard of proof which enables this principle to be maintained. However, there is relatively little attention given to the probability of false negatives.

---

[38] *Sustainable Development: The UK Strategy* (Cm. 1994 no. 2426).
[39] T. Page, 'A Generic View of Toxic Chemicals and Similar Risks' (1979) 7 Ecology LQ 207.

Scientific methodology may also suffer from the limitations set by the way the question is posed. Different formulations of the same question may provide different answers. Scientific data may also appear to offer objective or at any rate verifiable criteria that may go unquestioned in the way government may formulate its policy. This may result in government accepting scientific evidence and drawing their own conclusions without a proper inquiry into the hypothesis advanced by the scientist.

Conclusions

A crucial part of the future strategy for the environment is sustainable development, defined by the Brundland Commission in 1987 as intended to meet 'the needs of the present without compromising the ability of future generations to meet their own needs'. The recent UK Annual Report on *This Common Inheritance* has noted that the common theme in the sustainable development strategy adopted by the Government for the environment has been 'to establish more specific targets and objectives, together with quantified indicators of progress' for different parts of the environment[40] as among future priorities.[41]

The lessons from the nineteenth century are that setting objectives and adopting strategies for the environment are a multi-disciplined task. It relies on the collection of data to provide an adequate analysis. The nineteenth-century statistical societies provided the foundations for the study of the environment and the laws needed to remedy social problems. Its combination of law reform and statistical inquiry proved conclusive to the development of an effective legislative agenda.

[40] Cm. 1995 no. 2822, 12. Concerned about climate change and biodiversity, the UK ratified the Convention on Biological Diversity on 3 June 1994.
[41] There are a number of key elements in this strategy (*ibid.*, 9–38)—a high priority to the definition of environmental objectives and targets; publication of a set of indicators in areas such as air quality, water quality, land, wildlife, and habitats and the impact on these of social and economic change; education about the environment including the consideration of the Government's Panel on Sustainable Development; priority to improve relationships between industry and government; clarification of the need for environmental regulation and the use of fiscal instruments including taxation of pollution; the setting of the agenda and priorities for sustainable development; provision of advice and recommendations on actions to achieve sustainable development; the promotion of strong economic development in harmony with true stewardship of the environment.

In the present climate how might science and law be best combined? Monitoring how environmental laws are obeyed is the first step. This is an evolutionary process whereby learning how procedures and processes work will help ensure a better under-standing of regulation and law. Ensuring adequate enforcement of environmental law at national and European Community level sets immense challenges for the future of environmental law. It is also essential to set priorities that make environmental enforce-ment an essential value in society.[42]

Despite the inability of science to deal in absolutes, either in terms of proof or in standards of safety, science has a fundamental and important role in understanding environmental problems. This is particularly clear from the perspective of protecting the environment as well as diagnosing and attributing causes of pollution.

The techniques for predicting outcomes and consequences from existing data and information remain complex. Risk assessment techniques and mathematical modelling procedures attempt to establish predictive and quantitative assessments of the likely impact of man's activities on the local, regional, and global environment. It is on these predictions that future policies and regulations may be developed.

Scientists may have yet another role to perform in environmen-tal monitoring, that is, determining the probable source of a pollu-tant incident. Evaluating who is responsible for environmental damage may involve a degree of scientific detective work, but may not necessarily provide solutions as to how to clean up the envi-ronment or prevent harm in the future. The principle that 'the polluter pays' may simply result in clean up costs being borne by the end user who is able to pass costs on to the consumer. Thus a notional environmental 'overhead' may be built into pricing mechanisms. This does not provide long-term benefits for the environment. Scientists must also contribute to environmental management by meeting the challenge inherent in the development of economic remediation and restoration techniques.[43]

Environmental management techniques have adapted to accom-

[42] See L. Kramer, *European Environmental Law Casebook* (London, 1993), vi–vii.

[43] J. Steele, 'Remedies and Remediation: Foundational Issues in Environmental Liability' (1995) 58 Mod. LR 615.

modating a more problem-focused and policy-driven approach to the environment. Public education and forging inter-relations between science and industry, and government and law are an intrinsic part of the work of the environmental scientist today. Scientists may be able to determine the extent of 'harm' to the environment and suggest procedures to limit, control, or ameliorate the harmful effects. This knowledge is, however, only truly valuable if it is used to inform industry, policy-makers, and the public realistically and fully. The creation of new agencies, the Environment Agency and the Scottish Environment Protection Agency under the Environment Act 1995 and the European Environment Agency, is set to reflect public demands for standard-setting and auditing of the environment, demands that must ultimately be met by scientists.

There is also a further dimension to understanding environmental problems. All aspects of human activity including agriculture, industry, and population centres impinge on the environment in which we live. Environmental problems transcend national, European, and international legal systems. The global economy and the use of natural and energy resources must be confronted at every level, both local and global. The implementation of policies for sustainable development must measure the foreseen benefits as well as the detriments of man's activities, and attempt to predict unforeseen effects. Sustainable development must secure the best use of the world's resources measured in long-term as well as short-term strategies. Pro-active rather than reactive policy-making must be found in economic and scientific instruments that are sanctioned by law. The foundations of environmental law and its science-based methodology were firmly established by the end of the nineteenth century. At the end of the present century we should re-evaluate how far we have developed our thinking since then. Constructing our understanding of the environment is a complicated task. It is essential to understand the rich intellectual inheritance that was fundamental to the development of environment law. The curiosity that prompted the study of statistics to discover the problems of the environment in the nineteenth century needs re-kindling. The science of the nineties and the scepticism of the age should not prevent us from asking how reliable scientific evidence is in contributing to the protection of the environment.

THE BSE CRISIS: A STUDY OF THE PRECAUTIONARY PRINCIPLE AND THE POLITICS OF SCIENCE IN LAW

Jane Holder and Sue Elworthy

Introduction

The crisis over BSE (bovine spongiform encephalopathy) or 'mad-cow disease' provides fuel for several contemporary debates: the social and environmental impact of intensive farming; the survival of British sovereignty in the face of sweeping action by the European Union; and the nature of a modern 'Risk Society', in which perceptions of risk and the actuality of risk are conflated.[1] Underlying the Risk Society is an apparent failure of science to come up with the goods, in terms of providing solutions to public health and environmental problems, or at least reliable information on which to base regulation. Indeed, the manipulation of scientific knowledge in the BSE crisis shows up the uncertain and fragmentary quality of scientific, and other, knowledge that is said to be a hallmark of postmodernity.[2] The BSE emergency also reinforces some of the central premises of the sociology of science: that the creation and application of scientific knowledge is shaped by the social, economic, cultural, and legal contexts in which the processes of science take place.[3]

Looking at the legal context, the legislative responses to the BSE crisis are revealing as to the capacity of law to act in the face of scientific uncertainty, particularly when the situation has been

---

[1] U. Beck, *Risk Society: Towards a New Modernity* (London, 1992).

[2] A. Giddens, *The Consequences of Modernity* (Cambridge, 1990) and S. Crook, J Pakuski and M. Waters, *Postmodernization: Change in Industrial Society* (London, 1992).

[3] S. Jasanoff, *The Fifth Branch: Science Advisers as Policy Makers* (Cambridge, Mass., 1990).

exacerbated by political controversy. A significant feature of the European legal responses is that they have been grounded in the language of a principle of international environmental law—the precautionary principle. The principle was not invoked as such, perhaps because it had hitherto generally belonged to 'environmental' rather than 'agricultural' or 'food safety' matters, but also because it has uncertain legal status. Nevertheless, its (*de facto*) use during the BSE crisis has undoubtedly increased its legal importance, even though its scope and legal effects are still not precisely defined. It remains contentious whether precaution is a principle of administration, science, or law, or even culturally determined, being 'common sense' by another name. This paper uses the BSE crisis to explore the legal evolution of the precautionary principle. The emergence of BSE is exactly the sort of situation in which the precautionary principle should, in theory, operate; accordingly we consider the role that the principle appeared to play as events unfolded and suggest that the BSE crisis has, in turn, changed the law of precaution.

Having set the scene for the emergence of the BSE crisis by mapping the interests, evidence, and expertise involved in the production and communication of knowledge about the disease, we explain how the precautionary principle operated to relieve the crisis of uncertainty surrounding the supposed transmissibility of the disease to humans in the form of a new variant of Creutzfeld-Jakob Disease (v-CJD). The precautionary principle intervened at the 'prescientized' or pre-understanding stage of communication of knowledge of the disease, articulated by citizens and the media, and hastened legal responses to the crisis. In Habermas' schema of Rational Society this pre-scientific stage of communication is a precursor to the process of scientization of what are essentially political decisions—the reduction of political power to rational administration.[4] This leads us to tentatively suggest that, in describing science in modernity as capable of legitimating power, Habermas ascribes an authority to science which has since been displaced, largely because practical applications of science are perceived to have created the conditions for public health and environmental crises. Rather, we consider that the application of the precautionary principle to the 'prescientized' stage of communication of the BSE crisis

[4] J. Habermas, *Toward a Rational Society* (London, 1971), ch. 5.

liberated people (and the courts) to argue from belief and conviction and is therefore emblematic of post modern Risk Society.

The Precautionary Principle

The failure of politicians and experts to act to protect the environment and public health in conditions of scientific uncertainty has led to demands for a precautionary approach.[5] This requires that once there is the likelihood of harm, action should be taken to abate it even though there may still be uncertainty about the effects of activities or patterns of cause and effect. The conceptual premise of the principle is that the damaging effects of human activities may become irreversible before the scientific community can agree the precise nature and scope of their impact; taking precautionary action can help avoid the 'paralysis of uncertainty'.[6] The implications of the principle are potentially far-reaching: it has been identified with a major paradigm shift by which the prevailing perception of many activities changes from relatively harmless to capable of causing great harm to human health and the environment. The origins of the principle are in the West German concept of *Vorsorgeprinzip* (meaning 'precaution' or 'foresight' and encompassing 'good husbandry'), which was applied in its environmental policy of the mid-1970s.[7] Over the last twenty years the principle has been incorporated into many international legal documents concerning the environment, most notably Principle 15 of the Rio Declaration on Environment and Development, which is to guide decision-making.[8] It appears so

[5] For a review of the development of precautionary approaches, see M. Hession, 'Competence, Proportionality and Equality Applied to Decision Making Under Uncertainty: BSE and the European Court' (forthcoming).

[6] O. McIntyre and T. Mosedale, 'The Precautionary Principle as a Norm of Customary International Law' (1997) 9 (2) J Environmental Law 221 at 221.

[7] K. von Moltke, 'The *Vorsorgeprinzip* in West German Environmental Policy', in Royal Commission on Environmental Pollution, Twelfth Report, *Best Practicable Environmental Option* Cm. 310 (London, 1988).

[8] Declaration on Environment and Development, Adopted by the United Nations Conference on Environment and Development (UNCED) at Rio de Janeiro, 13 June 1992, UN Doc. A/Conf. 151/26 (Vol. 1) (1992) 31 International Legal Materials 874, Principle 15: 'In order to protect the environment, the precautionary principle shall be widely applied by states according to their capabilities. Where there are threats of serious or irreversible damage, lack of scientific certainty shall not be used as a reason for postponing cost-effective measures to prevent environmental degradation'.

often in international environmental law that there is some support for the argument that it has now crystallized into a norm of customary international law.[9] Another view is that the principle most easily fits the pattern of an administrative decision-making mechanism.[10] However, the development of the principle in environmental law[11] suggests that it has consequences beyond those of administration and may in some way be legally enforceable. It must be emphasized that the principle is still evolving, which means its legal status and scope are not fixed. In European Union law, the principle is described as guiding Community policy-making in Article 130r(2) of the Treaty Establishing the European Communities (EC Treaty).[12] Since it forms the basis of Community legislative action only, it is probably not justiciable and contains no binding rules which may be relied upon by individuals in their national courts.[13] Whether and how far Member States apply the principle is therefore to be judged by their adherence to Community law based upon the principle. The generalized nature of the precautionary principle, which so appeals to environmental and public-health campaigners, means that readings of the principle and its supposed implications are many. However, the main focus of this paper is the seepage of precaution, as a principle of law-making and administration, into judicial decision-making. The key issue is the cleavage between the different standards for scientific evidence for decision-making

[9] T. O'Riordan and J. Cameron (eds.), *Interpreting the Precautionary Principle* (London, 1994); McIntyre and Mosedale, 'Precautionary Principle as a Norm', n. 6 above.

[10] N. Haigh, 'The Introduction of the Precautionary Principle into the UK' in O'Riordan and Cameron, *Interpreting the Precautionary Principle*, n. 9 above.

[11] Variants of the principle may also be seen in other areas of law, e.g., the grounds for making a care order in the Children Act 1989, s. 31(2) are precautionary in nature: 'A Court may only make a care order if it is satisfied—(a) that the child is suffering, or is likely to suffer, significant harm'; in negligence the doctrine of foreseeability performs precautionary functions.

[12] Art. 130r(2) EC: 'Community policy making . . . shall be based on the precautionary principle.'

[13] See Case C–379/92, *Criminal Proceedings Re Peralta* [1994] ECR I–3453, in which the ECJ held, at para. 57: 'Article 130r confines itself to defining the general objectives of the Community in environmental matters. The responsibility for deciding upon the action to be taken is entrusted to the Council by Article 130s.' This interpretation of the legal scope of Article 130r was followed in the British courts in R v. *Secretary of State for Trade and Industry, ex parte Duddridge and Others* [1995] Environmental Law Reports 151, (1996) Property and Compensation Reports 350 (CA).

prior to taking regulatory action and the review of such action by the judiciary.

In considering these issues in the context of the BSE crisis, the European dimension becomes vital. The crisis is rooted in European policy and decision-making structures and is partly a consequence of the way that the unique institutions of the European Union use scientific knowledge to legislate on a European scale. A difficulty is the European courts' approach to scientific evidence. Unlike jurisdictions which have developed expertise in applying and interpreting rules of admissibility of scientific evidence in tort and criminal cases, the European courts, preferring a more inquisitorial approach, tend to defer to the opinions of various European Union expert committees on such matters. That these courts became engaged in assessing the 'real risk' of a link between BSE and its human equivalent, v-CJD, in the clutch of cases brought before them on the legality of the European Commission's export ban on British beef[14] suggests a new era of European judicial activism and reflects the politically charged background against which they made their decisions. The courts' reliance on the tenets of the precautionary principle to understand the legal measures taken and to resolve conflict as to their validity goes some way to revise the law's traditional and simplistic attitude to scientific uncertainty, but also poses new problems of the legal status of the principle and its persuasiveness in legal argument.

British Beef and Public Health

By March 1996, a bundle of related issues of animal welfare, public health, and consumer confidence had developed into a full-blown crisis. Ironically, by this time, the epidemic of the BSE disease in Britain appeared to be declining with only a quarter of the number of new cases being reported compared with the peak in 1993. The crisis over 'mad-cow disease' arose because of the fear of a link between BSE and a new form of the human disease

---

[14] Case C–180/96R *United Kingdom* v. *Commission*, not yet rep., jdgt 12 July 1996, Case T–76/96R *National Farmers' Union* v. *Commission*, not yet rep., jdgt 13 July 1996, and Case C–157/96 *National Farmers' Union* v. *Ministry of Agriculture, Fisheries and Food, the Commissioners for Customs and Excise* (pending) and Case C–180/96, *United Kingdom* v. *Commission* (pending); Opinion of AG Tesauro on Case C–157/96 and Case C–180/96 delivered on 30 Sept. 1997.

v-CJD. Both diseases are at the boundaries of scientific knowledge. BSE, a cattle disease, is very like the sheep disease scrapie, mink encephalopathy and kuru, a condition known amongst a group of Papuan New Guinean tribesmen who ritually ate human brains. All of these diseases are characterized by the microscopic appearance of sponge-like formations in brain tissue, leading to loss of co-ordination and degeneration of the brain. The leading scientific theory, but not the only one, is that this group of diseases is transmitted by an infectious protein called a prion. Again, not a great deal is yet known about prions, but the suggestion was that the prion jumped the species barrier from scrapie-infected sheep to cattle.[15] The scientific issue at the root of the crisis was whether BSE has now made the species jump to humans in the form of a new variant of Creutzfeld-Jacob Disease (CJD).

The occasional incident of a new disease would not have precipitated a crisis had Britain not experienced an epidemic of BSE. It should be emphasized that the cause of the epidemic is also disputed. However, the theory favoured by the committee formed to advise the United Kingdom Government (the Spongiform Encephalopathy Advisory Committee (SEAC)) is that this epidemic was caused by a combination of factors. First, cattle were given concentrated feed containing sheep brains infected with scrapie and, secondly, the rendered remains of these cattle were subsequently incorporated in the next generation of processed cattle-feed.[16] This raises the question of why cattle were being fed on animal remains. In the 1970s scientists suggested that milk production could be maximized if the first of a cow's four stomachs, which breaks down cellulose, were bypassed and protein introduced directly into the second stomach. Initially this was done by including soya and fishmeal in concentrated cattle-feed but the price of these ingredients rose steeply in the 1980s so sheep remains, as a cheap source of protein, were substituted.[17] The third significant factor is that the rendering process was

[15] 'Twists and Turns on the Trail of a Killer', *Guardian*, 21 Mar. 1996.

[16] See S. Elworthy and A. McCullogh, 'BSE in Britain: Science, Socio-Economics and European Law' (1996) 5(4) *Environmental Politics* 736 at 739; and R. Lacey, *Mad-Cow Disease: The History of BSE in Britain* (St Helier, Jersey, 1994).

[17] T. Radford 'Sifting Facts and Theory at the Boundary of Knowledge', *Guardian*, 22 Mar. 1996.

changed. To reduce costs, both the duration of processing and the temperature were reduced and an organic solvent extraction step was eliminated. The broader picture is that these practices are the logical conclusion of an agricultural policy based primarily on maximizing production which originated in the food shortages of the Second World War. Responsibility for the BSE crisis also lies in the structure of the European Union's agricultural policy, which reinforced the developments that had earlier taken place in Britain. The Common Agricultural Policy (CAP) was itself a response to war-time and post-war food shortages and was designed to reward production, thus resulting in the large, intensive farms that had already become the norm in Britain before joining the European Economic Community in 1972. Reducing costs through feeding contaminated meat to herbivores is a natural response to the British and European agricultural orthodoxy of super-production by any means. BSE may be seen as an irony of progress whereby the emphasis on maximising food production has led to the marginalization of beef.[18]

In March 1996 SEAC reported ten cases of a previously unrecognized variant of CJD. SEAC concluded that 'on current data and in the absence of any credible alternative, the most likely explanation at present is that these cases are linked to exposure to BSE infected beef before the introduction of the SBO (Specified Beef Offal) ban in 1989'[19] (that is between 1985 and 1989). Although emphasizing that this was only a small number of cases and that '*it is not possible to confirm* whether or not there is any causal link between BSE and the human disease', SEAC stated that this state of affairs 'is a cause for great concern'.[20] SEAC was unable to assess the risk of contracting CJD from BSE-infected beef because of a number of uncertainties: the duration of the incubation period; the uneven distribution of infection in any

[18] On the ironies of progress in food production from a US perspective, see G. Sager, ' "A Burger and A Coke" and Other Environmental Problems: Reflections on Diet and the Environmental Crisis' (1995) 3 *Sustainable Development* 149. However, in the UK extensive grass-fed beef production is environmentally beneficial: J. Lister-Kaye, 'Ill Fares the Land: a Sustainable Land Ethic for the Sporting Estates of the Highlands of Scotland' Occas. Paper No. 3 (Perth, 1994), 12. See also D. Nelkin, 'Science, Technology and Political Conflict: Analysing the Issues' in D. Nelkin (ed.), *Controversy* (London, 1984).

[19] Statement by SEAC, 24 Mar. 1996, 1.

[20] *Ibid.* (emphasis in original).

tissue; whether there is a dose below which there is no risk of infection; and the possibility of cumulative effects. The Minister of Agriculture reported SEAC's statement to Parliament but emphasized its central conclusion that it 'did not believe that additional measures are justified at this stage but the situation needs to be kept under careful review so that additional significant information can be taken into account as soon as it becomes available'.[21] The Government's reliance on 'sound science' as a basis for decision, as opposed to taking precautionary action, was reiterated in the light of SEAC's statement: 'throughout its considerations of these questions the Government has made it clear that it is our policy to base its own decisions on an up-to-date assessment of the scientific evidence. . . . [T]hat remains the position'.[22]

The immediate consequences of the public announcement of the SEAC statement were that consumers in Britain began avoiding British beef and that countries across Europe and beyond banned its import.[23] Once almost all of the Member States had unilaterally decided to ban beef from Britain, the European Commission was compelled to react by banning its export to other Member States and to the rest of the world.

Legal Responses: Suppositions made on Existing Evidence and Precaution

The state of scientific evidence of a causal link between BSE and v-CJD is characterized by causal uncertainty (as compared to conceptual or measurement uncertainty), since there is disagreement about the relationship between these two diseases. The drive for a causal analysis is to explain how the two conditions are connected, or whether they are connected at all, as opposed to assuming they do operate as part of a system and then merely predicting outcomes.[24] Some evidence of such a link was brought

---

[21] Statement to Parliament on BSE from the Secretary of State for Health, 4.

[22] *Ibid.*

[23] 'L'affaire de la "Vache Folle" Plonge L'Europe dans la Crise', *Le Monde*, 7 June 1996; panic over BSE continued over the following months, e.g. 'Du boeuf Britannique dans les Raviolis Panzani', *Le Parisien*, 24 Sept. 1997.

[24] V. R. Walker, 'The Siren Songs of Science: Toward A Taxonomy of Scientific Uncertainty for Decision Makers' (1991) 23 Connecticut LRev. 567 at 607; see also J. Lemon (ed.), *Scientific Uncertainty and Environmental Problem Solving* (Oxford, 1995).

to the Government's attention by the Chief Veterinary Officer in June 1987, which led to BSE being made a notifiable disease and requiring the isolation of cows suspected of having BSE when calving.[25] From the late 1980s more legal measures were taken in the United Kingdom, aimed at abating the spread of BSE. In contrast, a series of legal acts adopted by the European Community between the start of the BSE epidemic in Britain in 1989 and the height of the crisis in March 1996 attempted to prevent BSE and protect animal and human health. These culminated in the blanket ban on British cattle and beef exports, largely prompted by the unilateral boycotts by other Member States. An immediate distinction may therefore be drawn between the scale and precautionary nature of the European Community's legal responses (especially the export ban on cattle and beef) and the United Kingdom's more reactive, but arguably more measured, approach to the crisis.

Early legal responses by the European Community were concerned with establishing procedures for trade in animals and animal products. The key measure was Directive 89/662/EEC,[26] which required veterinary checks to be carried out by the 'state of dispatch' to assess the health of live animals transported between Member States, replacing veterinary checks at the Community's internal frontiers. The impetus for this measure was securing public health and animal welfare, with a view to completing the internal market. The measure is strongly precautionary since each Member State is to notify the other Member States and the Commission of any outbreak of disease in order that further action may be taken. An amending act, Council Directive 92/118/EEC,[27] laid down detailed rules for treatment, storage, and documentation of animal products. More significantly, the Directive introduced the concept of a 'real risk' of the spread of transmissible diseases, which was later relied upon by the

[25] Bovine Spongiform Encephalopathy Order 1988 (SI 1988 No. 1039).

[26] Directive 89/662/EEC concerning veterinary and zootechnical checks applicable in intra-Community trade in certain live animals and produce with a view to the completion of the internal market [1990] OJ L224/29, 18 Aug. 1990.

[27] Directive 92/118/EEC laying down animal health and public health requirements governing trade in and imports into the Community of products etc., [1992] OJ L62/49, 15 Mar. 1993.

European courts as justification for the Commission's export ban on British cattle and beef:[28]

The decisions . . . [governing trade and imports] must be taken on the basis of evaluation and, if appropriate, the opinion of the Scientific Veterinary Committee, of the real risk of the spread of serious transmissible diseases or of diseases transmissible to man which could result from movement of the product, not only for the species from which the product originates but also for other species which could carry the disease or become a focus of disease or a risk to public health.[29]

The procedures for establishing the 'real risk' of transmissible diseases suggest that the Directive conceives of risk assessment as not just a technocratic exercise, nor necessarily one in which a scientific consensus is arrived at. It is also a political exercise in which the Scientific Veterinary Committee, one of the many 'comitology' expert committees which advise the Commission and strongly influence the content of legislation, arrives at a decision by a qualified majority vote in accordance with the allocation of votes given to each Member State, on the 'real risk' of the spread of diseases. National representation on the Veterinary Committee inevitably leads to opportunities for the politicization of decisions on the 'real risk' of the spread of diseases such as BSE.

By 1994, legal measures were adopted specifically to prevent BSE spreading. Commission Decision 94/474/EEC[30] imposed a ban on the export from the United Kingdom to the other Member States of live cattle aged more than 6 months and the offspring of cows which had or might have BSE. These trade rules were supplemented by substantive measures concerning the preparation of meat and cattle-feed, such as trimming meat from animals from BSE-infected herds to remove tissues that might have the offending protein, banning the export of offal, and specifying that protein from cattle is not to be included in cattle-feed.

In contrast to this explicitly preventative approach, the United Kingdom engaged soft law and secondary legislation in response

[28] See 'Judicial review of precautionary action and scientific evidence', below, p. 141 et seq.

[29] Directive 92/118/EEC, n. 27 above, Art. 10(4).

[30] Commission Decision concerning certain protection measures relating to bovine spongiform encephalopathy and repealing Decisions 89/469/EEC and 90/200/EEC [1994] OJ L194/96, 29 July 1994, as amended by Commission Decision 95/287/EC, [1995] OJ L181/40, 18 July 1995.

to what was becoming a crisis. The first measures were that cattle suspected of having BSE were compulsorily slaughtered and their carcasses destroyed; milk produced by cows suspected of having BSE could not be used for human consumption and the sale of certain offal—the nervous and lymphatic tissue and the vertebral column (including offal later to be specified in European Union law)[31]—was banned.[32] The United Kingdom also banned the sale of cattle-feed containing proteins derived from ruminants and the feeding of ruminants with such feed.[33] Following SEAC's statement on the ten cases of v-CJD in Britain, the Government took additional measures: boning carcasses of cattle over 30 months in approved establishments monitored by the Meat Hygiene Service; and banning the use of bone meal from mammals in feed for all farm animals.[34]

A week after these measures, and implying their inadequacy, the European Commission banned the export of British cattle, beef, and beef products (gelatine, semen and tallow) to other Member States and the rest of the world by adopting Decision 96/239/EC.[35] The impetus for the ban was the new scientific evidence issued by SEAC and consumer concerns about the safety of eating British beef. The risk of contracting v-CJD from BSE-infected beef had been assessed by the Scientific Veterinary Committee of the European Union, as required by Directive 92/118/EC.[36] The Committee concluded that on the available data

[31] Directive 94/474/EC, [1994] OJ L194/96, 29 July 1994, art. 3: 'The United Kingdom shall not send from its territory to that of other Member States the following tissues and organs . . . derived from bovine animals aged more than 6 months at slaughter: brains, spinal cord, thymus, tonsils, spleen, intestine, placental tissue.'

[32] The Bovine Offal (Prohibition) Regulations 1989 (SI 1989 No. 2061), as amended. This prohibition was extended to the head of bovine animals, except the tongue, by the Specified Bovine Material Order 1996 (SI 1996 No. 963).

[33] SI 1988 No. 1039, n. 25 above, as amended, containing the Ruminant Feed Ban.

[34] Bovine Spongiform Encephalopathy (Amendment) Order 1996 (SI 1996 No. 962), amending Bovine Spongiform Encephalopathy Order 1991 (SI 1991 No. 2246).

[35] Commission Decision 96/239/EC on emergency measures to protect against bovine spongiform encephalopathy [1996] OJ L78/47, 27 Mar. 1996, art. 1, as amended by Commission Decision 96/362/EC [1996] OJ L139/17, 12 June 1996 which lifted the ban on bovine gelatine, semen, and tallow because scientific evidence suggested that they were safe with respect to BSE. Decision 96/239/EC also invites the UK to 'present further proposals to control bovine spongiform encephalopathy' (art. 4).   [36] N. 27 above.

it was not possible to prove that BSE was transmissible to humans, but that in view of the 'real risk' that existed of such transmissibility, the Community should ban the export of British beef. The fifth recital of the preamble to Decision 96/239/EC sets out the rationale for the export ban, using the language of risk, uncertainty, and precaution:

Whereas, under current circumstances, a definitive stance on the transmissibility of BSE to humans is not possible; whereas a risk of transmission cannot be excluded; whereas the resulting uncertainty has created serious concern among consumers; whereas, under the circumstances and as an emergency measure, the transport of all bovine animals and all beef and veal or derived products from the United Kingdom to the other Member States should be temporarily banned; whereas the same prohibitions should also apply to exports to non-Member countries so as to prevent deflections of trade.[37]

At first sight the ban is a profound reaction on the part of the European Community, an organization inspired by the liberation of trade between Member States. Underlying the ban, however, the objective of free trade prevails. Consumer confidence, essential for the proper functioning of the beef market in Europe, had to be restored. The centrality of consumer confidence to the decision to ban British beef is seen clearly in the Commission's concern that 'uncertainty has created serious concern among consumers'.[38] This was also a preoccupation of the Council of Ministers: an extraordinary meeting of the Council on the problems raised by BSE concluded, in agreeing a set of additional health and market support measures, that '(O)ur objective is to restore consumer confidence, stability in the markets and the Single Market'.[39]

In line with this saga of legal measure and counter legal measure, and in the backwash of the European Commission's export ban, in April 1996 the United Kingdom Government announced a beef cull programme for all cattle over 30 months (financed for the most part by the European Community),[40] which has kept incinerators busy ever since.

---

[37] N. 35 above. Preamble (5th recital).
[38] *Ibid.*
[39] Quoted in the judgment of Case C–180/96, n. 14 above, para. 23.
[40] Commission Regulation 96/716/EC adopting exceptional supplementary measures for the beef market in the United Kingdom, [1996] OJ L99/14, 19 Apr. 1996.

Judicial Review of Precautionary Action and Scientific Evidence

In May 1996 the United Kingdom lodged a case before the European Court of Justice, challenging the legality of the Commission's Decision banning the export of British cattle and beef,[41] and applied to the Court for an interim relief order to suspend the ban.[42] A corresponding case for interim relief was brought against the European Commission by the National Farmers' Union, heard by the Court of First Instance.[43] The National Farmers' Union also challenged the measures taken by the Ministry of Agriculture, Fisheries and Food and the Commissioners for Customs and Excise to give effect to the Commission's Decision. This led to the High Court requesting the Court of Justice's interpretation of the Decision.[44] All of these cases demonstrate the inherent difficulties involved in applying traditional principles of judicial review to a decision taken in conditions of scientific uncertainty.[45]

The United Kingdom's main position at the hearing for interim relief[46] was that the ban was made on economic grounds: to allay consumer fears of contracting CJD and therefore protect the European beef industry. It was not made on the grounds of a real risk to public health. As such it was not within the emergency powers available to the Commission. And, the United Kingdom argued, even if the Commission did have the requisite powers, the ban was not proportional to the problem of the likelihood of people contracting CJD from eating BSE-infected beef. The foundational issue, underlying these criteria of competence and proportionality, was whether the Commission was justified in acting to ban exports as a precautionary measure, in conditions in which 'a definitive stance on the transmissibility of BSE to humans is not possible'.[47]

The Court of Justice decided the issue of the Commission's competence to enact Decision 96/239/EC by reviewing the legal

---

[41] Case C–180/96, n. 14 above.
[42] Case C–180/96R, n. 14 above.
[43] Case C–76/96R, n. 14 above, in which the President of the Court of First Instance dismissed the National Farmers' Union's application for interim relief.
[44] Case C–157/96, n. 14 above.
[45] Hession, 'Competence, Proportionality and Equality', n. 5 above.
[46] Case C–180/96R, n. 14 above.
[47] N. 35 above, Preamble (5th recital).

basis of the act in the EC Treaty[48] and Directives[49] concerned with veterinary checks to safeguard animal and human health, discussed above. The Court was satisfied that, founded as it was on these Directives, the primary aim of the Decision was to 'have regard above all to protecting public health in the context of the internal market',[50] even though its preamble mentions 'consumer confidence' as a rationale. The Commission was therefore judged to possess the necessary powers to enact the Decision.

The criterion of proportionality, a general principle of European law, concerns what is the appropriate type and scale of action. Proportionality comprises three elements: a measure must be sufficient to achieve its objectives, it must be the least restrictive necessary, and the benefit achieved must be proportionate to the restriction imposed.[51] The United Kingdom argued that a total ban on exports breached the proportionality principle of European Community law because less restrictive measures could have secured the Commission's objectives, for example, a labelling or certification system so as to guarantee that beef or veal came from herds free from BSE. This argument was countered by the ineffectiveness of the United Kingdom's existing measures to prevent BSE, particularly the fact that despite the 1988 Specified Beef Offal ban[52] suspect meal was still fed to cattle for at least the following five years, and nearly half the slaughterhouses were still failing to comply with statutory requirements to separate offal from meat in 1995. The Court of Justice concluded that, given the

---

[48] Art. 43(3) EC empowers the Council to make regulations, issue directives or take decisions in regard to the development and implementation of the CAP.

[49] Directive 89/662/EEC, n. 26 above, 13; Directive 90/425/EEC [1990] OJ L224/29 and Directive 92/118/EEC, n. 27 above.

[50] Case C–180/96R, n. 14 above. para. 63. See similarly on this point, Case 68/86 *United Kingdom* v. *Commission* [1988] ECR 855 and Case C–331/88, *R* v. *Ministry for Agriculture, Fisheries and Food, ex parte Fedesa* [1990] ECR I-4023 in which the UK challenged a ban on the use of hormones in agricultural products.

[51] See Case 8/55, *Fedechar* v. *High Authority* [1954–56] ECR 245, Case 11/70, *Internationale Handelsgesellschaft* [1970] ECR 1125, and Case 114/76, *Bela Muhle Josef Bergmann KG* v. *Grows-Farm GmbH* [1977] ECR 1211. On the proportionality principle, see G. De Búrca, 'The Principle of Proportionality and its Application in EC Law' (1993) 13 Yearbook of European Law 105; J. Bengoetxea, *The Legal Reasoning of the European Court of Justice: Towards a European Jurisprudence* (Oxford, 1993), 77; in the environmental field, see O. McIntyre, 'Proportionality and Environmental Protection in EC Law' in J. Holder (ed.), *The Impact of EC Environmental Law in the United Kingdom* (Chichester, 1997).

[52] SI 1989 No. 2061, n. 32 above.

scale of infringements, a *total* export ban on beef was necessary to achieve the objective of protecting public health.

On the immediate issue, the application for interim relief, the Court was entitled to suspend the ban if this was justified in fact and law and in order 'to avoid serious and irreparable damage to the applicant's interests'.[53] The Court of Justice stated that although scientists have as yet only an imperfect knowledge of CJD, since the most likely explanation of this disease is exposure to BSE, 'there can be no hesitation'[54] in applying the precautionary measure of Decision 96/239/EC. A similar reliance on the language of precaution, particularly its central concept of irreversible harm, is seen clearly in the Court of Justice's balancing of the interests of public health against the economic interests of the United Kingdom as required to determine whether the interim order should be made: '[economic] damage cannot, however, outweigh the serious harm to public health which is liable to be caused by suspension of the contested decision, and which could not be remedied if the main action were subsequently dismissed'.[55] In the final analysis, the application for interim relief turned on the European Court of Justice's view of the need to take precautionary action in conditions of scientific uncertainty. Precaution operates both substantively and procedurally here: the Court's dismissal of interim relief was itself a precautionary measure.

The Court of Justice went beyond what was strictly necessary to decide the application for interim relief. The acceptance of the competence of the Commission to enact the ban and the finding that this act was proportionate means that the Court of Justice, contrary to its Rules of Procedure,[56] had prejudged, if not prejudiced, the decision of the Court on the substance of the case—the legality of the Decision. Although awaiting this judgment,[57] Advocate General Tesauro's Opinion[58] gives a reliable guide as to the Court's likely decision. An important feature of the Opinion, reinforcing the Court of Justice's judgment in the case for interim

[53] Case C–149/95 P(R) *Commission* v. *Atlantic Container Line and Others* [1995] ECR I–2165, para. 22. See Rules of Procedure (ECJ), Arts 83–90.
[54] Case C–149/95 P(R), n. 53 above, para. 93.
[55] *Ibid.*
[56] Art. 86(4) Rules of Procedure (ECJ).
[57] Case C–180/96, n. 14 above.
[58] Case C–180/96 and Case C–157/96, both n. 14 above.

relief, is the use of the language of precaution to determine the core issues of the Commission's competence to act and whether the Decision was proportionate. This has the effect of sanctioning precautionary action in a stronger sense than merely maintaining the ban until a decision in the main proceedings is made.

Advocate General Tesauro responded to the United Kingdom's (and the National Farmers' Union's) argument that the Commission only had competence to adopt measures that were intended to *guarantee* protection against a serious hazard to the health of humans and animals by referring to the concept of 'real risk' of transmissibility of the disease, derived from Directive 92/118/EEC:[59]

... [W]ithout there being any need to embark on scientific assessments as to the gravity of BSE and its transmissibility to man in the form of Creutzfeld–Jacob Disease . . . there is a real risk to human health . . . that may (and should) be sufficient to conclude that the Commission has not committed any misuse of power in adopting the Decision and that the latter falls within the scope of the powers conferred in adopting the Decision.[60]

The Commission was judged to have sufficient competence to act in order to prevent serious harm to human and animal health. This reasoning is in line with the basic premise of the precautionary principle: that action *should* be taken, even in conditions of scientific uncertainty, and indeed, 'without there being any need to embark on scientific assessments'.[61] The state of scientific knowledge of the link between BSE and v-CJD was also important in determining whether a total embargo on exporting cattle, beef, and beef products to all Member States and third countries was disproportionate. The Advocate General maintained that the Decision did not breach the principle of proportionality because, given the scientific uncertainty in this area and the absence of reliable national controls, the measure could not be regarded as manifestly inappropriate to ensure the attainment of the aim pursued, that is, the protection of public health.[62] Furthermore, in the absence of irrefutable scientific evidence, the Advocate General emphasized that the Commission has a sufficiently wide margin of discretion to enact precautionary measures with the assistance of

---

technical bodies. This strongly suggests that the precautionary principle does have legal effects when enforceable legislation, such as Decision 96/239/EC, has been made in accordance with it.

The Precautionary Principle Evolving

The justification for the European Commission's Decision to ban cattle and beef exports from the United Kingdom, set out in the fifth recital to the preamble and quoted above, is framed in the language of the precautionary principle. As well as characterizing the civil law's reliance upon general, guiding principles, this *de facto* grounding of the ban in the precautionary principle reveals the pro-activeness of the European response to the crisis when compared with the United Kingdom's slower and incomplete approach. This justification for the Decision was accepted by the Court:

Scientists have as yet only an imperfect knowledge of Creutzfeldt-Jakob disease and, more particularly, its recently-discovered variant. Its fatal consequences were reiterated several times at the hearing. There is at present no cure for it. Death ensues several months after diagnosis. Since the most likely explanation of this fatal disease is exposure to BSE, there can be no hesitation. Whilst acknowledging the economic and social difficulties caused by the Commission's Decision in the United Kingdom, the Court cannot but recognize the paramount importance to be accorded to the protection of health.[63]

The European Court of Justice's acceptance of the need for precautionary action, in the face of the 'real risk' of a link between BSE and v-CJD suggests some parity between the weight attributed to scientific evidence by the European Commission before taking regulatory action and by the European courts in their judicial review of that action. The Court of Justice adopted a particularly low threshold for the admissibility of scientific evidence. Initially this appears to be roughly akin to the United States' 'relevancy approach' rule, whereby any relevant conclusions which are supported by qualified expert witnesses are considered.[64] However, comparisons between US and European Community

[63] *Ibid.*, para. 93.
[64] D. E. Bernstein, 'Junk Science in the United States and the Commonwealth' (1996) 21 Yale J Internat. Law 123 at 127.

rules for the admissibility of scientific evidence are inevitably difficult to make because the European courts have not formulated
specific rules to guide their treatment of *scientific* evidence. This is
partly because the courts' jurisdiction is mainly confined to
reviewing the competence of the European institutions to enact
law and the legality of these measures. In formal terms, at least,
this jurisdiction does not extend to making judgements on the
admissibility or the quality of scientific knowledge. A further
reason is that the courts work within a particular institutional
framework in which much attention is paid to the considerations
of various 'Comitology' or expert committees.[65] These committees
provide scientific advice for drafting legislation and play a role in
formulating a judicial response to scientific evidence, thereby
limiting the need for expert witnesses to be called by the courts.[66]
However, although charged with providing independent scientific
advice, the committees' conclusions are determined by political
and economic agendas, influenced by conflicts of interest and
political negotiations.[67] As in the beef crisis cases, difficulties arise
when the courts defer to expert opinion in committees to aid their
review of action according to traditional legal rules and
principles.[68]

In the main, Community law does not lay down particular
requirements for proof, and the case law of the European Court of
Justice contains very few statements on the burden or standard of
proof to be satisfied.[69] Even in contentious proceedings, there is
generally no allocation of the burden of evidence between the
parties; both are under a duty to produce evidence relating to the
issues of fact in the case.[70] The beef crisis cases are no exception:

[65] See K. Bradley, 'Comitology and the Law: Through the Glass Darkly'
(1992) 29 CMLRev. 693–721. See also M. Gonçalves, 'Scientific Expertise and
European Community Regulatory Processes' (1995) 22 *Science and Public Policy*
183.

[66] Although the courts may acquire further evidence by prescribing measures
of inquiry which may amount to a request for further information: Rules of
Procedure (ECJ), art. 45(2) and Rules of Procedure (CFI), art. 65.

[67] J. Theys, 'Decision Making on a European Scale: What Has Changed in the
Relationship Between Science, Politics and Expertise?' (1995) 22 *Science and
Public Policy* 169; and P. Roqueplo, 'Scientific Expertise Among Political Powers,
Administrators and Public Opinion' (1995) 22 *Science and Public Policy* 175.

[68] Hession, 'Competence, Proportionality and Equality', n. 5 above.

[69] K. P. E. Lasok, *The European Court of Justice: Practice and Procedure*
(London, 1994), ch. 13.   [70] *Ibid.*, 422.

questions of the burden and standard of proof are not addressed explicitly. Instead, the Court of Justice adopts a 'common-sense' approach to the weight to be attributed to the scientific evidence as to a causal link between BSE and v-CJD. Such a common-sense approach was espoused by the Land and Environmental Court of New South Wales in *Leatch* v. *National Parks and Wildlife Service and Shoalhaven City Council*,[71] which concerned an appeal against a decision to 'take or kill' endangered fauna (the giant burrowing frog and the yellow-bellied glider). Although there was no express legal requirement to consider the precautionary principle, Justice Stein found that it should be applied as a matter of common sense and reasonableness. In the beef crisis cases, the Court of Justice's common-sense approach is to hold that 'the most likely explanation of the fatal disease is exposure to BSE'.[72] Advocate General Tesauro states similarly that 'without there being any need to embark on scientific assessments as to the gravity of BSE and its transmissibility . . . there is a real risk to human health'.[73] An immediate problem is that 'common sense', like reasonableness, is an open category, permitting value-laden judgements. This way of dealing with complex causal relationships highlights the inability of law to make sense of the beef crisis in a structured and reviewable way. A 'common-sense' approach represents a legal 'retreat from reason', or at the very least an entrenchment of scientific illiteracy in law.

The courts' approach to precautionary action in the BSE cases raises the possibility of a further relaxation of standards of scientific evidence before regulatory action is taken by the European Community. This might even lead to a crude reversal of the burden of proof so that an actor is required to show that harm will not occur before taking action.[74] In the BSE crisis, the precautionary principle also acted as a support mechanism or stratagem for those advancing a particular course of action. The principle

---

[71] 81 Local Govt Environmental Reports of Australia 270.
[72] *Ibid.*, para. 93.   [73] *Ibid.*
[74] G. Teubner, 'The Invisible Cupola: From Causal to Collective Attribution' in G. Teubner, L. Farmer and D. Murphy (eds.), *Environmental Law and Ecological Responsibility: the Concept and Practice of Ecological Responsibility: the Concept and Practice of Ecological Self-Organisation* (Chichester, 1994), 19–20.

may therefore be located within the 'advocacy science' debate[75] originating in the United States since both its adherents and detractors suggest it is capable of destabilizing existing standards for causation and the admissibility of scientific evidence. This also explains why the principle is charged by some with democratizing decision-making processes based on scientific knowledge by opening up space for distinctly non-scientific, or common-sense, views to be heard. In this respect, the principle works against the excesses of 'scientism' or the belief that the authority of scientific knowledge of the natural world makes it applicable in conventionally non-scientific realms.[76]

In their judgments in the beef crisis cases (and in contrast to the earlier approach to precaution and other environmental principles)[77] the European courts are developing, or perhaps crystallizing, precaution as a general principle of European law, particularly by aligning it with the principle of proportionality. This makes some sense: proportionality is concerned with what is appropriate action, the dilemma also of the precautionary principle. The courts' approach is an example of the distinct contribution which principles of *environmental* law are making to the general development of concepts in law.[78] The cases also illustrate how the precautionary principle can be used to negate objectivity in scientific judgements by giving undue weight to certain results, such as the ten cases of v-CJD, which although not statistically significant might show a possible link with BSE. The application of the principle allows value judgements on the acceptable level of risk to contribute to decisions about the suitability of certain legal responses in situations of uncertainty but might also create the conditions for the 'scientization' of political judgements.

[75] See Bernstein, 'Junk Science', n. 64 above, 123; A. D. Tarlock, 'The Futile Search for Environment Laws Based on "Good Science" ' (1996) 1 (1) *Internat. J Biosciences and the Law* 9; T. Horlick-Jones and B. De Marchi, 'The Crisis of Scientific Expertise in *Fin de Siècle* Europe' (1995) 22 (3) *Science and Public Policy* 139; and J. Gillott and M. Kumar, *Science and the Retreat from Reason* (London, 1995).

[76] S. Shackley, 'Mission to Model Earth' in S. Elworthy *et al.*, (eds.), *Perspectives on the Environment* (Aldershot, 1995), 11–23 at 11.

[77] For example, Case C–379/92, n. 13 above.

[78] See J. McEldowney below, p. 123.

European Politics and 'Pre-scientific' Communication of Risk

Whether there was a 'real risk' of BSE was ultimately a political decision, to be determined by the European institutions, on advice from the Scientific Veterinary Committee of the European Union. The political nature of this risk assessment is underlined by the denial that similar measures should apply to other Member States. This was reinforced by the Court of Justice's simple refusal to examine whether there was a danger to public health from the sale of beef from other Member States (France, Germany, Ireland, Portugal, and Switzerland) where there have been sporadic cases of BSE: '(S)uffice it to observe that . . . 97.9% of cases of BSE in Europe have been reported in the United Kingdom'.[79] Such an inadequate response added weight to the United Kingdom's argument that the ban gave rise to arbitrary discrimination between producers and consumers in the United Kingdom and those in other Member States, contrary to the EC Treaty.[80] Given the state of scientific uncertainty in this area, a fully precautionary approach would have sanctioned similar action against other Member States. It was this aspect of the beef crisis which so soured Britain's relations with the Commission, the Council, and other Member States.

The issue of consumer confidence—in the safety of beef, as well as the validity of Government advice—was central to the politics of the beef crisis. The part played by the issue of consumer confidence seems to approximate to a 'pre-scientific' or pre-understanding level of communication of knowledge of the disease by citizens and the media. In his assessment of the conditions for Rational Society, Habermas identifies this pre-scientific level of knowledge as essential to the 'scientization' of political decisions. In this process, political decisions are camouflaged by using science to make them appear objective and thereby increase the legitimacy of power.[81] This leads to the unreliable translation of scientific information into the language of practice and opinion.[82] In terms of the relationship between science and law, the main legal response to the BSE crisis, the export ban, was a very basic

---

79 Case C–180/96R, n. 14 above, para. 67.
80 See further P. Beaumont, 'BSE Crisis' (1996) 64 Scottish Law Gaz. 135.
81 Habermas, *Rational Society*, n. 4 above, ch. 5.
82 *Ibid.*, 70.

reaction to the pre-scientific communication of knowledge of the disease, commonly expressed as public opinion by the media, rather than a scientific evaluation of the 'real risk' of a causal link between BSE and v-CJD.

The significance of the precautionary principle here is that, as a rhetorical or communicative device, posited between politics and science and providing for legal action, it gave the European Union institutions, including the courts, a vocabulary with which they might legitimately express their concerns about the irreversible and serious nature of the threat posed by British beef. Perhaps we see here a shift from the conditions for Habermas' Rational Society, placed as it was firmly in the time of modernity when science could legitimate power. In a situation of such extreme uncertainties in scientific knowledge as the BSE crisis, the precautionary principle can be seen as a rational response. Recognizing that risk is about values as well as probabilities, a decision must be made as to whether it is worthwhile to run a particular risk, in this case the health of millions of consumers. The Court of Justice was clear that in such a situation action could be legitimated by values rather than sums. Possibly, in a post modern Risk Society, where applications of science are perceived to have caused dangers, 'scientization' does not deliver legitimacy for power.

Conclusions: Value Judgements and Precaution in Law

In cases of 'virtual risk' such as BSE, where scientists have identified possible problems but do not agree on the underlying causal mechanisms, the reality, or the extent of the problem, value judgements remain to fill the gap in public expectations left by the uncertainties of science. By giving space to value judgements, the precautionary principle offers a meeting point for law, science, and society. The principle may therefore be seen as a forum within which a range of concerns about environmental protection and public health might be expressed. These judgements may be overtly political as in the case of the Commission's Decision banning cattle and beef exports by Britain. This highlights the dilemma of invoking the precautionary principle as a replacement for 'scientism' since, by permitting value judgements to contribute to decision-making processes, it is capable of undermining the residual authority of science and thereby the seriousness and legitimacy of public-health problems and global environmental phenomena. The danger arises from the principle's openness: 'the precautionary principle can be shown to support almost any cause'[83] which raises the possibility of a US-style gridlock with experts adopting precaution as a central part of 'advocacy science' in conflicts.[84] The beef crisis cases illustrate that when law and science engage the relationship is a dynamic one: by upholding precautionary measures the European courts played as much a part in determining the science of BSE as scientific knowledge determined their legal judgments. This suggests a role for legal principles as a persuasive medium for pursuing certain interests. From this perspective, it is possible to see in the European Court of Justice's judgment on the legality of the export ban on British beef, the use of precaution as a persuasive, political device in much the same way as it is being used by environmental and public-health campaigning groups as they follow a particular agenda. Unfortunately the Court of Justice has not yet taken the opportunity to suggest some structure for sensible debate within the space opened up by the precautionary principle.

[83] J. Adams, 'Cars, Cholera and Cows: Virtual Risk and the Management of Uncertainty', Paper given at British Symposium on BSE/CJD, 10 Sept. 1996.

[84] Horlick-Jones and De Marchi, 'Crisis of Scientific Evidence', n. 75 above, 144.

A NEW CRITERION FOR THE ADMISSIBILITY OF SCIENTIFIC EVIDENCE

The Metamorphosis of Helpfulness

*Fiona E. Raitt**

Introduction

Many legal systems, including those of the United States and the United Kingdom,[1] have developed special rules for the admissibility of expert scientific opinion, one purpose of which is to control the quality of the science that is allowed into court. In recent decades there have been numerous calls to admit more science into the court-room.[2] The clamour for increasing use of expert scientific opinion has been met with equally vocal resistance, largely founded on fears that any changes in the rules for admissibility of expert evidence would inevitably lead to a deluge of junk science.[3] This debate has engendered a wide-ranging discussion particularly in the United States and, in a more muted form, in the United

---

* I am indebted to M. Suzanne Zeedyk for criticisms on earlier drafts of this chapter.

[1] For the purposes of this discussion the jurisdictions within the UK are England and Wales, Scotland, and Northern Ireland.

[2] See, e.g., S. M. Lloyd-Bostock, 'Psychology and the Law: A Critical Review of Research and Practice' (1981) 8 Brit. J. Law & Society 1; L. Walker and J. Monahan, 'Social Frameworks: a New Use of Social Science in Law' (1987) 73 Virginia LRev. 559; R. D. Mackay and A. M. Colman, 'Excluding Expert Evidence: a Tale of Ordinary Folk and Common Experience' [1991] Crim. LR 800; D. Sheldon and M. MacLeod, 'From Normative to Positive Data: Expert Evidence Re-examined' [1991] Crim. LR 811.

[3] J. C. Yuille, 'Expert Evidence by Psychologists: Sometimes Problematic and Often Premature' (1989) 7 Behavioral Science and the Law 181; M. McCloskey and H. Egeth (1983) 38 *Amer. Psychologist* 550; L. C. J. Taylor, 'The Lund Lecture' (1995) 35 Medicine Science and the Law 3.

Kingdom over the appropriate criteria that should govern the admissibility of science.[4] The two primary criteria for admissibility adopted in both systems are similar, although the emphasis given to these criteria differs between the systems. Specifically the criteria are (1) the helpfulness and (2) the reliability of expert testimony. Although these two criteria are generally presented as separate and distinct, this essay argues that helpfulness is actually reliability in another guise, and that, as used in the United Kingdom, the criterion for admissibility is inaccurately described as helpfulness. This inaccuracy distorts the fact-finding process. It is argued that a more transparent approach is needed which recognizes and acknowledges that reliability is the more appropriate criterion.

This essay focuses particularly on areas of expert evidence concerned with the behavioural sciences, for it is clear that the construction of guidelines for admissibility of science discourages these sciences in particular from entering the proof process. It is further argued that within the United Kingdom, adopting reliability as the primary criterion for admissibility, coupled with judicious use of the existing rules of evidence, would create greater clarity in the use of expert testimony. This would result in a more efficient regulator of science in the court-room and avert concerns about the consequences of changes in the parameters for admissibility.

The UK Position: Helpfulness as the Primary Admissibility Criterion

The traditional test applied in the United Kingdom governing the admissibility of science is its 'helpfulness' to the trier of fact. A body of evidence is deemed helpful or otherwise in terms of its capacity to add to the trier of fact's knowledge and to assist their deliberations. Applications to lead expert scientific testimony are

---

[4] P. C. Giannelli, 'The Admissibility of Novel Scientific Evidence: *Frye* v. *United States*, a Half-Century Later' (1980) 80 Columbia LR 1197; M. McCormick, 'Scientific Evidence: Defining a New Approach to Admissibility' (1982) 67 Iowa LRev. 879; E. F. Loftus, 'Resolving Legal Questions with Psychological Data' (1991) 47 *Amer. Psychologist* 1046; W. T. Pizzi, 'Expert Testimony in the US' (1995) 145 NLJ 82; E. J. Imwinkelried, 'Expert Testimony in the US: a Different Perspective' (1995) 145 NLJ 644; and 'Special Issue: Behavioral Science Evidence in the Wake of *Daubert*', the entire issue of (1995) 13 Behavioral Science and the Law.

more likely to arise in important cases such as those involving a significant point of law or a large sum of money, or serious criminal cases, where the trier of fact will be a jury rather than a judge. For example, experts may be called to speak to matters involving ballistics, bloodstains, and pathology in cases such as wounding, rape, and murder. 'Scientific testimony' is a broad term and there are several subject areas within its ambit where expert opinion is regularly admitted and welcomed. In particular, the physical sciences, such as engineering and thermodynamics, and the medical sciences, such as pathology and forensic medicine, make frequent appearances in legal proceedings.[5] But evidence from sources other than orthodox natural science or medicine is less happily received. The testimony of experts from the behavioural sciences, such as psychology, is often judged 'unhelpful' to the court.[6] It is charged that it has nothing to contribute because the trier of fact, whether judge or jury, is sufficiently informed through their personal experience of human behaviour to make decisions without reference to experts.

The preference of the UK courts for the helpfulness rule in governing the admissibility of science is derived from *R. v. Turner*.[7] Turner was charged with the murder of his girlfriend, whom he admitted killing with a hammer. His defence was provocation. It was to be based on psychiatric evidence that his personality was such that he would have been likely to have been provoked to murder by his girlfriend's account of her affairs with other men and her claim that the child she was expecting was not his. The evidence was ruled inadmissible at trial and that ruling was upheld on appeal. Relying on the precedent of *Folkes v. Chadd*, a 1782 case,[8] the Court of Appeal confirmed that

---

[5] In the field of forensic science in criminal cases in England, it has been estimated that some 30–40% of cases involve scientific evidence, which in 1992 translated into around 10,000 cases in the Crown Court: P. Roberts, 'Science in the Criminal Process' (1994) 14 OJLS 469. Professional law journals regularly devote considerable advertising and promotional space to expert witnesses, e.g. (1995) 145 NLJ 91–110, Spec. Supp.

[6] The leading case on this point is *R. v. Turner*, n. 7 below, where the expert in question was a psychiatrist and therefore, as a medically qualified person, arguably carried better scientific credentials than a mere psychologist or other expert from the behavioural sciences. Despite some inroads in subsequent case law, *Turner* still represents English, and probably Scots, law.

[7] [1975] 1 QB 834.   [8] 3 Doug. KB 157.

An expert's opinion is admissible to furnish the court with scientific information which is likely to be outside the experience or knowledge of a judge or jury. If on the proven facts a judge or jury can form their own conclusions without help, then the opinion of an expert is unnecessary. In such a case if it is given dressed up in scientific jargon it may make judgement more difficult.[9]

In relation to this particular case, Lawton LJ said,

We all know that both men and women who are deeply in love can, and sometimes do, have outbursts of blind rage when discovering unexpected wantonness on the part of their loved ones. . . . Jurors do not need psychiatrists to tell them how ordinary folk who are not suffering from any mental illness are likely to react to the stresses and strains of life.[10]

It was accepted by the trial and appeal courts that the expert evidence in *Turner* was relevant, and its reliability was not explicitly questioned. However, its helpfulness was questioned. It was felt the jury did not need the assistance of expert testimony to explain normal human reactions and emotions, which were deemed to be well within the common experience and understanding of jury members. *Turner* was ostensibly about preserving the authority of the jury as the trier of fact and preventing experts from trespassing on their preserve, especially where the issue was one relating to human behaviour. Courts in the United Kingdom are highly anxious to guard against this potential invasion of their territory. The authority of the trier of fact is absolute, and evidence deemed to intrude on that authority will be excluded.[11] Moreover, the *locus* and capacity of the jury to assess human behaviour is also deemed unimpeachable, and, in this respect, as Lawton LJ declared in *Turner*, 'the law assumes they can perform their duties properly', without expert assistance.[12] This view is endorsed even where relevant research in the behavioural sciences

---

[9] *Turner*, n. 7 above at 841.

[10] *Turner*, n. 7 above at 841. This is not the place to explore that judicial charge further, but it is precisely this assumption that the average juror has an informed awareness of the reactions of men and women who are 'deeply in love' and the circumstances in which they have 'outbursts of blind rage' that is dubious. Turner's reaction might have had just as much to do with power, possessiveness, and obsessive jealousy as a lover's blind rage sparked by infidelity.

[11] T. Hodgkinson, *Expert Evidence: Law and Practice* (London, 1990), 122.

[12] *Turner*, n. 7 above at 842.

domain has become well established[13] (and thus could reasonably be assumed to be reliable) and also where a dimension of that research indicates the existence of lay mythology or misunderstanding about the subject.[14]

The assumption that jurors are competent to evaluate human behaviour rests on a wholly false premise, namely that '[t]he behaviour of normal human beings is essentially transparent'.[15] Most psychologists would strongly challenge this notion. Their research has established that many areas of human behaviour, although occurring on a daily basis, are complex enough to confound simple comprehension. For example, research on eyewitness testimony will often be excluded on the basis that it is not 'helpful' as it concerns memory, visual recognition, and recall, activities in which we all engage daily and which are therefore presumed to be areas where common sense prevails and where jurors would not require professional guidance from psychologists or others researching in the field. Yet, as Colman and Mackay have shown, there is a substantial body of research to support the argument that much common sense is 'demonstratively counter-intuitive in the sense that "ordinary men and women" generally misunderstand [it]'.[16] They describe five examples of situations, including obedience to authority and bystander apathy, where the outcome of experiments was contrary to what the average person predicted, when invited to guess.[17]

Similarly, expert evidence of psychological syndromes arising

[13] S. M. Kassin, P. C. Ellsworth and V. L. Smith, 'The "General Acceptance" of Psychological Research on Eyewitness Testimony: a Survey of the Experts' (1989) 44 *Amer. Psychologist* 1089; S. D. Penrod, S. M. Fulero and B. L. Cutler, 'Expert Psychological Testimony on Eyewitness Reliability Before and After *Daubert*: the State of the Law and Science' (1995) 13 Behavioral Science and the Law 229.

[14] K. C. Gerbasi, M. Zuckerman and H. T. Reis, 'Justice Needs a New Blindfold: a Review of Mock Jury Research' (1977) 84 *Psychological Bulletin* 323; G. L. Wells, C. L. Lindsay and T. J. Ferguson, 'Confidence, Accuracy and Jurors' Perceptions in Eyewitness Testimony' (1979) 64 *J. Appl. Psychology* 440; K. A. Deffenbacher and E. F. Loftus, 'Do Jurors Share a Common Understanding concerning Eyewitness Behaviour?' (1982) 3 Law & Human Behavior 261; P. A. Tetreault, 'Rape Myth Acceptance: A Case for Providing the Expert Educational Testimony in Rape Jury Trials' (1989) 7 Behavioral Science and the Law 243.

[15] A. M. Colman and R. D. Mackay, 'Legal Issues Surrounding the Admissibility of Expert Psychological and Psychiatric Testimony' (1993) 20 Issues in Criminological and Legal Psychology 46.

[16] *Ibid.*, 48.   [17] *Ibid.*, 48–9.

from victims' responses to violence such as battered women's syndrome, rape trauma syndrome, or child sexual abuse syndrome is rarely heard in the United Kingdom, because it is deemed to contribute little to a juror's understanding of the issues as it is concerned with matters well within their knowledge. Although in the United Kingdom the Contempt of Court Act 1981 prevents research being conducted on jury deliberations or jurors' experiences, research of this nature carried out in the United States has consistently suggested the existence of jury bias and myth acceptance in numerous areas including witness accuracy in identification, witness credibility, and perceptions of rape victims. The unwillingness of courts to admit expert evidence describing such research, even to assist the jury from an educational perspective, stands in stark contrast to the observations made by judges in the types of cases where evidence from behavioural science would have been beneficial. Thus, in a recent case at Winchester Crown Court, Judge David Griffiths reportedly advised a man convicted of sexual assault, 'if you had had the courage and good manners to say you were sorry and sent a bunch of flowers all would have been forgiven'.[18]

These comments display a lamentable lack of comprehension of the issues of intimidation, power, and violence experienced by women in sexual assault cases. Similar misconceptions are apparent from the question frequently posed of a battered woman in a violent relationship—'but why doesn't she just leave?' Judges and jurors may think they know of the effects of being battered, but their level of awareness is limited and mythology remains rife. An example of this is apparent in the charge to the jury in *R. v. Thornton*:

[E]ven if Mrs Thornton had lost her self-control, you would still have to ask whether a reasonable woman in her position would have done what she did and, if you think . . . that she went out and found a knife and went back into the room and as a result of something said to her stabbed her husband as he lay defenceless on that settee deep into his stomach, it may be very difficult to come to the conclusion that that was, and I use the shorthand, a reasonable reaction. There are . . . many unhappy, indeed miserable, husbands and wives. It is a fact of life. It has to be faced, members of the jury. But on the whole it is hardly reasonable, you may think, to stab them fatally when there are other alternatives available, like walking out or going upstairs.[19]

---

[18] *Daily Telegraph*, 6 Oct. 1995.
[19] Referred to in the appeal hearing: [1992] 1 All ER 306 at 312.

It is highly questionable whether these purported 'alternatives' are serious options for a battered woman; it is this type of situation where expert testimony can aid juror understanding.

In the rare examples within the case law of expert behavioural-science evidence being permitted for limited purposes, the judicial logic is often hard to follow. One such case is *DPP* v. *A. and B. C. Chewing Gum Ltd.*,[20] a case about the effects which allegedly obscene pictures on bubble gum cards had on the children who collected them. The key issue was whether the evidence of experts in child psychiatry could be admitted, in regard to which Lord Parker said,

I can quite see that when considering the effect of something on an adult an adult jury may be able to judge just as well as an adult witness called on the point. Indeed, there is nothing more that a jury or justices need to know. But certainly when you are dealing with children of different age groups and children from five upwards, any jury and any justices need all the help they can get, information which they may not have, as to the effect on different children.[21]

The judicial reasoning here is fallacious. If adult jurors are deemed not to need expert assistance in relation to the effects of obscene pictures on adults on the grounds that, as adults themselves, they are fully cognizant with the effects of obscenity on all adults, then it is illogical to argue for an exception in the case of children. For indeed all adult jurors have also experienced childhood. It seems therefore that the helpfulness rule operates to the singular disadvantage of the behavioural sciences, yet it is these very sciences that have the capability of challenging the deeply-held but often misguided views of the trier of fact.[22]

Although the criterion of helpfulness is dominant in the United Kingdom, the criterion of reliability also has a role, as it features both in the assessment of precisely who is classified as an 'expert' and in the status of the scientific field about which the expert will testify. These two issues are considered next. They will be

---

[20] [1967] 1 QB 159. [21] *Ibid* at 164–5.

[22] Mackay and Colman, 'Excluding Expert Evidence', n. 2 above; Sheldon and MacLeod, 'From Normative to Positive Data', n. 2 above; Colman and Mackay, 'Legal Issues', n. 15 above; R. D. Mackay and A. D. Colman, 'Equivocal Rulings on Expert Psychological and Psychiatric Evidence: Turning a Muddle into a Nonsense' [1996] Crim LR 88.

discussed in the context of US procedures because they have been more explicitly addressed in that jurisdiction.

The US Position: Reliability as the Primary Admissibility Criterion

In the United States, reliability occupies the position of the dominant criterion for admissibility. Although some attention has been paid to the issue of helpfulness, within the United States (noticeably in the Federal Rules of Evidence, 1975)[23] most arguments about admissibility of scientific evidence in case law and in the academic literature focus on the reliability of the evidence. The recent Supreme Court decision in *Daubert* v. *Merrell Dow Pharmaceuticals Inc.*[24] revisited the criterion of reliability but gave little attention to that of helpfulness.

Reliability is an attribute central to the disciplines of both science and law. Scientists go to great lengths to ensure that their methodology of data collection, experimentation, replication, and analysis is one that is recognized and approved in its field, for reliability grants scientific findings internal validity. In law, unless a witness is considered reliable by a judge and/or jury, then the testimony will carry little weight and will be of no value in a case. For experts, this means that as a preliminary to having their testimony accepted by the court, their credentials as a witness must be established. In practice this involves providing the court with details of the expert's professional qualifications, academic and professional standing and publications. Equally, irrespective of the expert's background and qualifications, if the substance of his or her testimony is not rooted in a field of expertise 'sufficiently well-established to pass the ordinary tests of relevance and reliability', then it will not be deemed admissible.[25] These preliminaries of course guarantee neither the ultimate acceptance of the testimony of the expert nor the weight attached to it. Reliability is essentially an important mechanism by which evidentiary rulings can be kept uniform, uniformity being an obviously desirable attribute of any legal system that seeks predictability and certainty in its decision-making. It is arguably for this reason that reliability has domi-

---

[23] Federal Rules of Evidence (1975) (St. Paul, MN).
[24] 113 S. Ct. 2786 (1993); 125 L. Ed. 2d 469 (1993).
[25] C. Tapper, *Cross and Tapper on Evidence* (8th edn, London, 1995), 558.

nated in the debate within the United States this century concerning the admissibility of science.

In the United States the first judicial consideration of an appropriate standard for the admissibility of scientific evidence arose in the case of *Frye* v. *United States* in 1923.[26] This was a criminal case in which the defendant sought to introduce the results of a systolic blood-pressure test, a forerunner of the polygraph. This test was viewed as novel science, and the court refused to admit the evidence because it deemed that 'a scientific principle or discovery . . . must be sufficiently established to have gained general acceptance in the particular field in which it belongs'.[27] The evidence presented in that case did not achieve that standard. The *Frye* test of general acceptance became the main US standard by which novel science was evaluated. It remained so despite the enactment of the Federal Rules of Evidence in 1975, and it still retains a prominent role as a result of the Supreme Court decision in *Daubert*. This case was the first opportunity for the Supreme Court to adjudicate on key issues relating to the standards for admissibility, and while it appeared to bring some resolution to the debate, the abundant literature since the decision makes it clear that many issues were left unanswered.[28]

The *Frye* test of general acceptance was designed primarily as a measure for mechanical techniques, such as the polygraph in the *Frye* case, handwriting, voice-printing, and similar forensic procedures. With the expansion of the social science arena since 1923 and the subsequent pressure to admit evidence on a wide range of issues including, for example, eyewitness observation, the authenticity of confession evidence, and the effects of domestic violence on women who kill their abusive partners, increased confusion and disagreement arose about the application of this test. It was unclear what constituted scientific evidence, and there was disagreement in the courts over which aspects of scientific study were required to be generally accepted—was it the theory, the

[26] 293 F. 1013, 54 App. D.C. 46 (D.C. Cir. 1923).
[27] *Ibid.* at 1014.
[28] See e.g. Symposium Report (1994) 15 Cardoza LRev.; H. Zonana, *'Daubert v. Merrell Dow Pharmaceuticals*: A New Standard for Scientific Evidence in the Courts?' (1994) 22 Bull. of Amer. Academy of Psychiatry and the Law 304; and the Spec. Iss. (1995) 13 Behavioral Science and the Law.

technique, the conclusions, or all of these?[29] As the *Frye* test, with its narrow emphasis on reliability, became subject to academic and judicial criticism, it became increasingly discredited.[30]

The codification of the Federal Rules of Evidence in 1975 reflected a shift in emphasis away from reliability as the sole determinant of the evidence toward incorporation of relevancy and helpfulness. Rule 402 states that 'all relevant evidence is admissible, except as otherwise provided', and Rule 702 states that expert testimony should be permitted in any case where it 'will assist the trier of fact to understand the evidence or to determine a fact in issue'. These are relatively permissive rules. However the Rules did not explicitly address the continuing applicability of the general acceptance standard, resulting in ambiguity and uncertainty about its status. McCormick has shown how a succession of federal and state courts modified and changed the *Frye* general acceptance standard while purporting to apply it,[31] resulting in Giannelli's claim that there were 'several *Frye* tests'.[32] In the years following the enactment of the Federal Rules, an increasing number of courts rejected general acceptance altogether in favour of a standard of reliability. Thus, in the case of *United States* v. *Williams*, which concerned the admissibility of spectrographic voice identification evidence, the court ruled:

In testing for admissibility of a particular type of scientific evidence, whatever the scientific 'voting' pattern may be, the courts cannot surrender to scientists the responsibility for determining the reliability of that evidence. . . . The sole question is whether the spectrographic analysis has reached a level of reliability sufficient to warrant its use in the courtroom.[33]

An opportunity to remedy the status of the *Frye* test arrived with the Supreme Court ruling in *Daubert*. This case centred on allegations that the drug Bendectin, prescribed to pregnant mothers as an antidote to morning sickness, had caused serious birth defects in their children. In relation to expert testimony, the key

---

[29] S. Zeedyk and F. Raitt, 'Psychological Evidence in the Courtroom: Critical Reflections on the General Acceptance Standard' (1998) 8 *J Community and Appl. Social Psychology* 23.
[30] Giannelli, 'Admissibility of Novel Scientific Evidence', n. 4 above.
[31] McCormick, 'Scientific Evidence', n. 4 above, 895.
[32] Giannelli, 'Admissibility of Novel Scientific Evidence', n. 4 above, 1228.
[33] 583 F.2d 1194 (2d Cir. 1978) at 1198.

issue was whether or not re-analyses of epidemiological studies conducted by experts for the plaintiffs, which suggested Bendectin could cause birth defects, were competent. At the Court of Appeals it was held that since these re-analyses had neither been submitted to peer review nor published in a scientific journal, but had in effect been conducted purely for the purposes of the litigation, they did not meet the general acceptance standard of the *Frye* test. The issue for the Supreme Court was whether *Frye* was still authoritative, given the later enactment of the Federal Rules. The opinion of the Court, delivered by Blackman J, enunciated a set of principles to be deployed as guidelines in the admissibility of expert scientific evidence. These guidelines were presented as four questions which judges, in performing a gatekeeping role, could consider when deciding whether or not to admit expert opinion. These questions are:

1. Is the theory or technique at issue testable, or has it been tested?
2. Has the theory or technique been subjected to peer review and publication?
3. In the case of a particular technique, what is the known or potential rate of error?
4. What is the degree of general acceptance in the scientific community of the theory or technique?[34]

These guidelines all reinforce the focus on reliability. They highlight ways in which the reliability of scientific evidence can be affirmed before it is allowed into court. Extensive discussion has already arisen over the *Daubert* standard.[35] This included much speculation over whether the standard of general acceptance—the early hallmark of the scientific community's recognition of reliability—would continue to play a dominant role.[36] It is argued by many that it will continue to occupy a dominant position as it has been retained as the final criterion, and therefore perhaps one allocated the role of 'catch-all'. There is also much debate over the effect of what has been described as a 'two part reliability and

---

[34] *Daubert*, n. 24 above at 482–4.

[35] See literature cited at n. 28 above and n. 36 below.

[36] M. L. C. Feldman, 'May I Have the Next Dance, Mrs. *Frye*?' (1995) 69 Tulane LRev. 793; A. G. Gless, 'Some post-*Daubert* Trial Tribulations of a Simple Country Judge' (1995) 13 Behavioral Science and the Law 261.

helpfulness test in determining the admissibility of scientific evidence under Rule 702'.[37]

Until *Daubert*, almost every discussion of the requirement for scientific evidence to be helpful made reference to the terms of Rule 702. That rule is overt in its requirement that expert testimony must assist the trier of fact. However, interestingly, it is clear from a number of passages in the *Daubert* judgment discussing Rule 702 that the US position remains focused largely on reliability. For example, Blackman J, in confirming that the trial judge 'must ensure that any and all scientific testimony or evidence admitted is not only relevant, but reliable', stated that the 'primary locus of this obligation is Rule 702', thus depicting the helpfulness rule as one inextricably linked with reliability.[38] The lesson from the US debate is that it is not easy to craft concise criteria for admissibility of science. The efforts made by the Supreme Court to reconcile helpfulness as expressed in Rule 702 with the law's need for reliability are telling, and they reveal the inherent difficulties in distinguishing these criteria.

A Critique of the UK Position on Helpfulness

A superficial comparison of the criteria governing the admissibility of scientific evidence in the United States and the United Kingdom suggests two very different approaches in operation: the United Kingdom's attachment to helpfulness and the United States' preference for reliability. But if a closer comparison is made then it emerges that these approaches are not so diverse. For what exactly is 'helpfulness'? Is it so distinct from reliability? In assessing the helpfulness of testimony, the fundamental question that is posed is whether the evidence will add to the stock of juror knowledge, or ultimately create confusion and obscurity?

It seems odd to suggest that reliable evidence would not add to the overall stock of juror knowledge. Can reliable evidence be truly unhelpful? It may reinforce existing views, but if properly presented it ought not to confuse or misrepresent.[39] At worst, if

---

[37] D. E. Bernstein, 'Junk Science in the United States and the Commonwealth' (1996) 21 Yale J Internat. Law 123 at 135.

[38] *Daubert*, n. 24 above at 480.

[39] In other words the testimony must not be 'dressed up in scientific jargon', per Lawton LJ in *Turner*, n. 7 above at 841.

an expert is merely telling the jury what they already know, then his or her opinion will be superfluous but it will not be unhelpful. Alternatively, if an expert is telling jurors what they do not know, then the opinion proffered may disabuse them of deeply ingrained beliefs. The expert's challenge to these views may appear confusing from the juror's perspective, but if these deeply held beliefs are misconceived and rooted in mythology then they ought to be challenged. That is the very function of the expert. However, the statutory prohibition on research into jury deliberations or juror attitudes denies us the means of measuring juror competence or capability.

Why then was helpfulness selected in the United Kingdom as a criterion for admissibility, and why has it managed to survive for over twenty years relatively unscathed? I believe the answer lies in the relationship between law and science, which disguises an inherent competition between the disciplines and which has encouraged the growth of law's distrust of scientific evidence and scientific experts.[40] This competitiveness and distrust is revealed most sharply in law's relationship with the behavioural sciences. Law arguably has most to lose from conferring acceptability on these sciences, because both exist to interpret and assess human behaviour.

The function of the trier of fact is to evaluate the facts proven in court. As with all scientific evidence, the justification for excluding behavioural science research from the court-room is that the jury's authority as the trier of fact is paramount. Such reasoning assumes that the typical juror is educated and informed, perhaps even to a remarkably sophisticated degree, that he or she has diverse life experience, and that any lack of life experience can be compensated for by faultless insight. Moreover, these justifications assume that, as rational beings, jurors are equipped to evaluate the evidence objectively, ignoring the (human) tendency towards bias, prejudice, and partiality. These are not wholly convincing arguments. A more persuasive explanation is that the appeal to the pre-eminence of the authority of the trier of fact is a convenient device by which law is able to retain its privilege and status.

[40] R. Smith and B. Wynne (eds.), *Expert Evidence: Interpreting Science in the Law* (London, 1989).

It is through the principle of the authority of the trier of fact that the jury's status is protected from intrusion by other disciplines, especially cognate disciplines such as the social and behavioural sciences. Law is reluctant to confer authority on certain types of science. As Alldridge has observed, this reluctance has resulted in a 'pecking order of . . . respectability' among the sciences, which functions as a 'rough scale' that 'varies over time'[41] and reflects a wider academic and political dispute concerning which areas of knowledge are to command specialist expertise. There is little articulation of how the pecking order is determined, but it stems from what has been described as a power struggle between disciplines, a struggle that Jones believes is 'less to do with an ideological preference for the ordinary layperson, and more to do with professional power struggles between the judiciary and persons who have special knowledge'.[42]

Law is very protective of its domain, frequently reinforcing the executive role of the judge and protesting about its ability to penetrate dense, obtuse, or evasive testimony through skilful advocacy and forensic cross-examination.[43] This confidence in its truth-seeking skills was articulated in *Daubert* where we were reminded of the prowess of the adversarial system:

[V]igorous cross-examination, presentation of contrary evidence, and careful instruction on the burden of proof are the traditional and appropriate means of attacking shaky but admissible evidence.[44]

Thus for the judiciary, experts are regarded with relative cynicism, and faith is imbued in the jury system. Determining issues in the court-room (rather than the laboratory) is the pinnacle of dispute resolution for law, and a domain where it is reluctant to concede ground to any other discipline. It is especially defensive about encroachment upon its territory from another social science. It is one matter for law to acknowledge the need for expert evidence in the field of, for example, physics, but quite another to admit testimony that relates to human behaviour. After all, this is

[41] P. Alldridge, 'Forensic Science and Expert Evidence' (1994) 21(1) Brit. J Law & Society 136.

[42] C. A. G. Jones, *Expert Witnesses: Science, Medicine and the Practice of Law* (Oxford, 1994), 122. See too, S. Jasanoff, *Science at the Bar: Law, Science and Technology in America* (Cambridge, Mass., 1995).

[43] See e.g. R. du Cann, *The Art of the Advocate* (London, 1993).

[44] *Daubert*, n. 24 above at 484.

a field in which law itself is supposed to specialize. While the average juror is not expected to be conversant with the detail of the physical sciences, he or she is assumed to be at ease with all aspects of normal human behaviour.

As soon as law has to acknowledge the reliability of science it has immediately to concede ground and defer to superior knowledge. That is not a concession it makes lightly or happily for it involves giving up control, and traditionally law has tried to limit any concession of ground by using the criterion of helpfulness as a filter for admissibility. However, law's determination to retain the high ground is indicative of a power struggle that remains under cover. It would be too threatening for law to be explicit about its distrust of certain sciences, as this would bring it into direct confrontation with other disciplines.

Another explanation for law's attachment to helpfulness is the fear that admitting any expert evidence of human behaviour is the 'thin end of the wedge'. This is a separate but associated argument to that raised above and also stems from inter-disciplinary competition. If courts admit evidence of the instability of, for example, eyewitness testimony or confessions, then potentially all aspects of behaviour will come under scrutiny. This in turn could lead to the collapse of the process of proof as we know it. Thus, if experts were allowed to give evidence on the fallibility of witnesses' memory, or the capacity for witnesses' confusion induced by court-room nerves or through skilled cross-examination, then at a stroke the province of the court-room and the plethora of rules of evidence designed to locate 'the truth' would be undermined.

It is easier for law to reject such evidence as unhelpful than to enter into a debate about the reliability of the expert testimony. For if such testimony were accepted as reliable and informative by the scientific field, then the floodgates genuinely would be wide open. If the behavioural sciences were acknowledged to have something to say about human behaviour, pressure to explore these issues inside the court-room would be irresistible. The sanctuary and privilege of the court-room would be breached and all manner of legal activities might fall under the scrutiny of experts, including jury and judicial decision-making processes. Such a prospect is far too threatening for law, so it avoids the risk by keeping reliability out of the picture and the focus firmly on helpfulness.

The effect of preserving helpfulness as the primary criterion for admissibility within the United Kingdom is that law clings to an outdated and amorphous concept which is invoked to deprive law of a source of knowledge. This in turn inhibits and distorts fact-finding. If reliability were acknowledged as the real driving force behind admissibility, then a very different environment could emerge for bringing science into the court-room. Lawyers, professional experts and all those concerned with expert scientific testimony would benefit from there being a transparent and uniform threshold as the standard for admissibility. At present, case investigation and preparation often involves argument construction of the highest complexity and sophistication. When this construction entails expert scientific evidence, lawyers and scientists need to know what criteria they are expected to address. Is it the degree of helpfulness that the testimony offers, or is it the degree of reliability that it commands? A more explicit and accurate standard is required.

Reliability as an Explicit Criterion for Admissibility in the United Kingdom

The debate within the United Kingdom over standards for admissibility of expert evidence has not been nearly so wide-ranging, vociferous or influential as in the United States. Although there have been trenchant criticisms of the *Turner* decision, these have made little impact on admissibility criteria.[45] The concerns and interest evoked in the United States over the issue of expert evidence, most recently stimulated by the *Daubert* decision, are not replicated here. Perhaps the discussion in the United States seems too remote and disconnected from the position in the United Kingdom to have aroused interest. But if so, this is arguably due to a belief that the principles of reliability and helpfulness are divergent. Thus, because the United Kingdom ostensibly uses a different approach there would appear to be little to learn from recent developments in the United States. Such a belief of course overlooks the similarities between the criteria of reliability and helpfulness that I have examined above. Characterizing the helpfulness rule as a metamorphosed reliability rule enables a

---

[45] See literature cited at n. 22 above.

more useful analysis of the US debate for UK purposes. Since a far greater consideration of the issues raised by expert scientific testimony has occurred in the United States, there are undoubtedly lessons to be learnt.

The UK courts can afford to pursue a more liberal approach towards admissibility of science. This would not necessarily mean adopting complex *Daubert*-type guidelines. That solution would demand too major a shift in judicial attitudes towards science, and this is not likely to be achieved very quickly in the United Kingdom. However, rather than develop a new system of criteria for admissibility, I believe that a more imaginative deployment of the existing rules of evidence could provide an improved framework for admissibility. In particular, the existing rules such as those relating to burden of proof and corroboration can be mobilized to regulate admissibility of science. The final sections of this essay explore how this could be done.

BURDEN OF PROOF

The burden of proof is the obligation imposed by the law of evidence on a party seeking to prove a fact. The party must adduce sufficient evidence to discharge the burden and have the fact found proven.[46] At the conclusion of a case, the application of the burden of proof will determine whether the prosecutor or plaintiff has been successful. The consideration of whether the burden has been discharged is posed in the round, having gathered all the evidence. It is the totality of the evidence which is assessed to decide which party has proven their case. Burden of proof is an intrinsically flexible concept, which in practice has already been adapted to encompass two separate types of burden of proof, namely, the persuasive burden and the evidential burden. This flexibility makes the concept especially suitable for supporting a new framework for the admissibility of scientific evidence.

Some commentators have in the past proposed that expert testimony itself could carry an independent and enhanced burden of proof.[47] The burden would rest on the party seeking to adduce scientific evidence to demonstrate that it was sufficiently reliable

---

[46] Tapper, *Cross and Tapper on Evidence*, n. 25 above, 119–21.
[47] Giannelli, 'Admissibility of Novel Scientific Evidence', n. 4 above, 1245.

to be admitted. That party would have to decide what factors were relevant to reliability, and they would have to articulate that decision to the court. These might include factors similar to those identified in *Daubert* such as the level of general acceptance in the scientific community, the extent of replication of the research findings, the size of the sample group, the methodology employed, and statistical significance. Unlike the *Daubert* guidelines, however, these factors would not be a prescriptive list but would vary depending on the scientific issue in dispute.

Experts would have the opportunity and duty to explain why certain factors were relevant and why others were not. For example, parties seeking to admit evidence on eye-witness identification might choose to emphasise that twenty years' worth of research has established a rare measure of consensus in regard to findings which are rarely disputed and well-respected in the psychological community.[48] An expert on eyewitness testimony would probably stress the lengthy publication record and the extensive use of peer review in demonstrating reliability, because those are the features that best illustrate the reliability of this type of evidence. By comparison, those seeking to introduce evidence on environmental issues might stress 'the risk of future harm [as] a legitimate substitute for traditional scientific and legal standards', given that the relative infancy of such sciences prevent them from acquiring a substantial publication record or widespread peer review.[49] The essence of the application of burden of proof would be in the flexibility it permitted to experts in drawing on relevant aspects of their field to prove reliability.

Applying a criterion of reliability for admissibility of scientific evidence, achievable via a burden of proof, would encourage more direct accountability of scientists. It is they who would have the obligation of explaining to the court which factors should be used in evaluating the reliability of the evidence. It is not, as Rehnquist CJ feared in his dissenting opinion in *Daubert*, judges who should be responsible for such a task. The tools at experts' disposal should be variable, for, as acknowledged in *Daubert*, it is a

[48] Kassin *et al.*, ' "General Acceptance" of Psychological Research', n. 13 above.

[49] A. D. Tarlock, 'The Futile Search for Environment Laws based on "Good Science" ' (1996) 1 Internat. J Biosciences and the Law 9.

question of 'fit' and 'scientific validity for one purpose is not necessarily scientific validity for other, unrelated purposes'.[50]

This proposal for enhancing the burden of proof has two immediate attractions. First, it retains the law's control of the proof process by linking admissibility firmly to an established legal concept; and secondly, it confronts squarely the underlying distrust of certain sciences because it imposes a substantial additional hurdle for experts to overcome. The proposal would also increase the role of the judge who would inevitably be assigned the sort of gate-keeping role envisaged in *Daubert*. Although this new role has potential dangers, such as those alluded to in the dissenting opinion, where it was also observed that judges should not be expected to become 'amateur scientists' in order to perform their task,[51] there are advantages. Specifically, it reinforces the supremacy of law by installing a judicial gate-keeping function using familiar concepts and leaving judges with the ultimate say. Moreover, experts will quickly appreciate that in order to succeed in having scientific testimony admitted they will have to articulate their theories in a manner that elucidates and illuminates, rather than obfuscates and confuses. I do not share Rehnquist CJ's pessimism as expressed in the dissenting opinion that, for example, judges will necessarily be flummoxed when faced with the concepts and language typical of scientific research such as falsifiability or statistical significance.[52] It should not be beyond the wit of expert witnesses to explain such concepts clearly, or of judges to comprehend them.

This consideration of burden of proof has offered a glimpse of a new framework for admissibility. The proposal requires further development in order to address other major issues not examined here such as the appropriate standard of proof in civil and criminal cases, the compatibility of the burden of proof (a concept designed primarily to deal with matters of fact) with the question of admissibility (a concept which is a mixture of fact and law), and the continuing function of the jury as the trier of fact. However, this brief introduction is intended to show why such development could be valuable and fruitful.

---

[50] *Daubert*, n. 24 above at 482.
[51] *Ibid.* at 487.
[52] *Ibid.*

CORROBORATION

A second rule capable of regulating expert testimony is corroboration. It requires only a brief consideration because its application within the law of evidence is quite straightforward. Within the United Kingdom the rule of corroboration differs as between the jurisdictions of England and Scotland. It remains an important rule in Scotland, particularly in criminal matters where essential facts must still be corroborated.[53] In England the requirement for corroboration of essential facts in criminal cases has been much eroded, and there is now no general requirement for corroboration. Some lawyers have claimed that certain of the more notorious wrongful convictions in England arising through misuse of forensic science (for example, the Birmingham Six, the Maguire Seven, the Guildford Four) would not have occurred had the Scots rule of corroboration operated in these cases.[54]

In short, had the forensic evidence in those cases required corroboration from a separate and independent source for the essential facts in the cases to have been proved, then there would have been insufficient evidence for convictions.

Until recently English law recognized a number of well-established categories tempering the general rule that evidence from a single source is sufficient to secure a conviction. For example, at common law, in cases involving rape complainants or accomplices testifying for the prosecution, a judge was required to give the jury a warning about the dangers of convicting on uncorroborated evidence. While that requirement was removed by section 32 of the Criminal Justice and Public Order Act 1994, the judge retains a discretion to give such a warning if appropriate. There are also several statutory provisions where corroboration is required, such as in cases of perjury and criminal attempts. The principle of corroboration is therefore not unknown to English law and could be activated in relation to expert evidence. The corroboration would need to take the form of evidence from another, independent, source, that is, not simply more scientific evidence, as the quantity of available scientific data in support of the testifying

---

[53] There were some narrow exceptions to that rule introduced by the Criminal Procedure (Scotland) Act 1995.
[54] Jones, *Expert Witnesses*, n. 42 above.

expert would already be a factor in assessing the reliability of that expert testimony. Corroboration is an active safeguard against miscarriages of justice and has a distinctive contribution to make to admissibility of scientific evidence.

Conclusion

In its quest for 'truth' the judicial process seeks the impossible—the quest for certainty. This is an unattainable and ultimately pointless endeavour for, as some scientists have acknowledged, 'to keep silent until our understanding is perfect is to keep silent forever'.[55] Some judges in the United States have articulated a similar view. In *Daubert*, for instance, Blackman J agreed that 'it would be unreasonable to conclude that the subject of scientific testimony must be "known" to a certainty; arguably, there are no certainties in science'.[56] To insist on certainty is to deny the most recent knowledge an audience. The present rule in the United Kingdom governing the admissibility of expert scientific evidence with its emphasis on helpfulness is both misleading and unnecessarily restrictive. Despite repeated criticisms of the *Turner* rule, no reform is imminent. It is time to initiate change. We could do so by recognizing that there is little practical difference between the criteria of helpfulness and reliability. Instead it is an issue of power and status that differentiates them. By expressly endorsing reliability as a criterion we would encourage a more transparent and progressive debate that could be the genesis of a new framework for admissibility of science. This essay has outlined one such framework, suggesting how familiar legal concepts might be harnessed to provide a workable set of principles on which to admit scientific evidence whilst safeguarding against junk science. Such a framework is long overdue.

[55] P. C. Ellsworth, 'To Tell What we Know or Wait for Godot?' (1991) 15 Law and Human Behavior 77.
[56] *Daubert*, n. 24 above at 481.

EXPERT EVIDENCE IN CANADIAN CRIMINAL PROCEEDINGS

More Lessons from North America

Paul Roberts

1. Introduction: North American Comparisons

In an earlier article I suggested that English lawyers and law reformers might have something to learn from recent developments in United States law and practice regulating the admissibility of expert evidence.[1] The task of constructing evidential standards to meet 'the new challenges of scientific evidence'[2] seems well under way in America after the United States Supreme Court's landmark decision in *Daubert* v. *Merrell Dow Pharmaceuticals Inc.*[3] in 1993. *Daubert* and the voluminous academic commentary[4] which it spawned have propelled the American debate about the admissibility of expert evidence, and

---

[1] P. Roberts, 'The Admissibility of Expert Evidence: Lessons from America' (1996) 4 Expert Evid. 93.

[2] Cf. Note, 'Confronting the New Challenges of Scientific Evidence' (1995) 108 Harvard LR 1481.

[3] 113 S. Ct. 2786 (1993); 125 L. Ed. (2d) 469 (1993).

[4] The following articles provide useful introductions to this burgeoning literature: R. J. Allen, 'Expertise and the *Daubert* Decision' (1994) 84 J. Crim. Law and Criminology 1157; B. Black, F. J. Ayala and C. Saffran-Brinks, 'Science and the Law in the Wake of *Daubert*: A New Search for Scientific Knowledge' (1994) 72 Texas LR 715; D. L. Faigman, E. Porter and M. J. Saks, 'Check Your Crystal Ball at the Courthouse Door, Please: Exploring the Past, Understanding the Present, and Worrying about the Future of Scientific Evidence' (1994) 15 Cardozo LR 1799; D. E. Bernstein, 'The Admissibility of Scientific Evidence After *Daubert* v. *Merrell Dow Pharmaceuticals, Inc.*' (1994) 15 Cardozo LR 2139.

related issues such as judicial education and scientific literacy,[5] to a prominence which contrasts starkly with the intermittent and typically cursory attention afforded to these issues in England and Wales. And progress has been made. Although *Daubert* emphatically did *not* resolve all the difficulties associated with scientific evidence at a stroke,[6] it represents a significant contribution to a concerted and committed search for practical solutions. In England and Wales, meanwhile, these issues are rarely the subject of searching scrutiny or sustained analysis,[7] and that must change if we want to make the most of science in legal proceedings.

This essay aims to energize the debate about expert witness testimony in England and Wales through a comparative analysis of the admissibility of scientific evidence[8] in Canadian criminal cases. An indirect approach to our topic partly reflects the paucity of illuminating local decisions, for, as the leading English treatise on the law of evidence observes, almost apologetically,

The law relating to evidence of opinion is much less developed in the United Kingdom than it is in North America where as long ago as 1898, Thayer said, 'the quantity of decisions on the subject is most unreasonably

---

[5] See, e.g., S. Jasanoff, 'What Judges Should Know about the Sociology of Science' (1993) 77 Judicature 77; Federal Judicial Center, *Reference Manual on Scientific Evidence* (Federal Judicial Center, 1994); L. Walker and J. Monahan, '*Daubert* and the *Reference Manual*: An Essay on the Future of Science in Law' (1996) 82 Virginia LR 837.

[6] Some outstanding questions are discussed by J. T. Richardson, G. P. Ginsburg, S. Gatowski and S. A. Dobbin, 'The Problems of Applying *Daubert* to Psychological Syndrome Evidence' (1995) 79 Judicature 10; D. E. Bernstein, 'The Science of Forensic Psychiatry and Psychology' (1995) 2 Psychiatry, Psychology and Law 75; G. Edmond and D. Mercer, 'Keeping "Junk" History, Philosophy and Sociology of Science Out of the Court-room: Problems with the Reception of *Daubert* v. *Merrell Dow Pharmaceuticals Inc*' (1997) 20 Univ. New South Wales LJ 48.

[7] Notable exceptions include T. Hodgkinson, *Expert Evidence: Law and Practice* (London, 1990); JUSTICE (Chair: Judge Christopher Oddie), *Science and the Administration of Justice* (London, 1991). The 1993 Royal Commission on Criminal Justice devoted a whole chapter of its report to 'Forensic Science and Other Expert Evidence', but did not link this discussion to rules of admissibility; see Royal Commission on Criminal Justice, *Report,* (Cm. 2263, 1993), ch. 9. For an historical account of the role of expert witnesses in criminal proceedings in England and Wales, see C. A. G. Jones, *Expert Witnesses: Science, Medicine and the Practice of Law* (Oxford, 1994), chs. 2–5.

[8] In this essay I will use the terms 'expert evidence', 'scientific evidence' and 'expert witness testimony' interchangeably. Although they are not synonymous, nothing turns on the differences between them for the purposes of this essay.

swollen'. . . . In England, the reported decisions on the subject are comparatively few, and it is difficult to believe that the exclusionary rule gives rise to very much trouble in practice.[9]

So we will go west, where richer veins of jurisprudence may be found. But rather than looking to the United States, where the admissibility of expert evidence is primarily governed by statute[10] (as interpreted in *Daubert*) and the home-grown *Frye* rule,[11] the ideal site for our comparative exploration lies further north. Canada has imbibed much of its legal culture from the wellsprings of English common law, and doctrinal confluence is still particularly marked in the modern law of evidence. Canadian judges can be seen to draw upon the common stock of common-law rules and concepts in their approaches to expert witness testimony. Indeed, the leading English case, *Turner*,[12] is also frequently cited as an authority on the admissibility of expert evidence in Canada. Canadian appellate courts' recent attempts to get to grips with some of the most contemporary and intractable features of expert witness testimony are therefore worthy of our attention, not only for their intrinsic interest or because there are few English authorities, but more particularly because the Canadian experience bears directly on the law, and its development and reform, in England and Wales.

The general affinities between English and Canadian approaches to expert evidence are the subject of further elaboration in Section 2 of this essay. More detailed comparisons will be drawn in the sections that follow.

One final prefatory remark: this essay is concerned only with the admissibility of expert evidence in *criminal* proceedings, but that focus is not meant to imply that expert witness testimony in civil cases is uninteresting or unimportant. It simply reflects the

---

[9] C. Tapper, *Cross and Tapper on Evidence* (8th edn, London, 1995), 543 (footnote omitted). I agree with the first clause of the last sentence, but I fear that its second clause may be part of the problem.

[10] Federal Rule of Evidence 702 provides that: 'If scientific, technical, or other specialized knowledge will assist the trier of fact to understand the evidence or to determine a fact in issue, a witness qualified as an expert by knowledge, skill, experience, training or education, may testify thereto in the form of an opinion or otherwise.'

[11] *Frye* v. *United States* 293 F. 1013, 54 App. D.C. 46 (D.C. Cir. 1923). See P. C. Giannelli, 'The Admissibility of Novel Scientific Evidence: *Frye* v. *United States*, a Half-Century Later' (1980) 80 Columbia LR 1197.

[12] *R.* v. *Turner* [1975] 1 QB 834 (CA).

fact that the values and objectives of civil litigation, and the proper priorities between them, are very different from those which structure and animate criminal proceedings. To speak of an undifferentiated procedural law regulating both civil and criminal cases too often obscures more than it reveals.[13] It is, as Damaska has recently reminded us,[14] a peculiarity of common-law thought unknown to the Continental/civilian legal tradition.

2. The Structural Similarity of Admissibility Regimes in Canada and England

The Canadian rule governing the admissibility of expert evidence was succinctly stated by Sopinka J, delivering the judgment of the Supreme Court of Canada in *Mohan*:

Admission of expert evidence depends on the application of the following criteria:
  (a) relevance;
  (b) necessity in assisting the trier of fact;
  (c) the absence of any exclusionary rule;
  (d) a properly qualified expert.[15]

The individual components of this four-part test will be familiar to English common lawyers. Criteria (a) and (c), relevance and the absence of general exclusionary rules, form the backbone of the evidentiary skeleton of legal rules and principles in common-law systems, including England and Wales. 'Relevance' is a matter of logic and common-sense experience of the world and, generally speaking, evidence which is relevant to a fact in issue in the proceedings is admissible unless it falls foul of an applicable exclusionary rule. Expert qualification, the Canadian Supreme Court's criterion (d), is also an essential pre-condition of the admissibility of expert evidence in English law. In fact, expert qualification is essentially a function of relevance. The bogus testimony of a charlatan contributes nothing worthwhile to the proceedings, and as evidence

---

[13] The point is well made by A. A. S. Zuckerman, *The Principles of Criminal Evidence* (Oxford, 1989), ch. 1.

[14] M. R. Damaska, *Evidence Law Adrift* (New Haven, 1997), 110–13. For a radically different way of conceptualizing the Law of Evidence as a coherent subject of study, see W. Twining, *Rethinking Evidence: Exploratory Essays* (Evanston, Ill., 1994), 203–11 & ch. 11.

[15] *R. v. Mohan* (1994) 114 DLR (4th) 419 (SCC), at 427.

of neither truth nor falsehood it is, literally, irrelevant. If (d) is resolved into (a) we come very close to the structure of admissibility rules which (I contend)[16] governs the reception of expert evidence in England and Wales. That is to say, admissible expert evidence must:

(1) be relevant to a fact in issue;
(2) have greater probative value than (potential) prejudicial effect ('PV/PE'); and
(3) satisfy other generally applicable exclusionary rules of evidence, such as the rule against hearsay and the rules pertaining to character evidence.

In *Mohan* Sopinka J expressly identified the PV/PE exclusionary standard and distinguished it from the relevance inquiry with which it sometimes, improperly, becomes entangled:

> Although *prima facie* admissible if so related to a fact in issue that it tends to establish it, that does not end the inquiry. This merely determines the logical relevance of the evidence. Other considerations enter into the decision as to admissibility. This further inquiry may be described as a cost benefit analysis . . . Cost in this context is not used in its traditional economic sense but rather in terms of its impact on the trial process. Evidence that is otherwise logically relevant may be excluded on this basis, if its probative value is overborne by its prejudicial effect, if it involves an inordinate amount of time which is not commensurate with its value or if it is misleading in the sense that its effect on the trier of fact, particularly a jury, is out of proportion to its reliability. While frequently considered as an aspect of legal relevance, the exclusion of logically relevant evidence on these grounds is more properly regarded as a general exclusionary rule.[17]

This brings us to the most distinctive—and problematic—feature of the admissibility test laid down in *Mohan*, criterion (b): necessity in assisting the trier of fact.

---

[16] This formulation is controversial, but its defence must await another occasion.

[17] *Mohan*, n. 15 above at 427–8. Cf. US Federal Rules of Evidence, Rule 401: ' "Relevant evidence" means evidence having any tendency to make the existence of any fact that is of consequence to the determination of the action more probable or less probable than it would be without the evidence'. Lawyers sometimes refer to this definition of relevance as '*logical* relevance' (in contradistinction to '*legal* relevance'). On this question of definition I share Sopinka J's preference, which is also propounded by Thayer against Stephen, Wigmore and Cross. See further A. L.-T. Choo, 'The Notion of Relevance and Defence Evidence' [1993] Crim. LR 114; Tapper, *Evidence*, n. 9 above at 56–67; R. J. Delisle, *Evidence: Principles and Problems* (3rd edn, Toronto, 1993), at 23–31.

A Single Admissibility Standard: Helpfulness or Necessity?

Canadian courts have tried, without conspicuous success, to formulate a general criterion of admissibility which encapsulates the essential rationale for receiving expert witness testimony. The choice, as Canadian law presents it, is between 'helpfulness' and 'necessity'. Support for the former can be found in Dickson J's influential statement of the function of expert witnesses, made in delivering the Supreme Court's judgment in *Abbey*:

An expert's function is precisely this: to provide the judge and jury with a ready-made inference which the judge and jury, due to the technical nature of the facts, are unable to formulate. 'An expert's opinion is admissible to furnish the Court with scientific information which is likely to be outside the experience and knowledge of a judge or jury. If on the proven facts a judge or jury can form their own conclusions without help, then the opinion of the expert is unnecessary': (*R. v. Turner* (1974) 60 Cr. App. R. 80 at p. 83, *per* Lawton LJ).[18]

The idea of expert evidence supplying the jury with a ready-made inference of scientific fact seems to cast the expert in the role of juror's technical adviser or assistant, and the quotation from *Turner*, with its explicit reference to the jury's need for help, serves to reinforce a 'helpfulness' interpretation of the expert's function. 'It has been said', observes a Canadian Evidence Law text, 'that the hallmark of admissibility simply should be whether the experts' testimony would be helpful to the tribunal.'[19] However, in its more recent *Mohan* judgment the Supreme Court rejected 'helpfulness' as an accurate, practical translation of the basic admissibility standard. Having quoted the above passage from *Abbey*, Sopinka J explained his preference for a 'necessity' test of admissibility:

The word 'helpful' is not quite appropriate and sets too low a standard. However, I would not judge necessity by too strict a standard. What is required is that the opinion be necessary in the sense that it provide information 'which is likely to be outside the experience and knowledge of a

---

[18] *R. v. Abbey* (1982) 68 CCC (2d) 394 (SCC), at 409.
[19] J. Sopinka, S. N. Lederman and A. W. Bryant, *The Law of Evidence in Canada* (Toronto, 1992), 534. For a recent example, see *R. v. Lafferty* (1993) 80 CCC (3d) 150 (Northwest Territories Supreme Court): 'scientific evidence is put to the same test as other expert evidence, that being *indicia* of relevancy and helpfulness' (159).

judge or jury': as quoted by Dickson J in *R. v. Abbey, supra*. As stated by Dickson J, the evidence must be necessary to enable the trier of fact to appreciate the matters in issue due to their technical nature.[20]

Sopinka J elaborated on these remarks later in his judgment, when discussing the admissibility of novel scientific evidence:

[E]xpert evidence which advances a novel scientific theory or technique is subjected to special scrutiny to determine whether it meets a basic threshold of reliability and whether it is *essential* in the sense that the trier of fact will be unable to come to a satisfactory conclusion without the assistance of the expert.[21]

Yet the Supreme Court's endorsement of 'necessary' or 'essential' as the appropriate admissibility standard for expert evidence, and the supposed distinction between these concepts and 'helpfulness', remain perplexing. 'Necessary' and 'essential' are near-synonyms and surely imply an exacting standard. One might suppose there to be cases in which scientific evidence would be helpful to the jury, but not strictly essential or necessary to their deliberations (though it is difficult to imagine how one might attempt to calibrate something as elusive as the quality of (secret) jury decision-making with anything approaching the required degree of precision). If expert evidence would be *genuinely* helpful to the jury—that is, more help than hindrance *in the context of the proceedings* (PV > PE)—why not let the jury hear it? Perhaps this is the burden of Sopinka J's caution against judging necessity 'by too strict a standard'. It also bears observation that Lawton LJ, in the well-worn passage from *Turner* adopted in *Abbey*, apparently uses helpfulness and necessity interchangeably.

It seems fair to conclude that *Mohan* falls some way short of establishing the superiority of 'necessity' over 'helpfulness' as the key admissibility criterion for expert evidence. More fundamentally, however, it is, I suggest, an unhelpful and unnecessary diversion to frame the issue in terms of a choice between helpfulness and necessity. The challenge is to formulate a 'relevance-plus' admissibility standard which operationalizes the PV/PE test in a practical, informative way that trial judges can understand and

---

[20]   *Mohan*, n. 15 above at 429.
[21]   *Ibid.*, at 431 (emphasis added).

apply. Rather than looking for some all-encompassing word or phrase which communicates the fully articulated rule in a blinding flash of comprehension, courts of appeal might fare better by trying to spell out in greater detail the types of consideration to which tribunals of first instance should have regard when expert evidence is tendered at trial. This was the approach adopted by the US Supreme Court in *Daubert*, and in first instance Canadian decisions such as *Johnston*[22] and *Melaragni*.[23] On the other hand, it is essential to recognize that there are definite, if ill-defined, limits to how refined or conclusive these standards can usefully become. The admission of expert evidence in criminal cases is never simply a function of scientific validity or expert witnesses' qualifications, because its reception at trial is always partly determined by *the purpose(s)* for which the evidence is tendered and *the use(s)* to which it will or might be put. The discussion in this essay will emphasize the contextual factors influencing judicial approaches to expert evidence in particular cases, factors which tend to be overlooked or downplayed whenever evidentiary standards are discussed in the abstract.

In practice, expert witness testimony is often subject to the composite effect of two or more exclusionary rules of evidence. Moreover, the contextual nature of relevance implies that judicial determinations of (in)admissibility must remain provisional for the duration of the trial, subject to revision in the light of further evidential developments. Important issues of principle are also at stake. Decisions regarding the admissibility of expert evidence reflect the objectives and values of criminal proceedings, including perhaps the most fundamental procedural question of all, namely the extent to which truth-finding should be constrained by independent principles of political morality in the administration of criminal justice. These observations serve to indicate that the challenges posed by expert evidence in criminal trials are complex and multi-faceted. Solutions designed to meet these challenges must consequently be flexible and case-sensitive. We are unlikely to find

---

[22] R. v. *Johnston* (1992) 69 CCC (3d) 395 (Ontario Court (Gen. Div.)).

[23] R. v. *Melaragni* (1992) 73 CCC (3d) 348 (Ontario Court (Gen. Div.)). See, further, D. E. Bernstein, 'Junk Science in the United States and the Commonwealth' (1996) 21 Yale J Internat. Law 123, at 142–4; I. Freckelton, 'Science and the Legal Culture' (1993) 2 Expert Evid. 107, at 111.

some 'grand test'[24] or single set of criteria which can be applied more or less mechanically to every type of scientific evidence in every conceivable trial scenario. Instead, an element of judicial 'discretion' (judgement) to extend the general framework of rules and principles to particular types of evidence and particular types of cases is probably inevitable, and perhaps desirable.

These broader connections, issues and concerns will become more explicit in the following sections. We begin in Section 3 with a detailed illustration of the way in which the relevance and PV/PE standards may be applied to determine the admissibility of expert witness testimony in particular cases. Further sections addressing 'social framework evidence' (Section 4), hearsay (Section 5) and expert evidence of witness credibility (Section 6) will consolidate and develop this introduction to the Canadian courts' emerging jurisprudence on the admissibility of expert evidence.

3. Proof, Prejudice and Criminal Justice

The approach to expert evidence advocated by the Supreme Court of Canada in *Mohan*, requiring a judge (1) to identify the probative value of the evidence; (2) to assess its potential for prejudice; and then (3) to determine the balance between prejudice and weight, is well illustrated by a recent decision of the Court of Appeal for Ontario. In *Pascoe*[25] the accused was charged with sexual interference and sexual assault in relation to two boys, aged 8 and 11. On one occasion Pascoe had placed his hand on the younger boy's back and upper thigh for a matter of seconds. On other occasions he had asked the older boy to sit closer to him, lifted him up by the waist for a few seconds, and invited him to sit on his knee, an invitation which the boy declined. The boys were fully clothed on every occasion alleged to constitute an

---

[24] Bernstein, 'Junk Science', n. 23 above, at 146. I agree with Bernstein (and argue in this essay) that the Canadian courts' approach to scientific evidence sometimes leaves much to be desired. However, Bernstein's account of the 'chaos' (145) of Canadian law and his frustration with the courts' application of the relevance and PV/PE standards to the facts of particular cases—'deciding the admissibility of scientific evidence on a case-by-case basis depending on what [the Supreme Court] sees as the equities of the situation' (148)—seem to me to overlook the complexity of the issues and to underestimate the potential of this approach to address the validity of scientific evidence, and much else besides.

[25] *R. v. Pascoe* (1997) 32 OR (3d) 37 (Ont. CA).

assault; and, finally, any suspicions aroused by a middle-aged man forming friendships with young boys might in Pascoe's case have been dispelled by the fact that, according to a forensic psychologist who had examined him some years before, Pascoe was 'an inadequate personality . . . [with] below average intelligence and very poor social comprehension.'[26] However, Mr Pascoe was also a diagnosed homosexual paedophile with a history of sex crimes against young boys and repeat participation in sex-offender treatment programmes. Predictably, the prosecution sought to adduce expert psychiatric and psychological evidence of Pascoe's proclivities to establish a sexual motive for his conduct towards the boys. After hearing arguments on the *voir dire*, the trial judge (McIsaac J) ruled the evidence admissible, with the proviso that no specific mention be made of the defendant's criminal record. The prosecution called two psychiatrists at trial who testified to Pascoe's homosexual paedophilia, and he was duly convicted of one count of sexual interference with the 11-year-old boy, but acquitted of four related charges. Pascoe then launched a successful appeal against his conviction, based on the prosecution's use of expert evidence.

(A) EXTRANEOUS MISCONDUCT EVIDENCE

The admissibility of the expert evidence tendered by the prosecution in *Pascoe* was complicated by the fact that it constituted general evidence of the defendant's bad character, testimony which runs up against the exclusionary rule that 'mere' propensity evidence is inadmissible if its only purpose is to show, by reference to prior misconduct, that the defendant is 'the type of person' who would be likely to commit the offences charged. (This is the rule excluding extraneous evidence of the defendant's misconduct, or the 'similar facts' rule.) Expert evidence of a defendant's disposition had previously been considered by the Canadian Supreme Court in *Morin*,[27] where it was established that the trial judge should adopt the same approach towards prosecution evidence of the accused's bad character regardless of

---

[26] R. v. *Pascoe* (1997) 32 OR (3d) 37 (Ont. CA) at 43.
[27] R. v. *Morin* [1988] 2 SCR 345 (SCC).

its source or the status of the witness who testifies to it. The Supreme Court said:

It is illogical to treat evidence tending to show the accused's propensity to commit the crime differently because such propensity is introduced by expert evidence rather than by means of past similar conduct. If in the latter case the evidence is admitted provided its probative value exceeds its prejudicial effect, then the same test of admissibility should apply in the former case. Accordingly, when the prosecution tenders expert psychiatric evidence, the trial judge must determine whether it is relevant to an issue in the case apart from its tendency to show propensity. If it is relevant to another issue (e.g. identity), it must then be determined whether its probative value on that other issue outweighs its prejudicial effect on the propensity question.[28]

This approach was faithfully followed in *Pascoe* by Rosenberg JA, delivering the judgment of the Ontario Court of Appeal:

[T]he issues that the trial judge needed to resolve before admitting this evidence were as follows:
1. Was the evidence relevant to an issue other than mere propensity?
2. What is the probative value of the evidence in proving an issue other than propensity?
3. What is the prejudicial effect of the evidence?
4. Does the probative value of the evidence outweigh its prejudicial effect?[29]

Rosenberg JA agreed with the trial judge that the prosecution's psychiatric evidence could *in principle* be relevant to an issue other than mere propensity if it established the accused's membership of a class of persons—homosexual paedophiles—with a distinctive psychology or physiology predictive of their behaviour. If, for example, it could be said that when a homosexual paedophile touches a young boy's upper thigh he always, or nearly always, has a sexual motive, that would go to an issue in the case—intent— over and above mere propensity, and thus satisfy issue (1).[30] But this was as far as the Ontario Court of Appeal was prepared to travel along the road of McIsaac J's reasoning. For (the Court

---

[28] *Ibid.*, at 370.
[29] *Pascoe*, n. 25 above at 52.
[30] The Supreme Court's mode of reasoning in *Morin* follows the 'categories' approach to similar fact evidence, attributable to Lord Herschell LC's classic speech in *Makin* v. *Attorney-General for New South Wales* [1894] AC 57 (PC). More recently this approach to propensity evidence has, I think rightly, fallen out of favour with the courts: a straightforward PV/PE evaluation, which recognizes

held), in attempting to apply the PV/PE test to the prosecution's expert evidence, the trial judge had fallen into reversible error.

(B) PROBATIVE VALUE

McIsaac J's difficulties began with the 'necessity' test for the admission of expert evidence which, we saw above, was formulated by the Supreme Court in *Mohan*. McIsaac J apparently thought that the prosecution's psychiatric evidence satisfied the necessity test because without it the charges against Pascoe could never have been proved to the criminal standard of proof beyond reasonable doubt! Of course, this is not at all what the Supreme Court had in mind, as Rosenberg JA was quick to observe:

[W]hether or not the evidence was 'necessary' in the sense of being vital to the prosecution's case was not the sole consideration on the question of probative value. Obviously, if the evidence was unnecessary because the Crown could prove the case through other less prejudicial means then the evidence should be excluded if for no other reason than to avoid undue expenditure of time and confusion of issues. . . . The question was not whether the prosecution needed the evidence but the degree to which the evidence would prove the fact in issue for which it was tendered.[31]

McIsaac J had clearly failed to devote sufficiently careful attention to the true probative value of the expert evidence tendered by the prosecution. The Ontario Court of Appeal found, on closer inspection, that the psychiatrists' evidence at trial and on the *voir dire* 'was largely nothing more than evidence of propensity and expression of personal opinion rather than a careful examination of the particular characteristics of this abnormal group'.[32] Neither of the two psychiatrists who testified at trial nor the forensic psychologist who appeared on the *voir dire* had examined Pascoe in the previous five years. Consequently, none of them could tell

that evidence of the accused's disposition may be received if it has sufficient probative value, is now preferred both in Canada and in England and Wales; see, respectively, *R.* v. *B (CR)* (1990) 76 CR (3d) 1 (SCC); *DPP* v. *P* [1991] 2 AC 447 (HL). However, the point may be one more of form than substance, since the categories approach can reach the same result as the PV/PE test by equating '*mere* propensity' evidence with that which is of insufficient probative value to be admitted. Propensity evidence with very great probative value, on the other hand, can be said to go to a specific issue in the trial, such as identity or intent. This seems to have been the reasoning adopted by the Ontario Court of Appeal in *Pascoe*, applying *Morin*.

[31]   *Pascoe*, n. 25 above at 53.   [32] *Ibid.*

the court precisely what effect Pascoe's medication would be having on his sex drive or even, indeed, whether he was actually taking the drugs prescribed for him at the material times. More significantly still, these expert witnesses did not provide the jury with a psychiatric profile of homosexual paedophiles and their behavioural characteristics.[33] Instead, their evidence seemed chiefly to consist of speculations about the defendant's intentions, based on what could be inferred about his personality from his treatment history and criminal record. Thus, Dr McDonald told the court that Pascoe's medical file identified him as a 'stereotypical homosexual paedophile'. When asked what would have been going through the defendant's mind when he was in contact with the complainants, Dr McDonald replied:

Of course I am not a mind reader and the only person who knows for sure what is going on in a situation like that is the person who is doing it. . . . When you have, however, an overwhelming past history of sexual approaches to young boys, given that context, it would appear obvious that this is something that is motivated by sexual interest.[34]

Dr Dickie, for his part, thought that Pascoe could have been motivated by numerous factors, of which libido would probably be one:

I think that this is a limited lonely individual whose socialization is at some level of a child and I can see that there would be a need for friendship and companionship and numerous other motivators, I suppose, but over the extended period of time . . . I would think that there is a significant possibility that there was a sexual intent or motive. . . . [T]his is a lonely disabled individual who may well have a need for friendship and companionship whose alternatives in this sphere are limited, nevertheless I really think that to discount totally any sexual intent . . . would be somewhat naive.[35]

---

[33] Note that, since such evidence was never actually presented in this case, *Pascoe* provides no authority on the question whether expert evidence of propensity, in the form of a psychiatric or psychological profile, could be valid and sufficiently reliable to be admitted in a criminal trial. See, generally, D. C. Ormerod, 'The Evidential Implications of Psychological Profiling' [1996] Crim. LR 863; J. McEwan, ' "Similar Fact" Evidence and Psychology: Personality and Guilt' (1994) 3 Expert Evid. 113; K. J. Mair, 'Can a Profile Prove a Sex Offender Guilty?' (1995) 3 Expert Evid. 139; J. McEwan, 'Law Commission Dodges the Nettles in Consultation Paper No. 141' [1997] Crim. LR 93, at 95–7.

[34] *Pascoe*, n. 25 above at 45.   [35] *Ibid.*, at 46.

The Ontario Court of Appeal was less favourably impressed by this testimony than McIsaac J at first instance must have been. It judged the psychiatrists' evidence to have minimal probative value, notwithstanding the impressive qualifications and professional standing of the experts themselves:

Neither witness gave any evidence as to the characteristics of a homosexual paedophile. Nor did the witnesses provide any real basis for their opinion that the appellant had or might have had a sexual purpose in touching the complainants in this case, beyond the fact that he had been diagnosed as a homosexual paedophile over the last 20 years. . . . Neither expert defined for the judge the nature of this disorder or its characteristics. It was not enough in this case to show that the appellant has been reliably placed within the category of homosexual paedophile. There had to be some evidence as to the behavioural profile of this group or of the appellant as a member of that group from which the jury would then be able to make its own judgment as to the appellant's purpose at the time of the touching incidents.[36]

(C) PREJUDICIAL EFFECT

In addition to serious deficiencies in McIsaac J's analysis of the probative value side of the PV/PE calculus, the appellate court also found fault with his attention to the potential for prejudice in the psychiatrists' evidence.

McIsaac J did advert to the fact that the prosecution's expert evidence went to an 'ultimate issue'—in fact the *only* live issue—in the trial, the question of the defendant's intention (*mens rea*) accompanying acts which he fully admitted, but claimed were innocent. An old common-law doctrine of dubious provenance and uncertain rationale supposedly prohibited expert witnesses from stating an opinion on the central issues in the case, but nowadays the Canadian courts,[37] like the English Court of Appeal,[38] have dispensed with a formal rule mechanically exclud-

---

[36] *Pascoe*, n. 25 above at 54–5.

[37] '[I]t has long been accepted that expert evidence on matters of fact should not be excluded simply because it suggests answers to issues which are at the core of the dispute before the court.' *Burns* [1994] 1 SCR 656 (SCC), *per* McLachlin J at 666. 'Expert testimony is admissible even if it relates directly to the ultimate question which the trier of fact must answer.' *R. v. R (D)* (1996) 136 DLR (4th) 525 (SCC), *per* Major J at 540.

[38] *R. v. Stockwell* (1993) 97 Cr App R 260 (CA).

ing expert evidence on an ultimate issue. However, although the ultimate issue *rule* may be dead and buried, the concerns which inspired the courts to invent it are still very much alive. Fearing that jurors will too easily defer to an expert's opinion or, worse, relinquish their fact-finding responsibility altogether by accepting experts' conclusions uncritically, the judges remain vigilant to prevent experts usurping the role of the jury as fact-finder in criminal trials. In other words, the concerns which formerly supplied the best rationale for the ultimate issue rule have, with that rule's demise, become incorporated into the PV/PE ('necessity') test for the admission of expert evidence. Thus, in *Mohan* Sopinka J said,

[T]he criteria of relevance and necessity are applied strictly, on occasion, to exclude expert evidence as to an ultimate issue. . . . The closer the evidence approaches an opinion on an ultimate issue, the stricter the application of this principle.[39]

In *Pascoe* McIsaac J acknowledged the risk that, in so far as expert evidence constituted the whole of the prosecution's case on the crucial issue of intent, jurors might be tempted to accept it as an infallible surrogate for their own determination of what was 'going through the defendant's mind' at the material times. The trial judge took the view that this risk could be neutralized by the traditional common-law techniques of cross-examination and a stiff judicial warning to the jury, but the Ontario Court of Appeal, building on its finding of limited probative value, was less sanguine:

In this case, the psychiatrists were asked to give an opinion on the ultimate and only live issue in the case, the appellant's purpose in touching the complainants. As Sopinka J pointed out in *Mohan* this called for a very strict scrutiny of the expert evidence to ensure that it could be presented in a manner that would be of assistance to the jury and that it met the basic threshold of reliability. Left as it was, both experts, but particularly Dr McDonald, appear to be expressing nothing more than personal opinions, or to use Dr McDonald's term, educated guesses as to what was going through the appellant's mind at the time.[40]

The appeal court also discussed another source of prejudice which, it was said, ought to have figured more prominently in

[39] *Mohan*, n. 15 above at 430, 431.
[40] *Pascoe*, n. 25 above at 55.

McIsaac J's reasoning. The general ban on propensity evidence is designed to shield the defendant from three types of procedural unfairness:[41] the jury might condemn the defendant on his record as a 'bad man' who deserves punishment, regardless of whether the current charges against him are proved; the jury might give disproportionate weight to evidence of the defendant's propensity or disposition, immediately jumping to the conclusion that 'if he's done it before, he *must have* done it again'; or jurors could become confused about the central issues to be decided at trial, mistakenly substituting a finding of fact on a collateral matter for their verdict in the case. Adducing psychiatric expert testimony to inform the jury that the defendant is a confirmed homosexual paedophile is liable to create all three types of prejudice, but especially the first two. The risks of prejudice were heightened in *Pascoe*, moreover, because the documentary information on which the psychiatrists based their opinions was never revealed to the jury (partly, let it be noted, due to McIsaac J's entirely proper concern to suppress Pascoe's criminal record). Jurors were therefore deprived of the principal means of questioning the factual basis of the experts' opinions. In the eyes of the Ontario Court of Appeal this all amounted to a damning catalogue of prejudice which easily outweighed the meagre probative value of the psychiatric evidence:

In this case the jury were presented with the fact that the appellant was a homosexual paedophile and that in the opinion of the experts, both of whom had impressive credentials, his purpose was a sexual one notwithstanding the ambiguous nature of the conduct. . . . There was an overwhelming danger that the jury would give the expert evidence more weight than it deserves and, in any event, simply defer to the expert opinions. . . . [T]he manner in which the evidence was led, without any foundation facts, completely deprived the jury of the means of evaluating the expert opinion and deprived the appellant of the opportunity to fairly challenge the strength of those opinions.[42]

To summarize: (1) general evidence of bad character is inadmissible unless it has enhanced probative value which outweighs its potential for prejudice; (2) in addition, expert testimony going to

---

[41] *Pascoe*, n. 25 above at 56. See Tapper, *Evidence*, n. 9 above, at 382–5; Zuckerman, *Criminal Evidence*, n. 13 above, ch. 12.
[42] *Pascoe*, n. 25 above at 57, 56.

an ultimate issue must have sufficient probative value to offset its special dangers; (3) the prosecution's psychiatric evidence in *Pascoe* fell far short of satisfying these admissibility standards, because (4) its probative value was extremely limited, consisting, as it did, only of common sense inferences from general observations which lay jurors could readily have drawn for themselves if they had been told about Pascoe's clinical history and criminal record; but (5) these are the very matters to which jurors' access is restricted by the rule stated in (1). In these circumstances, expert evidence becomes, by accident if not design, little more than a device to circumvent the similar facts rule, and McIsaac J ought to have rejected it.

(D) Expert Evidence and Criminal Justice

We have considered the *Pascoe* judgment at some length because it exemplifies the process of judicial reasoning by which the PV/PE standard may be developed and applied, in conjunction with other procedural rules, to determine the admissibility of expert evidence in particular cases. The decision to receive or reject expert witness testimony requires a detailed, contextual inquiry, but that does not disqualify commentators or appellate judges from saying something more informative on the subject than 'everything turns on the facts'. The *Pascoe* appeal highlights several key issues— judicial assessments of probative value, the significance of testimony on ultimate questions and the prejudicial effects of bad character evidence—which are recurrent features of criminal cases involving scientific evidence. Procedural law and practice incorporate numerous other evidentiary norms and standards which, in appropriate cases, may also influence the admissibility of expert testimony. It is the task of legal analysis, and the special responsibility of courts of appeal, to identify these intermediate principles, and to develop the lines of reasoning, which link the abstract formulae of relevance and PV/PE with the decision to admit or exclude expert witness testimony in particular cases. Our investigation of these arguments and standards continues in the next two sections, but before leaving *Pascoe* we should venture some brief remarks on the merits.

Someone might reasonably ask how the Ontario Court of Appeal's decision can be held up as an exemplar of judicial method, when it resulted in the exclusion of what many people would regard as compelling evidence of guilt. Surely (the objection continues), on a common-sense view of the world, wasn't psychiatric evidence of Pascoe's homosexual paedophilia as conclusive evidence of his guilt as anyone could want or need? The first step in responding to this challenge is to concede that Pascoe was probably guilty of the offence of which he was convicted (and for the avoidance of doubt, by 'guilty' I mean that he did the act with the requisite mental state constituting the crime). In fact he was probably fortunate to be acquitted of the other four charges against him, to say nothing of the many other occasions on which he had no doubt offended without detection or complaint. Pascoe, in other words, was probably as guilty as the vast majority of other defendants in criminal cases, most of whom are, likewise, guilty as charged. Common sense tells us, without the trouble and expense of holding a criminal trial, that 'there is no smoke without fire', that the police and prosecution can usually be trusted to do their jobs effectively, and that chronic recidivists will probably re-offend. The point is that common-law rules of criminal evidence and procedure are predicated, not on these suspicions or presuppositions of guilt, but on the establishment of proof; and these procedural rules, in turn, embody a conception of criminal justice which places a very high premium on the avoidance of wrongful convictions[43] and requires that people be punished only for what they did, not for who they are[44] or what they can be fitted up[45]

[43] The philosophical foundations of this commitment are explored by Ronald Dworkin, 'Principle, Policy, Procedure' in C. Tapper (ed.), *Crime, Proof and Punishment* (London, 1981), 193 (and reprinted in R. Dworkin, *A Matter of Principle* (Oxford, 1986), ch. 3).

[44] This is a crude and philosophically controversial way of expressing the distinction between conduct and character conceptions of criminal liability, but it serves to capture the essence of my argument for present purposes.

[45] I use this provocative-sounding idiom primarily in its technical-sociological sense, to draw attention to the social construction of legal guilt through the workings of the criminal process; although, of course, it sometimes applies in a literal sense, too. A lively historical introduction to theorizing 'crime as a verb' is provided by C. Sumner, *The Sociology of Deviance: An Obituary* (Milton Keynes, 1994), ch. 9. For modern examples of this perspective, see M. McConville, A. Sanders and R. Leng, *The Case for the Prosecution: Police Suspects and the Construction of Criminality* (London, 1991); A. Sanders, 'Constructing the Case for the Prosecution' (1987) 14 J Law and Society 229; and for an account of the socio-legal construction of scientific evidence, see P. Roberts, 'Science in the Criminal Process' (1994) 14 OJLS 469.

with. Whenever a court is satisfied with suspicion or surmise in place of proof of guilt, it betrays the ideals of criminal justice and turns due process of law into an empty, ritualized, hypocritical charade. The only alternative is to remain faithful to existing principles of criminal procedure which, regrettably but inevitably, often allow guilty people to escape their just deserts. This is our chosen model of criminal procedure, and the courts are duty-bound to uphold it (unless they are at liberty to change the model; a question which I will revisit in the final section of this essay). So the Ontario Court of Appeal was astute to settle for nothing less than proof of guilt in service of these higher ideals. The final lessons to be drawn from *Pascoe*, then, are that expert evidence has the potential to subvert procedural guarantees which embody fundamental precepts of criminal justice, and that judges must be vigilant to prevent their erosion.

4. Social Framework Evidence

Some of the most complex and intractable problems surrounding expert witness testimony have confronted the Canadian courts in the guise of 'social framework evidence'[46] presented by psychiatrists, psychologists, or other behavioural or social scientists. In the leading case of *Lavallee*,[47] for example, the Supreme Court was asked to determine the admissibility of expert psychiatric testimony concerning the behaviour of women in abusive relationships—'battered woman/wife syndrome' ('BWS') evidence. Lyn Lavallee killed her abusive partner by shooting him at close range in the back of the head during a party at their house. At her subsequent murder trial, the defence called a psychologist, Dr Shane, who testified that this killing was the desperate act of a terrorized woman who truly believed that she was herself about to be the victim of a fatal attack unless she acted promptly and decisively in

---

[46] L. Walker and J. Monahan, 'Social Frameworks: a New Use of Social Science in Law' (1987) 73 Virginia LR 559. Professors Walker and Monahan coined the term 'social frameworks' to refer to evidence in which 'general research results are used to construct a frame of reference or background context for deciding factual issues crucial to the resolution of a specific case' (559). They described social framework evidence as an application of ' "off the rack" research studies' (568), but this useful terminology can also be applied to any clinical diagnosis which draws on behavioural science research data. See R. P. Mosteller, 'Legal Doctrines Governing the Admissibility of Expert Testimony Concerning Social Framework Evidence' (1989) 52 Law and Contemporary Problems 85, at 109–12.

[47] *R. v. Lavallee* [1990] 1 S.C.R. 852 (SCC).

self-defence. The jury acquitted, but the prosecution successfully applied to the Manitoba Court of Appeal for a re-trial on the basis that the judge had failed to draw sufficient attention to the unproven (hearsay) status of many of the facts on which Dr Shane based his opinion. The Supreme Court reinstated the acquittal, however, and Wilson J[48] took some time to explain why Dr Shane's evidence was both relevant and 'necessary' in this case:

Expert evidence on the psychological effect of battering on wives and common law partners must, it seems to me, be both relevant and necessary in the context of the present case. How can the mental state of the appellant be appreciated without it? The average member of the public (or of the jury) can be forgiven for asking: Why would a woman put up with this kind of treatment? Why should she continue to live with such a man? How could she love a partner who beat her to the point of requiring hospitalization? We would expect the woman to pack her bags and go. Where is her self-respect? Why does she not cut loose and make a new life for herself? Such is the reaction of the average person confronted with the so-called 'battered wife syndrome'. We need help to understand it and help is available from trained professionals.[49]

Linking the findings of BWS research to the applicable law, Wilson J demonstrated the pertinence of expert testimony to several material aspects of Lavallee's defence, including the reasonableness of her fear of being assaulted by the deceased and the eligibility of other possible courses of action, such as leaving home or shouting for assistance. This type of social framework evidence might help the jury to appreciate the defendant's perception of the circumstances in which she felt driven to kill and, in addition, dispel widespread misconceptions about the predicament of women in abusive relationships. In summary, the Court concluded:

1. Expert testimony is admissible to assist the fact-finder in drawing inferences in areas where the expert has relevant knowledge or experience beyond that of the lay person.
2. It is difficult for the lay person to comprehend the battered wife syndrome. It is commonly thought that battered women are not really beaten as badly as they claim, otherwise they would have left the relationship. Alternatively, some believe that women enjoy being beaten, that they have a masochist strain in them. Each of these stereotypes

---

[48] Delivering the judgment of Dickson CJ and Lamer, Wilson, L'Heureux-Dubé, Gonthier and Cory JJ.
[49] *Lavallee*, n. 47 above at 871–872 (*per* Wilson J).

may adversely affect consideration of a battered woman's claim to have acted in self-defence in killing her mate.

3. Expert evidence can assist the jury in dispelling these myths.

4. Expert testimony relating to the ability of an accused to perceive danger from her mate may go to the issue of whether she 'reasonably apprehended' death or grievous bodily harm on a particular occasion.

5. Expert testimony pertaining to why an accused remained in the battering relationship may be relevant in assessing the nature and extent of the alleged abuse.

6. By providing an explanation as to why an accused did not flee when she perceived her life to be in danger, expert testimony may also assist the jury in assessing the reasonableness of her belief that killing her batterer was the only way to save her own life.[50]

Wilson J's *Lavallee* judgment is notable for its wisdom and justice. Commentators have welcomed the advent of a more liberal approach to the admissibility of social framework evidence as a contribution to a more humane criminal law,[51] and *Lavallee* certainly presents tactical advantages to lawyers defending women charged with killing their abusive partners.[52] Yet, whatever else might be said about it, the implications of *Lavallee* for the admissibility of expert evidence are troubling in some respects and uncertain in others.

(A) SCIENTIFIC VALIDITY

Scientific validity is our first concern, as it should be of any court considering the admissibility of novel forms of scientific evidence. According to Dr Lenore Walker, the pioneer and leading exponent of BWS research, spousal abuse typically follows a three-stage

---

[50] *Ibid.*, at 889–890.

[51] Plaudits for *Lavallee* are, however, hedged with concern that whilst BWS testimony may reduce the culpability and punishment of individual defendants, it simultaneously draws upon and reinforces stereotypical representations of women as weak, submissive, neurotic, abnormal, and irresponsible (in the sense of lacking capacity to be judged as a responsible adult, like children or the insane) which in the long run work to the detriment of all women in society. See, e.g., I. Grant, 'The "Syndromization" of Women's Experience' (1991) 25 Univ. British Columbia LR 51; K. O'Donovan, 'Law's Knowledge: The Judge, The Expert, The Battered Woman and Her Syndrome' (1993) 20 J Law and Society 427; M. Fox, 'Legal Responses to Battered Women Who Kill' in J. Bridgeman and S. Millns (eds.), *Law and Body Politics: Regulating the Female Body* (Aldershot, 1995).

[52] See D. Nicolson and R. Sanghvi, 'Battered Women and Provocation: The Implications of *R. v. Ahluwalia*' [1993] Crim. LR 728.

cycle incorporating a tension-building phase, a violent battering incident and a period of contrition in which the abusive partner seeks forgiveness and makes empty promises not to batter again. Women in these abusive relationships may, according to the theory, develop a coping strategy known as 'learned helplessness', which is an attempt to limit the extent of their victimization, but which simultaneously renders them psychologically incapable of breaking the cycle of violence. In *Lavallee* the Supreme Court accepted the basic tenets of Walker's thesis, as relayed to the court by Dr Shane, without scrutinizing its epistemological or methodological credentials, and it would appear that the theory behind BWS was never challenged directly at any stage of the proceedings. The Canadian Supreme Court seems to have placed implicit trust in BWS as a valid description of human behaviour. But, if the court had chosen to look, it would soon have seen that the Walker cycle is predicated on equivocal empirical data, whilst its theoretical coherence is threatened by a striking internal tension between the concept of 'learned helplessness' and the violent events which precipitate legal proceedings. Women who kill their abusive partners, in self-defence or otherwise, are not 'helpless' in any ordinary sense of the word.

Whether the shortcomings of BWS theory and research are serious enough to warrant its complete exclusion from the courtroom, or merely reduce its evidential weight, is not a question we need to pursue here.[53] The most surprising and disturbing feature of the Canadian Supreme Court's approach to BWS evidence in *Lavallee* is that the issue of scientific validity was never raised at all. Evidence based on bogus or unreliable science will usually be inadmissible, either because it is irrelevant to any issue in the proceedings or because its marginal probative value is outweighed by its prejudicial effect, and these are questions for the judge. A

---

[53] For critical assessments of BWS research see I. Leader-Elliott, 'Battered But Not Beaten: Women Who Kill in Self Defence' (1993) 15 Sydney LR 403 at 407 *et seq.*; Note (D. L. Faigman), 'The Battered Woman Syndrome and Self Defense: A Legal and Empirical Dissent' (1986) 72 Virginia LR 619; R. A. Schuller and N. Vidmar, 'Battered Woman Syndrome Evidence in the Court-room: A Review of the Literature' (1992) 16 Law and Human Behavior 273; I. Freckelton, 'Contemporary Comment: When Plight Makes Right—The Forensic Abuse Syndrome' (1994) 18 Crim. LJ 29 at 32–6; D. L. Faigman, 'To Have and Have Not: Assessing the Value of Social Science to the Law as Science and Policy' (1989) 38 Emory LJ 1005 at 1072–4.

court's failure to satisfy itself of the scientific validity of expert testimony amounts to an abdication of judicial responsibility for regulating the admission of evidence at trial. Judges must therefore scrutinize all expert evidence with an appropriately sceptical eye to ensure that it satisfies the basic admissibility standards, relevance and PV/PE. Social or behavioural science evidence is no different in this respect to evidence derived from the 'hard' physical sciences, as Faigman has argued:

Laypersons, as much as social scientists, theorize about the determinants of human behavior. In order to claim a special role in the legal process, social scientists must demonstrate the greater validity of their theories.[54]

[I]n battered woman cases the court should at a minimum ensure that the evidence is genuinely relevant to a material aspect of the self-defense claim and that the researcher offering to testify has correctly applied the methodology of the general field of clinical psychology. To stop short of this inquiry, as courts and commentators have done, is to risk exposing the jury to unsound and potentially prejudicial evidence. . . . If research cloaks itself in the garb of an accepted scientific field, the court must examine the suitability of the fit. If the research violates basic tenets of its field, it should not go to the jury with the imprimatur of science.[55]

These concerns have been echoed in Canadian commentary on the use of social framework evidence in *Lavallee* and other cases:

As more and more 'expert' opinions are offered for consideration by the triers of fact, there is a real risk that old myths will simply be replaced by new ones that are even more insidious because of their appearance as scientific truths.[56]

That admitting the evidence is thought likely to be socially progressive or even 'politically correct'[57] is, needless to say, insufficient

---

[54] Faigman, 'To Have and Have Not', n. 53 above at 1052–3.

[55] Faigman, 'The Battered Woman Syndrome and Self-Defense', n. 53 above at 636.

[56] J. Norris and M. Edwardh, 'Myths, Hidden Facts and Common Sense: Expert Opinion Evidence and the Assessment of Credibility' (1995) 38 Crim. LQ 73 at 75. Also see G. H. Gudjonsson, 'The Implications of Poor Psychological Evidence in Court' (1993) 2 Expert Evid. 120.

[57] According to one (US) commentator the Supreme Court of Canada 'is known for its sympathy with feminist perspectives on law': Bernstein, 'Junk Science', n. 23 above at 148 n. 169. Some remarks of Peter Huber are worth quoting in this connection: 'No one should suppose that those who are liberal on consumer or environmental protection must be especially liberal about what passes for science in court. If it is politically convenient for chemophobes to embrace the

reason for allowing the judicial guard to slip. The quality of decision-making in the criminal process, and, by extension, the ideals
of criminal justice are at stake. In so far as courts are wont to
admit scientific evidence because other courts have admitted it in
the past,[58] *Lavallee* may turn out to be a bad precedent for receiving BWS testimony without adequately scrutinizing its claims to
scientific validity.[59] More generally, the Supreme Court missed a
golden opportunity to provide a lead to inferior courts by explaining the need for strict judicial scrutiny of novel forms of scientific
evidence.

Scientific validity is only the first, albeit a crucial, precondition of
the forensic reception of BWS evidence. Even if the validity question
could be resolved satisfactorily, it would remain necessary to think
carefully about what jurors need to be told, and how best to tell
them. Here again, *Lavallee* left important issues unaddressed. In
particular, the following four questions merit further consideration:

1. Should social framework evidence be admissible *per se* in relation to any issue on which it satisfies the relevance and PV/PE
   standards, or should its admissibility turn upon certain conditions precedent or 'triggering events' in the course of the trial?
2. If jurors need social framework information, should it be
   conveyed by expert witnesses or in some other way, for example by counsel putting questions to witnesses in the course of
   the trial, or by the judge in summing up to the jury at the close
   of evidence?

junk science of chemical AIDS, it is politically convenient for homophobes to
embrace the junk science of AIDS proper. Indeed, outside the liability system, liber-
als will often find themselves the front-line defenders of science against the world.'
P. W. Huber, *Galileo's Revenge: Junk Science in the Courtroom* (New York,
1991), 219.

   [58] It is notable that in at least one post-*Lavallee* case argued on appeal in
Canada expert psychological evidence of BWS was admitted without challenge or
objection. See *R. v. Malott* (1996) 30 OR (3d) 609 (Ont. CA).

   [59] Nor is this boot-strapping necessarily confined to courts within the same
national jurisdiction. It has been hypothesized that decisions on the admissibility of
scientific evidence may effectively become 'exported' to other common-law jurisdictions as part of a 'legal cultural diffusion process' whereby judicial decisions
and secondary literature discussing them are cited to and adopted by judges in
other countries: see S. I. Gatowski, S. A. Dobbin, J. T. Richardson, C. Nowlin and
G. P. Ginsburg, 'The Diffusion of Scientific Evidence: A Comparative Analysis of
Admissibility Standards in Australia, Canada, England, and the United States, and
their Impact on Social and Behavioural Sciences' (1996) 4 Expert Evid. 86.

3. Should social framework evidence be restricted to 'normative data',[60] reporting the results of research studies and conveying aggregated information about human behaviour under particular conditions, or may these data be applied directly to the events under consideration in the instant case, so that jurors are presented with ready-made inferences bearing on the issues that they have to determine to arrive at their verdict?

4. To what extent may social framework evidence bear, directly or indirectly, on witness credibility?

(B) LIMITED ADMISSIBILITY

The admissibility of evidence frequently turns on the sequence of events at trial, and some types of evidence only become admissible if a specified 'triggering' event occurs. For example, a defendant in England and Wales cannot be cross-examined on her previous record or bad character unless she first leads evidence of her own good character, attacks the character of a prosecution witness or gives evidence against a co-accused in the same proceedings.[61] But if she does any of these things, the 'character shield' is lost, and she can be cross-examined in the same way as any other witness. Another example, very close to present concerns, is provided by the difficult Privy Council judgment in *Lowery* v. *R*.[62] The *ratio* of this case is (probably) best explained by saying that King, Lowery's co-accused at their trial for murder, was allowed to adduce psychiatric evidence of his submissive personality only

---

[60] This terminology is borrowed from D. H. Sheldon and M. D. MacLeod, 'From Normative to Positive Data: Expert Psychological Evidence Re-Examined' [1991] Crim. LR 811. These authors argued that purely 'normative' or statistical data are inadmissible in a criminal trial because '[t]o exclude reasonable doubt as to the guilt of an individual, and to reach the required level of probability, positive data are required' (814). The argument is demonstrably mistaken, however, because statistical information, some of which has enormous probative value, is regularly received in criminal proceedings, for example in the form of population genetics underpinning DNA profiles: see M. Redmayne, 'Doubts and Burdens: DNA Evidence, Probability and the Courts' [1995] Crim. LR 464; and on probabilistic evidence generally, see B. Robertson and G. A. Vignaux, *Interpreting Evidence: Evaluating Forensic Science in the Courtroom* (Chichester, 1995). David Sheldon has since modified the original thesis: see D. Sheldon, 'Normative and Positive Data Re-Evaluated: Relevance and Probabilistic Reasoning in the Fact-Finding Process', forthcoming.

[61] Criminal Evidence Act 1898, s. 1(f)(ii) & (iii).

[62] [1974] AC 85 (PC).

after Lowery's testimony, in which he attempted to pin all the blame on King, had made their respective propensities for violence and manipulation the central issue in the case.[63]

Should the admissibility of social framework evidence also be limited by the course of events at trial? It bears observation that by expressly drawing the jury's attention to an impermissible argument or line of reasoning the court runs the risk that some jurors who might not otherwise have thought of it will now, perversely, fly in the face of the judge's instruction and adopt it anyway. Some things are best left unsaid. In *Lavallee* the Supreme Court of Canada assumed that misconceptions about the plight of battered women were so widespread that they stood in need of correction from the outset, before counsel or any witness had invoked stereotypical representations of the defendant. Was it sufficient for the Supreme Court, in effect, to take judicial notice of the existence of popular stereotypes? Two Canadian commentators think not:

If expert opinion evidence is to be admitted because it is required to forestall the trier of fact from drawing 'ordinary' unfounded inferences from the evidence, this should be done on a more secure foundation than merely the court's intuitive sense of what is commonly believed. Empirical evidence of the nature of the myths and misconceptions at issue and their prevalence in society should be required. If it is not forthcoming, the court should conclude that the basic requirement of necessity has not been met and the expert opinion evidence is therefore inadmissible if its only purpose is to 'educate' the trier of fact.[64]

Public perceptions are neither static nor immutable. As the general public from which jurors are drawn becomes better informed about the circumstances of (for example) battered women, the necessity or desirability of informing them about (what has become) common knowledge will diminish, ultimately to a point where the utility of such information is outweighed by its potential for mischief. At that point, where PV < PE, the evidence becomes inadmissible.

[63] See Tapper, *Evidence*, n. 9 above, at 551; A. W. Mewett, 'Character as a Fact in Issue in Criminal Cases' (1984–5) 27 Crim. LQ 29 at 47–8. The alternative, direct approach to admissibility is favoured by R. Pattenden, 'Conflicting Approaches to Psychiatric Evidence in Criminal Trials: England, Canada and Australia' [1986] Crim. LR 92 at 101–2.

[64] Norris and Edwardh, 'Myths, Hidden Facts and Common Sense', n. 56 above at 96–7. American courts have been prepared to make similar assumptions about jurors' beliefs in order to admit social framework evidence in rebuttal: see Mosteller, 'Social Framework Evidence', n. 46 above at 120–5.

(C) MEANS OF COMMUNICATION

What jurors should know is one thing; who should tell them is another. Paradigmatically, witnesses of fact testify to what they perceived with one or more of their five senses; legal experts—judges—instruct the jury on the law. Who should tell jurors about relevant scientific facts? Contrary to what might be supposed, the answer is not always 'scientific experts'. In England and Wales, for example, the findings of psychological research into the reliability of eyewitness identification have been incorporated into the '*Turnbull* warning'[65] which judges give to juries when summing up in cases involving eyewitness testimony. Of course, not all types of scientific knowledge are appropriately conveyed by judges: some science is too complex, difficult, labour-intensive or controversial to be explained by anyone other than *bona fide* experts with long years of training and experience. But judges are expert fact-managers. Good judging requires the ability to summarize, synthesize and draw out the legal significance of relevant evidence, including scientific evidence. We saw this in *Lavallee*: no psychiatrist could have improved upon Wilson J's clear and concise explanation of the relevance of BWS to the legal components of self-defence. If the science behind BWS is accepted, why not simply let judges tell juries the facts,[66] as they do with regard to eyewitness testimony? In the absence of empirical research it is impossible to tell whether this would be a fairer, more effective, or more efficient way of communicating information about BWS to juries. Has anybody ever tried to find out? Before we give in to the

---

[65] After the leading case, *R. v. Turnbull* [1977] QB 224 (CA). The 5-member Court of Appeal (Criminal Division) which handed down this judgment took cognizance of the Devlin Report on identification evidence, which itself made reference to contemporary psychological research. See *Report to the Secretary of State for the Home Department of the Departmental Committee on Evidence of Identification in Criminal Cases* (Chair: Lord Devlin), HC 338 (1976), paras. 4.12 *et seq.* There has, of course, been an enormous amount of new research since 1976, but there is no formal mechanism by which the latest findings can become incorporated into the *Turnbull* warning.

[66] Several US commentators have presented similar arguments: see Walker and Monahan, 'Social Frameworks', n. 46 above at 592–8; E. J. Imwinkelried, 'The Next Step in Conceptualizing the Presentation of Expert Evidence as Education: The Case for Didactic Trial Procedures' (1997) 1 Internat. J Evidence and Proof 128; Faigman, 'The Battered Woman Syndrome and Self-Defense', n. 53 above, at 645 n. 139.

assumption that more expert witnesses are needed in criminal trials, fully aware, as we are, of the additional problems they bring in their train, it seems to me that this issue deserves more careful attention than it has attracted to date.

(D) ULTIMATE ISSUES

My third question raises again the matter of expert evidence going to ultimate issues. In *Lavallee* Wilson J reaffirmed the traditional position:

Ultimately, it is up to the jury to decide whether, *in fact*, the accused's perceptions and actions were reasonable. Expert evidence does not and cannot usurp that function of the jury. The jury is not compelled to accept the opinions proffered by the expert about the effects of battering on the mental state of victims generally or on the mental state of the accused in particular.[67]

This is an unassailably accurate statement of the law, but how does it relate to the events at trial? Dr Shane did not confine his testimony to supplying normative data or explaining the conceptual apparatus of BWS and the theory behind it. He applied the theory directly to Lyn Lavallee, whom he had interviewed for a period of four hours in preparation for the trial. On the question of Lavallee's opportunities to run away or seek assistance, for example, he testified:

There was no out for her, this learned helplessness, if you will, the fact that she felt paralysed, she felt tyrannized. She felt, although there were obviously no steel fences around, keeping her in, there were steel fences in her mind which created for her an incredible barrier psychologically that prevented her from moving out. Although she had attempted [to leave] on occasion, she came back in a magnetic sort of a way.[68]

And on the crucial question of the need for self-defence at the material time, Dr Shane told the jury:

[S]he felt in the final tragic moment that her life was on the line, that unless she defended herself, unless she reacted in a violent way that she would die. I mean he made it very explicit to her . . . that she had, I think, to defend herself against his violence.[69]

---

[67] *Lavallee*, n. 47 above at 891 (*per* Wilson J) (original emphasis).
[68] As quoted by the Supreme Court, *ibid*. at 888.
[69] *Ibid*., at 859–60.

This is powerful testimony which, uncontradicted, must have had a strong influence on the jury's decision to acquit. If BWS provides a valid and reliable guide to the perceptions and behaviour of women in abusive relationships, if Dr Shane explained and applied the theory accurately using defensible diagnostic practice, and if the jury was appropriately critical in its assessment of Dr Shane's opinions and conclusions, there is nothing to be concerned about. But the stakes rise progressively as an expert witness's testimony approaches the central issue(s) in the case: flawed scientific evidence, or deficient interpretations of it by the jury, are all the more serious if they relate to the essential questions. Notwithstanding the (unlamented) demise of the ultimate issue rule,[70] judges should be particularly astute to unearth the shortcomings of expert evidence on an ultimate issue and ready, in appropriate cases, to restrict its admissibility or exclude it altogether under the PV/PE exclusionary standard.

(E) WITNESS CREDIBILITY

Lyn Lavallee chose not to testify at her trial, so the question of expert evidence bolstering witness credibility arose only indirectly in her case: there was no *testimonial* credibility for Dr Shane's evidence to support. Yet there is an obvious sense in which Dr Shane *was* supporting the truth of Lavallee's story,[71] and in a more direct and troubling fashion than the unremarkable case where scientific evidence such as a blood test or fingerprint provides independent corroboration of a witness's testimony. Dr Shane based his assessment of Lavallee's perceptions and behaviour at the time of the shooting on what Lyn Lavallee herself told him in four hours of interviews. Much of this information was uncorroborated and unproved at trial. Some of it could well have been detrimental to the accused, such as the disclosure that she had smoked marijuana earlier in the night. Other matters, like the

---

[70] Nn. 37–9 above and accompanying text.
[71] Also see *R.* v. *Lovie* (1995) 24 OR (3d) 836 (Ont. CA). Commenting on expert psychiatric testimony adduced by the defendant in support of his plea of diminished responsibility to a charge of murder, Finlayson JA said, 'pages of purely descriptive testimony do little except affirm the appellant's story and therefore his credibility. This testimony amounts to simple oath-helping and constitutes the very sort of expert testimony rejected by the Supreme Court of Canada in *R.* v. *Beland*' (848).

statement that her eight recorded visits to hospital casualty departments between 1983 and 1985 were not the result of accidents, as she had claimed at the time, would almost certainly have bolstered her plea of self-defence.

Now the jury heard all this, not, technically, as evidence in its own right, but as the factual substratum of Dr Shane's opinion evidence. No rules of evidence were breached, strictly speaking. But the result in *Lavallee* was a trial based on evidence far removed from the traditional procedural model in which facts are proved in court by the oral evidence of first-hand witnesses. From this perspective expert evidence is revealed as a potential Trojan horse which, in practice if not in theory, evades the familiar procedural guarantees and exclusionary rules of evidence.

These reflections on *Lavallee* foreground two evidentiary issues which merit closer attention. The following two sections consider, respectively, hearsay and witness credibility.

5. Hearsay in Expert Evidence

Generally speaking, a statement made by a person otherwise than in the course of giving evidence in the proceedings is inadmissible as proof of its contents. This is the rule against hearsay. Although any type of expert evidence could conceivably incorporate second-hand information, the hearsay problem is particularly acute in relation to psychiatric and behavioural science evidence, which is often based, at least in part, on unverified assertions made by the defendant, as it was in *Lavallee*. These extra-curial statements concerning, for example, the defendant's background or medical history can be introduced into court indirectly as the basis for an expert's opinion, but they are inadmissible in their own right. It remains incumbent upon the party adducing expert evidence incorporating hearsay to establish the factual basis of the expert's opinion by other evidence.

The leading cases on expert witness testimony, both in Canada and England, are more concerned with hearsay dangers than is commonly realized. Lawton LJ specifically drew attention to them in *Turner*, a case in which the defendant tried unsuccessfully to adduce psychiatric evidence to support his plea of provocation to a charge of murder:

[T]he judge commented that the report contained 'hearsay character evidence' which was inadmissible. He could have said that all the facts upon which the psychiatrist based his opinion were hearsay save for those which he observed himself during his examination of the defendant such as his appearance of depression and his becoming emotional when discussing the deceased girl and his own family. It is not for this court to instruct psychiatrists how to draft their reports, but those who call psychiatrists as witnesses should remember that the facts upon which they base their opinions must be proved by admissible evidence. This elementary principle is frequently overlooked.[72]

Lawton LJ went on to say that it is the duty of counsel in examination-in-chief to bring out the facts on which expert evidence is based, so that the foundation of the expert's opinion, either in hearsay or original evidence, is not obscured or overlooked: 'It is wrong to leave the other side to elicit the facts by cross-examination.'[73]

The Supreme Court of Canada addressed the same issues in *Abbey*, where the defendant adduced psychiatric testimony on a plea of insanity to charges of drug-trafficking. Having discussed *Turner*, Dickson J explained the rule in these terms:

While it is not questioned that medical experts are entitled to take into consideration all possible information in forming their opinions, this in no way removes from the party tendering such evidence the obligation of establishing, through properly admissible evidence, the factual basis on which such opinions are based. Before any weight can be given to an expert's opinion, the facts upon which the opinion is based must be found to exist.[74]

Canadian judges have tended to be more flexible than English courts in their respective interpretations of the hearsay prohibition,[75] and recent Canadian authority[76] has relaxed the general exclusionary rule still further. However, as Dickson J pithily explained in *Abbey*, facts recounted in expert opinions are not

---

[72] N. 12 above at 840.
[73] *Ibid.*, at 840.
[74] N. 18 above at 412.
[75] See, e.g., *Ares* v. *Venner* [1970] SCR 608 (SCC).
[76] *R.* v. *Khan* (1990) 59 CCC (3d) 92 (SCC); *R* v. *Smith* (1992) 94 DLR (4th) 590 (SCC), discussed by P. B. Carter, 'Hearsay: Whether and Whither?' (1993) 109 LQR 573.

even technically within the scope of the hearsay prohibition because they are not adduced for a hearsay purpose:

Testimony as to circumstances upon which the opinion is based is not introduced, and cannot be introduced, in order to establish the veracity of the second-hand evidence. It is thus not hearsay evidence.[77]

The correct analytical approach is to ask whether the probative value of an expert's opinion is diminished by the questionable status of the 'facts' on which it is based. The *Abbey* case affords an extreme example in which a psychiatrist's diagnosis of insanity was based *exclusively* on the defendant's own accounts of his previous behaviour. In these circumstances the Supreme Court found that the plea of insanity which had succeeded at first instance lacked any foundation of fact. It followed that 'the trial judge erred in law in treating as factual the hearsay evidence upon which the opinions of the psychiatrist were based',[78] and the verdict could not stand.

The lesson of *Abbey* is independent of the doctrinal contours of the hearsay rule, and will be no less instructive if in due course English law is reformed,[79] perhaps in a Canadian direction.[80] Expert opinions are only as good as the information on which they are based. If that information comes at one, two, or n removes from the original source, the probative value of the evidence typically diminishes correspondingly, and there will come a point when its basis in unsubstantiated hearsay renders the expert opinion more prejudicial than probative and therefore inadmissible.[81] In this way, the criteria of truthfulness and reliability which supply the rationale for the hearsay rule also bear on the admission of expert witness testimony. Judicial scrutiny extends to

[77] *Abbey*, n. 18 above at 410. This is a good illustration of the mantra I drill into my students: 'there is no such thing as hearsay *evidence*, only hearsay *uses*.'

[78] *Ibid.*, at 411–12.

[79] For the latest proposals see *Evidence in Criminal Proceedings: Hearsay and Related Topics* (Law Com. No. 245, Cm. 3670, 1997).

[80] *Ibid.*, paras. 8.136 *et seq.* And see Carter, 'Hearsay', n. 76 above.

[81] Cf. Sopinka J's observation in *Lavallee*, n. 47 above at 900 that '[w]here . . . the information upon which an expert forms his or her opinion comes from the mouth of a party to the litigation, or from any other source that is inherently suspect, a court ought to require independent proof of that information. The lack of such proof will, consistent with *Abbey*, have a direct effect on the weight to be given to the opinion, perhaps to the vanishing point.' Also see *Lovie*, n. 71 above at 845–6.

the facts supporting an expert's opinion as part of the PV/PE calculation and, in an extreme case,[82] may even trigger exclusion on grounds of irrelevance.

6. Expert Evidence of Witness Credibility

The opinion of one witness about the credibility or truthfulness of another witness is usually inadmissible in common-law criminal trials, for the simple and very good reason that such opinions are irrelevant. (A witness is allowed to testify to another witness's reputation for being a notorious liar, but this is not quite the same thing,[83] and in any event the modern status of this anachronism is doubtful and the rule is infrequently invoked.[84]) Most witnesses in criminal trials have no special qualifications for determining the truthfulness of what other people say, so why should we even entertain their opinions on the subject, let alone allow them to influence momentous public decisions about criminal liability and punishment? Such testimony would be irrelevant in the same way that the testimony of a charlatan or pseudo-expert is irrelevant: it has no rational connection with a fact in issue. But what of witnesses who are, in one sense or another, expert in the determination of witness credibility? Someone could be an 'expert' judge of a witness's credibility in one of two ways. He might have

---

[82] If an expert has based her opinion on reported 'facts' which are utter nonsense her evidence is, strictly speaking, irrelevant: rather than having *insufficient* probative value to offset its prejudicial effect, the evidence has no probative value whatever. Cf. *Lavallee*, n. 47 above: '[A]n expert opinion based *entirely* on unproven hearsay must, if anything, be inadmissible by reason of irrelevance, since the facts underlying the expert opinion are the only connection between the opinion and the case' (899 *per* Sopinka J) (original emphasis). Also see P. Wardle, '*R. v. Abbey* and Psychiatric Opinion Evidence: Requiring the Accused to Testify' (1984) 17 Ottawa LR 116 at 121–3.

[83] See Tapper, *Evidence*, n. 9 above, at 338–9.

[84] In *Toohey* v. *Metropolitan Police Commissioner* [1965] AC 595 (HL) Lord Pearce said, '[f]rom olden times it has been the practice to allow evidence of bad reputation to discredit a witness's testimony. It is perhaps not very logical and not very useful to allow such evidence founded on hearsay. None of your Lordships and none of the counsel before you could remember being concerned in a case where such evidence was called. But the rule has been sanctified through the centuries in legal examinations and textbooks and in some rare cases, and it does not create injustice' (605–6). But cf. *R.* v. *Richardson and Longman* [1969] 1 QB 299 (CA) (witness is allowed to express her own *opinion* about another's veracity) and *R.* v. *Bogie* [1992] Crim. LR 301 (CA) (modern example of extensive attacks on a witness's general credibility).

personal knowledge of a particular witness's character and past conduct from which her credibility may be inferred, or, alternatively, he could have access to some scientific means of judging witness credibility in general.

Judges in England and Wales are frequently heard to say that expert opinions regarding witness credibility threaten to usurp the jury's role as fact-finder and must be rejected on that account.[85] One of the best-known and most quoted statements to this effect was supplied by Lawton LJ in *Turner*:

[T]he proposed evidence was not admissible to establish that the defendant was likely to have been provoked. The same reasoning applies to its suggested admissibility on the issue of credibility. The jury had to decide what reliance they could put upon the defendant's evidence. He had to be judged as someone who was not mentally disordered. *This is what juries are empanelled to do. The law assumes they can perform their duties properly.* The jury in this case did not need, and should not have been offered, the evidence of a psychiatrist to help them decide whether the defendant's evidence was truthful.[86]

One interpretation of this passage is that juries are not in fact assisted by expert guidance on witness credibility. That, however, is an empirical proposition the truth of which is open to doubt, and commentators[87] and courts who understand the passage in this way have indeed doubted it. But another eligible interpretation of Lawton LJ's words, focusing on the italicized sentence, is that juries are *not permitted* by the received model of common-law criminal procedure to have the benefit of such assistance; and, *in that sense*, experts' opinions about the credibility or veracity of other witnesses are irrelevant to the proceedings, much as the judge's responsibility to make rulings on points of law leaves no room for the parties to adduce expert witness testimony on the law applicable to their case.[88] Witnesses are called to court to testify about facts which are under investigation in the

---

[85] For a recent example see *G.* v. *DPP* [1997] 2 All ER 755 at 759–80.

[86] N. 12 above at 841–2 (emphasis added).

[87] See e.g. F. Bates, 'Admissibility—Psychiatric Evidence—Towards a Coherent Policy' (1977) 55 Canadian Bar Rev. 178 at 184–5; R. D. Mackay and A. M. Colman, 'Excluding Expert Evidence: A Tale of Ordinary Folk and Common Experience' [1991] Crim. LR 800.

[88] Proof of foreign law, which is treated as a question of fact in England, is the exception where expert testimony is not only permitted, but usually required. See Hodgkinson, *Expert Evidence*, n. 7 above, ch. 16.

proceedings, facts which they themselves have *witnessed* (or about which they can bear witness). As assessing witness credibility is, by contrast, an integral part of the procedural architecture of criminal proceedings, and, in the traditional design, the job of deciding which witnesses to believe is vouchsafed exclusively to the court—paradigmatically, a jury properly directed by the judge.

Courts experience no difficulty in deploying either some variant of the irrelevance rationale or, alternatively, a PV/PE analysis to reject 'expert' evaluations of a witness's credibility based only on extensive personal knowledge of the witness. Witness credibility is collateral to the issues in the case and, as the Ontario Court of Appeal pointed out in its influential *Kyselka* judgment, evidence on collateral questions can be more trouble than it is worth:

[T]here is no warrant or authority for such oath-helping as occurred in the circumstances of this case. . . . If this sort of evidence were admissible in the case of either party no limit could be placed on the number of witnesses who could be called to testify about the credibility of witnesses as to facts. It would tend to produce, regardless of the number of such character witnesses who were called, undue confusion in the minds of the jury by directing their attention away from the real issues and the controversy would become so intricate that truth would be more likely to remain hidden than be discovered.[89]

Lay assessments of witness credibility have been the exclusive prerogative of the jury (or other fact-finder) since the roles of juror and witness became differentiated and clearly defined in the modern law. Today's judges, unsurprisingly, express little enthusiasm for 'a method of proving one's case that ante-dated the modern concept of trial by evidence'.[90] But what if science could supply a key to unlock the secrets of witness demeanour, an 'art to find the mind's construction in the face'[91]—or voice, or sweaty palms—of the witness? It is far from self-evident that the results of lie-detector tests, truth drugs and the like should either be irrelevant to legal proceedings or unfairly prejudicial to the

---

[89] R. v. *Kyselka* (1962) 133 CCC 103 (Ont. CA) at 108.
[90] *Beland and Phillips* (1987) 43 DLR (4th) 641 (SCC), *per* Wilson J (dissenting) at 657.
[91] *Macbeth*, I iv 7.

parties,[92] and it is with regard to these forms of evidence that the boundaries of traditional doctrine have been tested in the Canadian courts.

(A) SCIENTIFIC DEVICES FOR TESTING WITNESS CREDIBILITY

The admissibility of polygraph evidence fell to be determined by the Supreme Court of Canada in *Beland and Phillips*.[93] (Interestingly, as in *Frye v. United States*,[94] it was the *defendants* who were trying to support the credibility of their denials with this evidence.[95]) A majority[96] of the Court ruled polygraph evidence inadmissible on two grounds: first, it was said to infringe well-established rules of evidence, including the rule against oath-helping, the rule against narrative (previous consistent statements) and the rule limiting proof of good character to evidence of general reputation without reference to specific acts; and, secondly, it failed to satisfy the PV/PE standard:

[T]he admission of polygraph evidence will serve no purpose which is not already served. It will disrupt proceedings, cause delays, and lead to numerous complications which will result in no greater degree of certainty in the process than that which already exists.[97]

The majority's second ground for the decision appears, on first reading, to be the more persuasive, whilst Wilson J's dissenting opinion (in which Lamer J concurred) apparently has the better of

---

[92] Not least because lay jurors' assessments of a witness's demeanour are, at best, an unreliable guide to the credibility of the witness. See Olin Guy Wellborn III, 'Demeanor' (1991) 76 Cornell LR 1075; C. Fife-Schaw, 'The Influence of Witness Appearance and Demeanour on Witness Credibility: a Theoretical Framework' (1995) 35 Medicine, Science and the Law 107; M. Stone, 'Instant Lie Detection? Demeanour and Credibility in Criminal Trials' [1991] Crim. LR 821.

[93] *R. v. Beland and Phillips* (1987) 43 DLR (4th) 641 (SCC).

[94] N. 11 above.

[95] The admissibility issue is arguably easier, or at any rate clearer, with regard to scientific evidence proffered by the defence. When polygraph evidence is tendered by the prosecution the court must confront additional questions about the fairness of requiring the defendant to undergo extra-curial tests of his veracity on pain of adverse inferences being drawn from his refusal to co-operate. Similar issues attend the prosecution's recourse to other scientific techniques, e.g. hypnosis; see L. Haward and A. Ashworth, 'Some Problems of Evidence Obtained by Hypnosis' [1980] Crim. LR 469 at 482–3.

[96] Dickson CJ and McIntyre, Beetz and Le Dain JJ.

[97] *Beland*, n. 93 above at 655.

the argument on the first ground. Wilson J insisted that polygraph test results hardly bear comparison to the oaths made by compurgators in Norman England,[98] nor are they truly previous consistent statements or even evidence of character. They are scientific data presented to the court by an expert witness; and scientific evidence is not rendered inadmissible by application of the exclusionary rules cited by the majority, any more than (as we saw above)[99] opinion evidence based on second-hand information is subject to the rule against hearsay. Also dissenting from the majority's second ground, Wilson J thought that the defendants should have been allowed to adduce their polygraph evidence because the case turned on a credibility battle between the defendants and the prosecution's principal witness, one Grenier, an erstwhile accomplice who claimed to have joined the accused in a conspiracy to commit robbery:

The Crown, through Grenier, was impugning the credibility of the respondents by saying that they were lying under oath. It was his word against theirs. The respondents were, in effect, responding to an attack on their credibility by the Crown by offering to take a lie detector test. Indeed, the Crown's whole case was that the respondents were lying and that the informer Grenier was telling the truth.[100]

Her Ladyship concluded that 'in these circumstances it would be unjust to prevent the respondents from calling any evidence of probative value indicating that they were telling the truth',[101] polygraph evidence included:

Unless it can be established that polygraph tests are *per se* without probative value (and I do not think this has been or could be established), it would seem to me that the possibility of abuse should be a factor going to weight rather than to admissibility.[102]

Yet, with respect, it is difficult to see how the relevance or probative value—and therefore the *admissibility*—of polygraph evidence could be determined without first investigating the scientific credentials of polygraphy.[103] In *Beland* neither the validity

---

[98] On compurgation or 'trial by wager' see J. B. Thayer, *A Preliminary Treatise on Evidence at the Common Law* (Boston, 1898), 24–34.

[99] Sect. 5.   [100] *Beland*, n. 93 above at 658.

[101] *Ibid.*, at 665 (*per* Wilson J).   [102] *Ibid.*, at 659 (*per* Wilson J).

[103] Cf. E. Harnon, 'Evidence Obtained by Polygraph: An Israeli Perspective' [1982] Crim. LR 340, who observes at 345 that 'the question of validity is therefore the principal one'.

nor the reliability of the polygraph was fully canvassed before the court.[104] Even if the theory behind polygraph testing were shown to be scientifically valid, the questionable reliability of polygraph results, their scope for manipulation by witness coaching and 'examiner shopping', and their potential for misinterpretation by the jury might still lead to the exclusion of polygraph evidence under the PV/PE rubric.[105] It is submitted that the majority's approach is to be preferred, because Wilson J's argument moves too tersely from admissibility to weight. Be that as it may, however, the majority's rejection of polygraph evidence finds independent support in its first ground of decision. Although McIntyre J's judgment tends unhelpfully to elide the relevance and PV/PE standards,[106] it nevertheless clearly invokes the procedural irrelevance argument, outlined above, which the *Beland* dissentients were too quick to dismiss as a misconceived analogy to oath-helping. In fact, polygraphy *does* resemble compurgation inasmuch as neither is compatible with the traditional conception of a criminal trial.[107] As McIntyre J said,

> It is a basic tenet of our legal system that judges and juries are capable of assessing credibility and reliability of evidence. . . . I would seek to preserve the principle that in the resolution of disputes in litigation, issues of credibility will be decided by human triers of fact, using their experience of human affairs and basing judgment upon their assessment of the witness and on consideration of how an individual's evidence fits into the general picture revealed on a consideration of the whole of the case.[108]

Legal orthodoxy thus prevailed in *Beland*, but the Supreme Court of Canada has subsequently reconsidered its approach to expert

---

[104] McIntyre J explained, at 654, that the majority's decision was 'not based on a fear of the inaccuracies of the polygraph. *On that question we were not supplied with sufficient evidence to reach a conclusion*' (emphasis added).

[105] See to similar effect, E. S. Magner, 'Exclusion of Polygraph Evidence: Can it be Justified?' (1987–88) 30 Crim. LQ 412 at 426 *et seq.*

[106] McIntyre J's 'fear of turmoil in the courts' (656), for example, looks like part of an argument about the prejudicial effect of polygraph evidence, yet it falls in the middle of passages which argue that polygraph evidence is incompatible with traditional canons of jury fact-finding *irrespective of its accuracy*.

[107] An argument also noted by Harnon, 'Evidence Obtained by Polygraph', n. 103 above, at 346: 'adopting a system of polygraph examinations, including the admissibility of the results, means that the function of deciding the question whether a person is being truthful or lying would be removed from the courts and conferred upon the polygraph examiners; thus leading to "trial by polygraphers".'

[108] *Beland*, n. 93 above at 654, 656.

evidence of witness credibility in cases involving social framework evidence.

(B) SOCIAL FRAMEWORK EVIDENCE OF WITNESS CREDIBILITY

In *Marquard*[109] the defendant was convicted of causing serious facial burns to Debbie-Ann, her 3½-year-old granddaughter. The defendant claimed that the child had accidentally burned herself whilst playing with a cigarette lighter, and that version of events was initially confirmed to hospital staff by Debbie-Ann herself. But at trial Debbie-Ann testified that 'my nanna put me on the stove'. One ground of appeal against conviction argued before the Supreme Court concerned the evidence of a Dr Mian, who had been called *by the defence* to narrate Debbie-Ann's previous inconsistent statement. This assault on the complainant's credibility obviously back-fired, however, because under cross-examination Dr Mian candidly stated her opinion that Debbie-Ann had told the truth in court, an opinion based partly on the child's demeanour whilst giving evidence and partly on professional knowledge of the behaviour of abused children in general, who, Dr Mian explained, tended at first to support the lying excuses of their abusers until they were able to put sufficient trust in another adult to confide the truth. In the event, an 8-member majority of the Supreme Court agreed that the defendant's complaint against Dr Mian's testimony was well-founded, but in allowing the defendant's appeal partly on this ground the Court lent its blessing to some forms of expert testimony bearing on witness credibility.

Delivering the majority opinion, McLachlin J[110] began with a forthright and illuminating re-statement of the traditional position:

It is a fundamental axiom of our trial process that the ultimate conclusion as to the credibility or truthfulness of a particular witness is for the trier of fact, and is not the proper subject of expert opinion. . . . Credibility is a matter within the competence of lay people. Ordinary people draw conclusions about whether someone is lying or telling the truth on a daily basis. The expert who testifies on credibility is not sworn to the heavy duty of a judge or juror. Moreover, the expert's opinion may be founded

---

[109] *R. v. Marquard* (1993) 108 DLR (4th) 47 (SCC).
[110] Lamer CJ, La Forest, Sopinka, Gonthier, Cory, Iacobucci and Major JJ concurring.

on factors which are not in the evidence upon which the judge and juror are duty-bound to render a true verdict. Finally, credibility is a notoriously difficult problem, and the expert's opinion may be all too readily accepted by a frustrated jury as a convenient basis upon which to resolve its difficulties. All these considerations have contributed to the wise policy of the law in rejecting expert evidence on the truthfulness of witnesses.[111]

However, McLachlin J continued, this wise policy was subject to exceptions:

On the other hand, there may be features of a witness's evidence which go beyond the ability of a lay person to understand, and hence which may justify expert evidence. This is particularly the case in the evidence of children. . . . Expert evidence has been properly led to explain the reasons why young victims of sexual abuse often do not complain immediately. Such evidence is helpful; indeed it may be essential to a just verdict. For this reason, there is a growing consensus that while expert evidence on the ultimate credibility of a witness is not admissible, expert evidence on human conduct and the psychological and physical factors which may lead to certain behaviour relevant to credibility, is admissible, provided the testimony goes beyond the ordinary experience of the trier of fact.[112]

Dr Mian's evidence was unobjectionable, the Court concluded, so long as it was restricted to conveying general information about the behaviour of abused children and explaining, in general terms, how these social framework data should figure in jurors' assessments of witness credibility.[113] But Dr Mian should not have been permitted to apply her knowledge and experience to draw direct conclusions about Debbie-Ann's truthfulness, an error compounded in this case by the judge's defective direction to the jury:

---

[111] *Marquard*, n. 109 above at 81–2.

[112] *Ibid.*, at 82–3.

[113] This rationale for admitting evidence of witness credibility had previously been identified by Prof. Mewett, editor of the *Criminal Law Quarterly*, who argued that the witness who provides this testimony 'is not testifying as an expert in truth-telling. Nor is he oath-helping. The relevance of his testimony is to assist— no more—the jury in determining whether there is an explanation for what might otherwise be regarded as conduct that is inconsistent with that of a truthful witness. It does, of course, bolster the credibility of that witness, but it is evidence of how certain people react to certain experiences. Its relevance lies not in testimony that the prior witness is telling the truth but in testimony as to human behaviour': A. W. Mewett, 'Editorial: Credibility and Consistency' (1990–91) 33 Crim. LQ 385 at 386, quoted with approval in *Marquard*, n. 109 above, at 83 (*per* McLachlin J).

Dr Mian went further. She clearly indicated that she personally did not believe the first story of the child, preferring the second version which the child told at trial. In doing so, she crossed the line between expert testimony on human behaviour and assessment of credibility of the witness herself. Moreover, the trial judge failed to instruct the jury that it was their duty to decide on the child's credibility without being unduly influenced by the expert evidence. In fact, the trial judge's statement that Dr Mian gave 'evidence as an expert in child abuse and relating to the truthfulness of the testimony of small children' actually reinforced the effect of the inadmissible evidence.[114]

In setting up this distinction between evidence bearing on credibility in general (admissible) and evidence of a particular witness's credibility (inadmissible), the Supreme Court knew that it was renegotiating the boundaries of procedural law, but insisted that this was nothing more than a minor readjustment to the traditional model:

> To accept this approach is not to open the floodgates to expert testimony on whether witnesses are lying or telling the truth. It is rather to recognize that certain aspects of human behaviour which are important to the judge or jury's assessment of credibility may not be understood by the lay person and hence require elucidation by experts in human behaviour.[115]

But it is doubtful whether the majority's line in the sand will prove sufficiently robust to prevent expert testimony on witness credibility becoming an increasingly familiar feature of Canadian criminal proceedings, with the jury's role correspondingly diminished.[116] It is notable that the majority in *Marquard* did not limit its argument either (a) to evidence led in rebuttal of an attack on a witness's credibility[117] or (b) to the credibility of child witnesses, as it could easily have done on the facts. In the event it should, perhaps, come as no surprise to find the Supreme Court subsequently allowing a defendant's appeal against conviction partly on the ground that the trial judge improperly curtailed the scope of expert testimony challenging his accusers' credibility.

---

[114] *Marquard*, n. 109 above at 83.

[115] *Ibid.*

[116] Cf. L 'Heureux-Dubé J's dissenting observation, that Dr Mian's dual role as child abuse expert and Debbie-Ann's doctor 'made it difficult, *if not impossible*, for her to avoid testifying in a manner that touched, however slightly, on Debbie-Ann's credibility': *Marquard*, n. 109 above at 66 (emphasis added).

[117] Cf. Sect. 4(B) above.

In *R. v. R (D)*[118] an expert 'in the area of child development and characteristics of child abuse' was permitted to testify in general terms about children's memories and the indicia of their reliability, but was prevented by the trial judge from expressing conclusions about the credibility of particular allegations made by the complainants in that case. Although this would appear to be a faithful application of the distinction drawn in *Marquard* between general and specific evidence of credibility, a majority[119] of the Supreme Court found the judge to have been in error:

Dr Elterman's testimony was relevant to the issue of the reliability of the children's memories of their birth parents, memories which he suggested had been 'learned' and which could not be independently recalled. The credibility of the children was central to the disposition of the case, and considering the nature of the children's evidence, any explanation of their otherwise incredible behaviour could only aid the trier of fact in accurately assessing their credibility. Dr Elterman's testimony should have been admitted as an evidentiary basis upon which the children's credibility could have been judged.[120]

The (always frail) distinction between normative evidence of witness credibility in general and specific evidence of a particular witness's reliability and truthfulness seems here to have been abandoned in favour of returning to an unvarnished 'helpfulness' test.[121] In these circumstances, the Canadian Supreme Court's conviction that the floodgates remain fast against expert testimony of witness credibility reads more like an expression of hope than a statement of fact.

7. Expert Evidence Law and Law Reform

This essay began by observing that Canada and England share the same basic common-law approach to the admissibility of expert

---

[118] (1996) 136 DLR (4th) 525 (SCC).

[119] Major J, with Lamer CJ and Sopinka, Cory and Iacobucci JJ concurring.

[120] N. 118 above at 541.

[121] Note that L'Heureux-Dubé J., dissenting, held that the contested parts of Dr Elterman's evidence did not in any event satisfy the helpfulness test. Even on the assumption that the judge needed expert help to assess the complainants' credibility (which her Ladyship doubted), once Dr Elterman had explained his theory of memory to the court 'the application of the theory to actual testimony was quite straightforward and did not require any special knowledge or expertise.' *Ibid.*, at 551 (*per* L'Heureux-Dubé J).

evidence, from which it follows that developments in Canadian law and practice have special resonance for law and law reform in England and Wales. English appellate courts, like the senior Canadian judiciary whose work we have investigated in this essay, are (or soon will be) called upon to meet the challenges of scientific evidence: to develop and apply the relevance and PV/PE standards to social framework evidence and novel scientific techniques, to integrate these standards with other rules of evidence and procedure, and to work through the implications of expert testimony on witness credibility. Our survey of Canadian cases has enabled us to identify examples of best practice, but we also noted a range of issues which have so far eluded satisfactory resolution. The latter, no less than the former, have educational value.

An underlying theme of this review has been the apparent tension between traditional common-law rules of evidence and the emerging Canadian jurisprudence regulating the admissibility of expert witness testimony, a tension clearly evident in cases such as *Lavallee, Beland* and *Marquard*. This incompatibility does not necessarily imply the undesirability of recent developments, of course. One might just as well see the superiority of modern approaches to expert evidence as so much the worse for the traditional exclusionary rules, which have themselves attracted searching and frequently critical scrutiny in recent times. But this is not the place to begin speculating about the reasons for the supposed decline of common-law evidence doctrines in the last years of this century, or the prospects for their reform into the next.[122] Instead I want to conclude with the considerably more modest objective of posing another, related, set of questions about the appropriate techniques for reforming the law of evidence, including the law regulating expert witness testimony, in England and Wales.

Procedural law presents something of a paradox. On the one hand, it seems entirely sensible and appropriate for courts to regulate their own procedures. The rules of evidence in England and Wales (and, as we have seen, also in Canada) are traditionally thought of as judge-made law. It stands to reason that nobody is

[122] Such an inquiry might profitably begin with Damaska, *Evidence Law Adrift*, n. 14 above and Twining, 'What is the Law of Evidence?' in *Rethinking Evidence*, n. 14 above, ch. 6.

better placed to determine technical questions about, for example, the admissibility of character evidence or the scope of the hearsay rule than the judges who invented these doctrines in the first place. Yet, on the other hand, procedural law embodies some of the most cherished features of Anglo-American criminal justice. Defendants' rights to have the legality of their detention determined expeditiously by a judicial authority, to be informed of the charges against them, to have access to legal advice, to confront and question prosecution witnesses, to be tried by a jury of their peers, and to be presumed innocent until proven guilty are the stuff of national constitutions and international human rights conventions. These procedural guarantees cannot be watered down, much less abandoned, by judges in ordinary criminal proceedings. To be sure, at the extreme, it is sheer fantasy to suppose that five Law Lords hearing a criminal appeal would ever decide to abolish trial by jury, but it should be appreciated that the restriction on judge-made procedural innovation, as currently understood in England and Wales, penetrates much deeper into the doctrinal detail of the law. It constrains judicial reconsideration of key evidential doctrines, such as the scope of the hearsay prohibition and the existence of exceptions to it, even if in less rigorous times courts freely altered and developed them through case law.[123]

So the question arises: which, if any, of the issues which emerged from our review of Canadian approaches to expert evidence are appropriate for judicial resolution? If some of these issues should be left to the judges, but not others, which ones are which? And why? Have we been concerned only with technical matters best left to the lawyer-mechanic working with the tools of incremental common-law adjudication, or did we venture to the core of our procedural traditions where justice and transparency demand a different, perhaps more democratic and accountable, mechanism for their realignment? Reflections on the Canadian experience provide ample grounds to question whether English judges have either the scientific qualifications or the constitutional pedigree to settle the wider issues surrounding the admissibility of expert evidence without appropriate guidance, assistance, or

---

[123] A deservedly well-known example is *Myers* v. *DPP* [1965] AC 1001 (HL). The conservative position is well stated by Lord Reid, whilst Lord Pearce's dissent cogently argues the case for change.

constraint.[124] If the issues we have canvassed are symptoms of the struggle between law and science to predominate as 'the touchstone of social order',[125] which some have described, it is far from clear (to me at least) that judges have authority to cede the decision-making power conferred on them, or that entrusted to the jury, to expert witnesses: *delegatus non potest delegare*.[126] Perhaps the only real certainty in all of this is that the constitutional dimensions of expert witness testimony are another feature of procedural law reform which attracts too little attention in England and Wales.

[124] Cf. P. Alldridge, 'Recognising Novel Scientific Techniques: DNA as a Test Case' [1992] Crim. LR 687, who argues that the forensic use of novel science should be sanctioned by 'an extra-judicial committee' (698). For a review of American developments, see Note, 'Confronting the New Challenges of Scientific Evidence', n. 2 above at 1583–1604. In England, the Royal Commission on Criminal Justice discussed several proposals, including witness accreditation and more rigorous pre-trial preparation and disclosure of evidence, which would help trial judges to determine the admissibility of scientific evidence without requiring significant alterations to the traditional model of adversarial trial. For critical evaluations of the Commission's recommendations relating to expert witnesses, most of which remain unimplemented, see P. Roberts, 'Forensic Science Evidence After Runciman' [1994] Crim. LR 780; P. Roberts, 'What Price a Free Market in Forensic Science Services?' (1996) 36 Brit. J Criminology 37.

[125] Jones, *Expert Witnesses*, n. 7 above, at 96.

[126] 'A delegate cannot (does not have the power to) delegate.' My point is not that the division of political power between judges, juries, and expert witnesses can never be redrawn, but only that the judges have limited authority to alter the existing procedural architecture of criminal proceedings of their own motion.

THE RISKS AND DANGERS OF EXPERTS IN COURT

Michael King and Felicity Kaganas

Introduction

One of the remarkable achievements of modern law is the evolution of a concept of expertise which is both highly specific and, at the same time, is able to encompass an extraordinarily wide range of claimants to specialist knowledge. According to the law of evidence, what distinguishes experts from other witnesses is their knowledge of specialist matters which do not fall within the realm of the knowledge that judges (and juries) could be expected to possess.[1] It is this specialist knowledge which entitles them to give opinions in court instead of confining their evidence to factual matters.[2] In those areas of legal activity where the use of experts has become a common occurrence, the demands of legal rationality, as well as constraints of time and resources, require that considerable efforts are exerted in exercising and maintaining control over the border between law and what is seen in legal settings as expert knowledge.[3]

Law has succeeded in reconstructing as 'expertise' any body of knowledge which is not law[4] or 'common sense',[5] which might be

---

[1] *R.* v. *Turner* [1975] QB 834 at 841, cited with approval in *DPP* v. *Jordan* [1977] AC 699 at 718.

[2] *Sherrard* v. *Jacob* [1965] NI 151 at 157–8; Civil Evidence Act 1972, s. 1. For the admissibility of non-expert opinion, see M. Howard, P. Crane and D. Hochberg, *Phipson on Evidence* (14th edn, London, 1990) para. 32-53 et seq.

[3] See e.g., R. Slovenko, 'Surveying the Attacks on Psychiatry in the Legal Process' (1996) 48 Internat. J Evidence and Proof 71.

[4] Provided 'a field is sufficiently well-established to pass the ordinary tests of relevance and reliability' (C. Tapper, *Cross & Tapper on Evidence* (8th edn, London, 1995), 556).

[5] This does not exclude the possibility of law itself becoming the subject of expert knowledge where that knowledge relates to tribal or customary law or details of foreign legal codes.

relevant to the legal decision. This not only enables the legal system to draw a clear distinction between law and non-law, 'fact'[6] and 'opinion', between what ordinary people 'know' and what can only be 'known' by those who have the necessary professional qualifications; it also reduces complexity by allowing the courts, for the purposes of evidence and procedure, to treat all these specialist knowledge-holders as if they were *identical in kind*, whether they be accountants, architects, actuaries, archaeologists, biologists, chemists etc.

In this examination of the relationship between the legal system and 'expertise' we shall be drawing upon examples of expertise in relation to child protection and children's welfare. Here, those who appear as experts in the courts will have specialist medical or scientific academic qualifications and specific practising experience (for example, as psychologists, paediatricians and psychiatrists). These attributes are seen as qualifying them to provide knowledge about children's development and specific physical and psychological states which can be applied to the child in the case. Alternatively, they will be child care workers with professional qualifications who are acquainted with the particular child and family and whose occupational status and experience are seen by the law as entitling them to proffer opinions concerning allegations of harm and evaluations of risk to the child. These experts are likely to be social workers, welfare officers, health visitors or guardians *ad litem*.

The inclusion of guardians *ad litem* in this list is significant in that it illustrates the largesse of the legal system in extending the privileges of expert witness. Guardians *ad litem* are officers of the court appointed to protect the welfare of the child in the court proceedings. Their eligibility as experts is based upon nothing more than a qualification in social work, attendance at specialist training courses and experience in the field of child care. In court their role goes beyond that of advising on what might be a good or bad decision for the child in question. It includes also giving an assessment of the way that the local authority's child protection and/or care procedures have operated in relation to the particular child and the family. One of the directions that the evolution of

---

[6] Although some facts can be established only by the application of expert knowledge.

the notion of expertise in law has taken, then, is towards the recognition as experts of people whose expertise consists of *a knowledge and understanding of the way that other experts carry out their tasks.*[7]

Such an expansion of the concept of expertise appears to cause no problems for the operation of the legal system. The only concerns regarding the extension of the status of expert to new categories appear to be, first, that experts should not usurp the authority of the court by deciding the case in the place of the judge or jury,[8] secondly, that only those areas of knowledge that go beyond what a judge or jury could reasonably be expected to be familiar with should be the subject of expertise and, finally, that the expert evidence should be directly relevant to the issues in the case. As social life becomes increasingly complex and dependent upon technological and specialist knowledge, this leaves enormous scope for the law to construct an ever-growing regiment of potential experts. It is this phenomenon and its relationship with and effects on the world outside the law courts which concerns us in the remainder of this essay.

Proliferation of Expertise

The proliferation and ever-increasing influence of experts, in which the legal system has played its part, has been a prevailing theme for some of the most prominent social theorists of this century. Zygmunt Bauman, for example, has recently expressed his concern that the 'ethical competence' of ordinary people is being undermined by *moral experts* who claim that their ethical authority allows them 'to tell others what to do, to reproach them for doing wrong and to force them to do what is right'.[9] In Bauman's terms, therefore, the fact that judges appear increasingly reluctant to apply their own experience and common sense, and seem to have become more and more dependent upon the specialist knowledge

---

[7] This extension of the expert's role is particularly well developed in forensic evidence in criminal cases, as the O. J. Simpson trial illustrated only too well.

[8] It has often been stressed that the final decision is one for the court (see *Davie* v. *Edinburgh Magistrates* [1953] SC 34 at 40). On the 'ultimate issue' rule, however, see the Civil Evidence Act 1972, s. 3; *Re M and R (Minors) (Child Abuse: Evidence)* [1996] 2 FLR 195.

[9] Z. Bauman, *Life in Fragments* (Oxford, 1995), 12.

of experts, is symptomatic of a general social trend which down-grades personal experience in favour of technical or specialist expertise.

This, according to Bauman, eventually creates a dependency upon experts as *the only source of ethical authority*:

The experts pronounce the law, and judge whether the prescriptions have been followed faithfully and correctly. *They claim to be able to do it because they have access to knowledge not available to ordinary people.*[10]

Bauman's warning, however, is not simply to beware of the ethical experts taking over. Rather, his concern is that our reliance upon experts in time becomes self-reproducing to the extent that it ceases to be dependent upon the actual ability of the experts to deliver what they promise (in terms of certainty and reliability):

[S]ooner or later, we start seeking keenly and of our own accord reliable guidance from 'people in the know'. Once we stop trusting our own judgement, we grow susceptible to the fear of being in the wrong; we call what we dread sin, guilt or shame—but whatever the name we use we feel the need of the helpful hand of the expert to fetch us back into the comfort of certainty. It is out of such a fear that the dependency on exper-tise grows. But once the dependency has settled and taken root, the need of ethical expertise becomes 'self-evident', and above all self-reproducing.[11]

According to Bauman, we need experts whatever the effectiveness of the services they offer:

Paradoxically, the need grows bigger as the goods delivered are not fully up to the expectations and thus do not satisfy the need they were hoped to quell.[12]

What the experts are taking over in Bauman's scheme is 'ethics', which he describes as 'a code of law that prescribes correct behaviour "universally"—that is for all people at all times; one that sets apart good from evil once for all and everybody'.[13] Where this idealized notion of ethics comes from and how in past times it became common to all people he does not explain, but he is not the only theorist to sound the alarm bells, as they watch the experts take over.

---

[10] Bauman, *Life in Fragments* (Oxford, 1995), 11 (emphasis in original).
[11] *Ibid.*, 12.   [12] *Ibid.*
[13] *Ibid.*, 11.

Jürgen Habermas preceded Bauman in identifying a process of colonization within modern society—the imposition of the language of systems ('steering media') taking the place of the natural, spontaneous communications of ordinary people based on experience ('the lifeworld'). However, Habermas is concerned primarily with the contrast between 'the lifeworld' in which individuals are spontaneously motivated towards mutual understanding (even if they disagree with one another), and 'the system', which places individuals within a communicative world dominated by the systems of power and money to the point where 'lifeworld contexts, in which processes of reaching understanding are always embedded, are devalued in favour of media-steered interactions; the lifeworld is no longer needed for coordination of action'.[14] Although Habermas does not address the issue of 'expertise' in law directly, it is the impoverished communicative world of systems that endows with authority the judgement and opinions of technical and scientific experts to the detriment of the consensual ethics of the lifeworld. This situation, according to Habermas, can be reversed only through the reintroduction of truly democratic procedures.

In his later works law appears both negatively as a medium of communication and positively as an institution. As 'a medium' law is responsible, along with other media, for the colonization of the lifeworld, playing its part in imposing on it technological and scientific accounts of human behaviour, which in the final analysis belong to the power–money hegemony. As an institution connected to the lifeworld, law requires the validation of norms by reference, not to technical expertise or procedural mechanisms, but to 'valid authority and consensual rightness of decisions',[15] and invokes, for example, the universal value of equality. Like Bauman, Habermas sees 'technocratic consciousness' as reflecting 'the repression of ethics as such as a category of life'.[16] And so the experts take over.

Not surprisingly, Habermas is an admirer of Michel Foucault's analysis of the role of the human sciences in disciplining, checking

[14] J. Habermas, *The Theory of Communicative Action*, vol. 2 (Cambridge, 1987), 183.
[15] K. Raes, 'Legislation, Communication and Strategy: a Critique of Habermas' Approach to Law' (1986) 13 J Law and Society 183.
[16] J. Habermas, *Toward a Rational Society* (London, 1971), 112.

and controlling the human psyche.[17] For Foucault and his disciples the evolution and growing influence of 'expertise' on the minds and bodies of human subjects is a central theme.[18] Experts in these fields both operate within and help to sustain a panoply of medical-scientific 'knowledge' about people and their behaviour. They disseminate and promote this 'knowledge' so that it takes on the appearance of incontestable fact, the taken-for-granted world, governing expectations and practices. It is the unchallengeable nature of this medical-scientific *epistème* which gives experts their power and authority. For Foucault the concepts upon which such power and authority depend are not confined to particular disciplines or institutions, but are all-pervasive, characterizing and defining knowledge for a given intellectual era.[19]

In his later work Foucault considers the role of experts in the new art of government, which he identifies as having emerged in the eighteenth century around forms of bio-power directed at the phenomenon of population.[20] He identifies the emergence of the family, formerly the model for government, as the target for 'a range of new techniques aimed at securing the management of population as the ultimate end for government'.[21] These techniques include the practices of law, medicine, psychology, etc. Law and human scientific discourses thus become coupled within a political rationality which has as its objective the management of populations. By invoking the neutrality and sanctity of science, government, through its institutions (including the legal system) is able to extend the possibilities of permissible intervention in the family, continually redefining the division between the private, where intervention is unlawful, and

[17]   J. Habermas, *The Philosophical Discourse. Twelve Lectures* (Oxford, 1987).

[18]   See Foucault's writings on madness and on medicine (M. Foucault, *Madness and Civilization* (New York, 1965); *id.*, *The Birth of the Clinic* (New York, 1973); *id.*, *The History of Sexuality, Vol I: An Introduction* (London, 1979)) and the works of the many social scientists who have applied his theoretical constructs and methods to the modern world by constructing a 'History of the Present'.

[19]   G. Gutting, *The Cambridge Companion to Foucault* (Cambridge, 1994), 9.

[20]   M. Foucault, 'Governmentality' (1979) 6 *Ideology and Consciousness* 5; *id.*, *Power/Knowledge: Selected Writings 1972–1977* (Brighton, 1980).

[21]   S. Ashenden, 'Reflexive Governance and Child Sexual Abuse: Liberal and Welfare Rationality and the Cleveland Inquiry' (1996) 25 *Economy and Society* 64 at 69.

the public, where it is not only permitted but is also seen as being normal and necessary.[22]

Legitimation through science also emerges as a strategy for resolving conflict between disciplinary methods of control and the legal system:

[D]isciplinary normalizations come into ever greater conflict with the juridical systems of sovereignty: their incompatibility with each other is ever more acutely felt and apparent; some kind of arbitrating discourse is made ever more necessary, a type of power and of knowledge that the sanctity of science would render neutral.[23]

In a similar vein, but within a rather less sophisticated theoretical framework, Mary Douglas, focusing on the concept of risk, depicts each different society as vesting authority in different experts. This authority allows them a power, which gives their decisions the appearance of being legitimated by forces outside the political order, so that '[a]ppealing to degrees of risk assessed by accredited experts, is appealing to an external arbiter, an independent, objective judge of the rights and wrongs of the case'.[24] Experts then conceal the wider implications of decisions concerning danger by presenting them as technical solutions to issues of risk and probability. According to Douglas, an anthropological analysis using cultural theory is capable of exposing the moral and political implications which lurk behind the technological screen.[25] While all societies have their 'experts', modern Western society is particularly generous in the extent of the decision-making power that it confers on them through this presentation of moral and political issues as matters of risk and probability, with the implication that only those with the necessary expertise are able to understand the complexity of these issues and make informed decisions. Douglas believes that 'it would usually be preferable to have the choices directly presented as political questions, instead of sanitized

---

[22] 'It is the tactics of Governmentality which make possible the continual definition and redefinition of what is within the competence of the State and what is not, the public versus the private, and so on; the State can only be understood in its survival and its limits on the basis of the general tactics of Governmentality' (M. Foucault, 'Governmentality', Lecture at the Collège de France (1978) *Aut Aut* 167).

[23] *Ibid.*

[24] M. Douglas, *Risk and Blame. Essays in Cultural Theory* (London, 1994), 33.   [25] *Ibid.*, 51.

and disguised in probability theory terms'.[26] Applying Mary Douglas' approach, the use of experts within the legal system may be seen in a similar manner. These experts wrap the moral judgements of law in a cloak of technology which makes it difficult (without the aid of cultural theory) to uncover and question the political and moral nature of legal decisions.

Autopoietic theory, by contrast, sees the legal system's use of expert knowledge in less sinister terms. Experts become experts because their knowledge is necessary to law's processing of external events for the production of legal decisions.[27] This process occurs quite independently of the selfish interests of governments or particular professional groups. It is also independent of morality, which may co-exist and co-evolve with law, but does not directly affect the operations of the legal system.

Teubner writes of the 'enslavement of science' by law[28] and King and Piper describe the way that this 'enslavement' may involve the distortion and simplification of the complexities of what they call 'child welfare science'.[29] In autopoietic terms, the explosion of expertise in child welfare cases cannot be explained simply by notions of the concealment of power or the management of populations. Rather, it is the inevitable result of the growing complexity of society, to which law, as a social function system, is obliged to respond. No longer is it possible for courts to apply simple, universalistic, notions of right and wrong or good for children/bad for children in their decisions, for the knowledge of what is to the benefit and detriment of children has become incorporated within a scientific system. In order to apply its code of lawful/unlawful to situations within its environment, therefore, law increasingly finds itself having to reconstitute scientific knowledge about what is beneficial and detrimental to children as legal communications. As law becomes increasingly dependent upon the complexities of science, its own structures (and communications) become more complex, taking the form, for example, of specialist courts and judges, specialised court officers such as guardians *ad*

---

26   Douglas, *Risk and Blame*, 39.
27   G. Teubner, 'How the Law Thinks: Toward a Constructivist Epistemology of Law' (1989) 23 *Law & Society Rev.* 727.
28   *Ibid.* at 745.
29   M. King and C. Piper, *How the Law Thinks about Children* (2nd edn, Aldershot, 1995), 50.

litem, funds to pay for experts and rules and procedures to govern their evidence. This dependence on science in turn generates distinctions between expert and non-expert that create the expectation that experts will be a necessary feature of child welfare cases and results in the demand for more and more specialist expertise. As legal communications reflect this growth in scientific knowledge about children's welfare, they become reconstructed within science as demands to increase further the pool of knowledge on those issues which present themselves as problems to be solved by the legal system. Once set in motion this 'structural coupling' of law and child welfare science develops into what Teubner has termed a 'hypercycle' with its attendant self-perpetuating increase in complexity.[30]

We shall return to some of these theoretical ideas at a later stage in this essay when we assess the more general effects of the present proliferation of experts in the courts upon the way in which problems are conceptualized and solved in modern society. For the moment, however, let us turn specifically to the English legal system and the way in which English judges have faced up to the challenge of averting what is perceived as a threat to justice presented by this situation.

The Recent English Experience

Lord Woolf, in the recent report on the Administration of Justice,[31] presents the problem for the English legal system as follows:

A large litigation support industry, generating a multi-million pound fee income, has grown up among professions such as accountants, architects and others, and new professions have developed such as accident reconstruction and care experts. *This goes against all principles of proportionality and access to justice.* . . . Many potential litigants do not even start litigation because of the advice they are given about cost, and in my view *this is as great a social ill as the actual cost of pursuing litigation.*[32]

---

[30] Teubner, n. 27 above at 742; *id., Law as an Autopoietic System* (Oxford, 1993), ch. 3.

[31] Sir Henry Woolf, *Access to Justice: Final Report to the Lord Chancellor on the Civil Justice System in England and Wales* (London, 1996).

[32] *Ibid.*, ch. 2, para. 2 (emphasis added).

Moreover, it is not simply that the proliferation of experts presents an impediment to access to justice. According to Woolf, expert evidence is one of 'the principal weapons used by litigators' who choose to take advantage of the other side's lack of resources.[33] And the problems posed by expert evidence are further compounded by the fact that some experts may be partisan.

Experts then emerge from the Woolf Report as resembling a powerful drug. They are clearly necessary, but they are also potentially dangerous. The objectives for law must be to regulate expertise, first by keeping the costs down and secondly by guaranteeing the reliability of experts.

According to the Report, the first objective is achievable through procedural regulation. Woolf recommends more control by the courts, over both the selection and acceptance of experts and over the scope of their expertise. Under his system 'the court will have *complete control* over the use of evidence, including expert evidence'.[34] Remedies to the crisis of too much expertise are sought and found in 'limiting the scope of expert evidence' by directing that 'no expert evidence . . . at all or no expert evidence of a particular type or relating to a particular issue' shall be adduced; by limiting the number of expert witnesses per party; by 'directing that evidence is to be given by one or more experts chosen by agreement between the parties or appointed by the court'; and by requiring evidence to be given in writing.[35]

The second objective, that of quality control, is fully realizable, according to Woolf, through the training of experts,[36] by ensuring that solicitors give experts adequate instructions[37] and, above all, by vigorous cross-examination in the courtroom, which is 'an essential safeguard to ensure the quality and reliability of evidence'.[38]

The 'social ill' that Woolf highlights, therefore, appears at first glance far removed from the concerns of those social theorists critical of the increasing power of experts and anxious at the way moral and political issues are concealed behind a curtain of exper-

---

[33] Sir Henry Woolf, *Access to Justice*, ch. 3, para. 7.
[34] *Ibid.*, ch. 3, para. 13 (emphasis added).
[35] *Ibid.*
[36] *Ibid.*, ch. 2, para. 54.
[37] *Ibid.*, ch. 2, para. 56.
[38] *Ibid.*, ch. 2, para. 17.

tise. It is perhaps not surprising for Lord Woolf (or for that matter any other judge) to see the present proliferation of expert evidence as a threat to justice. It is also not surprising that, in contrast to the radical critiques of modern society of those social theorists who were quoted earlier, the threats that the Woolf Report identifies are of a quite different order and are of a kind that may be effectively avoided through rational reforms of the legal process. It would have been unthinkable for Woolf to suggest that the process of justice was dependent upon scientific expertise to a degree that would cast doubt on the likelihood of success of any control mechanisms. It was not possible for him to question the assumption on which law relies that 'reliable' expert evidence represents nothing other than objective knowledge. It would have been unthinkable to do so, because the courts rely on science for consensual legitimation of their decisions. Like so many lawyers before him, Lord Woolf succeeds therefore, with exemplary rationality, in transforming a potential crisis for justice into the familiar administrative problem of lack of adequate controls—a problem which the legal system, given sufficient powers and resources, is well able to solve.

Children's Welfare

Let us now focus our attention specifically on expertise in relation to cases before the courts concerning children and their welfare. Strict procedures exist governing the behaviour of experts inside and outside the court-room. They must accept the framework that the legal actors provide and also tailor their knowledge to the needs of the legal process. What experts both know and say about a case are constrained by the legal rules of relevance and procedural fairness. The adversarial nature of the process means that the task of briefing the experts is given to the solicitors and barristers acting for the parties. They instruct the experts as to the relevant facts that they should consider and the questions they are to address.[39] More importantly, however, experts are also subject to the control of the courts. It is the judges who ultimately have the

---

[39] See *Re M (Minors) (Care Proceedings: Child's Wishes)* [1994] 1 FLR 749; *Re T and E (Proceedings: Conflicting Interests)* [1995] 1 FLR 581; *Re CS (Expert Witnesses)* [1996] 2 FLR 115. See also C. Goodwin Jones 'Men of Science v. Men of Law: Some Comments on Recent Cases' (1986) 26 Medical Science Law 13 at 14.

power to decide upon whether expert evidence is or is not relevant to the issues in the case, to determine the areas in which expert evidence is necessary, to limit expert evidence to specific categories of expertise, to specify the number of experts that are called and to decide whether a child may be examined by, or documents shown to, an expert.[40] The increasing use of directions hearings provides ample scope for this kind of control. In addition, in presenting their evidence to the court, experts are expected to distinguish clearly between fact and opinion, to confine themselves strictly to their area of expertise and to ensure that their testimony accords with legal conceptions of relevance.[41]

Employing the legal distinction between 'facts' and 'opinions', judges have been able to introduce extensive controls over what they define as 'the fact-finding activities' of experts as opposed to the formulating of opinions. For example, both courts and judicially chaired public inquiries have laid down guidelines for 'good practice' to cover the interviewing techniques of social workers and psychiatrists in cases of suspected sexual or ritual abuse,[42] much in the same way as the courts, through the old Judges' Rules, attempted to control police interviews of criminal suspects. Any contravention of these guidelines[43] will cast doubt on 'the facts' as presented by the expert since evidence will not have been *'obtained in a reliable form'.*[44]

---

[40] See *Re G (Minors) (Expert Witnesses)* [1994] 2 FLR 291.

[41] 'It is very important to control what the witness does . . . unless they are properly guided they may go off on a tangent' (David Corker, partner at Peters & Peters, quoted in Peter Weiss, 'Filling the Knowledge Gap', *The Lawyer*, Nov. 1996, 14).

[42] See e.g. E. Butler-Sloss, *Report into Child Abuse in Cleveland*, Cm. 412 1988; *Rochdale Borough Council* v. *A and Others* [1991] 2 FLR 192; *Note. Re R (A Minor) (Experts' Evidence)* [1991] 1 FLR 291; *Re A and Others (Minors) (Child Abuse: Guidelines)* [1992] 1 FLR 439 at 442–3. See also *Re E (A Minor) (Child Abuse: Evidence)* [1991] 1 FLR 420 at 456.

[43] For instance, the inadequate audio- or video-recording of interviews, contamination caused by the interviewers' preconceptions, the use of leading questions or the use of untrained or inexperienced interviewers. In *Re A and Others* (n. 42 above) the court criticized the effect on questioning of what it described as the interviewers' obsessive belief that they were investigating a case of group satanic ritual abuse (443).

[44] *Rochdale*, n. 42 above at 205 (emphasis added). Or at least something that can responsibly be relied upon. Courts in the US and Australia appear to accept that reliability is not necessarily synonymous with certainty. See *Daubert* v. *Merrell Dow Pharmaceuticals Inc* 113 S. Ct. 2786 (1993), 125 L. Ed. 2d 469 (1993); *R.* v. *Gilmore* [1977] 2 NSWLR 935 at 941.

Experts' opinions too are, in turn, tested for their reliability. This reliability is judged, and conflicting expert evidence evaluated, through the application of criteria devised to distinguish between 'good' and 'bad' experts. For example, experts may be designated insufficiently competent, and therefore unreliable, on the basis of their qualifications and/or experience.[45] In addition, a witness' competence might be impugned because the opinion he or she offers is seen to be based on incomplete facts or inadequate research. Alternatively, an opinion may be suspect because it reflects an unorthodox position.[46] Ideological bias or partisanship may, on occasions, be another reason for refusing to accept an expert's evidence or for preferring one expert over another.[47]

Yet there are probably few people working in the field of child welfare today, even among the ranks of the judiciary or legal academics, who would claim that scientific facts in relation to children's emotional well-being or mental health exist independent of social contexts. Nor would many argue that the opinions of experts in child care cases are value-free. Using the logic of science, therefore, one might expect little or no use of experts in such cases. Yet in fact the last twenty years have seen a major growth both in the kinds of experts who give evidence in children's cases and in their numbers. It would appear that the absence of a universally accepted consensus over what is good for children paradoxically makes it all the more important for the legal system to give the impression that right answers exist. Furthermore, this impression may be reinforced by the legal system providing copious and detailed procedures and restrictions which are based on the unchallenged (and unchallengeable) assumption that maintaining a tight rein over the evidence of experts operates as an effective quality control mechanism to ensure that courts reach the right answers.[48]

---

[45] See e.g. *Re E*, n. 42 above; *Rochdale*, n. 42 above; *Manchester City Council v. B* [1996] 1 FLR 324 at 331. See also P. Roberts, 'Science in the Criminal Process' (1994) 14 OJLS 468 at 498–500.

[46] In *Re R*, n. 42 above, Cazalet J noted the need for proper research and observed that opinions differ, but usually only 'within a legitimate area of disagreement' (at 292). See also *Re AB (Child Abuse: Expert Witnesses)* [1995] 1 FLR 181.

[47] *Rochdale*, n. 42 above at 212–3 and 218; *Re E*, n. 42 above at 456; *Re R*, n. 42 above at 292–3; *Re AB*, n. 46 above at 199.

[48] See *Re AB*, n. 46 above; L. Askowitz and M. Graham, 'The Reliability of Expert Psychological Testimony in Child Sexual Abuse Prosecutions' (1994) 15

Social Constructionism

A sociological observer of the English legal system's existing rules for dealing with expert witnesses or Lord Woolf's recommended reforms will recognize that these procedural and administrative solutions appear convincing only if one accepts the prior definition of the problem. Here, the definition of the problem relies upon the existence of an idealized notion of 'reliable experts' and 'reliable' here denotes not merely neutral and impartial (that is, not partisan or biased) but the ability to apply a body of objective knowledge to the issues in the case in such a way that 'the right answer' will emerge.[49] Yet when lawyers claim to have reached 'the right answer' its rightness is not, as they would have us believe, rooted in objective or scientific facts. Rather, it is likely to be of a more limited nature, a *rightness in the eyes of the beholders*, a rightness that appears convincing according to the social context, and to the particular form of rationality that is applied to the facts of the case—*a constructed rightness*.

While the lawyers' quest for objective facts may well take them in the direction of science, social construction theorists and sociologists of knowledge suggest that the very intrusion of law into science and the attempt to bring science into the legal process constitutes a 'social negotiation of scientific consensus'.[50] The 'objective facts' generated by technical experts in court therefore are not, according to this view, independent of the legal context but very much a part of it. The apparent ability of courts to determine what constitutes reliable scientific opinion reinforces the assumption within the legal system that there are 'objective facts out there' and that their presentation as reliable evidence flows directly from the development of efficient controls over the scope of expertise and procedures for validating the truth. To abandon this belief would be to plunge the legal system into a state of

Cardozo LR 2027; M. Hayes, 'Reconciling Protection of Children with Justice for Parents in Cases of Alleged Child Abuse' (1997) 17 Legal Studies 1; S. Jasanoff, *Science at the Bar: Law, Science and Technology in America* (Cambridge, Mass., 1995); N. Wall, 'Judicial Attitudes to Expert Evidence in Children's Cases' (1997) 76 *Archives of Disease in Childhood* 485.

[49]   *Access to Justice*, n. 31 above, ch. 2, paras. 8 and 9.
[50]   B. Wynne, 'Establishing the Rules of Laws: Constructing Expert Authority' in R. Smith and B. Wynne, (eds.), *Establishing the Rules of Laws: Constructing Expert Authority* (London & New York, 1989), 23 at 47.

chaos, where facts, opinions, and values would become indistinguishable and where scepticism and uncertainty would run riot. No one would know whether truth existed or, if it did exist, where to find it.

An alliance of critical legal theory and social constructionism may conclude that the preservation by the courts of the fiction that objective truths may be discovered with the assistance of expert evidence has the effect of undermining the moral or normative function of law and handing power to a non-accountable élite. But such an interpretation is not to be assumed from the application of social construction theory on its own. What social constructionism reveals may be seen as politically far less critical, but, at the same time, epistemologically far more radical. What it shows us is *law's construction of different forms of specialist knowledge,* which does not mean that the facts uncovered as a result of the legal process are not 'true', but rather that their truth is dependent upon the social context of the enquiry. Other truths about the same events exist if one asks different questions or asks the same questions differently and if the objectives for which the answers are sought are different from the legal system's objectives. Brian Wynne eloquently understates the issue by suggesting that there is a tendency in the rhetoric and practices of law

to treat 'science' or 'expertise' as an autonomous, objective entity which has authority independent of the institutional settings in which it is used. This may be a practically necessary mythology for legal institutions to employ, but that does not mean that more reflective discourse should ignore its mythological qualities.[51]

Risk Management

Sociological observations of science and of the proliferation of expertise in modern society have forced us, then, to question fundamental assumptions concerning the nature of truth and knowledge. Critical observers such as Bauman, Douglas, Habermas, and Foucault have succeeded in opening our eyes to the power that experts exert in all areas of social decision-making and to the political agendas that may be concealed behind the screen of scientific and technological complexity. The relationship

---

[51] *Ibid.* at 29.

between law and 'expertise', as we have seen, has also received attention from social construction theorists, such as Wynne, who take delight, through 'reflective discourses', in exploding the myth of scientific knowledge that the legal system relies upon to provide it with objective facts and truths and to legitimate publicly its decisions. What appears to be lacking in all these observations, however, is any detailed account of the processes by which the expert knowledge becomes disseminated throughout society as laying down a framework for understanding and for problem-solving. To put it crudely, experts today may well be indispensable as part of the machinery of government and social control, if only to give an aura of respectability and scientific legitimacy to decisions. But this in itself does not explain the social processes by which the population being governed or controlled so willingly accepts the need for and the validity of such scientific legitimation. Michel Foucault probably comes closest to providing such an account in the attention he gives to the exercise of power in every-day practices, but, as critics of Foucault point out, what one is left with are a series of vignettes of the practices that have existed and, in some cases, continue to exist in the governance of sexuality, mental illness, and crime, with no overriding or linking concepts, except for the generalized notions of power and knowledge. For Foucault, accounts of law's governance of the activities of expert witnesses would probably suffice to confirm the existence of a framework of belief and understanding within which both lawyers and scientists (or purveyors of technical knowledge) practise. There could, for example, be no co-operation between them with-out a commitment to a shared belief in the possibility of achieving 'the right answer' through the submission of specialist knowledge to the rigours of law. What Foucauldian accounts tell us is that the negotiations and accommodations between lawyers and experts carried out within this epistemological framework (even where they expose and challenge expert opinion) actually help to construct, sustain, and develop the very shared expectations and understandings that come to represent reality. Yet what these accounts do not identify are specific social mechanisms which call this reality into existence in the first place and then permit it to extend way beyond the boundaries of the legal system. Foucault, together with many other social theorists, manages to avoid such difficult issues by positing a broad-brush interpretation of the history of Western society since the Enlightenment. Law, politics, and science are all seen to exist as part of an overarching *epistème*, a seamless scientific-legal-political complex which determines the way that everyone (within a specified locality) understands events and relationships, makes decisions for themselves and others and even settles the form that resistance to the existing social order will take.

Mary Douglas comes close to identifying a possible social mechanism for the translation of professional practice into unquestioned reality when she compares blame attribution for disasters and future dangers across different societies. Power in all these societies devolves to those who are able to give the impression that they are capable of identifying the causes of these misfortunes and offering reassurances as to their future avoidance. Those who have gained power are able to retain and increase such power by fostering anxiety about the future among their subjects and then claiming to be able to foresee and control that future. In modern society this management of uncertainty, she argues, takes the form of risk-assessment:

The idea of risk could have been custom-made [to fill the needs of justice and welfare in the modern world]. Its universalizing terminology, its abstractness, its power of condensation, its scientificity, its connection with objective analysis make it perfect. Above all, its forensic uses fit the tool to the task of building a culture that supports a modern industrial society.[52]

Risk-assessment, according to Douglas, offers a supposedly scientific way of conceptualizing dangers, giving 'the pretension of a possible precise calculation'.[53] We do not need, however, to follow Mary Douglas in her attempt to present risk management as socially significant solely through its use and misuse by politicians. Her claim that cultural theory is able to strip away the technology and expose the moral or political controversies that lie hidden beneath the rhetoric of probability theory should not blind us to the wider implications of what Ulrich Beck famously calls 'the Risk Society'.[54] 'Risks are always political'[55] and risk-assessment always conceals the iron hand of power within the velvet

---

[52] Douglas, *Risk*, n. 24 above, 15.   [53] *Ibid.*, 25.
[54] U. Beck, *Risk Society. Towards a New Modernity* (London, 1992).
[55] Douglas, *Risk*, n. 24 above, 44.

glove of scientific neutrality only when observed by an anthropologist who insists on seeing societies only or predominantly as different forms of political organization. There is, however, no obligation to view them in this way. Nevertheless, we should be grateful to Mary Douglas for drawing our attention to the important mechanism of risk-assessment and its role in managing anxiety in modern society.

Risks and Dangers

It is at this point that Niklas Luhmann's ideas offer an opportunity to progress from a concept of risk evaluation and multiplication for covert political ends to one which makes no assertions as to who might be exercising power to control whom for whose benefit. Luhmann distinguishes between risks and dangers. He conceptualizes risks as losses that social processes attribute to decisions,[56] while 'dangers' are defined as those losses which are seen as occurring independently of decisions. Being injured by the actions of a negligent driver, for example, would be seen as a risk, because it has been categorized socially as one of those events which, while perhaps not predictable, is amenable to retrospective analysis to determine the cause and identify that cause as attributable to human decision-making. Being struck by a thunder bolt, by contrast, would be seen as a danger. Using this distinction, it is possible to talk of 'the production of risk', meaning the process by which the factors that are seen as contributing to future loss become identifiable as knowable, and once known, controllable through decisions. From this point onwards the danger of that loss may be perceived in terms of risk. For this to occur there is no requirement of certainty as to how losses are to be averted, but merely the belief that the knowledge, necessary for such loss-avoidance, exists.

The translation of dangers into risk in Luhmann's scheme is not just a matter of applying probability theory to known dangers. It involves the substitution of decisions or the possibility of decisions for what were previously seen as events which occurred through the random operations of nature, the mysteries of God's will or the playing out of fate. Of course, theoretically, there is no need

---

[56] N. Luhmann, *Risk: A Sociological Theory* (New York, 1993), ch. 6.

for the formal institutions of politics and law to exist in order for dangers to be converted into risks—science is quite capable of managing such operations on its own. Without the normative communications of law, politics, and economics, however, making distinctions as to what is and what is not risky would itself be a risky business, for how would we know upon what risks to concentrate our attention at any one time, whether certain risks were unavoidable, and which risks were worth taking in order to avoid others which involve the possibility of even greater loss?

The publication of scientific papers alone does little to resolve these difficulties. Even the wide dissemination of 'new discoveries' in the mass media is a random, haphazard process which pays little or no attention to the use to be made of such discoveries by society or the weight that they should carry in decision-making. Seen in this light, the role of the expert in court takes on a new significance. Wynne hinted at this when he wrote of science in the legal process as 'a social negotiation of scientific consensus'.[57] The expert in court should not simply be seen as representing science helping law to do its work effectively.[58] What is also occurring is a validation of science or technical knowledge as being capable of producing 'facts' for society. Even if the particular expert is unsound, reliable expertise is nevertheless believed to exist. Where risks are concerned, the legal system in its pronouncements on crime, negligence, fraud, and child abuse arouses public anxieties concerning possible future loss, but, at the same time through the introduction of experts is able to give the impression that these losses are, at least to some extent, avoidable if only the proper decisions are made.[59] Yet even this is not all that takes place when experts give evidence in court.

If we apply Luhmann's sociological theory of risk to the role of child welfare experts in child abuse cases, it becomes apparent that the very process of bringing the matter before a court has the immediate effect of producing the expectation that the events surrounding the harm to the child were not chance happenings. The legal process applies the risk/danger distinction by transposing

[57] Wynne, 'Establishing the Rules', n. 50 above at 47.
[58] See Hayes, 'Reconciling Protection', n. 48 above.
[59] The political system is also able to pass legislation with the intention of preventing or controlling what were previously seen as dangers. Economics will take dangers and translate them into the risk of monetary loss.

the loss to the child from the side of danger to that of risk. From that point on, the expectation is that the events were not of a kind for which nobody could be held responsible. Of course, until the moment when the court pronounces its decision that someone or some legal body was responsible, there is always the possibility, however remote, that the loss will be reclassified as a danger.

Calling for an expert opinion assumes that knowledge concerning the risk/danger question is indeed available. This issue of risk on the one side of the distinction and danger on the other may itself become a matter of debate among experts, as in cases of brittle-bones, the onset of mental illness, or childhood suicide. More often, however, the experts operate as second-order observers of other people's risk-averting decisions. Should the parents have taken the child to hospital? Should the social services department have offered more support to the family? Should a social worker have recognized the signs of sexual abuse? Should a mother have taken steps to protect her child against the physical violence of the step-father? In these cases the expert starts, therefore, from the belief that if the right decision had been taken by the right people at the right time, the loss or harm to the child could have been averted or at least reduced in severity.

Within the court setting the risk/danger distinction could be re-read as losses for which expert knowledge exists on the one side and those for which it does not exist on the other (for by definition nobody can tell when or where dangers are likely to strike). Once classified as a risk-associated loss, the expectation arises that somewhere there will be experts with the knowledge to explain how the loss came about and, in the concern for the child's future safety, what steps should be taken to avoid further loss. A lawyer's ignorance of or refusal to contemplate the existence of any such expertise may in its turn give rise to risk of loss—the loss of losing the case, which in child protection cases may mean that the parents lose their child.[60] The judge too may run risks by not

---

[60] This is not to suggest that medical or psychological practitioners are a driving force for the creation of so much expertise, but that once the wheels have been set in motion, it is very difficult to halt the machine or even to slow it down. Its progress soon takes it out of the control of individual practitioners, as the author of a recent research report into delays in children's cases in England writes, 'Many medical practitioners, including experienced practitioners, were said to feel uncomfortable with the concept of setting themselves up as 'experts', although it

asking for an expert opinion, for future loss to the child (if, for example, he or she is returned to the parents) could well be attributed to that judge's failure to recognize or fully appreciate the seriousness of the risk. Once the possibility of expert knowledge has been recognized by a court, therefore, one cannot turn the clock back and declare such knowledge to be useless or too expensive. On the contrary, the tendency is always in the opposite direction—that of acknowledging more and more events as susceptible to expert opinion and that of refining, through further distinctions, which experts should give opinions on which kinds of event. The creation of new risks appears to go in one direction only. Once created, it is extremely difficult, if not impossible, to reverse the process and declare that what was previously believed to be a decision-avoidable loss should now be seen as a matter of chance or the result of totally uncontrollable events.

A decision to convert or reconvert risks into dangers is always available as a possible, if unlikely, path for law to take. Taking this path may appear to contradict the general trend of increasing risks, but such an interpretation ignores the possibility that other social systems, such as economics, politics, or science, may continue to observe the situation as risky, that is as giving rise to losses which are attributable to decisions regardless of, or even as a result of, law's action.[61] The consequence for society is an ever-growing catalogue of risky situations and an ever-increasing deployment of resources towards their identification, monitoring, and attempted control. In principle, the legal system is no more immune than other social systems from this inexorable progression towards increasing risk-regulation. Having helped to create the monster, it cannot absolve itself from all future responsibility for its excesses. All it can do is to pass the risks on to other

was observed that if they did not do so those less specialist than themselves would be consulted instead.' (D. M. Booth, *Avoiding Delay in Children Act Cases* (London, 1996), 40).

[61] We are indebted to Elena Esposito for pointing out the possibility of law converting risks into dangers. An example of such a process would perhaps be the withdrawal of law in most Western countries from the unpleasant task of establishing responsibility for the breakdown of marriage in divorce cases. This does not mean, however, that nobody now is ever responsible for such breakdowns and divorce, like an earthquake or tidal wave, simply happens. On the contrary, intense efforts are being made within politics, psychological science, and religion to establish causes and introduce preventative measures.

systems by making it appear as if they possess the knowledge and capacity that are needed to attribute causes to past losses (in our case, harms to children) and to provide guidance on ways to avoid future loss.

Seen in this light, it is no longer possible to accept the law's perception of its own operations. Legal decisions on the use of experts can no longer be seen merely as innocent mediators in the interface between law and scientific or technological knowledge, or even as a method of controlling the quality and the admissibility into normative decisions of different bodies of technical knowledge.[62] A sociological account of risk as a social construct would observe law *actually helping to create the very risks for which expert opinions become necessary* (for what will happen to the child, if the 'right decision' is not taken?). These newly produced risks then make it possible for increasingly extensive and specialist forms of expertise to develop, which in their turn are likely to enter the legal arena as expert evidence and emerge as new risks for law as well as for society. Once set in motion this process is carried forward by its own dynamic—the need to make decisions based on the awareness of risk. Seen in this light, the only chance of slowing down the inexorable process of risk creation with all its attendant anxieties lies, not in legal, administrative, or political controls, but in quite the opposite direction, the reduction of decisions. This may be possible in some areas of social activity, as the deregulation policies of right-wing governments have recently demonstrated. It seems highly unlikely, however, in those situations where decisions serve in the short term to quieten deep-seated anxieties, such as those concerning children's well-being, and operate as a reassurance that future risks or harms can indeed be brought under control.

[62] See Jasanoff, *Science at the Bar*, n. 48 above.

LAW'S TRUTH, LAY TRUTH AND MEDICAL SCIENCE

Three Case Studies

Tony Ward

Tom Wolfe displayed severe historical amnesia when he wrote recently that 'we now live in an age in which science is a court from which there is no appeal. And the issue this time around, at the end of the twentieth century, is . . . the nature of our precious inner selves.'[1] The same could have been said last time around, when similar claims were advanced about Freudian psychoanalysis, and the time before that, when Wolfe's kind of 'scientific naturalism' was at its height in the Victorian era.[2] Ever since then, courts of law have had to grapple with the cognitive authority claimed by the 'court' of science, especially over our 'precious inner selves'.[3]

One way which courts have found to reconcile the claims of science and law has been described in broadly similar terms by Brian Wynne and Carol Jones.[4] In essence, courts can accept the

---

[1] Tom Wolfe, 'Sorry, but your Soul just Died', *Independent on Sunday,* 2 Feb. 1997, 7.

[2] F. M. Turner, *Between Science and Religion: The Reaction to Scientific Naturalism in Late Victorian England* (New Haven, 1974); L. S. Jacyna, 'Somatic Theories of Mind and the Interests of Medicine in Britain, 1850–1879' (1982) 26 *Medical History* 335. On psychoanalysis, see e.g. E. Glover, 'The Roots of Crime' (1922), reprinted in his *The Roots of Crime* (London, 1960).

[3] R. Smith, *Trial by Medicine: Insanity and Responsibility in Victorian Trials* (Edinburgh, 1981); M. S. Moore, *Law and Psychiatry: Rethinking the Relationship* (Cambridge, 1984).

[4] B. Wynne, *Rationality and Ritual: The Windscale Inquiry and Nuclear Decisions in Britain* (Chalfont St. Giles, 1982), ch. 7; B. Wynne, 'Establishing the Rules of Laws: Constructing Expert Authority' in R. Smith and B. Wynne (eds.), *Expert Evidence: Interpreting Science in the Law* (London, 1989); C. Jones, *Expert Witnesses* (Oxford, 1994).

claims of 'science' in the abstract to provide objective and reliable knowledge, without extending such recognition automatically to the individual scientist. Law's own cognitive methods (cross-examination, observation of the demeanour of witnesses, etc.)[5] can then be deployed to establish whether a particular expert truly represents the claims of science, or is biased, incompetent, or a downright charlatan. In this way the law can, as Wynne puts it, both 'deconstruct' the expert's testimony and 'reconstruct' the social authority of science.[6] Individual experts become scapegoats for the failure of science to live up to its 'scientistic' image as a repository of value-free, consensual truth.

What law's deference to the authority of science fails to recognize, according to Wynne and other sociological critics,[7] is the contingent nature of all acts of classification:

Assignments of cases to general classes, or evidence to theories, are usually presented as natural, inescapable meanings, merely 'revealed' by expert analysis. Certain properties are highlighted, others tacitly neglected, resulting in the perception of similarity or difference between cases and classes. Yet these 'natural' logical pathways can be shown to be the result of social conventions which have achieved closure around one set of classifications rather than another.[8]

There is, however, another legal response to science which takes as its starting-point precisely the fact that law and science classify phenomena according to different conventions, that, in Nelken's terms, 'law's truth' is not the same as the truth of science.[9] Perhaps the clearest example is the insanity defence. The criminal law classifies people as insane according to quite different criteria from those used to define what is now called mental illness and has not accepted the claims of medicine to reveal a uniquely true classification of mental phenomena.[10]

---

[5]   See e.g. *Loveday* v. *Renton* [1990] 1 Med. LR 117 at 125.

[6]   Wynne, 'Establishing the Rules', n. 4 above at 32–7.

[7]   H. Collins, *Changing Order* (London, 1985), 152–3; H. Collins and T. Pinch, *The Golem: What Everyone Should Know About Science* (Oxford, 1994), 145–8.

[8]   Wynne, 'Establishing the Rules', n. 4 above at 24. For fuller discussion of this argument see B. Barnes, D. Bloor and J. Henry, *Scientific Knowledge: A Sociological Perspective* (London, 1996).

[9]   D. Nelken, *The Truth About Law's Truth* (Florence, 1990).

[10]   H. Oppenheimer, *The Criminal Responsibility of Lunatics* (London, 1909); H. Fingarette, *The Meaning of Criminal Insanity* (Berkeley, 1972).

But studies of the actual operation of the insanity defence, both historically (see below) and in present-day England[11] and the United States,[12] show that it does not reflect a doctrinaire adherence to a legal definition of insanity. Rather, whatever the precise test the law may lay down, the sane are divided from the insane according to juries' and judges' ideas about moral responsibility and 'folk psychology'.[13] It is 'lay truth' rather than 'law's truth' or 'medical truth' which ultimately prevails.

The first of the three case studies which follow expands on this argument about the insanity defence; the other two suggest that it may have a wider application. The first study is of a decisive series of events in the long debate about reform of the insanity defence: the trial of Ronald True and its aftermath in 1922–4. The second is of a recent case in an area of the law of tort, liability for psychiatric injury, which has certain similarities with the law on criminal insanity. The third case is about as different as it could be while still remaining mainly within the ambit of medical science: it concerns the alleged carcinogenic effects of radiation from a nuclear power plant. I argue that in all three cases the same broad pattern can be discerned: rather than deferring to the authority of science, law upholds its prerogative of classifying phenomena in its own way, but ultimately classifies them not according to rigorous criteria of either law or science, but rather according to what purports to be common sense. Of course, three case studies are not a basis for any sweeping generalization about law's relationship to science, even if valid generalizations of this kind are possible.[14] What they can do, I hope, is to convey some idea of the complexity of that relationship, and specifically to suggest that it needs to be analysed as a relationship among three forms of knowledge rather than just two supposedly 'autopoietic' discourses.[15]

[11] R. D. Mackay, *Mental Condition Defences in the Criminal Law* (Oxford, 1995).

[12] N. Finkel, *Insanity on Trial* (New York, 1988).

[13] D. N. Robinson, *Wild Beasts & Idle Humours* (Cambridge, Mass., 1996), ch. 6.

[14] Cf. M. Valverde, 'Social Facticity and the Law: A Social Expert's Eyewitness Account of Law' (1996) 5 Social & Legal Studies 201 at 203.

[15] Three exemplary studies in this respect are: R. Harris, *Murders and Madness: Medicine, Law and Society in the Fin de Siècle* (Oxford, 1989); P. Guarnieri, *A Case of Child Murder: Law and Science in Nineteenth-Century Tuscany* (Cambridge, 1993); and S. Jasanoff, *Science at the Bar: Law, Science and Technology in America* (Cambridge, Mass., 1995).

Mad or Monstrous Murders, 1922–4

The M'Naghten Rules, stipulating that insanity is a defence to a criminal charge only where a disease of the mind prevents the defendant from knowing the nature and quality of their act or that it is wrong, were created by the judges in response to pressure to limit the influence of medical experts.[16] The judges transformed a loose common-law principle into a rigid formula which accorded both with early Victorian morality[17] and with the Austinian 'command' theory of law (according to which a subject who could not understand the sovereign's commands or relate them to their actions could not be said to disobey those commands).[18] Later in the nineteenth century, as middle-class opinion became more receptive to medical explanations of crime,[19] some judges—most influentially Stephen J[20]—came to believe that the Rules should be relaxed to reflect public morality. After 1886, the prosecution in capital cases was required to ensure that medical evidence was called if there was any suggestion of possible insanity, and the apparent neutrality of evidence introduced in this way contributed to a relaxation of judicial attitudes.[21] For some years the liberal application of the rules in practice took the heat out of the debate over reform.[22] Around the time of the First World War a number of factors combined to revive the debate, including the creation of the Court of Criminal Appeal in 1907, the rise of psychoanalysis, and the rivalry between prison medical officers (who took a relatively narrow

[16] J. M. Quen, 'An Historical View of the M'Naghten Trial' (1968) 43 *Bull. Hist. Medicine* 43; R. Moran, *Knowing Right from Wrong: The Insanity Defense of Daniel McNaughtan* (London, 1981).

[17] M. Wiener, *Reconstructing the Criminal: Culture, Law and Policy in England, 1830–1914* (Cambridge, 1990), 83–91.

[18] J. Austin, *Lectures,* vol. 1 (2nd edn, London, 1885), Lecture XXVI; 'Second Report of the Commissioners for Revision and Consolidation of the Criminal Law' (1845) 24 *Parl. Papers* 107; E. C. Clark, *An Analysis of Criminal Liability* (Cambridge, 1880), 63–7.

[19] Wiener, *Reconstructing the Criminal,* n. 17 above, chs. 4–7.

[20] R. v. *Davis* (1881) 14 Cox CC 563; Sir James Fitzjames Stephen, *A History of the Criminal Law of England,* vol. 2 (London, 1883), ch. 19.

[21] T. Ward, 'Law, Common Sense and the Authority of Science: Expert Witnesses and Criminal Insanity in England, ca. 1840–1940' (1997) 6 (3) Social and Legal Studies 343.

[22] See e.g. Medico-Psychological Association, 'Report of the Criminal Responsibility Committee' (1896) 42 *J Mental Science* 863.

view of insanity) and the lunacy specialists instructed on behalf of some defendants.[23]

The controversy came to a head in 1922 over the case of Ronald True, a spectacularly unsuccessful aviator and flamboyant liar who brutally murdered a prostitute and stole her jewellery.[24] The trial was unusual in that all the medical witnesses agreed that True was insane but their view was vigorously contested by the prosecution (who may have rightly anticipated that any leniency shown to True would be attributed to his wealthy connections). The medical witnesses considered that a combination of innate mental defect, head injury, morphine addiction, and perhaps syphilis had robbed True of any appreciation of moral right and wrong; two lunacy experts also thought him unable to control his actions. Under cross-examination, however, they all had to concede that he knew what he was doing and that it was wrong according to the 'ordinary views of mankind'. Therefore, argued the prosecution, he was sane according to the M'Naghten Rules as interpreted by the Court of Criminal Appeal.[25] As the editor of the published transcript of the trial perceptively observed:

Had the temper of the jury been different, this insistence on a technical point would have been worse than useless. But as the case proceeded it became clear that the facts which to medical men were so eloquent of profound mental disorder would convey to the jury only the picture of a depraved and callous monster who, being in need of ready money, thought to raise a few pounds by murdering and robbing a defenceless woman.[26]

After lengthy legal argument, McCardie J directed the jury on the lines advocated by Stephen J, that in addition to the grounds specified in the Rules, True would have a defence if he was 'deprived of the power of controlling his actions', though this test should be applied 'with great care'.[27] The jury nevertheless found True guilty. In order to challenge the judge's summing-up on appeal the defence argued that the jury should have been directed that it must return a special verdict where there was unanimous medical

---

[23] T. Ward, 'Psychiatry and Criminal Responsibility in England, 1843–1939', unpub. PhD. thesis (De Montfort Univ., Leicester, 1996), chs. 4–5.

[24] D. Carswell (ed.), *The Trial of Ronald True* (Edinburgh, 1925).

[25] In *R. v. Codère* (1916) 12 Cr. App. R. 21.

[26] Carswell, *Trial*, n. 24 above, 38.   [27] *Ibid.*, 253–4.

evidence of insanity. The Court of Criminal Appeal dismissed this argument and also declined to endorse McCardie J's 'self-control' test.[28] Further controversy was aroused when the Home Secretary, as was practically (but not legally) inevitable in the light of his medical advisers' view that True was certifiably insane, reprieved him from execution. A Committee was then appointed, chaired by Atkin LJ (as he then was), to examine the law on criminal insanity.

Shortly after True's case there was another murder trial which was in some ways more typical of criminal insanity cases.[29] Ernest Walker, a 17-year old domestic servant, telephoned for a messenger-boy. On the boy's arrival Walker struck him fatally on the head with an iron bar. He took a train from London to Kent and gave himself up to a policeman with the words 'I think I've done a murder in London'. A suicide note and a numbered 'programme' for the murder were found near the body, indicating that Walker had planned not to kill the boy immediately but to tie him up and torture him first. What may strike the reader today as an obvious indication of sexual sadism did not prevent defence counsel from arguing that there was 'no motive whatever for the attack'. Letitia Fairfield, in an incisive commentary on the case, suggested that 'Walker's motive was the gratification of abnormal desires, unintelligible to the average man and therefore accepted as *prima facie* evidence of insanity'.[30] Had the victim been a girl whom Walker wanted to rape, she suggested, the defence would have had a harder task.

The defence called a Harley Street physician to testify that Walker had a history of epilepsy and had acted in a condition of 'epileptic automatism or psychic equivalent'. This was quite a common defence at the time,[31] and the prosecution sought to rebut it in the usual way, by calling a prison medical officer (Dr Norwood East, who had been a key defence witness at True's trial) to testify that he had carefully observed Walker in prison

[28] R. v. *True* (1922) 16 Cr. App. R. 164.
[29] *The Times* 22 June 1922. See also (1922) 68 *J Mental Science* 399–400; (1923) 69 *J Mental Science* 142–3.
[30] L. Fairfield, 'The Criminal Law and the Criminal Insane' (1922) 4 *J Compar. Legislation and Internat. Law* (3rd ser.), 191 at 194.
[31] W. Norwood East, 'Some Forensic Aspects of Epilepsy' (1926) 72 *J Mental Science* 533.

and seen no signs of epilepsy or insanity. The judge considered East's evidence 'not very strong'. The jury took just five minutes to find Walker guilty, but insane.

Here was a case where both the law and the medical evidence provided strong grounds for conviction. The similarity between the murder and the plan was hard to explain if Walker did not know what he was doing. At least by the time he got to Kent, he knew it was legally wrong. East's diagnosis was based on a scientific test—he administered a combination of medication and food which would be expected to induce a fit in a genuine epileptic[32]— whereas the defence case rested on vague evidence that Walker had suffered fits in childhood. Defence counsel put the real basis of the defence succinctly when he asked Dr East whether this was not 'a very mad murder'.

Walker's case illustrated what was well understood on all sides in the debate over criminal insanity: that whatever the legal test and whatever the scientific evidence, judges and juries would stretch the law to find defendants insane who appeared obviously mad from a lay point of view.[33] The Court of Criminal Appeal was less flexible than many trial judges, but in at least two cases it found the facts sufficiently redolent of insanity to substitute special verdicts for convictions with little attempt to satisfy the letter of the Rules.[34] Atkin LJ and his Committee, while insisting that the insanity defence should reflect the law's concern with *mens rea* rather than a medical definition of insanity, wanted to narrow the gap between doctrine and practice by adding an 'irresistible impulse' defence to the M'Naghten Rules.[35] But when Lord Darling, a retired judge, introduced a bill into the House of Lords to implement Atkin's proposal, a succession of Law Lords rose to speak against it, including Lord Hewart CJ who claimed to speak for the great majority of the Queen's Bench judges.[36]

[32] W. C. Sullivan, *Crime and Insanity* (London, 1925), 143.

[33] See e.g. T. Humphreys, 'The Criminal Responsibility of the Alleged Insane' (1922) 1 CLJ 302; Lord Atkin, speech to the Medico-Legal Society (1925) 159 Law Times 436; C. S. Kenny, *Outlines of Criminal Law* (13th edn, Cambridge, 1929), 55; W. Norwood East, 'Murder, from the Point of View of the Psychiatrist' (1935) 3 Medico-Legal and Criminological Rev. 61.

[34] *R. v. Jefferson* (1908) 1 Cr. App. R. 95; *R. v. Lloyd* (1927) 20 Cr. App. R. 139.

[35] *Report of the Committee on Insanity and Crime* (1923) 12 *Parl. Papers* 787.   [36] (1924) HL Debs., 15 May, cols. 443–76.

The reasoning of Lord Hewart and his supporters appeared contradictory. On the one hand, Hewart in particular insisted on the need for 'clear proof' of the precise matters stated in the M'Naghten Rules.[37] But, almost in the next breath, he was defending the law for its flexibility:

In cases where there is evidence of real mental disease antecedent to the commission of the alleged crime, and there is no evidence of a motive which might influence a sane person, juries have no difficulty in finding either that the accused did not know the nature and quality of its act or that it was wrong.[38]

This informal 'no sane motive' test fell far short of 'clear proof' of the matters covered by the Rules, and in many cases amounted to a laxer definition of insanity than that proposed by Atkin and Darling, which in Hewart's view was merely 'a more exact formula to justify a few verdicts which are already returned'.[39] What really troubled Hewart and his allies was not that juries would apply a loose definition of insanity but that they would defer to a medical definition.

These scientists are excellent servants, but they are not always reliable masters, and . . . in a very large number of cases there would always be people who would come forward and say that mental disease was present, rendering the act uncontrollable. What is the unfortunate jury to do? A tender-hearted jury . . . would be likely to say that they were not in a position to contradict the evidence of these eminent scientific gentlemen, and would therefore accept it.[40]

Thus, in defending legal formalism the judges were also defending the cognitive authority of lay psychology and lay morality in the face of what Hewart in another context dubbed 'the new despotism' of benevolent experts.[41] As Jerome Frank argued a few years after the trial, the practice of leaving apparently rigid rules to be interpreted by juries was a way for the law to have its cake and eat it by preserving the 'self-delusion of legal fixity and

[37] (1924) HL Debs., 15 May, col. 465.
[38] *Ibid.*, col. 468. See also Lord Sumner, cols. 457–8.
[39] *Ibid.*, cols. 470–1.
[40] Lord Haldane, LC, *ibid.*, col. 473; see also Lord Sumner, col. 461; Lord Hewart cols. 468, 470; and for a well-argued defence of their position, J. Hall, 'Mental Disease and Criminal Responsibility' (1945) 45 Columbia LR 677, at 702–5.
[41] Lord Hewart of Bury, *The New Despotism* (London, 1929).

certainty' alongside the reality of uncertainty and flexibility.[42] The discretionary powers of the Home Secretary allowed any apparent triumph of lay retributivism over medical knowledge to be quickly reversed, and also allowed the Court of Criminal Appeal to uphold the letter of the law without appearing unduly inhumane.[43] They also ensured the quiet triumph of Dr Norwood East, whose evidence was rejected in the *True* and *Walker* cases but who played a leading role for many years behind the scenes in deciding whether convicted murderers would live or die.[44]

Vernon v. *Bosley:* the Judge as Biographer

The definition of 'nervous shock' or 'psychiatric injury' in the law of tort involves an interaction between legal and psychiatric discourse not unlike that seen in the insanity defence. In both areas a 'disease of the mind' (insanity) or 'recognized psychiatric illness' (nervous shock) is a necessary but not sufficient condition for membership of the relevant legal category. A more rigorous test must be satisfied before the defendant is excused from criminal responsibility or the tortfeasor is held responsible for the illness. In *Vernon* v. *Bosley*,[45] the plaintiff claimed that his career had been destroyed by the psychiatric consequences of watching the unsuccessful efforts to save his children from drowning after the defendant negligently caused the car in which they were travelling to fall into a river. The defendant admitted negligence but argued that the plaintiff's psychiatric condition would sound in damages only if it amounted to post-traumatic stress disorder, as distinct from pathological grief disorder or a pre-existing disorder of personality exacerbated by stress. Much of the sixty-eight days of evidence heard by Sedley J was taken up with conflicting expert opinions as to the diagnosis and aetiology of the plaintiff's condition. The plaintiff was awarded over £1m in damages and the defendant appealed.

---

[42]   J. Frank, *Law and the Modern Mind* (New York, 1930), 177.

[43]   The Court repeatedly emphasized that the Home Secretary was better placed than it was to make inquiries about a prisoner's sanity, and in dismissing appeals based on insanity would occasionally drop a public hint that the prisoner should be reprieved: e.g. *R.* v. *Atherley* (1909) 2 Cr. App. R. 165; *R.* v. *Coelho* (1914) 10 Cr. App. R. 10.

[44]   P. Bowden, 'William Norwood East: the Acceptable Face of Psychiatry' (1991) 2 *J Forensic Psychiatry* 59.

[45]   (1995) 28 BMLR 1 (QBD); [1997] 1 All ER 577 (CA).

In a dissenting judgment in the Court of Appeal, Stuart Smith LJ accepted the defendant's view of the relation between law and medicine.

[T]he plaintiff must suffer from a recognised psychiatric illness. Over the last 15 years psychiatrists have come to call this illness post traumatic stress disorder (PTSD). . . .

[Grief and bereavement do not, however,] become actionable even if the grief becomes so severe as to be regarded as abnormal and gives rise to psychiatric illness, the symptoms of which may include depression and anxiety. Such an illness is referred to as pathological grief disorder (PGD).[46]

Having equated legal with medical categories in this surprisingly crude fashion,[47] Stuart Smith LJ was driven into a posture close to that described by Wynne and Jones. Medical science ought to be able to provide an objective answer to the question of whether the plaintiff had PTSD or not. But it could not do so, partly 'because psychiatry is not a precise science';[48] partly because '[i]n the field of psychiatry it may be more difficult for those who have treated the Plaintiff to approach the case with true objectivity';[49] and partly because the particular experts called for both sides were unacceptably partisan. As a result, in Stuart Smith LJ's view, 'the Judge was presented with an almost impossible task'; but in the absence of 'acceptable medical evidence' he ought to have found that the plaintiff had failed to discharge his burden of proof.[50]

The trial judge and the majority of the Court of Appeal preferred to assert the independence of legal categories from medical ones. As Thorpe LJ put it, 'PTSD is not a bespoke measure for the purpose of nervous shock litigation. . . . The fact that it is a diagnosis that necessarily involves a shock is not a reason for elevating it to the exclusion of other psychiatric illnesses that may be shock induced.'[51] Both he and Sedley J, the trial judge, pointed out that the definition of PTSD in the diagnostic manual known as DSM III-R—which on several counts Mr Vernon's condition did not fit—differed from that given in

---

46 [1997] 1 All ER 577 at 584-5.
47 Especially surprising in view of the judgment of Stuart-Smith J (as he then was) in *Brice* v. *Brown* [1984] 1 All ER 997.
48 [1997] 1 All ER at 586.   49 *Ibid.* at 591.
50 *Ibid.*   51 *Ibid.* at 610.

another widely used manual, *The International Classification of Diseases*, and was open to dissent and revision within the psychiatric profession. Sedley J did not consider that he was 'limited to answering Yes or No to a particular diagnosis posited by one or other party. . . . Among the competing diagnoses and aetiologies are the signposts to a conclusion which must in the end be my own.'[52]

Sedley J's route to a conclusion began not from the expert evidence but from his own impressions of the plaintiff as a witness: 'a tragic figure' whose rambling and untruthful evidence ironically helped his case.[53] Sedley J then embarked on a lengthy biography[54] of the plaintiff from his schooldays to the time of the trial, in which he deliberately eschewed the use of psychiatric or psychological terminology.[55] The judge skilfully evoked a personality which, he repeatedly insisted, was too complex to be described by any psychiatric label.

The peculiarity of Mr Vernon's case lies in the complexity and fragility of the man: throughout his life personality and mental state have reacted upon one another, so that one cannot look in him for textbook conditions in isolation but must try, with the help of expert evidence, to understand as best one can the whole individual.[56]

Sedley J's understanding of Mr Vernon was that he always had flaws in his make-up (whether or not these amounted to a 'personality disorder') but that without the tragedy of his children's death he would not be the unemployable wreck who had stood in the witness box. But in order to draw the line between 'nervous shock' and 'grief' the judge considered himself bound by the authority of *Hinz* v. *Berry*[57] to answer the 'unattractive' if not 'pointless'[58] question whether the plaintiff's mental state would have been the same if his children had died but he had not experienced the trauma of seeing them drown. This required him to point to some medical aetiology linking Mr Vernon's 'recognized

---

[52] (1995) 28 BMLR at 110.   [53] *Ibid.* at 4.
[54] Described as such in [1997] 1 All ER by Stuart Smith LJ at 591 and by Evans LJ at 597.   [55] 28 BMLR at 12.
[56] *Ibid.* at 122.   [57] [1970] 1 All ER 1074 at 1075.
[58] The words are Hidden J's in *Alcock* v. *Chief Constable of the South Yorkshire Police* [1991] 1 All ER 353 at 382. Sedley J remarked that while the exercise on which he was embarking 'might well attract the same comment . . . the decision in *Hinz* v. *Berry* requires it to be attempted' ((1995) 28 BMLR at 120).

illness' to the traumatic event, and he found what he was looking for in a particular article from the *British Journal of Psychiatry*.[59] Although the article does not specifically discuss the kind of trauma suffered by Mr Vernon, it provided a 'linkage between the circumstances of the bereavement and the personality of the survivor, a linkage which may then produce a variety of reactive states, depression and anxiety prominent among them.' The judge also drew on some psychological theory about 'learned helplessness'.

These citations, however, provide only limited support to a judgment which relies heavily on a skilfully constructed narrative to convince the audience of the causes of the plaintiff's present state. One reader who was not convinced was Stuart Smith LJ. While paying tribute to Sedley J's 'biography' of Vernon as 'a *tour de force*', he considered that it ultimately relied on 'speculation and guesswork'.[60]

Evans LJ, on the other hand, commended Sedley J for relying on 'common sense' rather than psychiatry. He pointed out that the symptoms of the kind of illness at issue in the case were

conduct or speech which is regarded as 'inappropriate', meaning, as I understand it, not to be expected from a 'normal' person. This factor has some implications for the admissible scope of expert psychiatric evidence, because it may mean that ultimately the psychiatrist is expressing his or her own view as to the extent to which the observed behaviour departs from what is normal. ... It is for this reason in my judgment that the starting point for this particular inquiry is not the opinions of expert witnesses but the factual evidence of what the plaintiff said and did—how he behaved—during the periods in question.[61]

The role of the experts—to which those at the trial should have been more strictly confined—was to 'inform' the judge, who 'must decide the issues to the best of his judgment, depending ultimately on the exercise of common sense in the light of the evidence he has heard'. The limits of liability for nervous shock should be drawn not by medical diagnoses, but by the 'good sense' of the judge.[62] *Hinz* v. *Berry* did not require the judge to subtract the effects of

---

[59] M. Parkes, 'Bereavement' (1985) 146 *British J Psychiatry* 11, cited in (1995) 28 BMLR at 117.   [60] [1997] 1 All ER at 592.
[61] *Ibid.* at 598.
[62] *Ibid.* at 603, quoting Lord Wright in *Bourhill* v. *Young* [1943] AC 92.

bereavement from the effects of trauma, because it was 'impossible as a matter of common sense to draw such a distinction' in a case like the present, and because there was no good policy reason to do so, 'particularly when the line between recovery and non-recovery would or might depend upon a detailed psychiatric inquiry in every case'.[63]

In contrast to the criminal insanity cases, Evans LJ's desire to curb the role of the experts had less to do with upholding other forms of authority than with pragmatic issues about the length and cost of litigation.[64] But the method adopted by the majority of the judges to avoid deferring to medical expertise was similar to the insanity cases: first emphasize that legal classifications of phenomena do not correspond to scientific ones, then assign the facts to the appropriate legal category on the basis of 'common sense', by assessing the plausibility of competing narratives and moral judgements of responsibility. Unlike the insanity defence, however, *Vernon* v. *Bosley* explicitly makes the judge's 'good sense' the ultimate legal test, rather than leaving it to the good sense of a jury to modify the apparent precision of the law.

'An Attempt to Systemize Common Sense': *Reay v. BNFL*

The nature of the dispute in *Reay and Hope* v. *British Nuclear Fuels p.l.c.*,[65] said to have been 'the longest and most expensive personal injury action mounted in the British courts',[66] created a very different relationship between expertise and lay knowledge from that seen in the area of psychiatry. That a father may 'go to pieces' after witnessing the death of his children is the kind of risk that a layperson can recognize without the help of experts. The possibility, as alleged by the plaintiffs in *Reay*, that the exposure of a father to radiation prior to conception may cause his children to contract leukaemia or non-Hodgkin's lymphoma is the kind of risk which Ulrich Beck sees as a pervasive feature of late modern

---

[63] *Ibid.* at 606, 605.

[64] All 4 judges expressed concerns about the use and abuse of expert evidence similar to those discussed by Lord Woolf, *Access to Justice: Interim Report* (London, 1994). See also *Vernon* v. *Bosley (No. 2)* [1997] 1 All ER 614, for further strictures on the conduct of the plaintiff's experts.

[65] (1994) 5 Med LR 1.

[66] C. Dyer, 'Court Rejects Cancer Link', *Guardian,* 9 Oct. 1993, 5. The court heard 90 days of evidence over a period of 9 months.

societies: a risk created by applied science and knowable only through science. In this case the risk was identified in a study by Professor Gardner and colleagues[67] but his findings were disputed by other epidemiologists.[68]

Beck sees scientific and political disputes over this type of risk as bringing about 'a momentous *demonopolization of scientific knowledge claims* . . . science becomes more and more *necessary*, but at the same time, *less and less sufficient* for the socially binding definition of truth.'[69] In a process which Beck terms 'reflexive modernization', laypeople are said to become increasingly adept at playing off scientific claims against one another, applying to science the kind of methodological scepticism which was previously confined to internal debates within the scientific community. Beck also sees this process—especially in relation to nuclear power—as leading to increasing autonomy and politicization of the judiciary as they are obliged to settle irreconcilable conflicts between experts.[70]

Reay's case could be taken as an example of the process described by Beck, in so far as it shows the lawyers and the judge (who from a scientific point of view are laypeople) adroitly employing the sceptical idiom of science, for example in detailed methodological criticisms of the Gardner study, to construct their own assessment of the alleged risk and ultimately arrive at a 'socially binding definition of truth'. It shows a very different attitude towards science from that which Wynne depicted in a discussion of an earlier dispute about the same reactor, in which science was dichotomized by the judge into objective truth and the products of individual bias on the part of scientists,[71] but it also shows

[67]　M. J. Gardner, M. P. Snee, C. A. Powell, S. Downes and J. D. Terrell, 'Results of a Case-Control Study of Leukaemia and Lymphoma among Young People near Sellafield Nuclear Plant in West Cumbria' (1990) 300 *B.M.J.* 423. Prof. Gardner died shortly before the trial and the plaintiffs did not call any of his collaborators to defend their work, attracting adverse comment from the judge.

[68]　E.g. L. J. Kinlen, 'Can Paternal Preconceptional Irradiation Account for the Increase of Leukaemia and Non-Hodgkin's Lymphoma in Seascale?' (1993) 306 *B.M.J.* 1718. For a summary of the scientific case against Gardner, written shortly after the trial, see R. Doll, H. J. Evans and S. C. Darby, 'Paternal Exposure Not to Blame' (1994) 367 *Nature* 678.

[69]　U. Beck, *Risk Society. Towards a New Modernity* (London, 1992), 156 (emphasis in original).

[70]　*Ibid.,* 196.

[71]　Wynne, *Rationality and Ritual,* n. 4 above, ch. 7.

certain continuities with the approach to 'softer' forms of scientific knowledge discussed above.

One point of similarity is the way French J began his discussion of the epidemiological evidence in his judgment by pointing out the differences between the classification of phenomena for scientific and for legal purposes: '[t]he fact that an epidemiologist or another scientist would not find an association and/or a cause to be established to his satisfaction is, of course, most helpful to the Judge but only within the limits imposed by their respective disciplines'. He quoted one of the expert witnesses as giving a clear expression of the epidemiological concept of causation:

Rarely can we be certain that a causal relationship exists but by assembling evidence from many different angles we may build a body of support sufficient to convince most reasonable people that it is more prudent to act as though the association were causal than to assume it is not. The point in the accumulation of evidence at which this decision is reached depends in considerable part on the consequences of the alternative actions to be taken as a result of the judgment.

French J contrasted this view with his own duty 'to decide each of these cases on the balance of probabilities'. [72]

The contrast between scientific and legal probabilities drawn here is the exact reverse of that drawn by Ormrod LJ in *Re JS (a minor)*. In that case science was said to be concerned with objective, mathematical probability, while probability in law depends on whether the evidence is sufficient to 'satisfy the court that it is reasonably safe in all the circumstances of the case to act on the evidence, bearing in mind the consequences that will follow'.[73] In *Reay*, science appears, far from being value-free, to make judgements of causation depend upon value judgements, unlike the law's objective measure of probability.[74] Whichever way round the contrast is drawn, it serves to free the judge from any need to defer to science: legal probability is for judges and not scientists to determine.

[72] (1994) 5 Med LR at 10, quoting the evidence of Prof. MacMahon.
[73] [1981] Fam. 22 at 29.
[74] Some epidemiologists have indeed argued that whether an association should be considered causal is a matter of public policy rather than science: see K. J. Rothman, *Modern Epidemiology* (Boston, 1986), 20; L. A. Bailey, L. Gordis and M. Green, 'Reference Guide to Epidemiology' in Federal Judicial Center, *Reference Manual on Scientific Evidence* (Washington DC, 1994), 157.

Because of the complex and technical nature of the evidence, *Reay*'s case posed even more acutely than the cases considered above the question raised in a classic article by Learned Hand: how can a jury or judge be competent to decide between the conflicting statements of experts when '[i]t is just because they are incompetent for such a task that the expert is necessary at all'?[75] In a study of personal injury practitioners, Jeremy Green found that they did not consider Hand's paradox a serious embarrassment, at least with respect to the supposedly 'easy' science of medicine. They saw medical expertise as consisting of the possession of a large body of factual information, the relevant aspects of which lawyers and judges were able to master and from which they could draw valid inferences on the basis of 'logic' and 'common sense'. As 'intelligent and logically trained individuals', lawyers considered themselves competent to make such inferences without needing to be socialized into the interpretative frameworks of science.[76]

The *Medical Law Reports'* commentary on *Reay*'s case[77] describes it as an admirable application of the approach to conflicts of scientific evidence set out by Finlay CJ of the Irish Supreme Court in *Best* v. *Wellcome Foundation* (in which the Court upheld the trial judge's finding that whooping-cough vaccine could cause brain damage). Finlay CJ's attempt to resolve Hand's paradox superficially resembles that described by Green:

it is not possible . . . for a . . . court to take upon itself the role of a determining, scientific authority resolving disputes between distinguished scientists in any particular line of technical expertise. The function which a court can and must perform in the trial of a case in order to acquire a just result, is to apply common sense and a careful understanding of the logic and likelihood of events to conflicting opinions and conflicting theories concerning a matter of this kind.[78]

It is notable, however, that while Finlay CJ claims that judges are competent to draw inferences from scientific facts on the basis of 'logic' and 'common sense', he concedes that such inferences

[75] L. Hand, 'Historical and Practical Considerations Regarding Expert Testimony' (1901) 15 Harvard LR 40.
[76] J. Green, 'Industrial Ill-health, Expertise and the Law' in Smith and Wynne, *Expert Evidence*, n. 4 above, 115–6.
[77] Margaret Puxon QC, 'Commentary' (1994) 5 Med LR 55.
[78] (1994) 5 Med LR 81 at 98.

cannot have the same cognitive authority as those made by trained scientists. The aim is not scientific truth, but 'a just result' to a dispute in which law cannot wait for science to provide a definitive answer. The judgment in *Reay* draws no such contrast between scientific truth and lay truth, but rather—at least so far as the epidemiological evidence is concerned[79]—seeks to minimize the difference between them.

The core of the judgment consists of French J's summary and assessment of the interim submission of counsel on the epidemiological and genetic evidence. Had the 'highly complex and technical' scientific evidence not been translated into legal argument in this way, the judge would have found the task of reading and reviewing it 'utterly intolerable'.[80] In contrast to Sedley J's avoidance of technical vocabulary in *Vernon* v. *Bosley*, French J made a point of using such vocabulary having first explained it in lay terms. The lawyers' submissions on, and the judge's conclusions about, the epidemiological evidence were largely based on the criteria proposed in 1965 by Sir Austin Bradford Hill to determine whether a statistical association is likely to be causal.[81] These criteria could, in the judge's view, 'be regarded as an attempt to systemise common sense'.[82] Thus, where at first we seem to see a layperson claiming the competence to resolve a complex argument between scientists, we find instead a judge applying reason and common sense to the arguments of lawyers—and who could question his competence to do that?

The image of epidemiology as 'informed common sense' (a phrase used in evidence by the eminent epidemiologist Sir Richard Doll, and taken up by the plaintiffs' counsel and the judge)[83] is very different from Collins and Pinch's caricature of lay and judicial attitudes to science, according to which scientists are either infallible 'gods' or biased, incompetent 'charlatans'.[84] French J's judgment portrays scientists as fallible human beings, who if they work for the nuclear industry may not be perfectly objective but

---

[79] For convenience, French J. divided the expert evidence into 2 categories, 'epidemiology' and 'genetics'.   [80] (1994) 5 Med LR at 15.

[81] *Ibid.* at 16 20, 24–9, 49–50; A. B. Bradford-Hill, 'The Environment and Disease: Association or Causation?' (1965) 58 *Proc. of Royal Society of Medicine* 295. For a sceptical view of the usefulness of these criteria as a 'checklist' see Rothman, *Modern Epidemiology*, n. 74 above, 17–20.

[82] (1994) 5 Med LR at 13.   [83] *Ibid.* at 17.

[84] Collins and Pinch, *The Golem*, n. 7 above, 145.

do their 'honest and expert best',[85] and who, even in 'a good study, well carried out and presented' by 'an epidemiologist of the highest distinction' are prone to occasional 'lapses of judgment':

I doubt whether any epidemiological study has ever been subjected to so lengthy or rigorous an examination as the Gardner study has undergone in this Court. Equally, I doubt whether, if so subjected, any epidemiological study would emerge unscathed.[86]

(Note, too, what a strong claim is made here for the rigour of the legal process as compared to the process of scientific debate.)

What does 'common sense' mean in such a context? Ordinarily it might be supposed to refer largely to the jury's or judge's knowledge and experience of human social behaviour,[87] but such knowledge is of little use when considering the possible effect of radiation upon chromosomes. Drawing upon the insights of Bennett and Feldman, Jackson, and others,[88] we can see that what the reasoning in *Reay* has in common with other instances of forensic common sense is a concern with the structural coherence of the 'stories' told by the lawyers and their witnesses. The 'Gardner hypothesis' on which the plaintiffs' case rested conformed to the basic structure which Jackson, following Greimas and others, sees as a universal feature of legal (and other) narratives, but with a natural phenomenon rather than a human actor as the 'subject'.[89] Radiation is invested by the laws of nature with the 'goal'[90] of causing leukaemia in children and the 'competence' to do so via their fathers' sperm ('contract'); when given the opportunity by BNFL it duly causes leukaemia ('performance'); and its contribution is discovered by Gardner and his colleagues

---

[85]   (1994) 5 Med LR at 8.   [86]   *Ibid.* at 48–9.

[87]   See Ward, 'Law, Common Sense and Science', n. 21 above.

[88]   W. L. Bennett and M. S. Feldman, *Reconstructing Reality in the Courtroom* (New Brunswick, NJ, 1981); B. S. Jackson, *Law, Fact and Narrative Coherence* (Merseyside, 1988); N. Pennington and R. Hastie, 'The Story Model of Juror Decision making' in R. Hastie (ed.), *Inside the Juror* (Cambridge, 1993), 192–224; J. Sanders, 'From Science to Evidence: the Testimony of Causation in the Bendectin cases' (1993) 46 Stanford LR 1 (applying the 'story model' to a scientific dispute).

[89]   B. S. Jackson, *Making Sense in Law* (Liverpool, 1995), 145–8. For a semiotic approach to science which treats natural phenomena in a similar way to human actors see B. Latour, *Science in Action* (Milton Keynes, 1987).

[90]   Jackson (*Making Sense*, n. 89 above, 147–8) stresses that a 'goal' need not be a conscious intention and the 'sender' that sets the goal may be an impersonal force.

('recognition'). Some of the weaknesses which French J detects in this narrative are those which, in a story about a human villain, would indeed be matters of common sense. For example, how exactly does radiation perform its diabolical trick of striking at the child through the father (in semiotic terms, what is its *pouvoir faire*)? In French J's judgement the plaintiffs failed to demonstrate any biological mechanism convincingly. And why does the radiation cause a leukaemia cluster only in Seascale, when 'high dose' fathers live in other villages around Sellafield as well?[91] It is like a whodunit in which the detective unmasks the murderer but cannot find the murder weapon or explain the choice of victim.[92]

On the other hand, the defendant's story also displayed serious structural weaknesses. For one thing, the defendant's experts could not agree, as the plaintiffs' counsel pointed out, on any common 'story' to explain the Seascale leukaemia cluster. For another, they had to explain away the statistical association between leukaemia and paternal radiation doses in the Seascale cases as a mere coincidence. Indeed there was, in the plaintiffs' submission, a whole 'chain of coincidences' which rendered the defendant's case implausible. It was this which gave French J his 'greatest cause for pause and reflection' before he decided for the defendant.[93]

While French J's judgment spells out the arguments on each side of the case with impressive clarity and detail, it is less explicit and thorough in explaining why the defendant's arguments finally outweighed the plaintiffs'. French J's conclusion moves abruptly from finding the explanation of the Seascale cluster put forward by one of the defendant's experts 'no less plausible than the Gardner hypothesis', through an acknowledgement of the problem posed by the element of coincidence in the defendant's scenario, to a pronouncement that 'in my judgement, on the evidence before me the scales tilt decisively in favour of the Defendants'.[94] What went into the scales on each side (including much that has been

---

[91] (1994) 5 Med LR at 23, 48. The plaintiffs did put forward an explanation for this point (17, 20) which was rejected by French J as 'speculative' (52).

[92] And in which there appears to be another killer with a similar *modus operandi* operating in the same area: hence the significance of the 'Egremont cluster' which could *not* be explained by paternal irradiation.

[93] (1994) 5 BMLR at 53.   [94] *Ibid.*

omitted from this résumé) is clear, but exactly why the scales tilted so 'decisively', rather than ending up somewhere close to equipoise between two equally plausible theories, is not.[95]

As we have seen, the judge was unwilling to adopt the view of some epidemiologists that whether an association should be interpreted as causal is largely a matter of policy,[96] and it is easy to see why. A decision based on the grounds, for example, that the evidence was insufficient to justify the damage which a finding for the plaintiffs would have inflicted on the nuclear industry[97] would have been of questionable legitimacy, to say the least. If there was, by some objective standard, a clear preponderance of scientific evidence and argument on one side of the issue, a layperson might well ask why all reasonable experts were not persuaded. The explanation to which Jones shows other judges resorting—that the experts on the 'wrong' side must be incompetent or biased[98]—was rejected by French J. Another option for judges faced with such unresolved scientific conflicts might be to say that where the arguments are finely balanced the plaintiffs have not met the burden of proof; but this would be a confession of incompetence in the face of Hand's paradox, and a thinly disguised answer in favour of defendants to the political question of 'who should bear the costs of society's inability to ascertain the relevant facts with any degree of certainty'.[99] It is difficult to see any other way to break the deadlock except to fall back on 'common sense', impressionistic assessments of the witnesses, and what Finlay CJ in *Best* called 'the logic and likelihood of events',[100] or in other words the coherence and plausibility of narratives. Such judgements of common sense and plausibility seem, almost by definition, incapable of being fully articulated. The ineffable quality of judicial fact-finding has recently been affirmed, in the context of another complex scientific dispute, by Lord Hoffman:

[95] For an argument that 'common sense' should have tipped the balance of probabilities in favour of the plaintiffs, see J. Holder, 'The Sellafield Litigation and Questions of Causation in Environmental Law' (1994) 47 Current Legal Problems 287.   [96] See above, nn. 72, 74 and accompanying text.
[97] See H. Bolter, *Inside Sellafield* (London, 1996), 156–67.
[98] Jones, *Expert Witnesses*, n. 4 above, 97–102.
[99] Jasanoff, *Science at the Bar,* n. 14 above, 123.
[100] (1994) 5 Med LR 81 at 98.

[S]pecific findings of fact, even by the most meticulous of judges, are an inherently incomplete statement of the impression that was made upon him by the evidence. His expressed findings are always surrounded by a penumbra of imprecision as to emphasis, relative weight, minor qualification and nuance . . . which time and language do not permit exact expression, but which may play an important part in the judge's overall evaluation.[101]

Conclusion

This has been a tentative, exploratory paper, and has attempted neither to propose any general theory about law and science nor to prescribe how courts ought to deal with conflicts of expert evidence. I shall conclude with some brief comments on issues which might merit further consideration.

The three case studies I have presented suggest that while the 'scientistic' judicial attitude discussed by Jones and Wynne is one possible way for law to maintain its cognitive authority in the face of the challenge of science, it is not the only one. A strategy which combines assertion of the autonomy of legal categories with the application of 'common sense' criteria of plausibility to competing narratives appears to work equally well. These may well be only two out of a much wider range of possibilities. It would be interesting to inquire whether courts tend to adopt different responses to different types of scientific evidence (is epidemiology more amenable than genetics to a 'common-sense' approach?), and whether any trend is discernible over time. For example Beck's account of 'reflexive modernization' might lead one to expect a decline in simplistic 'scientism' and a greater readiness on the part of judges to criticize scientific evidence on methodological grounds (developments in the United States since *Daubert*[102] might be pertinent here). Of course any such inquiry would need to look at a much larger sample of cases than I have done.

The normative issues raised by expert evidence include not only how far the law ought to defer to the cognitive authority of science, but how far it should defer to lay 'common sense', especially as

---

[101] *Biogen Inc.* v. *Medeva p.l.c.* [1997] RPC 1 at 45. (The case concerns a disputed patent in the field of genetic engineering.)
[102] *Daubert* v. *Merrell Dow Pharmaceuticals Inc.* 113 S. Ct. 2786 (1993); 125 L. Ed. 2d 469 (1993).

embodied in the jury.[103] Epistemology and political values intersect in this area. There seems to be something democratic and egalitarian about the claim that laypeople, and particularly juries, are competent to decide scientific questions,[104] and conversely something authoritarian and élitist in the claim that scientific rationality is beyond the grasp of untrained minds.[105] (This is one reason that Lewis Wolpert's sharp antithesis between science and common sense is controversial.)[106] Faith in the common sense of jurors is easier to justify in an area such as criminal responsibility where the issues at stake are ultimately moral rather than medical, than in areas where it helps to secure convictions for serious crimes on the basis of dubious scientific evidence,[107] and there is no evident democratic or egalitarian argument (nor much basis in the light of their record of recent miscarriages of justice) for placing such faith in the common sense of judges.[108]

[103] For a searching examination of this issue see D. Schiff and R. Nobles, *Reassessing Expert Evidence on Appeal* (unpub. submission to the Royal Commission on Criminal Justice, 1993); R. Nobles, D. Schiff and N. Shaldon, 'The Inevitability of Crisis in Criminal Appeals' (1993) 21 Internat. J Sociology of Law 1.

[104] P. Feyerabend, *Science in a Free Society* (London, 1978), 97–8; M. S. Jacob, 'Testing the Assumptions Underlying the Debate about Scientific Evidence: Juror Incompetence and Scientific Objectivity' (1993) 25 Connecticut LR 1083.

[105] See e.g. Steve Fuller, *Social Epistemology* (London, 1988) on the 'Authoritarian Theory of Knowledge'; D. Shuman, A. Champaign and E. Whittaker, 'Juror Assessments of the Believability of Expert Evidence: A Literature Review' (1995) 36 Jurimetrics Journal 371 at 382 (scepticism about jury competence is 'élitist and anti-democratic').

[106] L. Wolpert, *The Unnatural Nature of Science* (London, 1992); S. Fuller, 'Can Science Studies be Spoken in a Civil Tongue?' (1994) 24 *Social Studies of Science* 143 (denouncing Wolpert's argument as 'outrageous'); M. Lynch, 'Detoxifying the "Poison Pen Effect" ' in A. Ross (ed.), *Science Wars* (Durham, NC, 1996).

[107] As in the notorious 'Birmingham Six' and 'dingo baby' cases: *R. v. McIlkenny and Others* (1991) 93 Cr. App. R. 287; *Chamberlain* v. *R.* (1984) 51 ALR 225. D. E. Bernstein, 'Junk Science in the United States and the Commonwealth' (1996) 21 Yale J Internat. Law 123 at 174–8 uses these and similar cases to support the 'jury incompetence' thesis.

[108] Thanks to David Schiff for his constructive criticism of an earlier version of this paper, to Barbara Harvey for discussions of 'nervous shock', and to several participants in the Law and Science Seminar for some very helpful comments.

'BRAINWASHING' EVIDENCE IN LIGHT OF *DAUBERT*

Science and Unpopular Religions

Gerald Ginsburg and James Richardson

Introduction

A revolution occurred in American evidence law in 1993 when the United States Supreme Court rendered the *Daubert* decision, over-turning 70 years of law governing the area of novel scientific evidence.[1] Previously, admissibility of expert evidence had been governed in federal courts (and many state courts as well) by the *Frye* rule of 'general acceptance', which meant that novel scientific evidence could not be admitted unless the methods and principles under which it was found had achieved general acceptance within the relevant discipline(s).[2] The *Frye* rule was conservative and was subjected to much criticism.[3]

The *Frye* rule was incorporated into the *Daubert* guidelines, so the notion of general acceptance was not entirely abandoned. However, other guidelines included by the *Daubert* court go far beyond *Frye*, and have major implications for all scientific evidence, including, we will claim, social and behavioural evidence being proffered to courts.[4]

---

[1] *Daubert v. Merrell Dow Pharmaceuticals Inc*, 113 S. Ct. 2786 (1993); 125 L. Ed. 2d 469 (1993).

[2] *Frye* v. *United States*, 293 F. 1013; 54 App. D.C. 46 (D.C. Cir. 1923).

[3] A major reason for criticism of the *Frye* rule that is germane here concerns the fact that general acceptance does not always equate with scientific reliability. As M. Saks, 'Enhancing and Restraining Accuracy in Adjudication' (1988) 51 Law and Contemporary Problems 243, has noted, some forms of forensic evidence that are readily accepted in courts have little scientific research to support them, while other, more scientifically based, techniques may not be acceptable.

[4] See J. T Richardson, G. P. Ginsburg, S. Gatowski, and S. A. Dobbin, 'Problems Applying *Daubert* to Psychological Syndrome Evidence' (1995) 79(1) Judicature 10.

The other three guidelines include: (1) establishing the 'falsifiability' of a theory being presented; (2) the 'known or potential error rate' associated with applying the theory; and (3) whether the findings have been subjected to peer review and publication in scientific forums. This list is not exhaustive, as the court also said that other sound criteria have been suggested and: '[t]o the extent that they focus on the reliability of evidence as insured by the scientific validity of its underlying principles, all these versions may well have merit'.[5] Thus the US Supreme Court has weighed in heavily in favour of judges being required to make sound, scientifically based decisions concerning admissibility of proffered evidence claimed to be scientific.[6]

The issue of admissibility of scientific evidence is not confined to the US. It is clear that most Western countries, at least, are grappling with how to handle such evidence.[7] Courts in many other countries are dealing with this issue and related issues, as more and more allegedly scientific evidence is offered in various types of court cases. Interest in this issue is evidenced by the amount of attention which has been given to the *Daubert* decision itself outside the US.[8]

---

[5] N. 1 above, 2796–7, n. 12.

[6] Not all the justices shared this view, however, as Rhenquist CJ filed a dissent (joined by Stevens J) to this part of the opinion, which said, 'I defer to no one in my confidence in federal judges; but I am at a loss to know what is meant when it is said that the scientific status of a theory depends on its 'falsifiability,' and I suspect some of them will be too. I do not doubt the Rule 702 confides to the judge some gatekeeping responsibility in deciding questions of the admissibility of proffered expert testimony. But I do not think it imposes on them either the obligation or the authority to become amateur scientists in order to perform that role' (at 4811).

[7] See S. Gatowski, S. A. Dobbin, J. T. Richardson, C. Nowlin, and G. R. Ginsburg, 'Diffusion of Scientific Evidence: A Comparative Analysis of Admissibility Standards in Australia, Canada, England, and the United States' (1995) 4 Expert Evid. 86.

[8] See S. Odgers and J. T. Richardson, 'Keeping Bad Science out of the Courtroom: Changes in American and Australian Expert Evidence Law' (1995) 18 Univ. of New South Wales LJ 108; J. T. Richardson, 'Dramatic Changes in American Expert Evidence Law: From *Frye* to *Daubert*' (1994) 2 The Judicial Review: J Judicial Commission of New South Wales 13; I. Freckleton, 'When Plight makes Right: The Forensic Abuse Syndrome' (1994) 18 Crim. LJ 29; P. Roberts, 'Admissibility of Expert Evidence: Lessons from America' (1995) 4 Expert Evid. 93, for examples. The first author has been asked to make presentations on the implications of *Daubert* to appeal court judges in Canada and in 4 of the 6 states in Australia, as well as to contribute to scholarly publications from other countries on the topic.

Daubert and Social and Behavioural Science Evidence

A problem immediately arose with the *Daubert* decision in the United States because it was not clear whether the court intended to apply the decision to social and behavioural science evidence. Some have claimed that this was not the intention of the court, and that such evidence falls under the 'technical, or other specialized knowledge' phrase of Federal Rule of Evidence 702.[9] Others, including the present authors, believe that the social and behavioural sciences are indeed sciences, and that social and behavioural evidence should be forced to meet the more rigorous guidelines of *Daubert*.[10] There are court decisions on both sides of this issue, as well, which leaves the situation ambiguous. Richardson *et al*.[11] note that the Supreme Court itself referred several times in the *Daubert* decision to a case that turned on admissibility of evidence concerning the efficacy of eyewitness testimony,[12] which suggests that the court did not intend to differentiate between types of scientific evidence.

Psychological Syndromes and Scientific Validity

It is true that nowhere in *Daubert* did the court refer to psychological syndromes, thus leaving open the interpretation of its applicability to such evidence. For reasons given elsewhere,[13] we assume the applicability of *Daubert* to social and behavioural science evidence, including psychological syndromes.[14] Furthermore, we

[9] See T. Renaker, 'Evidentiary Legerdemain: Deciding when *Daubert* should Apply to Social Science Evidence' (1996) 84 California LR 1657; but see also D. Faigman, 'The Evidentiary Status of Social Science under *Daubert*: Is it "Scientific, Technical, or Other" Knowledge?' (1995) 1 Psychology, Public Policy, and Law 960.

[10] See R. Underwager and H. Wakefield, 'A Paradigm Shift for Expert Witnesses' (1993) 5 *Issues in Child Sex Abuse Accusations* 156; Richardson, 'Dramatic Changes' n. 8 above; Richardson *et al*., 'Problems Applying *Daubert*', n. 4 above; T. Moore, 'Scientific Consensus & Expert Testimony: Lessons from the Judas Priest Trial' (1997) 17 Amer. Psychology-Law News 3.

[11] See Richardson, 'Dramatic Changes', n. 8 above, 12.

[12] *US* v. *Downing*, 753 F.2d 1224 (3d Cir. 1985).

[13] See Richardson *et al*., 'Problems Applying *Daubert*', n. 4 above.

[14] The term 'syndrome' implies that the condition being so described is a medical entity or has a medical basis. Thus, successfully designating some characteristic or behaviour as a syndrome has value, both economically and in terms of social control.

argue that psychological syndromes are based on claims that can only be viewed as scientific, and that therefore the claims should be subjected to rigorous criteria such as appear in *Daubert* before they are accepted as scientific evidence.

To take this position suggests that we are dubious about much psychological syndrome evidence, and that we generally agree with several other critics of such evidence being admitted.[15] Our reasoning is based on the failure of most such evidence to meet the key criteria of falsifiability and reliable error rates. Psychological evidence, including syndrome evidence, can sometimes meet the other guidelines of *Daubert*—that is, it might be generally accepted within certain disciplinary groups and published in peer review journals for those groups. But we argue here that these characteristics by themselves do not guarantee the scientific validity of evidence.

Indeed, we would even suggest that political and popular opinion about certain issues can influence decisions to admit allegedly scientific evidence. For instance, it seems clear that decisions to admit Child Sex Abuse Accommodation Syndrome evidence have been influenced by popular concern about child sex abuse.[16] And similar considerations may have influenced the rapid spread of acceptance of repressed-memory evidence by the courts.[17]

For the purpose of this paper, we examine in some detail the evidentiary basis for one type of purportedly scientific evidence offered in cases involving controversial new religions—organizations that have sometimes been called 'cults'.[18] Despite the fact that such evidence in 'cult' cases has a weak scientific basis, the

---

[15] See I. Freckleton, 'Battered Woman Syndrome' (1992) 17 Alternative LJ 39; Freckleton, 'Forensic Abuse Syndrome', n. 8 above; Underwager and Wakefield, 'Paradigm Shift', n. 10 above. Similar comments might be made about psychological profiles, such as those of airline hijackers or drug couriers, etc.

[16] See Freckleton, 'Forensic Abuse Syndrome', n. 8 above.

[17] See E. Loftus, 'The Reality of Repressed Memories' (1993) 48 *Amer Psychologist* 518. See J. Richardson, ' "Brainwashing" Claims and Minority Religions outside the United States: Cultural Diffusion of a Questionable Concept in the Legal Arena' (1996) Brigham Young Univ. LR 873 and S. A. Gatowski, S. T. Dobbin, J. Richardson, and G. P. Ginsburg, 'Globalization of Behavioral Science Evidence about Battered Women: A Theory of Production and Diffusion' (1997) 15 Behavioral Science and the Law 273 for other examples of syndrome evidence that are scientifically problematic.

[18] See J. T. Richardson, 'Definitions of Cult: From Sociological-Technical to Popular Negative' (1993) 34 *Rev. of Religious Research* 348; J. Dillon and J. T. Richardson, 'The "Cult" Concept: A Politics of Representation Analysis' (1994) 3 *SYZYGY: J Alternative Religion and Culture* 185.

underlying ideas enjoy considerable popular support,[19] and have
been accepted in courts of law.[20]

'Brainwashing', 'Mind Control', and 'Destructive Cultism'

There have been hundreds of court cases involving controversial new
religions over the past several decades, since they came into prominence in the late 1960s.[21] Many of the cases involve claims that
participation in the new religious groups was coerced and destructive, an evidentiary theory often referred to as 'brainwashing' or
'mind control'. These are popularized notions sometimes associated
with what has been claimed to be a new psychological syndrome—
'destructive cultism'.[22] It is supposed that 'cult' recruiters use this
powerful psychotechnology to recruit unsuspecting youth, who then
evidence 'destructive cultism' in their behaviours.[23]

[19] See D. Bromley and E. Breschel, 'General Population and Institutional Élite
Support for Control of New Religious Movements: Evidence from National Survey
Data' (1992) 10 Behavioral Science and the Law 39; J. T. Richardson, 'Public
Opinion and the Tax Evasion Trial of Reverend Moon' (1992) 10 Behavioral
Science and the Law 53.

[20] See F. Flynn, 'Criminalizing Conversion: The Legislative Assault on New
Religions' in J. Dayand and W. Laufer (eds.), Crime, Values, and Religion
(Norwood, NJ, 1987), 153; J. T. Richardson, 'Minority Religions ("Cults") and
the Law: Comparisons of the United States, Europe, and Australia' (1995) 18 Univ.
of Queensland LJ 183; Richardson, 'Brainwashing Claims', n. 17 above; J. T.
Richardson, 'Cult/Brainwashing Cases and the Freedom of Religion' (1991) 33 J
Church and State 55; D. Anthony, 'Religious Movements and Brainwashing
Litigation: Evaluating Key Testimony' in T. Robbins and D. Anthony (eds.), In
Gods We Trust (2nd edn, New Brunswick, 1990), 295; D. Anthony and T.
Robbins, 'Law, Social Science, and the "Brainwashing" Exception in the First
Amendment' (1992) 10 Behavioral Sciences and the Law 5; D. Anthony and T.
Robbins, 'Negligence, Coercion, and the Protection of Religious Belief' (1995) 37 J
Church and State 509.

[21] See Flynn, 'Legislative Assault', n. 20 above; J. T. Richardson, 'Legal Status of
Minority Religions in the United States' (1995) 42 Social Compass 249; D. Bromley
and T. Robbins, 'The Role of Government in Regulating New and Unconventional
Religions' in J. Wood and D. Davis, (eds.), The Role of Government in Monitoring
and Regulating Religion in Public Life (Waco, Texas, 1993).

[22] See R. Shapiro, 'Of Robots, Persons, and the Protection of Religious Beliefs'
(1983) 56 Southern Calif. LR 1277; J. Clark, 'Problems in Referral of Cult
Members' (1978) 9(4) J National Assoc. of Private Psychiatric Hospitals 19; J.
Clark, 'Cults' (1979) 242 J Amer. Medical Assoc. 279.

[23] But see R. Straus, 'Religious Conversion as a Personal and Collective
Accomplishment' (1979) 40 Sociological Analysis 158; J. T. Richardson and B.
Kilbourne, 'Classical and Contemporary Applications of Brainwashing Theories: A
Comparison and Critique' in D. Bromley and J. T. Richardson, (eds.), The
Brainwashing/Deprogramming Controversy (Toronto, 1983), 29; R. Shapiro, 'Of

In the early court cases involving such ideas there was a willingness to accept the claims that brainwashing and mind control were being used, sometimes with apparently dramatic effects. Such evidence seemed relevant to cases involving the 'cult problem', and it was often offered by a professional mental health specialist such as a psychologist or psychiatrist, usually with little effective rebuttal testimony.[24]

Initially, such evidence was used to undergird requests for conservatorships, to assist in obtaining court orders sanctioning 'deprogramming' of participants.[25] Later, accusations of 'brainwashing' and 'mind control' supported civil action claims of inten-

Robots', n. 22 above; E. Barker, *The Making of a Moonie: Brainwashing or Choice?* (Oxford, 1984); J. Richardson, 'A Social Psychological Critique of "Brainwashing" Claims about Recruitment to New Religions' in J. Hadden and D. Bromley (eds.), *The Handbook of Cults and Sects in America* (Greenwich, CT, 1993), 75; J. T. Richardson, 'Religiosity as Deviance: Use and Misuse of the DSM with Participants in New Religions' (1993) 14 *Deviant Behavior* 1; J. T. Richardson, 'Active versus Passive Converts: Paradigm Conflict in Conversion/Recruitment Research' (1985) 24 *J for Scientific Study of Religion* 163; J. Saliba, 'The New Religions and Mental Health' in Hadden and Bromley, *Handbook*, above, 99; J. Muffler, J. Langrod, J. T. Richardson, and P. Ruiz, 'Religion', in J. Lowinson, P. Ruiz, R. Millman, and J. Langrod (eds.), *Substance Abuse: A Comprehensive Textbook* (3rd edn, Baltimore, 1997), 492; B. Kilbourne and J. T. Richardson, 'A Social Psychological Analysis of Healing' (1988) 7 *J Integrative and Eclectic Psychotherapy* 20; B. Kilbourne and J. T. Richardson, 'Cults versus Families: A Case of Misattribution of Cause?' (1981) 4 *Marriage and Family Rev.* 81; Bromley and Richardson, *The Brainwashing/Deprogramming Controversy* (above); M. Galanter, R. Rabkin, F. Rabkin, and A. Deutsch, 'The "Moonies": A Psychological Study of Conversion and Membership in a Contemporary Religious Sect' (1979) 136 *Amer. J Psychiatry* 165.

[24] One clinical psychologist claims to have testified in over 40 such cases. See Richardson, 'Cult/Brainwashing cases', n. 20 above.

[25] A conservatorship is a method whereby a court can grant control of the financial affairs of a person to another. The laws were developed many years ago to deal with situations involving elderly people who were becoming senile and could not manage their own financial and personal affairs. Under such laws courts could grant the legal right for such persons to be cared for personally and financially by someone else, usually their children. In the 3 decades during which so-called 'new religions' have existed in the US such laws have been used on occasion by parents seeking control of their children, even those who are of age, who have joined these unpopular groups. Such use of conservatorship laws has now generally ceased as a result of court decisions overruling such practices on the grounds that they violate the religious freedom of the person over whom the conservatorship is sought. See D. Bromley, 'Conservatorships and Deprogramming: Legal and Political Prospects' and J. LeMoult, 'Deprogramming Members of Religious Sects', both in Bromley and Richardson (eds.), *Brainwashing/Deprogramming Controversy*, n. 23 above, 267, 234; Anthony and Robbins, 'Negligence, Coercion' n. 20 above.

tional infliction of emotional distress or false imprisonment.[26] Also, some deprogrammers who were charged with kidnapping in criminal actions or with false imprisonment in civil actions used brainwashing notions to underpin their 'necessity' defences.[27] For about two decades, these brainwashing-based claims and defences were generally accepted. Eventually, though, those being negatively affected by the acceptance of such evidence tried to rebut it, or even have it disallowed completely,[28] and its acceptance became less certain.

Brainwashing and the *Frye* Rule

The use of brainwashing-based testimony was developed under a climate of admissibility dominated by the *Frye* rule of general acceptance. Those offering brainwashing-based testimony were usually seated as experts and allowed to offer their views either because judges thought such testimony particularly relevant or because they thought it was generally accepted among relevant disciplines. In cases during the late 1960s and through the 1970s, there was not much serious effort to rebut testimony attesting to the occurrence of brainwashing, and typically judges and juries agreed with such views. Appeal courts sometimes disagreed with jury decisions, but overall, triers of fact seemed willing to accept a view of reality concerning 'cults' that included notions of brainwashing and mind control.

Later, however, a number of social and behavioural scientists and some professional organizations became concerned about such testimony, which they viewed as prejudicial and not scientifically sound, as well as misrepresenting the relevant disciplines. A

---

[26] See Richardson, 'Cult/Brainwashing cases', n. 20 above.

[27] See Anthony, 'Religious Movements', n. 20 above; Richardson, 'Legal Status', n. 21 above. A necessity defence basically claims that if a law is not broken then a greater harm will result. The classic example often used in law school classes is that it is all right to 'break and enter' a burning building to rescue people in the building. Apparently the analogous logic is that a greater harm is caused by leaving an adult in a new religious group than by forcibly removing him or her for purposes of deprogramming. Such defences represent a way to avoid the constitutional provisions against evaluation of religious beliefs and practices. That is, if such defences are allowed, triers of fact are required to evaluate the extent of the harm that would be done by not removing the person, and that assessment seems to call for learning about the beliefs and practices of the group in question.

[28] See Anthony and Robbins, 'Negligence, Coercion', n. 20 above.

few scientists worked on cases as rebuttal witnesses or as consultants, assisting attorneys in handling such evidence when it was offered.[29] Some social scientists also helped develop a few *amicus* briefs that were submitted in some cases on appeal, usually for professional organizations and individual scholars in the field.[30]

At the trial level it was found that just asking better cross-examination questions or offering rebuttal witnesses was generally not adequate, because juries would none the less find in favour of the side offering brainwashing-based perspectives.[31] Given this circumstance, in a few cases a new effort was made to seek a separate hearing on the validity and reliability of brainwashing-based testimony. This was done via requests for '*Frye*' hearings on the specific claims that made use of brainwashing-based testimony. Thus, pre-trial hearings were held in some cases to determine whether or not the brainwashing evidence should be accepted, and in other cases, a ruling might be entered on appeal that a retrial was required after there had been a separate evaluation of brainwashing-based testimony that had been offered and which was significant to the case.[32]

In one major case, *United States* v. *Fishman*,[33] a decision was made to flatly reject brainwashing-based testimony on the basis of the *Frye* rule of general acceptance. The plaintiff in a mail fraud case had sought to use as a defence that he had been brainwashed by Scientology and that this was what led to his breaking the law.

---

[29] See Anthony, 'Religious Movements', n. 20 above; J. T. Richardson, 'Sociology, "Brainwashing" Claims about New Religions, and Freedom of Religion' in P. Jenkins and S. Kroll-Smith, (eds.), *Sociology on Trial: Sociologists as Expert Witnesses* (New York, 1997), 115.

[30] See Richardson, 'Sociology', n. 29 above. The first author participated in the activities described in this paragraph. The *amicus* briefs, which are available from the first author, presented data-based research conclusions refuting the brainwashing theories being offered. See Anthony, 'Religious Movements' (n. 20 above) for the most thorough critical analysis of brainwashing-based testimony, and also see Richardson and Kilbourne, 'Applications of Brainwashing Theories' (n. 23 above) for a comparison of classical and contemporary uses of such theories as ideological weapons and J. Fort, 'What is "Brainwashing", and Who says so?' in B. Kilbourne, (ed.), *Scientific Research and New Religions: Divergent Perspectives* (San Francisco, 1985), 57 for a contemporary history of use of the term.

[31] See J. DeWitt, J. Richardson, and L. Warner, 'Novel Scientific Evidence in Controversial Cases: A Social Psychological Examination' (1997) 21 Law and Psychology Rev. 1 for evidence relevant to this point.

[32] See Anthony, 'Religious Movements', n. 20 above.

[33] (1990) Case No. CAR–88–0616–DLJ No. Cal.

This defence was rejected after a spirited exchange during the pre-trial phase of the case that included submission of considerable material critical of brainwashing theories.[34]

In a case decided after *Fishman* and referring to it as precedent, *Green and Ryan v. Maharishi et al.*,[35] brainwashing-based testimony was again rejected. This time the rejection occurred after an initial trial court decision in favour of civil plaintiffs who sought damages for being brainwashed into participating in the Divine Light Mission. On appeal, the decision was overturned and the case remanded for further evaluation of the testimony of a well-known brainwashing 'expert'.[36] The trial court's subsequent review of brainwashing testimony applied a criterion of 'substantial acceptance', a lesser standard than general acceptance, but the testimony was still rejected.

These two federal court decisions have since been cited in other cases, and the decisions have apparently had something of a deterrent effect. Claims of brainwashing and mind control are heard less in courts across America now.[37]

Brainwashing Evidence and *Daubert*

Anthony and Robbins raised an interesting question concerning application of *Daubert* to brainwashing-based testimony and claims in 'cult cases'.[38] They suggest that the 1993 decision might allow a 'regression' to a time when more brainwashing-based testimony was admitted. They may be suggesting that the greater discretion granted to judges under *Daubert* could allow those who were not sympathetic to 'cults' to admit more evidence against

---

[34] See Anthony and Robbins, 'Law, Social Science' and Anthony and Robbins, 'Negligence, Coercion', both n. 20 above.

[35] USDC No. 87–0015 and 0016 (1991).

[36] The expert in this case was also one of the two experts disallowed from offering brainwashing-based testimony in the *Fishman* case.

[37] See Anthony and Robbins, 'Negligence, Coercion', n. 20 above. However, negative sentiments against newer controversial religious groups run deep, fed by such events as the tragic death of nearly 100 people at Waco in 1993 and more recently the mass suicide of 39 Heaven's Gate members at San Diego (1997). Thus, although there are fewer overt uses of brainwashing-based claims in contemporary court actions, new religions still do not fare well in court cases, as judges and juries act out their concerns and biases about such phenomena. See Richardson, 'Legal Status' n. 21 above and Bromley and Robbins, 'Regulating Religions', n. 21 above.

[38] See Anthony and Robbins, 'Negligence, Coercion', n. 20 above, 523.

them. However, later in the same paper they seem to suggest that *Daubert* will not work in a more liberal fashion;[39] that is, it will not let in more of the kinds of testimony that had finally been ruled inadmissible under *Frye*. They say:

Vague and indeterminate identifications of the purported theoretical foundation of proffered testimony . . . will probably fail to meet criteria of falsifiability. More precise applications of 'classical' models of brain-washing and related constructs to formally voluntary associations may also fail to pass muster due to the difficulty of specifying precisely how much non-physical coercion produces involuntariness. . . . Also pertinent is the general vagueness and lack of reliable diagnostic criteria for 'Atypical Associative Disorder' supposedly produced by cultist mind control.[40]

Richardson, in a lengthy critique of brainwashing ideas and how they have spread to other legal systems around the world, says, '[u]nder recent, more rigorous, criteria established in Daubert . . . for the acceptance of scientific evidence, brainwashing-based claims should . . . be excluded.'[41] In another paper, after a discussion of the consequences of applying *Daubert* criteria to child sex abuse cases, Richardson further notes:

In another area of high emotion and considerable misinformation, a new syndrome of 'destructive cultism' has seen use. The author and others have been involved in criticizing questionable psychological and psychiatric testimony alleging negative effects of participation in new religious groups (. . . 'cults') that cannot be substantiated by well-done research.[42]

Thus we have seen several comments made in passing, usually in footnotes, to the issue of the application of *Daubert* criteria to brainwashing-based testimony. In the present paper, we apply the four guidelines of scientific reliability from *Daubert* to such testimony in a more direct fashion, in an effort to establish with more precision whether such testimony meets the *Daubert* criteria. We focus on the two more complex guidelines, falsifiability and error rates, but with comments on the other two guidelines as well.

[39] Anthony and Robbins, 'Negligence, Coercion', n. 20 above, 531.
[40] *Ibid.*, n. 74 (references omitted). A similar footnote appears in Odgers and Richardson, 'Bad Science', n. 8 above, 119, n. 51.
[41] See Richardson, ' "Brainwashing" Claims', n. 17 above, 883, n. 37.
[42] See Richardson, 'Dramatic Changes', n. 8 above, 34, n. 50 (references omitted).

Falsifiability and Brainwashing

As far as we are aware no case has yet seen the evaluation of brainwashing-based testimony in light of *Daubert*. But if this were done the analysis would probably start with the most fundamental of the criteria, falsifiability.

Richardson discusses the concept of falsifiability in some detail, including its application to social and behavioural science evidence.[43] He notes that the *Daubert* opinion cites major figures in the philosophy of science, including Sir Karl Popper, whose writings made the term falsifiability well-known. Popper claimed that scientific knowledge in a given area developed incrementally, by the establishment of testable hypotheses at the boundaries of knowledge. By 'testable' Popper meant that a method could be devised to test the hypothesis such that the hypothesis could actually fail the test.

This kind of precision requires a clear statement about what is predicted by the theory being tested. For instance, it is not scientifically defensible to make both of the following claims about the effects of child sex abuse:

1. If a child being examined for possible sex abuse does not like his or her genitals being examined, this is evidence of the child having experienced sexual trauma through sex abuse and thus of having been sexually abused.
2. If a child seems not to mind having its genitals examined this means that the child is accustomed to such activity, which is evidence that the child has been sexually abused.

Similarly, the following statements about actions of a perpetrator of child sex abuse cannot jointly be defended as scientifically justified:

1. He shows guilt and remorse, which indicates his guilt.
2. He shows no guilt and remorse, indicating that he is in denial about the abuse he perpetrated, a sure sign of his guilt.[44]

These examples are not just a problem of logic in that both A and not-A are claimed, but illustrate a problem with the falsifiability

---

[43] *Ibid.*, 19–27.
[44] See Underwager and Wakefield, 'Paradigm Shift' (n. 10 above) for a discussion of this and the previous example and Richardson *et al.*, 'Problems applying *Daubert*' (n. 4 above) for related discussion.

of a supposedly scientific theory. That is, in each example, the referent person (the child, or the perpetrator) need not be the same person; one perpetrator could show remorse, while another might not. The important point is that the theory in each case makes two opposite predictions—that a behaviour is evidence of a prior act, and that the absence of that behaviour is evidence of that same prior act. If all behaviours, including exactly opposite behaviours, can be said to support a theory, then the theory cannot be falsified. If a theory cannot be falsified, according to Popper it is not a scientific theory. Under *Daubert* such theories should not be admissible as scientific evidence.

Popper used Marxism and Freudian thought as two examples of major theories that cannot, by definition, be tested.[45] The latter is directly relevant to our concerns, since much of modern psychiatry and clinical psychology is Freudian-based. For instance, the frequently cited *Diagnostic and Statistical Manual* ('*DSM*') of the American Psychiatric Association[46] is derived in large part from Freudian thought, and its many entries of mental disorders often lack solid scientific basis.[47] To the extent that testimony based on the *DSM* is not supported by sound science, such evidence should not be admitted as scientific under *Daubert*.[48]

The issue of brainwashing testimony raises a serious falsifiability problem. Part of the problem is definitional: what does the claim that participants have been brainwashed really mean? This problem makes it difficult to state a hypothesis about the brainwashing of participants that is truly falsifiable.

Some would apparently say that anyone in a new religion has been brainwashed, by definition, because otherwise it is not logical that they would choose to participate in such strange groups.[49]

[45] See K. Popper, *The Open Society and Its Enemies* (Lawrenceville, NJ, 1952).

[46] American Psychiatric Association, *The Diagnostic and Statistical Manual* (4th edn rev., Washington, DC, 1995).

[47] See S. Kurt and H. Kutchins, *The Selling of DSM: The Rhetoric of Science in Psychiatry* (New York, 1992); Richardson, 'Religiosity as Deviance', n. 23 above.

[48] Such evidence might be admitted on other grounds, of course, but not as scientifically based. Admission of such testimony on other grounds would, however, be controversial. See Underwager and Wakefield, 'Paradigm Shift', n. 10 above.

[49] See M. Singer, 'Therapy with Ex-Cult Members' (1978) 9 (4) *J National Association of Private Psychiatric Hospitals* 14; M. Singer, 'Coming out of the Cults' (1979) 12 *Psychology Today* 72; Clark, 'Problems in Referral', n. 22 above.

Others might say that anyone who gives up a promising career to join an exotic religious group and sell flowers and books on streets and in airports has been brainwashed. These are not testable notions, but instead are normative statements that reveal a view of human volition that some may find offensive. Such statements are saying, in effect, that because a person is not doing what was expected, and because their behaviour is not easily understood, they have been brainwashed.

If one claims that brainwashing causes a fundamental and permanent change in a person, that claim is testable, although its testability requires specification about the kind of change, what is meant by 'fundamental', and what is meant by 'permanent'. For instance, one could assert that some basic and negative personality change will occur with people who have been brainwashed. This might be demonstrated through longitudinal research showing change over time that could be attributed to a process that people agree is brainwashing.[50] Little such research has been done, and much of what there is seems to show either ameliorative effects of participation[51] or no long-lasting negative effects.[52]

Other acceptable scientific procedures that could yield evidence on the effects of joining make use of standardized personality assessment instruments. One could hypothesize that those who join new religions end up being significantly different from 'normals' against whom the tests were standardized. Research of this sort has been done, but the results usually do not confirm the negative effects predicted by a brainwashing-based hypothesis.[53]

---

[50] Getting agreement on what constitutes brainwashing would be quite difficult, however, since the term itself is a popular and not a scientific term. See Richardson and Kilbourne, 'Brainwashing Theories', n. 23 above; Anthony, 'Religious Movements', n. 20 above; Richardson, 'Cult/Brainwashing Cases', n. 17 above; Richardson, ' "Brainwashing" Claims', n. 17 above.

[51] See M. Galanter, 'The "Relief Effect": A Sociobiological Model of Neurotic Distress and Large Group Therapy' (1978) 135 *Amer. J Psychiatry* 588; B. Kilbourne and J. T. Richardson, 'Psychotherapy and New Religions in a Pluralistic Society' (1984) 39 *Amer. Psychologist* 237.

[52] See C. Taslimi, R. Hood, and P. Watson, 'Assessment of Former Members of Shiloh: The Adjective Checklist 17 years later' (1991) 30 *J for Scientific Study of Religion* 306.

[53] See J. T. Richardson, 'Clinical and Personality Assessment of Participants in New Religions' (1995) 5 *Internat. J for the Psychology of Religion* 145; J. T. Richardson, 'Psychological and Psychiatric Studies of New Religions' in L. Brown, (ed.), *Advances in Psychology of Religion* (New York, 1985), 209 for reviews of a large amount of such research.

Few differences with normals have been found and even some of those are hard to characterize in negative terms.[54] Thus, when tested in this way the hypothesis of major damaging change is not confirmed.

If one assumes that brainwashing leads to *permanent* changes, then again the evidence refutes the notion and falsifies the assertion. Most of the controversial groups are small and suffer extremely high attrition rates.[55] If brainwashing, whatever it is, does take place in those groups, it seems rather ineffectual, with most participants leaving of their own volition after a time. The brainwashing hypothesis, so far as it implies permanency, fails a straightforward test of that permanent effect.

Non-falsifiability is also apparent in the claim that participants in exotic religions have been brainwashed and are consequently suffering from a newly proposed syndrome called 'destructive cultism'.[56] Richardson and Stewart offer the following synopsis of the new syndrome,[57] using language from Shapiro:[58]

He described destructive cultism as a distinct *syndrome* with a number of discernible characteristics. It strikes most commonly during adolescence or young adulthood, among 'idealistic people under stresses of rapid physical and emotional development.' 'Change in personality is the most prominent characteristic of this syndrome,' and the change may happen suddenly or gradually. People suffering from destructive cultism 'may adopt new and unusual eating habits and peculiarities in dress and hair style.' They may engage in begging for support, and they may develop 'hatred and disrespect for the family, the parents, and society in general.'

---

[54] For instance, A. Rosen and T. Nordquist, 'Ego Developmental Level and Values in a Yogic Community' (1980) 39 *J Personality and Social Psychology* 1152 found that participants in Ananda Cooperative Village, a Hindu-based communal group in Northern California, were more compassionate than conventionally religious people in the US.

[55] See F. Bird and B. Reimer, 'Participation Rates in New Religious Movements and Para-Religious Movements' (1982) 21 *J for Scientific Study of Religion* 1; J. T. Richardson, J. van der Lans, and F. Derks, 'Leaving and Labeling: Voluntary and Coerced Disaffiliation from Religious Social Movements' in K. Land and G. Lang (eds.), *Research in Social Movements, Conflicts, and Change*, vol. 9 (Greenwich, CT, 1986).

[56] See E. Shapiro, 'Destructive Cultism' (1977) 15(2) *American Family Physician* 80.

[57] See J. T. Richardson and M. Stewart, 'Medicalization of Participation in New Religions: A Test and Extension of the Conrad and Schneider Model' (1997), unpub. paper.

[58] See Shapiro, 'Destructive Cultism', n. 56 above at 83.

They may display 'a constantly sombre and grave attitude' and become preoccupied with religious rituals and beliefs. Sufferers may also lose personal identity and 'change in mannerisms is common.' Some afflicted with destructive cultism enter into a 'trance-like state, which is intensified during periods of prayer, meditation and rituals.' Shapiro closed his section on the syndrome by stating: 'Destructive cultism is a sociopathic illness which is spreading rapidly throughout the US and the rest of the world in the form of a pandemic.'

Clearly, the claim of a 'destructive cultism' syndrome is not falsifiable, nor is the claim that it is produced by 'brainwashing'. The syndrome can happen 'suddenly or gradually', and it may or may not entail a number of different behaviours.[59]

Although the 'newly discovered' syndrome has not yet been placed in the DSM, one prominent clinical psychologist who has testified in dozens of 'cult cases' has inserted references to 'cults' in the DSM itself;[60] she and others[61] regularly use the DSM as a basis for testimony, even citing DSM mental disorders that make no reference to 'cults'.[62] Coupled with the scientifically question-able basis of some aspects of the DSM,[63] this raises a serious ques-tion about the admissibility as scientific evidence under Daubert of any brainwashing-based assertions about the deleterious effects of participation in new religions.

Specifically, it appears that the assertion that participants in new religions are brainwashed lacks scientific merit. What research has been done refutes such claims, and leads to other conclusions about why people participate and to what effect(s). In terms of falsifiability:

[59] The description is also overtly anti-religious, of course, and efforts to promote such views have been very disquieting to a number of religionists and civil libertarians. See D. Kelley, 'Deprogramming and Religious Liberty' in Bromley and Richardson, Brainwashing/Deprogramming, n. 23 above, 309; J. Guttman, 'The Legislative Assault on New Religions' in T. Robbins, W. Shepherd, and J. McBride, (eds.), Cults, Culture, and the Law (Chico, Calif., 1985); T. Bohm and J. Guttman, 'The Civil Liberties of Religious Minorities' in M. Galanter (ed.), Cults and Religions (Washington, DC, 1989), 211, for examples.

[60] See M. Singer, 'Transcript of Testimony in George v. ISKCON' (1983) Los Angeles District Court, 248 pages; Richardson, 'Religiosity as Deviance', n. 23 above.

[61] See Anthony and Robbins, 'Negligence, Coercion', n. 20 above.

[62] See Anthony, 'Religious Movements', n. 20 above; Richardson, 'Cult/Brainwashing Cases' n. 20 above; Richardson, 'Religiosity as Deviance', n. 23 above.

[63] See Kurt and Kutchins, The Selling of DSM, n. 47 above; Underwager and Wakefield, 'Paradigm Shift', n. 10 above.

(1) properly designed empirical studies do not support the brain-washing-based hypothesis of long-term deleterious effects of participation (thus, to the extent that the theory is testable, it has not been supported); and

(2) brainwashing theories of 'cult religion' indoctrination and participation often allow for the derivation of mutually incompatible hypotheses, as exemplified by the 'destructive cultism' concept; (thus, major aspects of those brainwashing theories are untestable, therefore unfalsifiable).

On both prongs of the falsifiability criterion, then, brainwashing-based testimony about participation in 'cult religions' should be inadmissible as scientific evidence.

Error Rates and Brainwashing

Daubert instructs judges, who are given a definite 'gatekeeping' role, to consider the 'known and potential rate of error' of a scientific theory offered as evidence. Voice spectrography is used as an example in *Daubert*, in which the error-rate concept involves the probability of wrongly classifying someone. There are two forms of misclassification:

1. A decision can be made that someone who is actually speaking is not doing so (a 'false negative').
2. A decision can be made that someone who is not speaking is doing so (a 'false positive').

Many examples of error-rate classification problems can be cited from the social and behavioural science literature. Earlier, we discussed difficulties in deciding whether a child has been sexually abused and whether someone is a perpetrator of sexual abuse. Similar classification problems can arise with regard to whether someone is a spouse batterer, or a drug courier, or suffering from some psychological syndrome such as rape trauma syndrome. These types of classifications have immense legal implications. They can cause, or at least contribute to, a person losing freedom and being labelled an abuser, a rapist, or a drug dealer, or to a child undergoing years of therapy for a trauma that never occurred. Thus, the costs to individuals of false positive errors can be immense, so the negative utility of a false positive misclassification must be taken very seriously, and the probability of a classification error should clearly be specifiable. (Parenthetically, false negatives also pose serious problems and can have high costs, often for potential future victims and society as well as for current victims, but it is the false positives that are most relevant to the focus of this paper.)

Brainwashing-based testimony has severe problems passing muster on the error rate guideline, unless one adopts the problematic logic cited above that anyone who participates has, by definition, been brainwashed. If that approach is not applied then any claim that someone has been brainwashed must be accompanied by a list of specific indicators of the state of being brainwashed, so that people can be accurately classified through properly designed research.

One approach sometimes taken by brainwashing proponents is to use the *DSM*, citing characteristics of selected disorders such as Atypical Associative Disorder, which does include a mention of 'cults' in its description, or Post-Traumatic Stress Disorder, which does not mention involvement in 'cults'.[64] This type of reliance on *DSM* categories with regard to brainwashing is fraught with difficulties, since criteria for inclusion and exclusion are not clearly specified, and false positive rates are indeterminable. Both beauty and mental disorder are in the eye of the beholder. If one is looking for signs of mental disorder then one can probably find them,[65] especially given the vagueness of such concepts as Shapiro's 'destructive cultism'.[66]

Shapiro's development of the term 'destructive cultism' is quite instructive on the point of classification and error rates. Shapiro's son Edward was incarcerated and transported from New York to Boston on the basis of having been classified as suffering from membership of the Hare Krishna making him 'incompetent as a result of mind control'. That opinion was tendered by another psychiatrist, John Clark, after very limited contact with the son.[67]

Edward Shapiro was kept in a mental institution, McLean Hospital in Boston, for two weeks while a team of mental health

[64] See Richardson, 'Religiosity as Deviance', n. 23 above.
[65] See D. Rosenhan, 'On Being Sane in Insane Places' (1973) 179 *Science* 250.
[66] See Shapiro, 'Destructive Cultism', n. 56 above.
[67] See J. T. Richardson, 'Mental Health of Cult Consumers: Legal and Scientific Controversy' in J. Schumaker (ed.), *Religion and Mental Health* (New York, 1992), 233 at 236.

professionals at the hospital evaluated him. When those doctors then testified in a conservatorship hearing that he was not suffering from any mental disorder and that he should be released, Dr Clark insisted that mind-control techniques were so powerful that they could actually conceal mental illness (a claim with implications for falsifiability, of course). Clark recommended that Edward be kept in the hospital for further observation under conditions of 'stress testing', which meant that Shapiro was not to be allowed to see any friends or attorneys, and he could not practise his religion.[68]

The Shapiro case clearly shows a classification disagreement. Psychiatrist Clark, as well as the father who was also a psychiatrist, were attempting to gain court approval of a certain classification of the son Edward. To do so would undergird the request for a permanent conservatorship of the son by the father. But a team of doctors from McLean Hospital disagreed with that classification. They testified that Edward was not suffering from any mental disorder at all, and that he was competent to manage his personal affairs.

The court decided to follow the expert advice of the McLean team of mental health professionals, perhaps because of the plain outrageousness of some of the assertions of Dr Clark. But this sort of outcome does not always pertain;[69] judges and juries have often shown a willingness to accept brainwashing-based testimony in less egregious circumstances.[70]

The acceptance of such assertions risks false positive errors of classification. People who are not 'brainwashed' are said to be, and leaders of religious groups are said to 'brainwash' when they recruit members. These misclassifications provide definitions of reality that have significant implications for public policy and individual freedom. Such classification schemes fail to recognize the normality of the recruitment and persuasion processes used in most newer religious groups, and that many other human groups

---

[68] Shapiro was ordered to be released by the court, which did not accept Clark's expert advice, and Clark was eventually reprimanded by his state medical board for apparently equating participation in a religious group with mental illness. See Richardson, 'Mental Health of Cult Consumers', n. 67 above.

[69] See Bromley, 'Conservatorships and Deprogramming', n. 25 above; LeMoult, 'Deprogramming', n. 25 above.

[70] See Richardson, 'Cult/Brainwashing Cases', n. 20 above; Anthony and Robbins, 'Negligence, Coercion', n. 20 above.

use similar techniques to gain and socialize participants.[71] College fraternities and sororities are examples, but so are various community groups as well as the military, correction institutions, and some forms of group therapy. The 'brainwash' misclassifications, then, have serious costs associated with them, both for the alleged 'brainwasher(s)' and for the 'brainwashed' victim; but although it is clear that such misclassifications have occurred in court proceedings, the probability of such errors is unknown.

It seems clear that brainwashing-based testimony does not meet the 'known and potential error rate' guideline from *Daubert*. Therefore, such testimony should be disallowed as scientific evidence, even though it might mesh well with the values and normative positions of the gatekeepers and triers of fact in cases involving exotic religions.

Peer Review and Publication

This guideline seems straightforward on its face, but contains some problematic elements. It would seem reasonable simply to see what was published in the major refereed journals in a field of scientific endeavour. Similarly, it would seem reasonable to examine the resumés of proposed experts to see if they had published their results in major journals in their field of study. This is the approach taken by judges when they evaluate most scientific testimony and the experts offering it.

In the field of social and behavioural science this straightforward approach has some value. The most prominent scientific journal in the world, *Science*, has, for instance, published at least one article extremely critical of much of the clinical psychological testimony offered in courts of law in America.[72] On the specific issue of participation in new religions, the refereed journal with the largest circulation of any in the field of behavioural sciences, *The American Psychologist*, has published a paper quite critical of brainwashing-based theories as they apply to contemporary religious groups.[73]

[71] See Richardson, 'Active v. Passive Converts', n. 23 above; *id*. 'Social Psychological Critique', n. 23 above.
[72] See D. Faust and J. Ziskin, 'The Expert Witness in Psychology and Psychiatry' (1988) 241 *Science* 31.
[73] See Kilbourne and Richardson, 'Psychotherapy and New Religions', n. 51 above.

However, problems arise with the assessment of peer review and publication, specifically with respect to what disciplines are relevant and who are the peers of those offering testimony. The *Science* article mentioned earlier aroused strong reaction, especially from clinical psychologists, who defended their turf vigorously. The *American Psychologist* article that critiqued brainwashing-based theories was itself criticized in a newer 'anti-cult' journal that is attempting to achieve respectability.[74]

There appear to be major disciplinary differences on the issue of cult brainwashing. Most sociologists and psychologists of religion reject brainwashing theories, whereas many clinical psychologists and psychiatrists apparently give them some credence.[75] The views of psychiatrists and clinical psychologists are widely accepted among the general public, journalists, and organs of mass media,[76] a circumstance with important implications for admissibility.[77]

Thus, journals in the field of psychiatry may publish brainwashing-based articles with no suggestion of the problematic nature of the evidence for such theories. Also, more popular 'anti-cult' publications and the lay media disseminate brainwashing theories readily. Relatively few people are aware of the vast literature from sociology and psychology of religion which refute brainwashing theories, and which use more mundane and well-substantiated theories to explain participation in such groups and movements.

Similar comments can be made about peer review. When the difference of opinion about the efficacy of expert evidence breaks down along disciplinary lines, this means that apparent peers can probably be found who share the perspective of the one offering the testimony. Indeed, a clinical psychologist or a psychiatrist might even disagree that a sociologist or social psychologist would be a peer (and the sociologist or social psychologist might return the favour).

Thus, gatekeeper judges deciding about admission of brainwashing-based testimony can admit evidence that is questionable

---

[74] See Richardson and Stewart, 'Medicalization', n. 57 above.

[75] See Richardson, 'Sociology', n. 29 above.

[76] See J. T. Richardson, 'Journalistic Bias toward New Religious Movements in Australia' (1996) 11 *J Contemporary Religion* 289.

[77] See Gatowski *et al.*, 'Globalization', n. 17 above.

to many, but do so under *Daubert* by simply referring to journals or to peer groups that reflect values supportive of those offering the evidence. Because of this problem, it is important that judges making admissibility decisions are informed about the science behind whatever evidence is being presented. Judges must be able to ascertain what disciplines can and should have something relevant to say about the admissibility of testimony being offered as scientifically based evidence.[78] If information necessary to make a proper admissibility decision is not being proffered then the judge must consider how to obtain that information. To decide the admissibility of brainwashing-based testimony under *Daubert* guidelines for scientific evidence, a judge should consider whether the theory or hypothesis being proffered has been published in peer-reviewed scientific journals, but not just in those journals of the proffered expert's discipline or profession. To do so could bias the decision process in favour of the discipline which has a vested interest in the outcome of the decision.[79]

General Acceptance

This criterion from the 1923 *Frye* decision was retained in *Daubert*, with the understanding that it does make a difference how widely supported a scientific conclusion is among an identified 'relevant scientific community'. The court said that widespread acceptance can be an important factor in ruling particular evidence admissible. The implication of the term 'widespread' is one of inclusiveness, but the court does not explicitly note the problem referred to above of possible disciplinary differences on the value and soundness of a given piece of scientific evidence. And there is no apparent recognition of the fact that popular opinion can potentially influence admissibility decisions in cases involving issues of great interest to the general public or to official authorities.[80]

---

[78] This problem also pertains in the physical and biological sciences. See R. Bjur and J. Richardson, 'Chemistry in Court: Admissibility Decisions Concerning Chemical Evidence' (1997), paper presented at annual meeting of the American Chemical Society, Las Vegas.

[79] See Kilbourne and Richardson, 'Psychotherapy and New Religions', n. 51 above.

[80] See Dewitt *et al.*, 'Novel Scientific Evidence', n. 31 above; Gatowski *et al.*, 'Globalization', n. 51 above.

We have seen some troubling admissibility decisions made in recent years in controversial, high interest areas such as child sex abuse, repressed memories, and rape trauma syndrome, as well as in so-called 'cult/brainwashing' cases. Judges acting as gatekeepers need to overcome pressures from the media or other sources to accept allegedly scientific evidence, and instead assess the scientific basis of such evidence and make decisions accordingly.

In the particular case of brainwashing-based testimony, a number of interest groups would favour admitting evidence that might be useful in exerting social control over exotic religions or in offering therapy to participants. Some of those interest groups would be represented by people with impressive professional credentials. However, given the strong social values that surround this particular area of knowledge it seems imperative also to seek information based on serious empirical research done in the field by researchers operating without any preconceived normative notions about the groups being studied. General acceptance in this circumstance, then, should encompass more than just the therapeutic community.

Expansion of the notion of relevant scientific community contributed to the decisions cited earlier rejecting brainwashing-based testimony under the *Frye* rule.[81] When psychologists and sociologists of religion became involved, and when their research results were presented to the court, this contributed to an awareness on the part of the court that other relevant information for the court was available, and that the brainwashing-based testimony being offered did not therefore meet the general acceptance criterion.[82]

Conclusions

Simply put, brainwashing-based testimony was eventually ruled inadmissible under *Frye*, and it should also be ruled inadmissible under *Daubert*. Such evidence does not meet any of the four guidelines. Ambiguity of the brainwashing concept and the exis-

---

[81] See *Fishman*, n. 33 above and *Green*, n. 35 above.

[82] It is worth noting that legal and constitutional arguments also played a major role in these key cases (Anthony and Robbins, 'Law, Social Science', n. 20 above), but it also seems probable that evidence about research which did not support the brainwashing theory was important.

tence of mutually incompatible hypotheses from it make major portions of any brainwashing theory of religious indoctrination unfalsifiable. Furthermore, to the extent that testable, operational hypotheses about effects have been generated from it, they have been explicitly disconfirmed. Also, error-rate data do not support brainwashing-based hypotheses, and indeed it is even difficult to devise a plausible test of a classification scheme that makes any sense. The peer review publication guideline is not met when it is properly understood as involving a broader range of disciplines, and that is also the case with the general acceptance criterion.

Given the problematic nature of scientific support for brainwashing-based theories as they are applied to participants in new religions, it is reasonable to ask why such evidence was ever admitted, and why it is sometimes still admitted.[83] The most plausible answer has to do with the operation of biases, prejudices, and misinformation in cases that involve controversial parties and issues, or, as Kassin and Wrightsman say, cases 'involving emotional topics over which public opinion is polarized'.[84]

'Cult/brainwashing' cases fit such a description, raising the possibility alluded to earlier that judges and juries may on occasion have acted out of bias or misinformation in cases involving controversial groups. Their judgement about the scientific viability of the brainwashing-based testimony may have been clouded by values and views about the role of such groups in society. Considerable anecdotal evidence about specific cases suggests that this may be the case,[85] and there is also some experimental evidence supporting the point.[86] Furthermore, the popularization of the term 'brainwashing' by news media,[87] from the Korean War to the present, has made the brainwashing concept highly

---

[83] See Richardson, ' "Brainwashing" Claims' n. 17 above; Anthony and Robbins, 'Negligence, Coercion', n. 20 above.

[84] See S. M. Kassin and L. Wrightsman, *The American Jury on Trial* (New York, 1988).

[85] See Anthony and Robbins, 'Law, Social Science', n. 20 above; Richardson, 'Cult/Brainwashing Cases', n. 20 above.

[86] See J. Pfieffer, 'The Psychological Framing of Cults: Schematic Representations and Cult Evaluation' (1992) 22 *J Appl. Psychology* 531; DeWitt *et al.*, 'Novel Scientific Evidence', n. 31 above.

[87] See B. van Driel and J. Richardson, 'Print Media Treatment of New Religious Movements' (1988) 38 *J Communication* 377.

familiar and therefore not likely to be seen by a judge or juror as needing scientific validation.[88]

The very possibility that admissibility decisions about proffered scientific testimony might be affected by such extraneous factors should give all involved with the legal system pause for thought.[89] At the very least, this examination of brainwashing theories under *Daubert* guidelines makes clear the importance of enhancing not only the scientific education of judges, but their sensitivity to the special problems which scientific evidence poses in the social and behavioural sciences.

[88] Interestingly, the construct has not been subjected to scientific scrutiny in which conventional scientific procedures are used to establish its validity. See Fort, 'What is "Brainwashing"?', n. 30 above; P. London, Deposition in *Fishman*, n. 33 above; Anthony, 'Religious Movements', n. 20 above.

[89] See T. Robbins, and D. Bromley, 'Social Experimentation and the Significance of American New Religions' in M. Lynn and D. Moberg (eds.), *Research in the Social Scientific Study of Religion,* vol. 4 (Greenwich, CT, 1992), 1.

WHAT LAWYERS NEED TO
KNOW ABOUT SCIENCE

Lewis Wolpert

Science is the best way to understand the way the world works. It has had enormous success in explaining physical, chemical, and biological processes, and even the behavioural sciences, though there remain great areas of ignorance. In biology too there are lacunas and uncertainties. Even in the so-called harder sciences like physics and chemistry, while there is much greater certainty that the ideas are correct, there remains in some areas some little room for a little doubt. In part this success is because science is a social process in which there is constant critical evaluation.

Science compared, for example, to art, is progressive; science approaches closer and closer to understanding the nature of the world. Art, by contrast, is about change. There are many other differences: a work of art has a high emotional content, the original production is crucial, and it can have multiple interpretations. David Hilbert pointed out that the measure of a good scientific paper is how many other scientific papers it makes irrelevant. If there had not been Shakespeare, nobody would have written Hamlet. Ultimately, however, all scientists are anonymous and irrelevant for a community of scientists will make the discoveries sooner or later. With the structure of deoxyribonucleic acid (DNA), if it hadn't been Watson and Crick, we know it would have been Franklin and Klug within a year. Simultaneous discovery is common in science.

Unnatural Nature

Science is, ironically, unnatural, requiring an unnatural mode of thought and leading to unnatural ideas.[1] What I mean by unnatural

---

[1] See generally L.Wolpert, *The Unnatural Nature of Science* (London, 1992).

is that it goes against one's natural expectations, against common sense. If an idea fits with common sense, then scientifically it is almost certain to be false. It just so happens that the world, the Universe, is not constructed on a common-sense basis.

If you can see the sun during the day, it is absolutely obvious that the sun goes round the earth, and I think you would be going against common sense not to assume that that was true. Surveys show that only 70 per cent of the British population actually believe that it is that way round. It is very hard for non-scientists to come up with a good explanation as to why it is the earth that moves rather than the sun.

Quite a lot of our so called common sense about science these days is really by authority. We all say with great confidence that it is the moon that causes the tides. The moon attracts the water, and so it is high tide on the side where the moon is. But why is it high tide over on the opposite side? The explanation for this is quite complex and Galileo failed to solve it.

Newton's and Galileo's ideas about moving bodies have been around for over three hundred years, yet many people still have quite a lot of difficulty making predictions as to how moving bodies actually behave. Many people, even those trained in physics, think that when a ball is thrown into the air, there is an impressed force on it which gets less and then it begins to return under gravity. The correct answer is, of course, that there is only one force acting on it all the time—gravity. Again, if you kick a football, what happens to its velocity from the moment it leaves your foot? The answer is that it decreases from the moment you kick it, and that is quite counter-intuitive. The reason that the velocity decreases is that force produces acceleration and there is no force on the ball after it has left the foot. Why it is counter-intuitive is perhaps because acceleration is about second derivatives, whereas speed is about first derivatives, and it is very difficult to be intuitive about second derivatives. A great deal of science depends on mathematics and, unfortunately, mathematics is not an intuitive subject.

With really difficult topics like quantum mechanics everyday analogies break down. For the Big Bang, black holes and so forth, there are no everyday metaphors and they are highly mathematical. Even biological ideas like the theory of evolution do not fit with common sense. Is it really easy to believe deep down that humankind has been achieved by random changes and natural selection? It is highly significant that science only had one origin and that was in Greece; no other society ever developed a scientific approach to the world. The fact that it only happened once supports my argument that science is an unnatural mode of thought. Somebody once wrote to Albert Einstein, asking him why it was only in Greece and Europe that science flourished. His reply was as follows:

Dear Sir,
the development of western science has been based on two great achievements: the invention of the formal logical system in Euclidian geometry by the Greek philosophers, and the discovery of the possibility of finding out causal relationships by systematic experiments at the Renaissance. In my opinion, one need not be astonished that the Chinese sages did not make these steps; the astonishing thing is that these discoveries were made at all.[2]

Unnatural Thinking

The whole process of doing science also requires a particular mind set, a particular way of thinking about the world. Probability, for example, which scientists use a great deal, does not fit with common sense. Many people who are not familiar with it believe that, if you have an evenly weighted coin, six heads in a row is less probable than heads, tails, heads, tails, heads, tails. In fact, they are equally probable. How many people in a room do you require in order to have the probability of one half, that is evens, of two of them having the same birthday? The answer is twenty-three. Such issues are important when it comes to assessing risk, considered below. Problems of scale in science, too, are difficult. It turns out that molecules are very small. There are more molecules in a glass of water than there are glasses of water in all the seas. Even quite simple puzzles which involve quantification do not fit easily with common sense. You tie a piece of string 20,000 miles long around the equator and pull it tight, and now you increase its length by 36 inches, so it is 20,000 miles plus 36 inches. What's the gap between the string and the earth all the way round? The answer is about six inches.

[2] *Ibid.*, ch. 3.

Psychologists have studied the way people make judgements when they have not got total information. One of their most interesting ideas is what is called representativeness, that is, we tend to give undue weight to the most recently acquired information, or that information which we know best. So, if I ask you if there are more words in English which begin with 'r', or in which 'r' is the third letter, you would be an unusual audience not to plump for the first but in fact you would be wrong. There are more words with 'r' as the third letter than with 'r' as the first. Another example which illustrates the same point is this: you go to a group of people and ask them to estimate quickly what is $8 \times 7 \times 5$, and so forth all the way down to 1. Then you go to another group and ask them to estimate $1 \times 2 \times 3$, up to 8. You'll get a much higher estimate from the first group than from the second group. Both groups will estimate far too low; the answer is, in fact, 40,320.

Estimating risk is a risky business even for experts. Consider the problems doctors have to face when estimating the probability that one of their patients has a particular disease when the diagnosis is positive. Consider that a disease affects one per cent of the population and the probability of the test detecting the disease in someone who has it is 80 per cent. But the chance of a false positive—that is the test indicating that someone has the disease even though they do not have it—is 10 per cent. What should the doctor tell a patient who tests positive and asks what the probability is that they have the disease? Most doctors estimate the probability as around 75 per cent. Are they correct? If we take 1,000 people at random, then we expect 10 to have the disease. Of these 10 only 8 will be detected by the test. Tests on the other 990 will give 100 false positives. Thus only 8 out of 108 with a positive test will have the disease, that is, less than 8 per cent! The patient, contrary to what most doctors think, should be quite reassured.

All the evidence says that we are very bad at such judgements, and yet there are even some clinicians who will say 'Well, the clinical trials show that this drug doesn't work but in my experience . . .'. That you can convince yourself of the efficacy of a particular activity is all too easy and most unreliable.

Evidence-based Medicine

The most reliable way to assess any medical treatment is by random clinical trials, preferably double blind. The treatment is given to some patients and not to others and so its effectiveness measured. The patients are assigned to one or other treatment randomly, and neither the patients nor the doctors should know who has been given which treatment. This anonymity is essential, for if either group knows what is going on this can significantly affect the outcome in all sorts of subtle ways: not least, the placebo effect can greatly alter patients' responses.

Such trials are a relatively recent procedure, only having started in this country in the 1940s. And trials of any sort to find out if a medical treatment works were virtually unknown until the pioneering work of Pierre Louis in Paris in the 1830s where he showed, at last, that blood-letting on the basis of the ancient belief that the patient had too much of one of the humours did them harm not good. Now the situation is very different, for roughly one million randomized clinical trials have been conducted over the last fifty years. Clinicians need important new information far more often than they realize; studies show that in a typical day as many as eight decisions would have been different if the necessary information had been available. Their problem is that they just do not have the time to go searching and the solution lies in evidence-based medicine.

Practising evidence-based medicine requires doctors to adopt an evidence-oriented attitude and to become more determined to seek the relevant information. Hitherto this has not been easily available and traditional review articles have been found to be unreliable. The more self-confident the author, it was found, the more unreliable was the article. Two new sources of information are now available to those who wish to practise evidence-based medicine. There is a new journal, *Evidence-Based Medicine*, that screens many other journals, and rigorously filters and summarizes the key points. The second comes from what is known as the Cochrane Collaboration—an international group that provides systematic reviews by collating the numerous clinical trials.

Not every new treatment needs a fully fledged clinical trial. In some rare cases the results are so dramatic that it would be improper to withhold treatment from those in a trial. An example is the use of a drug based on platinum to treat testicular cancer.

Science is not the same as Technology

It is very easy to conflate science and technology, and particularly when ethical issues arise in relation to the applications of science a clear distinction can be helpful.[3] Many people do not like this distinction since over the last hundred years science has had an enormous impact on technology. But much of what we would think of as technology, that is metal-making and agriculture, goes back about 10,000 years and owes absolutely nothing to science. Until the late eighteenth century, science, and by science I mean understanding in some mechanistic and causal way, played almost no role in advancing technology. Certainly with regard to metal-making and agriculture, you needed to understand nothing.

The great Chinese inventions, gun powder, the compass, and printing, required no understanding of science. The great mediaeval buildings and churches were built with no understanding of mechanics. They were built on what Professor Hayman calls 'the five minute theorem',[4] that is, you put up one of these buildings, you took away the props, you waited for five minutes and if it lasted for five minutes you could assume it would last for ever. It has been argued that the Greeks could have built the steam engine. You do not have to have any science to make a steam engine; the thermodynamicists came along later to explain why it worked.

A strong argument comes from evolution. You can have amazing technology with zero understanding. No one could deny that elephants are a remarkable technological achievement—consider its heart, muscles, and so forth—yet it has been invented by natural selection from random changes during evolution, and evolution understands no science whatsoever.

I also have Galileo on my side: 'We are certain that the first inventor of the telescope was a simple spectacle maker who, handling by chance different forms of glasses, looked also by chance through two of them, one convex, one concave, held at

3 Wolpert, *The Unnatural Nature of Science,* ch. 2.
4 *Ibid.,* 29.

different distances from the eye, saw and noted the unexpected result, and thus found the instrument'.[5]

The claim that science had no impact on technology until the nineteenth century is not true for medicine. Physical methods of treatment from Greek times, blood-letting in particular, were based on humoralism to disastrous effect.

Philosophy and Sociology of Science

Having recognized that science is peculiar, one might have thought that either the philosophers of science or the sociologists of science, those professionals who devote their time not to doing science but to thinking about science, might have illuminated its nature. The philosophers of science this century, however, have made virtually no contribution to the understanding of science. Popper's idea that the only way science progresses is by falsification is itself flawed, because as Francis Crick made clear, 'a theory that fits all the facts is bound to be wrong, as some of the facts will be wrong.'[6] How does one know a falsification is correct? Moreover, the emphasis on falsification fails to deal with discovery. Science is a very complicated process; there is no algorithm for doing science, no general scientific method.

The sociologists of science are a somewhat different group. There is a group who support what is called the Strong Programme in the Sociology of Science, who take a very curious view of science. Science, they say, is assumed to be the form of knowledge which *par excellence* remains unaffected by changes in social contact, culture, and so on. The recent social study of science, they claim, challenges this assumption. Their argument now is that the universalism of scientific truth is a myth. We should abandon the idea of science as privileged or even a separate domain of activity and enquiry. For some of them, the natural world has had little influence on the construction of scientific theories.

The portentously named Strong Programme in the Sociology of Science essentially claims that science is little more than a social construct, another set of myths, little different from any other beliefs. This extreme relativist view of science is with little foundation, and

[5] *Ibid.*, 28.   [6] *Ibid.*, 97.

two physicists have examined the claims of one of these sociologists that 'there is no obligation upon anyone framing a view of the world to take account of what 20th century science has to say',[7] a view that is widely held by many sociologists of science. It essentially says that science tells us nothing, nothing at all, about the way the world works. On this view the idea that DNA is the genetic material is no different from astrology and the periodic table of the same nature as the *Odyssey*. It is not unreasonable to ask for the grounds on which these so-called academics base their claims. They almost always deal with issues at the edge of science and never with the core.

One of the claims of these sociologists is that 'scientists at the research front cannot settle their disagreements through better experiments, more knowledge, more advanced theories, or clearer thinking ... [but transmute] wildly varying results ... into neat and tidy scientific myth.' For someone like myself who works in cell and developmental biology this is such unmitigated nonsense that it does not bear discussing for we continually have to change our ideas as new results appear.

This is not to say that science is not a social process—no one is more aware of this than scientists themselves. We compete, collaborate, try to get our papers into the best journals, persuade grant bodies to give us money. We also do not like to give up our favourite ideas on which we have lavished so much effort. But the individual in science is ultimately irrelevant and it is the group consensus that matters. Do these sociologists really believe that the astonishing success of molecular biology and genetics in explaining how organisms work is a mere figment of our imaginations? Do not the applications of science to technologies that have changed our lives—electronics, jet aircraft, techniques for body-scanning, hormones produced by bacteria—give them just a little confidence that reality may be involved?

For their part the sociologists of science claim that they have virtually no disagreements within their field, which suggests to me that they live in total isolation from other disciplines. It is a comfortable inward-looking self-sustaining world.

Why should any of this matter as it presents no threat to

[7] K. Gottfried and K. G. Wilson, 'Science as a Cultural Construct' (1997) 386 *Nature* 545–7.

science? It does, for as the authors of *The Higher Superstition: The Academic Left and its Quarrels with Science* point out,[8] it teaches a systematic flight from reason and science in the universities where it is taught. This relativist approach to science has also had a pernicious influence on feminism, and alternative medicine and other post-modernist cults. I fear that it dominates many science studies courses and may even influence the law.

Science and Reliability

But how reliable is science? Do not scientific ideas change constantly? This is true in principle and scientists accept that new evidence can change scientific ideas, no matter how long the ideas have been held. In almost all cases in which science changes, the old ideas are not so much discarded as incorporated into the new. Thus Newton's mechanics is a special case of Einstein's theory. Changes usually occur at the advancing fronts of science and the core can be regarded as very secure. Archimedes' laws of floating bodies and levers, or the idea that DNA is the genetic material, is not really open to doubt any more. The periodic table is secure, and it is probably the case that most of chemistry is correct and will be so for ever.

How then can one explain the disagreements amongst scientists? This again is mainly in areas where advances are being made. Since science is a social process in which ideas are incorporated into a common body of knowledge the consensus at any stage will be the most reliable guide. Maverick views of individuals should be treated with great caution.

Law is often concerned with individual events and their causation. Science by contrast is rarely interested in single events but rather in general understanding, laws that apply to a wide variety of events. The spinning of a coin can illustrate the differences that this involves. Using classical mechanics the scientist can predict whether the coin will come down heads or tails if the initial conditions are known, but these are rarely available. What the law might want to know is why it was heads rather than tails. The analogy is with the question whether a chemical or treatment could have caused some damage or illness in an individual, or

---

[8] P. Gross and N. Levitt (Baltimore, 1994).

whether a child is likely to be abused. This raises very difficult problems.

Morals and Ethics

Leo Tolstoy has written: 'Science is meaningless because it gives no answer to our question, the only question important for us: "What shall we do and how shall we be?" '[9] Tolstoy is correct in that science has very severe limitations as it cannot tell you how to live your life; it has zero to say about ethics and moral issues.

But what about scientists and their social responsibility? There is at the moment a great deal of anxiety about scientists being socially responsible. The big issues are nuclear energy, nuclear weapons, and genetic engineering. I suggest that the only social responsibility scientists have, because they have access to privileged knowledge, is to explain to the public what the implications of that knowledge are and how reliable that knowledge is. It is not up to them to make the decisions. I would argue that, in relation to the atom bomb, the scientists behaved with great moral responsibility. Robert Oppenheimer made the position very clear when he said:

The scientist is not responsible for the laws of nature, but it is the scientist's job to find out how these laws operate. It is the scientist's job to find the ways in which these laws can serve the human will. However, it is not the scientist's responsibility to determine whether a hydrogen bomb should be used. That responsibility rests with the American people and their chosen representatives.[10] It is to society as a whole and lawyers in particular that we must look for the framing and enforcing of moral codes of conduct.

[9] Wolpert, *Unnatural Nature*, n. 1 above, 144.
[10] *Ibid.*, 157.

INDEX